Music in American Life

A list of volumes in the series Music in American Life appears at the end of this book.

Pickin'
on
Peachtree

To:
Peg and Dave, —
I hope you find
something of interest
in this book.
Best Wishes and
Happy Reading!!
Wayne W Daniel
Atlanta, GA
March 12, 2006

Pickin' on Peachtree

A History of Country Music in Atlanta, Georgia

Wayne W. Daniel

University of Illinois Press

Urbana and Chicago

First paperback edition, 2001
© 1990 by the Board of Trustees of the University of Illinois
Manufactured in the United States of America
⊚ This book is printed on acid-free paper.

Library of Congress Cataloging-in-Publication Data
Daniel, Wayne W., 1929–
Pickin' on Peachtree : a history of country music in Atlanta, Georgia /
by Wayne W. Daniel.
p.   cm. — (Music in American Life)
ISBN 0-252-06968-4 (alk. paper)
1. Country music—Georgia—Atlanta—History and criticism.
2. Radio and music. I. Title. II. Series.
ML3524.D36   1990
781.642'09758'231—dc20   89-20278

P 5 4 3 2 1

University of Illinois Press
1325 South Oak Street
Champaign, IL 61820-6903
www.press.uillinois.edu

To
Atlanta's country music artists,
past and present,
and their families

Contents

Preface

IF I HAD BEEN BLESSED with an iota of musical talent this book would never have been written. I would have been too busy picking a guitar and singing country songs. Since it was not meant for me to make music, I have done other things to keep me close to the art. I could not be content just listening to music. I had to become actively involved. I found that writing about country music and country musicians allowed me to enjoy vicariously something that I could not actually do myself. I am eternally grateful to those musicians who, over the years, have been willing to talk to me about their craft.

I probably don't fully understand why country music has been such an important force in my life. It was the first poetry I knew. The first country song I remember hearing was "My Clinch Mountain Home," by the Carter Family. I was probably four or five years old. I must have heard it many times for I learned by heart the last half of the first verse: "She clung to me and trembled when I told her we must part. She says, 'Don't go my darling, it almost breaks my heart to think of you so far apart.'" Over the years those words have popped into my mind in some of the most unusual situations. I later learned that the Carter Family first recorded the song (the version that I first heard) on the day I was born.

My exposure to country music was only sporadic during the next several years. These were the Depression years and phonograph records were low priority items. In fact, I think the ones I did hear were borrowed. It was not until around 1939 or 1940 that my family became sufficiently affluent to purchase a radio, a battery-operated table model that required an outside antenna and a ground wire. As we talked about one day owning a radio I knew what delights lay in store for me. I had sampled the offerings of the airwaves through the courtesy of the two or three families in the neighborhood who already had receiving sets. Once we had our own radio I became totally immersed in country music. Not a country music program within reach of that vacuum-tubed wonder escaped my twistings of the dial. In the wee hours of the morning I reveled in the hymns, heartsongs, and breakdowns from such far-away (from Georgia) places as Cincinnati, Ohio; Shenandoah, Iowa; and New Orleans, Louisiana. My favorite evening programs came from WJJD in Chicago and from the Mexican border stations. On Saturday nights I incurred the wrath of the rest of the family as I switched back and forth between the "Grand Ole Opry," the "National Barn Dance," the "Renfro Valley Barn Dance," and the "WSB Barn Dance" in my efforts to hear, frequently in defiance of such obstacles as dying batteries, static, and interfering stations, every song by every performer.

During the day I had to be content with Birmingham, Chattanooga, and Atlanta. But I was not disappointed. Beginning with the "Dixie Farm and Home Hour" that came on before daylight, through the mid-morning "Cracker Barrel," "Barnyard Jamboree," and "Little Country Church" programs, to the noontime "Georgia Jubilee," the radio for the most part stayed tuned to WSB. That's when Harpo Kidwell, James and Martha Carson, Jane and Cotton Carrier, the Swanee River Boys, Pete Cassell, the Sunshine Boys, and all those other Atlanta artists you can read about in this book became my heroes.

Just listening to the radio stars was not enough. I had to learn the words to all the songs they sang. I had to write them letters and send them jokes to read on the air. I wheedled my mother out of butter-and-egg money to send off for their songbooks. I bought cold medicines and hair dyes that I neither needed nor could afford just to get the box tops that I could mail to some radio station and receive in return a picture of the Carter Family, or Mainer's Mountaineers, or dozens of other pickers and singers. While other kids were collecting baseball cards I was collecting pictures of such idols as Roy Acuff, Bill Monroe, and Ernest Tubb.

I eventually grew up, and other adventures such as getting an education, making a living, and raising a family forced my obsession with country music into the background. When I had about finished with those jobs I discovered that radio programming had changed. I could no longer pick up live country music except for the "Grand Ole Opry." And I began to wonder what had happened to Hank Penny, Grady and Hazel Cole, and those other Atlanta-area country entertainers who had brought me so much pleasure during my formative years. So I started tracking them down. It dawned on me that there might be others in the country like myself who would also like to have an update on the Blue Sky Boys and the Hoot Owl Hollow Girls. That's when I started interviewing and writing stories about performers like the Holden Brothers and the Pine Ridge Boys. Fortunately the editors of such publications as *Bluegrass Unlimited, Old Time Music*, the *Journal of Country Music*, the *JEMF Quarterly, Atlanta Weekly*, and the *Devil's Box* were kind enough to publish my articles. A few sympathetic readers asked, "Why don't you write a book?" I didn't have any more sense than to try, and you're now holding the result in your hands. I hope you enjoy it half as much as I enjoyed writing it.

I am grateful to all those past and present Atlanta-area country musicians (and others connected with country music in Atlanta) and their families who talked to me in person and on the telephone and answered my letters while I was collecting the data on which this book is based. They are mentioned in the book proper or in the notes, and I will not repeat their names here. Many other people helped with the writing of this book, and I would like to list their names here in recognition of that assistance. Their help took many forms. Some of them told me how to get in touch with a musician or a member of a musician's family. Others shared with me their collections of country music records and memorabilia. Some offered much-needed words of encouragement and advice. Among these helpers are Lee Roy Abernathy, Eugene Akers, Joann Allen, Jerry W. Bethel, Romeo Brinkley, Ray Brown, Professor John Burrison, Joe Bussard, Jr., Tony Cianciola, Phyllis Cole, Bob Pinson and Ronnie Pugh at the Country Music Foundation, Joe DePriest, Mary Englett, Sylvia Etheridge, Joe Ford, David Freeman, Paul Harper,

Ken Hawkins, T. P. Hollomon, Jimmy Jones, Benny Kissinger, Marjorie Kizer, Bill McMichen, Guthrie T. Meade, Ray Melton, Don Naylor, Robert Nobley, Helen Parker, Professor Daniel W. Patterson of the University of North Carolina at Chapel Hill, Mrs. Helen Petro, Mrs. Odell Rakestraw, Don Rhodes, Mike Seeger, Mrs. Dora Smith, Jack Sorrells, Ernest Spearman, Phil Tanner, Ann Tant, Mrs. Andy Thomas, Jimmy Timmes, Professor Ivan Tribe, Jerry Vandeventer, Cecil White, Dr. Gene Wiggins, and Mrs. J. D. Williams.

If I have failed to mention the name of someone who deserves to be remembered, I offer my sincere apologies and assurances that such an oversight was not intentional.

Special thanks are due the reference librarians at Georgia State University who never lost their composure as they plowed the fields of knowledge trying to turn up rare and sometimes near nonexistent documents and other printed matter for me.

I am also grateful to my wife, Mary, who helped with the typing and other clerical duties necessary to organize the massive amount of material that I accumulated while researching the subject of this book. But most of all I'm grateful to her for her understanding and acceptance of that other woman in my life—country music.

Finally I would like to thank Norm Cohen and Charles Wolfe, who read early drafts of the book and made valuable suggestions for its improvement. They, however, cannot be held responsible for any deficiencies that still exist.

Introduction

COUNTRY MUSIC, ACCORDING TO a brochure published by the Country Music Foundation of Nashville, Tennessee, "is the commercial extension of Anglo-American folksong. In its first commercial appearances in the 1920s country music carried this rich British and American folk music tradition at its heart, but even then contained a wealth of songs and performance styles drawn from the blues of Southern Blacks and from nineteenth-century popular music." That there exists an organization such as the Country Music Foundation to inform a reading public about the subject is a striking testimony to the importance of country music in the fabric of American culture. This is the music that, each year, sells millions of dollars' worth of record albums and cassette tapes; attracts millions of devotees to nightclubs and auditoriums of all sizes where the purveyors of this music can be seen and heard; and sends to Nashville every summer more than twenty thousand ardent fans who spend a week as participants in an organized celebrity-worship service called Fan Fair in which farmers from Iowa, assembly-line workers from Detroit, and secretaries from North Carolina seek autographs, photographs, and souvenirs of, handshakes and hugs from, and close-up looks at their favorite disseminators of the art form. This is the music the history of which is filled with rags-to-riches stories in which superstars such as Eddy Arnold and Dolly Parton escaped from childhoods of modest means or near abject poverty to become millionaires. This is the music that has spawned a spate of subgenres such as bluegrass, western swing, rockabilly, honky-tonk, cowboy, and country gospel. This is the music that has nourished the careers of a number of cult artists (Willie Nelson and Dwight Yoakam readily come to mind). This is the music whose existence at one time was not acknowledged in polite society, but today is the subject of doctoral dissertations by university students and of serious study and analysis by scholars and critics of popular culture. This is the music that could not be contained within the borders of the region or the nation that gave it birth. This is the music that has large followings in Europe, Asia, Australia, and elsewhere around the world.

The story of country music from a national perspective has been accurately and entertainingly narrated by Bill C. Malone in his book *Country Music, U.S.A.*[1] But the big picture that is American country music is a montage of numerous genres, performers, and regional differences. The need for a closer, in-depth look at these components of country music has been partially met through the works of such scholars as Robert Cantwell (*Bluegrass Breakdown: The Making of the Old Southern Sound*),[2] Nolan Porterfield (*Jimmie Rodgers: The Life and Times of America's Blue Yodeler*),[3] Neil Rosenberg (*Bluegrass: A History*),[4] Elizabeth Schlappi (*Roy Acuff: The Smoky Mountain Boy*),[5] Charles Townsend (*San Antonio Rose: The Life and Music of Bob Wills*),[6] Ivan Tribe (*Mountain Jamboree: Country Music in West Virginia*),[7] Gene Wiggins (*Fiddlin' Georgia Crazy: Fiddlin' John Carson, His Real World, and the World of His Songs*),[8] and Charles Wolfe (*Kentucky Country: Folk and Country Music of Kentucky*[9] and *Tennessee Strings: The Story of Country Music in Tennessee*).[10] The subject of country music, however, still abounds with untold stories. Consider just the regional aspect of the topic, for example. The general public has not yet been provided with the details of the importance to the development of country music of such places as Dallas, Charlotte, Cincinnati, Birmingham, and Oklahoma City. The motivation for the present book was a desire to try to fill in one of the blank spaces in the mosaic of country music history. It is an account of the development of the genre in Atlanta, Georgia, one of the cities besides Nashville that played an important role in the evolution of today's commercial country music.

Introduction

Necessary for the birth, development, and nurture of any cultural or commercial structure are, of course, people. In order for any geographical area to attract people in sufficient numbers to foster the development of identifiable cultural entities it must provide easy access. From as far back as the early 1700s the spot on the map that is now known as Atlanta has been characterized by the convergence of a system of pathways conducive to the free flow of man and materials. An eighteenth-century map of Georgia shows nearly a dozen roads crisscrossing at, and in the immediate vicinity of, the present city.[11] These early thoroughfares were Indian trails and the pathways hewn from the wilderness by westward-bound pioneers. Those migrants who, for one reason or another, decided to halt their westward trek at the confluence of these arteries of social intercourse became Atlanta's first residents.

Next came the railroads. The initial action in a chain of events that would lead to Atlanta's becoming the "Gate City" and the "Chicago of the South" took place in 1837. Sometime in September of that year an engineer for the then recently chartered and state-owned Western and Atlantic Railroad decided that the southern terminus of a track originating in Chattanooga, Tennessee, should be located on the east bank of the Chattahoochee River.[12] Perhaps not totally coincidental, the spot was located near the village that had grown up in the vicinity of the intersection of the Indian and pioneer trails to which we have already alluded. Ten years later the railroad village that grew up around the stake marking the Western and Atlantic southern terminal point had become the hub of a transportation system the spokes of which were three converging railroads. By 1852 the number of railroads terminating in the heart of present-day Atlanta had grown to four, making the city the largest railroad center in the South.[13] Within a year after Sherman departed the city in 1864 trains were entering and leaving Atlanta on the tracks of five railroads.[14] By the early 1900s the city could boast of a total of eight railroads and a reputation as one of the nation's key transportation centers.[15]

While this settlement was developing as a rail center the problem of importing and exporting people and goods by animal-drawn conveyances—and later by the automobile—received due attention by the state and local governments in the area. A state highway department map of Georgia for 1920 shows seven state-supported highways connecting the city in all directions with every major population center of Georgia and surrounding states.[16] As the federal highway system evolved, Atlanta emerged as a major connector in the north-south movement of interstate traffic.[17]

Over the roads and rails came entrepreneurs with visions of fortunes to be made in industry, banking, and real estate. In their wake was a host of supporting tradesmen and craftsmen. And Atlanta grew. A community of just over 2,500 souls in 1850, she was a burgeoning metropolis with a population of almost 8,000 a decade later. Atlanta was home to more than 37,000 persons in 1880; the number had expanded to almost 90,000 by 1900 and had reached more than 200,000 by 1920.[18]

Thus early on, Atlanta became, according to sociologists, one of those "Southern cities [that] served as repositories of regional culture—including, many would argue, the primitive values and instincts of rural society—and as links between the traditional South and the contrary influences of northern capitalism and the American 'mainstream.'"[19] Among the "primitive values and instincts of rural society" that found their way to Atlanta were those having to do with music.

With the breakdown of the plantation system following the Civil War, the rural areas of Georgia suddenly became populated by a contingent of displaced and disgruntled citizenry to whom the attractions of life in cities like Atlanta appeared more promising than a hardscrabble existence in red clay fields and the piney woods.[20] Consequently Atlanta, during the first quarter of the twentieth century, could be described, in the words of folklorist John Burrison, as "largely a town of rural refugees."[21] Large assemblages of these rustic emigrants set up housekeeping in the near vicinity of available sources of employment. Notable among such communities of former tillers of the soil were the villages that flourished around the textile mills that began operation in the Atlanta area around the turn of the century. Three such mill villages that enjoyed considerable longevity and the later attention of sociologists and urban historians were Cabbagetown, Chattahoochee, and Scottdale, communities that still exist, having outlived the stimuli that gave them birth. Cabbagetown, located a mere mile and a half due east of downtown Atlanta, grew up around the Fulton Bag and Cotton Mill which, including its antecedents on the same premises, provided employment for sometimes as many as 2,500 persons, into the 1970s. Chattahoochee was the residential adjunct of the Old Whittier's Mill located on the Southern Railroad near the Chatta-hoochee River approximately seven miles northwest of the center of Atlanta. Founded in 1900 the mill remained in operation well into the 1960s. Some eight miles roughly northeast of Atlanta, Scott-dale provided housing for employees of Scottdale Mills for more than seventy years, beginning in 1900.[22] As the country music scene in Atlanta unfolded, residents of these three communities provided many of the actors in the form of both audiences and artists.

Atlanta's brand of commercial country music bore the imprint of folk traditions, black influences (notably the blues), and gospel styles. Although this fact has been acknowledged, specific details have not been adequately documented. Especially lacking are com-prehensive studies of Georgia's folk music legacy and the interaction between black and white country musicians.

Writing in 1972, Killion and Waller noted that up until then no single printed volume had centered on Georgia's folklore.[23] Their 267-page book, covering a broad spectrum of folkloristic topics, presents material, never previously catalogued or organized, that was collected as part of the 1930s WPA Writer's Project. The vol-ume contains one thirty-two-page chapter devoted to folk songs collected in Georgia. The chapter's one-and-a-half-page introduc-tion is followed by the words to fifty-six songs and song fragments grouped into the following categories: work songs, songs for play, spirituals and hymns, English and Scottish songs, and two murder crimes. The latter category contains five verses of "Frank Dupree" and two verses of "Little Mary Fagan [sic]." Killion and Waller state that the traditional songs to which Georgia residents have been exposed "comment on the changing culture of Georgia and Georgians for over three centuries. Their transmission is traceable largely to numerous waves of immigration into and around the state, first from literally every country in Europe, then from Africa, and finally the steady but considerable influx from the Virginias and the Carolinas."[24]

In a later venture, folklorist and folk music performer Art Rosenbaum spent several years, beginning in 1977, collecting songs and tunes from singers and musicians residing in north Georgia. In the introduction to the published account and results of his endeavor Rosenbaum states that this area of the state "has given rise to and nurtured a variety of impressive musical traditions, emblematic of southern folk music, and well-springs of later American music. Among these are the stirring antebellum spirituals and lined-out hymns of black country churches, the old-time black frolic tunes and bottleneck blues, the bitter hammer-and-pick songs that helped build the railroads and highways, the ebullient dance music of the Piedmont fiddle bands, the mournful and tragic unaccompanied mountain ballads, [and] the raucous backwoods banjo tunes and songs."[25]

If one is willing to wade through mounds of likely sources, other references, frequently made merely in passing, to folk music activity in Georgia may be found. In "The Dance," one of the sketches in Longstreet's *Georgia Scenes, Characters, Incidents &c.*, first published in 1835, we meet a fiddle player whose repertoire includes at least a reel or two.[26] The author of another collection titled *Saturday Night Sketches: Stories of Old Wiregrass Georgia*, published in 1918, seeks "to tell posterity something of a people who have passed. To put in form more permanent than tradition something of those hardy pioneers who initiated the development of a wilderness into a land of fertility and plenty."[27] In this collection the vignettes concerned with music include a description of hymn singing in a church service following a baptism in a nearby stream.[28] The sketch called "An Old-Time Wiregrass Frolic" tells the story of a country dance that takes place in a one-room cabin from which the furniture had been removed. The music was furnished by two fiddlers and two straw beaters. We are led to believe that the musicians knew at least two tunes—"Old Dan Tucker" and "Cotton Eyed Joe."[29] In "The Singing School" we are taken inside a "log schoolhouse, used alike for occasional religious services and the three-months annual term of semi-public school." There we are introduced to an "itinerant singing teacher" whose class, consisting of "barely a dozen" pupils who "atoned in zeal for any lack in number," attempts to learn the rudiments of the do-re-mi vocal music system with the aid of "the time-honored 'Sacred Harp'" songbook.[30] Fiddle playing with straw beating and congregational hymn singing are described, respectively, in two other of the pieces, "The Homefolks Dance"[31] and "The Revival's Close."[32]

A short narrative titled "Among the Georgia Crackers" that

appeared in the collection *Highways and Byways of the South*, published in 1904, contains a description of an all-day Sunday singing at a village church. The songbook used by this congregation was *The Old Christian Harmony*.[33] In the same composition the author gives an account of a party in which games were played to the tune of a fiddle. "Of co'se," explains one of the characters in the story, "these games ain't regular dancing. That wouldn't be allowed at most houses. They're Christian dancing."[34]

On the basis of such evidence, meager though it may be, it seems reasonable to assume that the native Georgia musicians who are discussed in this book were exposed to a wide range of folk music traditions before they ventured into the world of commercial country music. Documentation of interaction between these musicians, all of whom were white, and black musicians, however, is sparse. During the interviews conducted in preparation for this book, not one individual ever mentioned having been influenced in any way by black musicians. One cannot imagine, however, that in Georgia and Atlanta, the two racial groups coexisted without some swapping of materials and styles. Blues historian Pete Lowry states that "white and black traditions certainly interacted, both in musical styles, as well as instruments—whites borrowed blues and banjos from blacks; blacks borrowed ballads and fiddles from whites."[35] This undoubtedly describes the situation with respect to Georgia and Atlanta musicians. In one newspaper story we are told that Gid Tanner made quite a hit at a fiddlers' convention with his imitations of some "Decatur Street types" who, presumably, were black. As we shall see, folk music scholar Gene Wiggins elicited from the Cofer Brothers, country musicians from middle Georgia, acknowledgment of some indebtedness to a black musician. A popular Atlanta guitarist of the 1920s and 30s, John Dilleshaw, also learned from a black man. It is known that white progressive-country guitar picker Hoke Rice accompanied blues singers on recordings in the late 1920s and early 1930s. In the liner notes to some of the LP album reissues of recordings of Atlanta-connected artists a few references are made to black influences on the white man's music. These comments are noted later in this book.

Atlanta's role in the development and commercialization of black blues appears to be equally as important as its role in the history of the country music of whites. According to Lowry, "the first

'country blues' recording seems to have been one by Ed Andrews
—'Barrel House Blues'/'Time Ain't Gonna Make Me Stay' (OKeh
8137)—which was recorded in Atlanta in 1924."[36] The city subsequently became a center for blues recording activity. However
interesting it might be, to pursue further the subject of black music
in Atlanta is beyond the scope of the present book. The interested
reader is referred to the books by Oakley[37] and Bastin[38] and to the
journal articles written by Frangiamore and Durban,[39] Lowry,[40] and
Pettigrew.[41] An album of sixteen early recordings by Atlanta blues
artists is also available.[42] A booklet accompanying the album contains an overview of the blues in Atlanta as well as biographical
sketches of the featured artists.

Shortly after the turn of the century it became evident that
Atlanta was well blessed with musicians whose styles and repertoires can be labeled as folk-oriented. The sound that evolved
from their type of music would in turn be referred to as hillbilly,
country-western, and finally country. As we shall see, Atlanta subsequently developed into a center for the commercial exploitation
of this music. First there were the annual fiddlers' conventions that
drew large audiences to the City Auditorium. Then came radio, and
through the far-reaching signal of WSB, Atlanta became known
as home to a number of musicians whose appeal was primarily
to a rural or rural-oriented audience. Finally the city became one
of the most active field-recording centers of the New York-based
phonograph companies.

So important was Atlanta's role in the development of country
music that it has been referred to as "a pre-Nashville Nashville"[43]
and a one-time "country music capital."[44] A question often asked
is why, with such an auspicious beginning, did not Atlanta, rather
than Nashville, become the country music capital of the world? The
deciding factor seems to have been the philosophies and attitudes of
the personalities behind the programming policies of those pioneer
radio stations—WSB in Atlanta and WSM in Nashville. At WSB
Lambdin Kay and, perhaps to some lesser extent, his close associate, Ernest Rogers, decided who would perform on the station,
when, and for how long. At WSM, the person performing a similar
role was George D. Hay.

Lambdin Kay, station manager at WSB from 1922 to 1940,
was born in Brooklyn, New York, in 1889, the son of a civil engi-

neer father and a pianist/composer mother who performed light classics as well as her own compositions on WSB during its early years. A graduate of the Prosso Preparatory School in Kansas City, Kay attended (and was perhaps graduated from) the University of Georgia. In 1909 he was graduated from Draughon's Business College in Atlanta. He was associated with the *Atlanta Journal*, owner of WSB, when the station went on the air.[45] Ernest Rogers, who was associated with WSB in various capacities from 1922 until 1940, was born in 1897. His father, a Methodist minister and holder of a doctoral degree, was educated at Vanderbilt University. The younger Rogers was a *cum laude* graduate of Emory University.[46]

George D. Hay was born in Attica, Indiana, in 1895. His father, a jeweler, died when the younger Hay was ten years old. Forced to drop out of high school in order to support himself, Hay held a variety of jobs prior to 1924 when he became an announcer at radio station WLS in Chicago, a position that brought him in contact with the "WLS Barn Dance" program. He became station manager at WSM in 1925. October of that year marked the debut of the station's Saturday night program featuring the music of a country fiddler that eventually evolved into the the "Grand Ole Opry," a program still heard on the station.[47]

Insight into the attitudes toward country music and its performers held by these early arbiters of the airwaves in Atlanta and Nashville can be gleaned from their writings. In a memoir published in 1956, Ernest Rogers, reminiscing about his tenure at WSB, writes, "Credit—*if such it may be called*—goes to WSB for having introduced hillbilly music to radio, or vice versa. It arrived in the person of Fiddlin' John Carson, an itinerant musician who enjoyed a reputation *of sorts* in the back country" (emphasis added).[48] He later refers to Carson as a "man of somewhat unstable habits," and ends his sketch of WSB's first country music artist by noting that "in his latter years Fiddlin' John joined the entourage of the Talmadges —Gene and Herman—and his fiddling and singing added the *corn pone flavor* to many a political rally up and down and across Georgia" (emphasis added).[49] From the many anecdotes about Carson from which Rogers must have been able to select for his book, he chose one that depicted the musician as an intemperate guzzler of "corn squeezings."[50]

While no printed comments by Lambdin Kay about country

music appear to have survived, George D. Hay left written accounts of the early days. In his booklet *A Story of the Grand Ole Opry*, published in 1953, Hay writes, "It (the 'Grand Ole Opry') has a universal appeal because it is built upon good will and with folk music expresses the heart-beat of a large percentage of Americans who labor for a living."[51] Writing in the third person about himself and the program that can be called the first "Grand Ole Opry" broadcast, he recalls that "realizing the wealth of folk music material and performers in the Tennessee Hills he [Hay] *welcomed* the appearance of Uncle Jimmy Thomson and his blue ribbon fiddle who went on the air at eight o'clock, Saturday night, November 28, 1925" (emphasis added).[52] His characterization of brothers Sam and Kirk McGee, one-time performers on the "Grand Ole Opry," appears to express his general feeling about the artists who were heard on the program. "They are," he wrote, "fine citizens, who are well thought of in their county."[53]

George D. Hay was a person who, according to his daughter, had a warm and understanding attitude toward the folk-oriented music to which he was devoted. In the words of his daughter, "His [Hay's] argument to the directors of WSM was that his country cousins were authentic representatives of whatever America was all about; it had its origins in the early settlers and it was a part of the blood stream of America."[54] In short, George D. Hay had an appreciation for the worth and importance of folk music.

Lambdin Kay and Ernest Rogers possessed the credentials of the culturally elite—college educations and upper-middle-class upbringings. There is no evidence that Rogers perceived in the music of Carson and the other purveyors of country music at WSB any intrinsic value or significant merit. This "corn pone" noise that passed for music was to be tolerated in the interest of holding radio listeners, but it was not to be taken seriously. When he looked at Fiddlin' John Carson, Rogers seems to have seen not a folk music artist, but an unlettered hillbilly.

Now, more than a half century later, it is pleasant to speculate that if George D. Hay had gone to Atlanta's WSB rather than to Nashville in 1925, what we now know as the "Nashville sound" might, instead, be called the "Atlanta sound," and Georgia's capital city, not Tennessee's, might be known as "Music City, U.S.A."

Although Atlanta did not become the country music capital of the world, the city did, as we have already noted, play an important role in the development of commercial country music. At this point we may well ask ourselves a number of questions. What was it about Atlanta that enabled it to enjoy for four decades so prominent a position in the field of country music? What made the city attractive to country music artists from other states? Why was Atlanta so popular as a regional recording center? As we have seen, Atlanta was, from the beginning, easy to get into and out of. In addition, the city fathers made a point of selling the city to anyone who would listen, promoting its virtues with the fervor of civic piety.[55] Soon after the Civil War "there developed what came to be called 'the Atlanta Spirit.' It ran the gamut from crass boosterism to genuine vision, from outright tub-thumping to careful planning, from smugness to a spirit of sacrifice."[56] An International Cotton Exposition held in Atlanta in 1881 "focused national attention upon the [city] and highlighted the growing importance of the city as a transportation, distribution and manufacturing center."[57] A similar event, the Cotton States and International Exposition of 1895, contributed further to the attractive aura with which Atlanta officials wished to drape their city. A public relations tour de force of the 1920s called the Forward Atlanta Campaign broadened Atlanta's image to that of a "cosmopolitan, progressive, commercially vibrant city."[58] Skyscrapers that first made their appearance in the city in the 1890s and were added to through the 1920s became symbols of vitality that boosters used to promote the city through such devices as picture postcards and ads in nationally circulated magazines.[59] In short, Atlanta, from the 1880s through the period covered by this book, was touted as a good place to live and work. And apparently the city was so perceived by those who heard the story.

Particularly attractive to country music artists after 1922 was the power of radio station WSB. Even the weaker stations that followed WSB into the ether could be heard for relatively long distances, for Atlanta was not hemmed in, as were some other cities, by mountains that could interrupt radio signals. With the exception of Denver, Colorado, Atlanta, sitting 1,050 feet above sea level, is the highest large city in the United States. This fact, no doubt, gave those early signals from the city's radio stations an added boost. The further a radio station could be heard, the greater was the area in which country music artists on the station could book the personal appearances that were frequently their sole sources of income.

Undoubtedly a major reason for Atlanta's success as a regional recording center was the wealth of talent to be found in the city and surrounding area. But perhaps there is more to the story. The talent scouts and engineers sent into the field by the New York record companies found in Atlanta not crude provincialism, but a big-city ambience in which they could feel at home. For example, as early as the 1880s one found in the city hotels, such as the Kimball House and the Markham House, genteel surroundings that "gave the visitor an instant impression of urban elegance."[60]

The purpose of the present book is to document the role that Atlanta played in the development of country music. I have brought together the facts of the story from a variety of sources, mainly contemporary newspaper articles and the recollections and memorabilia of the drama's principal actors and/or their descendants. The order of presentation is basically chronological, but not strictly so because of inevitable overlaps and the need to emphasize some aspects of the story without regard to a time sequence. I begin with a chapter on the Georgia old-time fiddlers' conventions which, in 1913, were formalized into an annual series of events under the aegis of a structured organization. These events were well established and apparently attracting large crowds when the radio and recording industries came to Atlanta in the early 1920s. The second chapter, covering the early days of radio, begins with the first broadcast from the city in 1922 and ends in 1929. With the waxing of the first country music record in Atlanta in 1923 began the city's era as a regional recording center lasting until the early 1940s. I devote a chapter to this period in the history of country music in Atlanta. Thus, chapters two and three cover essentially the same time span. In chapter four I digress from the chronological sequence to concentrate on the four most popular country music pioneers who called the Atlanta area home. They are Fiddlin' John Carson, Riley Puckett, Gid Tanner, and Clayton McMichen. In chapters four and five I cover the radio activity at WSB during the decade of the thirties. Chapter six, covering the period from 1936 to 1940, emphasizes the "Cross Roads Follies," WSB's longest running and most formally organized country music program up to that time. By 1930 other radio stations, albeit weaker ones with respect to power output, were beginning to operate in Atlanta to compete with WSB for the ear attuned to the sounds of the fiddle, banjo, and mountain-style vocalizations. I devote a chapter to the hillbilly acts that were heard on these stations. For although the stations were weaker than WSB, their country music artists were not necessarily inferior to those heard on the stronger station, a notable example being the Blue Sky Boys who were heard on WGST. The last two chapters are chronological. Chapter eight covers mainly the 1940s, in which Atlanta's country music scene was dominated by the "WSB Barn Dance" and related radio programs. The last chapter begins with the advent of television in the late 1940s and takes the reader up to the late 1980s.

For readers not intimately acquainted with Atlanta an explanation of the title of this book is in order. It has been said that "everything that's ever happened in Atlanta had some connection with Peachtree [Street],"[61] and that "this celebrated street is unique in having become the symbol of a city."[62] Activities associated with country music were no exception. The origin of the name "Peachtree" as it applies to Atlanta's famous thoroughfare is uncertain. According to one story, which was current more than a hundred years ago, the name comes from the Indians who frequented the area around present-day Atlanta. One of their choice resting places afforded the convenience of a stream and a large tree that was particularly popular as the target in a favorite game involving the pitching of tomahawks. Over time the tree became known as the Pitchtree and the nearby stream acquired the name Pitchtree Creek. Little in the way of translation skills was required for the later white settlers to convert Pitchtree to Peachtree.[63] The trail that crossed Peachtree Creek, nee Pitchtree Creek, eventually was dubbed Peachtree Street, and over the years "Peachtree" proliferated as a name for Atlanta streets, avenues, and cul de sacs: By the mid-1980s, maps of the city, to the amusement and sometimes confusion of visitors, showed more than twenty arteries of social and commercial intercourse bearing the word "Peachtree" as part of their names.

Much of the activity associated with the progress of country music in Atlanta took place in and around Peachtree Street and its namesakes. For much of the period covered in this book WSB was located in the Biltmore Hotel, on West Peachtree Street. The Erlanger Theater and the Woman's Club Auditorium, longtime homes of the "WSB Barn Dance" and other country music shows, were both located on Peachtree Street. The Kimball House Hotel, scene of frequent recording sessions, sat a mere block to the east of Peachtree Street. Arriving in Atlanta by train, even visitors who were not bound for this famous strip of cement would often have to cross it to reach their destinations. No wonder then that one of Atlanta's most popular country music groups decided to call themselves the Peachtree Cowboys.

At this point a word is perhaps appropriate regarding the amount of space allotted to the personalities who inhabit the pages of this book. As a rule, group leaders and solo artists receive more coverage than performers who worked primarily as band members and backup musicians. Generally, I believe, the amount of space I have devoted to a performer is in proportion to the length of time the performer worked in Atlanta as a musician. The scrutinizing reader, no doubt, will find exceptions to these rules. When such is the case, the reader will, I hope, agree that it is for a good reason. For example, I have probably written about Cousin Emmy out of proportion to her relatively short stay in Atlanta. However, her impact on the country music scene in Atlanta was also probably out of proportion to her stay there. Few of the musicians who worked with her while she was at WSB failed to mention her during the interviews for this book. Similarly, listeners to WSB during her stints in Atlanta also remember her, both from her broadcasts and from her stage shows that they attended.

Finally, in this history the reader will encounter more fact than interpretation. With respect to the subject under consideration I find myself in the position of popular historian Barbara W. Tuchman who is reputed to have once said, "I am a seeker of the small facts, not the big Explanation; a narrator, not a philosopher."[64]

CHAPTER

1

The Georgia Old-Time Fiddlers' Conventions, 1913–35

ON MARCH 4, 1913, Woodrow Wilson became the twenty-eighth president of the United States, assuming his leadership role during a period in American history that has been characterized as one of prosperity and economic expansion.[1] The Gay Nineties were only a fond memory, and World War I was an unimagined future reality.

With a great deal of interest, Americans—of whom more and more in 1913 were becoming urban dwellers—watched the progress being made in the development of affordable automobiles. While luxury cars such as Packard, Pierce Arrow, White, Franklin, Locomobile, and Peerless were selling for $2,500 to $7,500, some new Ford models could be had for as little as $550. The ten-year-old Ford Motor Company was adapting the conveyor-belt system to its production process and would soon be turning out a thousand cars per day. By 1924 Americans would be buying Model T's for $290.

The country's infatuation with sports was well established in 1913, and news of the completion on October 10 of the Panama Canal did not seem nearly as important to many baseball enthusiasts as the fact that during the same week Philadephia defeated New York 4 to 1 in the tenth annual World Series. The following month, in their first encounter ever, the relatively unknown Notre Dame football team defeated the powerful Army eleven.

Entertainment history was made in 1913 when Cecil B. de-

· 15 ·

Mille's *The Squaw Man* became the first full-length movie to be filmed in Hollywood, California.

If the weatherman can be believed, Sunday, March 30, 1913, was a cloudy day in Georgia's capital city, and the temperature did not get above fifty-eight degrees. If this did not provide sufficient reason to keep the more than 150,000 folks who called Atlanta home indoors, they had yet another excuse. The city's movie houses would be closed that day in compliance with a state law forbidding the showing of motion pictures on Sunday. The afternoon, however, could be spent listening to the latest supply of phonograph records or reading one of Atlanta's three daily newspapers, the *Journal*, the *Constitution*, and the *Georgian*.

Those turning to the newspapers for information and entertainment were reminded of the hazards of residing in a large city. The night before, three masked "highwaymen" robbed a pedestrian on Juniper Street of seven dollars and three pennies, and in the early morning hours a Courtland Street landlord deemed it necessary to shoot and seriously wound a tenant who allegedly was trying surreptitiously to move out of his apartment without paying five-weeks' back rent.

But the most celebrated crime in Atlanta's history would be committed within the coming month. On April 26, a not yet fourteen-year-old Mary Phagan, an employee of the city's National Pencil Company, was seen alive for the last time. The next day her lifeless body was found in the basement of the building where she had worked. Her murder and the events connected with the trial and execution of her alleged murderer would be recounted in story and song for decades to come.

Such villainy likely did not go unmentioned from the pulpit of the Wesley Memorial Church during the first week in April 1913 when that congregation of worshippers conducted what many citizens no doubt felt was a much-needed revival.

In the event a desire for spiritual rejuvenation was not pressing, the Atlanta resident might wish to consider shopping as an alternate activity while the revival was going on, even if the city did have the second-highest cost of living in the nation. According to the ads in the Sunday papers those visiting the M. Rich and Bros. Co. department store would find a sale in progress where silk stockings were selling for a dollar up. At the Davison-Paxon-Stokes store ladies' spring coats could be bought for $4.75, and grocery shoppers could buy sugar-cured hams at 19 cents a pound and a peck of yams for a mere 24 cents.

Those who chose to have lunch in downtown restaurants would, after Tuesday, April 1, 1913, be less likely to find a winged intruder in their soup. Beginning that day a city ordinance would require all "places where food is sold [to install] screen doors and windows to keep out flies."[2]

If a movie was on the shopper's itinerary as a reward for not having been able to attend one on Sunday, he or she could choose from among such offerings as *The Spy's Defeat*, a romance of the Franco-German War, showing at the Alcazar; *A Night of Anguish*, at the Savoy; or *The Judge's Vindication*, the Vaudette's "magnificant drama" from the book by Marion Brooks.

City residents with ties to the hinterlands might be ready for a spring visit to relatives in Augusta, Savannah, Columbus, Macon, or some point in between. Frequent train departures and arrivals provided convenient access to many towns, cities, and rural areas throughout the state. No less than eight trains ran daily between Atlanta and Macon.

Readers of the Sunday paper, winding up their afternoon diversion with the comic section, could chuckle at the slapstick antics of "Ike and Mike," the misadventures of the hapless "Mr. Hobby," and the daring deeds of "Hawkshaw, the Detective."

Careful readers that last Sunday afternoon in March would have noted—with, one wonders, what reaction—two upcoming cultural events. The Metropolitan Opera Company would come to Atlanta in April, and on the first through the third of the same month the Georgia Old-Time Fiddlers' Convention would be held at the City Auditorium.[3]

There had been other fiddling conventions, or contests, in Atlanta—some say a fiddlers' convention had been held in the city as far back as 1885[4]—but no previous one seems to have received the publicity enjoyed by the affair that took place in 1913. Reporters with the daily newspapers covered the three-day event in a total of at least fifteen articles in which they analyzed and described in detail not only the entertainers, but the entertained as well.

The fiddlers at the 1913 convention and at those held in the following years came mainly from the northern half of Georgia, while those who came to listen were primarily city and suburban residents mixed with a smattering of out-of-towners who came to hear and root for their local contenders. Most Atlanta residents who attended the fiddlers' conventions were not long off the farm, having been attracted to Atlanta in their search for a steady income and a better standard of living. By the turn of the century word had spread to the state's tenant farmers, sharecroppers, and mountaineers that jobs could be found in Atlanta—jobs in the railroad yards, in construction, and in the city's numerous factories. As a result, hordes of rural refugees, flocking to the city in search of employment, became the nucleus of Cabbagetown, Chattahoochee, Scottdale, and other blue-collar neighborhoods.[5]

The men and women from the mountains, the red clay hills of middle Georgia, and the wiregrass region and swamplands to the south who came to Atlanta to set up residence in these mill villages and other working-class neighborhoods brought with them the hallmarks of their rural culture. One of these was a love for traditional country music. Not only did they enjoy listening to the sounds of the fiddle, the banjo, and the guitar; many of these former residents of Gilmer, Paulding, Pike, Walton, and other outlying counties were accomplished performers as well. Bringing their instruments with them when they came, they continued in the urban setting the long-standing tradition of gathering together in living rooms and on front porches for informal jam sessions and sing-alongs. Thus the fabric of folk music tradition not only remained intact but was strengthened through the interweaving of songs and styles from the different parts of the state.

With a potential appreciative audience of considerable size close at hand and with a seemingly limitless reservoir of talent not only willing, but eager to entertain, it is not surprising to find that the Georgia Old-Time Fiddlers' Conventions were popular annual events for many years. They disappeared from the scene only after the appearance of alternate forms of entertainment with similar appeal to the rural taste in music.

The 1913 Atlanta fiddlers' convention, like those of subsequent years, was held at the Municipal Auditorium, or City Auditorium as it was sometimes called, located at the corner of Courtland and Gilmer streets, a few blocks east of the center of town. Completed in 1909, the original structure, referred to officially as the Atlanta Auditorium-Armory, was designed to serve both as an auditorium and as the headquarters for the Georgia National Guard. In addition to the main auditorium, which could accommodate an audience of more than five thousand, the building also housed Taft Hall, a convention room with a seating capacity of five hundred. The horseshoe-shaped arena of the main auditorium was surrounded by box seats, a dress circle, and a balcony. An Austin organ with six thousand pipes ranging in length from a few inches to thirty-two feet was installed in 1911. Over the years the auditorium provided the setting for a wide variety of cultural, commercial, and political events, including not only the fiddlers' conventions, but symphony orchestra concerts, operas, political rallies, automobile shows, wrestling matches, basketball tournaments, roller skating derbies, ice skating shows, high school graduation exercises, and circuses. In 1979 the auditorium was acquired by nearby Georgia State University, and the main auditorium was subsequently razed to make room for a parking lot. The assembly rooms, including Taft Hall, were remodeled to accommodate the university's Office of Alumni and Development.[6]

By the time the first session of the fiddlers' convention opened on Tuesday night, April 1, a considerable amount of advance publicity had been generated for the event. The articles that had appeared in the papers stressed the rural and traditional flavor of the evening performances, and promised that "there will be no classic music on the program." They vowed, "Indeed, half the numbers to be played have never been written or printed. They have been handed down from father to son for generations, played by ear, memory and main strength and awkwardness."[7]

In the way of tunes, the papers continued, the audience could expect "old favorites [such] as 'Soldiers' Joy,' 'Billy in the Low Grounds,' 'Chickens Before Day,' 'Bacon and Collards,' and scores of others your granddaddies used to dance to in the country cabins before they moved to Atlanta and got rich in real estate and turned to grand opera lovers."[8]

Tuesday evening's program, like the one on Wednesday, served as a warm-up session for the main event—the contest to be held on Thursday night. It was, according to one observer, a "continuous stream of joy"[9] in which "an epidemic of dancing broke out" among members of the audience who displayed the symptoms at various spots around the auditorium. "We're getting further and further back into the woods every minute," one of those in attendance was heard to observe. On stage, each performer was working his hardest to outdo his colleagues, creating "a revel of fiddling, with every piece better than the one before it."[10]

The following "nearly complete" summary of the Tuesday evening program appeared in the *Journal* of Wednesday, April 2:

Col. A. V. Poole—"Fishers Hornpipe."
J. B. Singley, Logansville [*sic*]—"Jackson's March."
P. D. Ludwig, Cobb Co.—"Nigger in the Woodpile."
M. Y. Robinson, Dunwoody—"Going Down to Town,"
Wiley Harper, Monroe—"Polly Put the Kettle On."
Bob Young, Newton County—"Hog in the Cane Break."
J. D. Crenshaw, Covington—"Hop Light Ladies."
Elmira Mack Eddleman, Madison (4 years old)—recitation.
J. V. Tyson, Hogansville—"Snapfinger."
John Block, Lawrenceville—"Arkansas Traveler."
Mack and Bonnie Singley—"Dixie" and "Casey Jones."
C. C. Moon—"Shanghai."
W. M. Ware, Atlanta—"Sweet Bye and Bye" with harmonica accompaniment and encores.
Fiddling John Carson, Blue Ridge, "S'annee River," "Run, Nigger, Run," and encores.
W. Buck Nash, Atlanta, "Forked Deer."
B. E. Day, Cartersville—"Soldier's Joy."
J. O. Hudson, Macon—"Cotton Eyed Joe."
Wiley Harper—"Bonaparte's Retreat."
Cliff Singley, Logansville [*sic*]—Strawbeating accompaniments.[11]

Despite "very wet" weather, the Wednesday crowd of some three thousand was larger than that of the previous evening. Reputedly the second program was every bit as entertaining as the first, with the old fiddlers "a little bit more keenly on their mettle," perhaps in anticipation of the big contest that was then only twenty-four hours away.[12]

It was reported that on Thursday evening an even greater number of old-time fiddling enthusiasts made their way to the auditorium to witness the contest that would bring the convention to a close. Not only was the final evening's audience bigger, it was also said to have been "more enthusiastic, and quicker to cheer the old fiddlers on" than those of the two preceding evenings.[13] Meanwhile the fiddlers could almost taste the delights of fame and fortune awaiting them, and they unloosed a veritable floodgate of artistic devices calculated to win the favor of the presiding judges. Contestants were allowed to play three pieces, but the judges based their decisions on the last-played tune.

According to the *Constitution*, Thursday evening's program was as follows:

Overture by M. Y. Robinson, son and daughter.
A. V. Poole, of Oxford, Polka, accompanied by the Singley children.
Contestants:
Wiley (Shorty) Harper, Monroe, "Sailor's Hornpipe,"
R. M. Stanley, Dacula, "Bile Them Cabbage Down,"
C. L. Hutchins, Sewanee, "Kill Crankie,"
M. Y. Robinson, Dunwoody, "Pretty Betty Martin,"
P. A. Ludwig, Marietta, "Nigger in the Woodpile,"
R. H. Young, Jersey, "Billy in the Low Ground,"
J. B. Singley, Logansville, [*sic*] "Leather Breeches,"
John M. Carlton, Cartersville, "Nigger Dan,"
C. C. Moon, Logansville, [*sic*] "Rye Straw,"
Master Mack Singley, Logansville [*sic*], "Soldiers' Joy,"
J. R. Simonton, Logansville, [*sic*] "Shanghi Chicken,"
W. B. Childs, Yatesville, "Mississippi Sawyer,"
H. W. Bullard, Fairburn, "Arkansas Traveler,"
John Bloch, Lawrenceville, "Forked Deer,"
"Fiddlin'" John Carson, Blue Ridge, "Cacklin' Hen,"
E. S. Cown, Hogansville, "Nancy Rollin,"
J. M. Mathews, East Point, "Lady's Fancy,"
J. O. Hudson, Atlanta, "Johnson's Steamboat,"
J. H. Strickland, Atlanta, "June Apple."
Special features:
James Dodd, College Park, recitation, "Nebuchadnezzar."
Tom Corwine, Alkahest Lyceum, imitations.
A. V. Pool, presided.[14]

From among the fifty fiddlers who had attended the convention, the following prizewinners and their prizes were announced:

First prize, J. B. Singley, Logansville [*sic*], $20.
Second prize, John Block, Lawrenceville, $17.

Third prize, P. A. Ludwig, Marietta, $15.
Fourth prize, John Carson, Blue Ridge, $12.
Fifth prize, J. M. Mathews, East Point, $10.
Sixth prize, R. H. Young, Jersey, $8.
Seventh prize, C. C. Moon, Logansville, [sic] $7.
Eighth prize, Mark Singley, Logansville, [sic] $5.
Ninth prize, Wiley B. Harper, Monroe, $3.
Tenth prize, John M. Carlton, Cartersville, $2.[15]

Serving as judges of the contest were two actual jurists, Judge Dick Russell, of the State Court of Appeals, and Judge Andy Calhoun, of the Atlanta City Court, as well as Timsey Warren from Rockdale County.

Following the contest a square dance was held at which Shorty Harper, from Monroe, directed "an orchestra" of six fiddlers and John Carson "called the figures." Proceeds from the convention went to the Fifth Infantry Regiment of the Georgia National Guard.

Before leaving Atlanta approximately forty of the fiddlers met in order to organize themselves permanently into the Georgia Fiddlers' Association. The following officers were elected: President—Timsey Warren, Rockdale; First Vice President—A. V. Poole, Oxford; Second Vice President—P. A. Ludwig, Marietta; Secretary—H. J. Weaver, Atlanta.

An executive committee consisted of R. M. Stanley, Dacula, chairman; John Bloch, Lawrenceville; R. M. Simonton, Logansville [sic]; E. S. Cown, Hogansville; and John M. Carlton, Cartersville. Elected to the committee on constitution and by-laws were J. T. Holland, Madison, chairman; T. J. Low, Lithonia; C. C. Moon, Logansville [sic]; M. Y. Robinson, Dunwoody; and H. J. Weaver, Atlanta.[16] Members of the new organization agreed that they would thereafter hold a convention each year, a commitment that was dutifully kept, with one possible exception, for the next twenty-two years.

The 1913 Georgia Old-Time Fiddlers' Convention was fairly typical of those that took place over the next several years. From forty to a hundred picturesque musicians flocked to the city auditorium to clown and fiddle—each hoping to win the title of state fiddling champion, a gold medal, and a monetary prize of about fifty dollars. A convention official reported in 1916 that he "had more fiddlers on his list than he could find time for without extending the contest past last trolley time." It was suggested that he probably would have to "arrange for elimination contests and cut down on the entrants." [17]

"It's hard to describe a fiddlers' convention," wrote a newspaper reporter after attending one of the annual contests. "It is not exactly like a wampus chorus, neither does it resemble a shebang. You could not say that it looks like a shindig. It's more like a cross between a thingamajig and a dololly. It ain't like nothing else. The only way to grasp a fiddlers' convention is to see it." [18]

One year a *Journal* editorial writer, anticipating an upcoming convention, promised his readers that the fiddlers' music would cause its listeners to "feel the thrill of forest throats, and mountain wind," and to "hear the whisperings of April voices in the leaves or raindrops dripping from the eaves of some lone cabin on the hill." [19]

Another convention enthusiast, apparently overcome by a wave of nostalgia, described a scene in which every one of the "several dozen" fiddlers carried "the feel of the old red hills of Georgia and the little old cabin with the golden corn swaying in the wind across the patch and the sour mash still bubbling out its distilled sunshine just over the brow of the hill, where the revenooers haven't looked yet. Shut your eyes," he continued, warming to his subject, "and you forget you are in Atlanta's big auditorium. You can see the rafters of the old barn and smell the hay up in the mow and 'most hear the lowing of the cattle and the rustle of the hen who complains about her disturbed nest. You can hear the callers' 'swing your partners,' 'all hands aroun',' 'choose the lady you like best.' [You] remember the girls in the print calico—yes, bare feet, some of them, the dears; and the uneven floor that used to ring like a sounding board to the 'highsteppin' snorters.'" [20]

One witness to the annual contests wrote that "a fiddlers' convention [is] as much a Georgia classic as a barbecue," that "every year the mountaineers who play 100 year old tunes on still older violins gather to decide the state championship and compete for $100 in prizes"; that "each meeting draws to the city the queerest collection of odd characters that Atlanta ever has seen"; that "rich folk and poor folk, society leaders and plain people throng to the auditorium to hear the fiddlers." [21]

The musicians who congregated at the auditorium each year formed a colorful cast of entertainers, exhibiting a wide variety of ages and styles of dress. There were "aged granddaddies whose grizzled beards must needs be tucked inside their hickory shirts to keep them out of the way of the flying bows; young men whose muscles bulge through store-bought coats they have purchased for the great occasion"; and "boys in short trousers who have been taught the fiddle tunes handed down through generation after generation of 'natural musicians.' "[22]

An article in *Hearst's Sunday American* (the Sunday edition of the *Georgian*) described the fiddlers attending the 1918 convention as "gaunt seven-footers from the mountains of north Georgia; slap-sided fishermen from the marshes of the coast; silent ploughboys from middle Georgia farms; and everyone a devil of a fiddler in his own hometown."[23] At the 1914 convention many "wore medals and exhibited certificates proclaiming them the champion fiddlers of county contests."[24]

Typical of one contingent of fiddlers who made the annual pilgrimage to Atlanta's City Auditorium was "Uncle Bud" Littlefield of Hickory Gap, located "at the foot of Pine Mountain in north Georgia's Rabun County." "Uncle Bud" was one of the first contestants to reach the city for the 1920 convention. Arriving at one of the train stations with a burlap bag thrown over his shoulder and carrying his fiddle in a pillowcase tucked under his arm, he said this was his first trip to Atlanta and that he had "come down a little ahead of time" to visit a nephew who was then living in the city. He noted that he had come to Atlanta "to show the people of Georgia what regular fiddling is." Mr. Littlefield, whose countenance was adorned with "two feet of white whiskers," informed his listeners that up where he came from "we raise corn, hell and fiddlers, and we had a pretty good crop this year, all around."[25]

Among the not-so-typical contestants was Rev. A. G. Alloway, also of Rabun County, who entered the 1929 contest. His friends stated that he was not only an able evangelist, but an equally accomplished fiddler who used his instrument to lead the music in his revival meetings. "We certainly will be glad to have brother Alloway with us," said an official of the Georgia Old-Time Fiddlers' Association. "I hope he can help me keep the boys in line."[26]

The personalities and backgrounds of the contestants provided only part of the variety to be observed at the fiddlers' conventions. Even the instruments on which they performed were a heterogeneous lot and objects of considerable interest among the musicians and their friends. Fiddles of reputed ancient vintage and crude homemade specimens were exhibited with equal pride by their owners. In 1914 one J. D. Bobo appeared at the convention displaying an instrument which he claimed to be "a genuine Stradivarius, 241 years old and worth $4,000 to a collector." Bobo stated that he had played his way "around the world and back."[27]

Representative of the homemade instruments that could be found at the fiddlers' conventions was the one fashioned in time for the 1920 contest by Jim [*sic*, probably John] Goolsby of Peavine. It was, wrote a newspaper reporter, "a fiddle such as Kriesler never saw and Kubelik never dreamed of touching. It was built by his own hands from a cigar box, a hoe handle and assorted sizes of wire strings, and when tickled with a bow made of half a barrel hoop and well-rosined horsehair" it reputedly emitted "sounds guaranteed to make a $90 saxophone in a jazz band sob with envy." Mr. Goolsby announced that his home-crafted fiddle was for "exhibition purposes only" and would not be played in the official contest for state champion. For that event, he explained, he would borrow a regular instrument from one of his fellow fiddlers. "Fiddles are all just alike, except this one I made," said Goolsby. "If a fiddler's a fiddler he can play any fiddle," he philosophized. "It's a bad workman that blames his tools."[28]

One of the more original and successful of the home-produced instruments was created by Atlanta resident C. S. Brook, a carpenter by trade. Brook and his instrument appear to have made their convention debut in 1918. Later dubbed a "broomaphone," Brook's device consisted of a broomstick and one string. He could charm a tune from his homemade device by rubbing a cigar box up and down the string. Mr. Brook's offerings at the 1918 convention, which included "It's a Long Way to Tipperary," "elicited roars of approval." From time to time Brook performed on his broomaphone at subsequent annual fiddlers' conventions. He and his novel instrument also became familiar sights at other old-time music events in Atlanta.

Many of the fiddles played at the Georgia Old-Time Fiddlers' conventions, wrote an *Atlanta Journal Magazine* contributor in 1915, had "come down from father to son through several generations, and . . . are heirlooms more highly prized than a Highlander's bagpipes. There are no Cremonas in the mountains. No famous Italian name is to be found scrawled inside the brown belly of a Georgia fiddle. Most of them have been patched with pine head-pieces and cedar thumb keys, and their wire strings, snapping in the midst of the jig, have cut deep scars in the shining violin which has played reels and jigs for generations. One could hardly imagine a musician coaxing Rubenstein or Liszt from one of them." To illustrate his point the writer mentioned the fiddle proudly exhibited by one Charley Randall. "Yes, sir, that fiddle is older than the United States," Mr. Randall was quoted. "My granddaddy is more'n ninety —going on ninety-four to be exact—and he says his granddaddy brought that fiddle down the ridge from No'th C'eliny before they fought the British in the war." [29]

The contestant whose instrument was not quite to his liking no doubt tried harder in 1921 to win the coveted first-place position in the competition. For, in addition to the usual cash award, the winner of the fiddling contest that year received a violin valued at $100, a gift of the Cable Piano Company, Atlanta's leading music store at the time. Said William L. Brownlee, president of the company, in announcing the prize, "These country fiddlers are doing something more than merely providing entertainment for a crowd of city folks; they are preserving the traditional music of our forefathers, the old melodies which their ancestors brought into the mountains more than a hundred years ago. I know no other state in which the old tunes, the folklore of the pioneers, is being thus preserved. These annual conventions of the fiddlers, from which all modern music is excluded, are doing a great deal to keep up this tradition, and we are glad to have a share in it by offering an instrument which may play 'Chicken in the Bread Tray' and 'Bonaparte's Retreat' for many generations yet unborn." [30] Violins donated by the Cable Piano Company were given as prizes for several subsequent years.

Contestants not having the good fortune to win the prize fiddle in 1921 could have placed an order for a new instrument with T. H. Gamble. He and his two sons were violin makers from Cherokee County, and samples of their handiwork were on display at the auditorium during the convention. Mr. Gamble, who "learned his art from his grandfather who made fiddles more than 50 years ago," carved his instruments by hand from Georgia timber. We are told that several of the Gamble instruments had previously won prizes at the Georgia Old-Time Fiddlers' Conventions and that they were "famous for their resonance and the volume of tone, two qualities especially in demand for fiddling at country dances."[31]

No matter the origin of the instrument played by a Georgia old-time fiddler it was called a fiddle—not a violin. Sometimes, for the unenlightened, the difference between the two had to be explained. An Atlanta lawyer, Col. Eb T. Williams, who served as a judge at some of the early fiddlers' contests, and who was, himself, both a fiddler and a violinist, once addressed the subject. "A fiddle," he said "is an old, common instrument, clumsily and roughly finished with wire strings, the bridge a thick piece of wood set in the wrong place, the sound post sometimes in front instead of behind the bridge, and not infrequently a mouse hole gnawed in the 'F' holes as big as a goose egg, where several generations of mice were born and raised. A violin," he continued, "is, on the other hand, a thing of beauty, the most dainty and exquisitely finished instrument in the world, made of the most beautiful grained maple and spruce pine, with old Cremona varnish that has foiled the centuries; beautiful, fresh and oily . . . and it has a divine voice that appeals to you like the voice of an angel, and in the hands of a master wails with sorrow or laughs with joy, having concealed in its body a human soul sounding every depth of the human heart."[32]

In less-polished language the difference between a fiddler and a violinist was explained to a reporter at the 1920 convention by "Judge" Tump Jackson, a contestant from the mountains of Towns County on Georgia's border with Tennessee. (The title "Judge" derived from the days when he had been a justice of the peace.) "The difference between a fiddler and one of these here violinists is that a violinist plays by note and a fiddler by plain natural disposition and elbow grease," said "Judge" Jackson. "You might go on to say," he continued, "that a violinist draws down about a thousand a night, a week, a month or whatever it is, if it's so, and a fiddler is lucky to get the neck of the chicken and what's left in the bottle after it's done been around the room. There's an old saying that the devil pays the fiddler, but if that's the case, he owes me for about 40 years of back debts."[33]

"Judge" Jackson, who was described as a "widely known character" in his home county and "something of a philosopher," had first-hand experience on which to base his opinions regarding fiddlers and violinists. "I had the pleasure of hearing one of these fancy violinists last year," Mr. Jackson stated. "He came a pesterin' around through the mountains on the trail of what he called folk music. He got three or four of us fiddlers together and prevailed on us to play for him, and he put down little crooked notes in a black book. Everytime I'd get good started on a tune, he'd stop me while he caught up, and then tell me to start over. When he got through I asked him to play us a tune and he took my fiddle and projected with it a little bit and then sawed the bow up and down and seemed to be huntin' around for something he never could find, and then he quit. Uncle Jim Watson asked him why he didn't go ahead and play something.

" 'Why, I've just played it,' this fellow said. But I don't know but what he was joking. If he played any tune whatsoever, I clean missed it." [34]

If the fiddlers and the instruments on which they performed provided a study in contrasts, the many ways in which these rosin-and-bow experts executed their skills ran the gamut in instrument and body manipulation. In their efforts to extract music from a wooden box some of the fiddlers even held their instruments under their chins in the conventional manner of the violinist. The majority, however, it was said, held them "against their wishbone or anywhere else." [35] Remarked one spectator, "The difference between a fiddler and a violinist is that a violinist stands up, but a fiddler's just got to sit down so he can pat his feet—or he couldn't play." [36] A *Georgian* reporter, attending a fiddlers' convention for the first time, wrote that he "learned a number of things. I learned, for example, that footwork is a prime feature of elderly fiddling. Some pat with the left foot. Some pat with the right. Some . . . pat with both feet, with a wealth of syncopation. Some pat with the fore part of the foot, some with the heel. But they all pat, prodigiously. Feet are as necessary to an old fiddler as to a ballet dancer." According to this reporter the fiddlers, who sat in chairs as they performed, were provided with "patting platforms" on which to execute the footwork which so captured his attention. [37]

In describing the 1913 fiddlers' convention, a reporter for the *Constitution* noted:

There were those who must introduce their selections by bewildering flourishes of the bow and labyrinthian mazes of musical runs, and there were others who, already keyed to the point of inspiration, dived head first, as it were, in the placid midst of a melody and by the same token past the ending place and wound up in the middle of a bar.

There were those contestants who could not make fittin' melody until they had shifted the chair to just the right angle and reposed the fiddle in their laps, and still others stood up in all their majesty and poured the strains of "Turkey in the Straw" over the heads of the multitude assembled. One of the musicians found it necessary to walk several miles up and down the platform during his preliminary bars before he could work himself up to the proper frenzy to do himself justice. For others most of the music seemed to emanate from a syncopating elbow.[38]

Like many of the instruments on which they performed, the tunes played by the contestants at the old-time fiddlers' conventions were of ancient origin. In fact, noted one observer, they were "even older [than the fiddles], and that is strange," he commented, "when one considers that they have never been set down in black and white. The composer of 'Soldiers' Joy,'" he elaborated, "may have been in the camps of the cavaliers, or the blockhouses of Daniel Boone. It is rather well established that the air was a favorite in the War of the Revolution, and played on the shrill fife, inspired the volunteers of the colonies in many a famous charge." [39]

Another chronicler of the conventions reported that "the tunes the fiddlers play are jigs and reels and breakdowns, with an occasional old ballad air. There is little of the melancholy of the Scotch or Irish folk song. Most of the tunes," he added, "are riotous, breakneck melodies, used to spur on the dancers in [a] Virginia reel or quadrille, the same tunes that for a hundred years or more have furnished the accompaniment for the 'barndances' of the country gatherings, where the customary refreshments consisted of a barrel of moonshine mountain dew with a gourd hanging on its rim. There are," he concluded, "quaint names fitted to these old tunes, [such as] 'Devil Before Day' and 'Grey Hoss in the Wilderness' and 'Billy in the Low Ground.'" [40]

Old-time string bands added variety to the annual fiddlers'

conventions as well as providing the music for the square dances that always ended each evening's entertainment bill. Hailing from various parts of the state these musical aggregations were identified by such bucolic appellations as the Hoe Cake Orchestra, the Moo-Cow Band, the Sorghum Band, and the Smoky Ridge Band. The apparent favorite among the convention bands was the Lick Skillet Orchestra. Year after year its presence at the auditorium was reported by the local press. In 1919 the band was described as consisting of "three fiddles, a couple of banjos, two straw beaters and a 'bull fiddle' taller than the man who plays it, and who comes from the upper corner of Cobb County." We are told, "It has played at every country breakdown in that section for years, and it provides the music for the dances which follow the night sessions of the fiddlers' conventions at the auditorium."[41] A reporter once wrote that, in keeping with the spirit of the conventions, the band "usually . . . is swelled by the joining in of every other fiddle in the room, for the mountaineers are quite quick to pick up an air, and before the evening is over it is the size of the Metropolitan Orchestra, though perhaps not as well balanced."[42]

Through the years several persons served as master of ceremonies at the Georgia Old-Time Fiddlers' Conventions. The most frequent and most colorful of these was a man who went by the name of Professor Aleck (sometimes reported as Alec or Alex) Smart, allegedly a teacher at "the little red school house" in the Cove, near Woodbury.

Smart made his initial convention appearance in 1915 when he was described as a "quaint character . . . who . . . plays a melodeon and sings ancient ballads, which end in a yodel that climbs clear out through the roof and wanders among the stars."[43] He was said to have long hair and a long neck. His clothing, the most prominent feature of which was a frock coat from another era, hung loosely on his "slight and frail" frame, and his striped pants failed "to connect with his shoe tops by some three inches."[44] Gold-rimmed spectacles habitually rested far down on his nose, and a tall silk hat topped off his attire. His stage delivery, it was reported, was a masterpiece of "old school oratory."[45]

It was Smart's responsibility to "keep watch over the Atlanta convention," to see that "every fiddle is tuned properly before the owner strikes the first note, and keep order on the big stage, where fiddlers' jealousies frequently give rise to trouble." [46] In those days that preceded the era of modern amplification devices, Smart directed his ensemble of fiddlers and other performers through the skillful use of a cowbell and a megaphone. Between fiddlers' conventions in Atlanta Smart stayed busy in other parts of the state conducting singing schools, giving lessons in elocution, and organizing county branches of the Georgia Old-Time Fiddlers' Association. [47]

"There was no doubt," wrote a newspaper reporter in 1914, "that Atlanta welcomed the fiddlers." Devotees of old-time music, we are told, arrived at the auditorium in limousines and trolley cars while others "hoofed it." [48] The gatherings were usually described as a veritable montage of humanity as ladies in silks and expensive furs mixed with working folk "in plain attire," as city folk and country folk "rubbed elbows, quarrelled over the merits of rival favorites and patted their feet as one man" to the strains of the music they had come to hear. At one of the performances in 1914 a row or two of the younger society set, conspicuous in their evening clothes, were spotted among the congregation. They had, concluded a reporter, dropped in on their way to a tango. [49]

A *Constitution* reporter once wrote that although the fiddlers put on a good show, the audience provided "a better one. They didn't applaud," explained the scribe, "they bawled, they howled, they shrieked, they crowed.

"Practically three thousand persons filled to overflowing the lower part of the building, and created an atmosphere that was something like the enthusiasm of a prize fight, added to the getting happy of [an] old time camp meeting. Members of the audience got the spirit and moved out into the aisles, for a double shuffle. Encouragement was yelled back and forth over the footlights to professional and impromptu performers." [50]

Inspired by the enthusiasm of the crowd, the fiddlers on stage outdid themselves in the execution of their musical talents. "They fiddled in solos, in duets, in deafening ensembles. They fiddled in the regular way, on their knees, backward and forward, and blindfolded. Since the burning of Rome," concluded the reporter, "there has never been such fiddling." [51]

When they were not performing on the auditorium stage the fiddlers spent their time in a variety of ways. They got together in informal jam sessions, they entertained at civic clubs and for other organizations, and they partied. While the convention was in session numerous small groups of fiddlers and other musicians could be found in and around the auditorium jamming, practicing, and warming up. By the time the evening shows began the fiddlers usually had been on the premises all day. "In every nook and corner of the big Atlanta auditorium Thursday," wrote a reporter in 1918, "the scrape of bow over catgut made it hard for the janitors and scrubwomen to make their feet be still." [52]

If the day were warm the fiddlers gathered in the alley outside, "holding a reunion, swapping yarns, and picking up new tunes to take home and play at corn shuckings and barn dances." [53] One observer of such jam sessions concluded that the fiddlers were not enjoying the music—they were "studying it," for it was said that "as a pianist goes to Chicago or Boston for a post-graduate course with a famous master, so do the Georgia fiddlers attend the Atlanta conventions." [54]

The old fiddlers did not limit their entertaining to the performances at the auditorium. On a Wednesday afternoon in 1915, for example, about sixty of the fiddlers boarded a chartered streetcar that took them to the Atlanta Federal Prison where they entertained the inmates in the prison chapel. There "the famous old songs of the rural districts were played and brought back fond remembrances to many a gray-haired prisoner whose younger days were spent around the country store." [55] On the following Thursday afternoon from 4:30 to 6:30, the fiddlers gave a reception in the auditorium's Taft Hall for the Atlanta chapter of the Daughters of the Confederacy, an occasion promised to be one of "unique and delightful interest." [56] Counting the people who heard the fiddlers at the auditorium and those who were entertained at the prison, in Taft Hall, and at other places, one reporter estimated that the fiddlers would have reached an audience of thirty thousand by the end of their four-day convention. [57]

The fame of the Georgia Old-Time Fiddlers' conventions and their stars spread to all parts of the country as the events and the performers became the subjects of articles in several publications with nationwide circulations. At least two articles appeared in *Musical America*, a magazine usually concerned with matters pertaining to classical music. This magazine featured the convention in a 1919 article that also covered Atlanta's Metropolitan Grand Opera season and the appearance in the city of violinist Fritz Kreisler, the Cincinnati Symphony, and the then popular Irish tenor, John McCormack. "The fiddlers," the article noted, "know almost nothing of modernity or cities; and their rendition is pure, even antique, often accompanying their fiddled tunes with untrained and old-fashioned but quaintly charming voices."[58] Allegedly the *New York Times* once "sent a special representative to the convention, and he devoted a page of pictures and text to the unusual exposition of old-fashioned music."[59] Stories on individual performers appeared in several other popular publications.

The conventions were not neglected by the other communications media. In 1928, the *Journal* reported that arrangements were being made "for filming a group of the fiddlers and reproducing their music through the medium of movietone." The group was to include more than a dozen of the fiddling favorites. An official of the Georgia Old-Time Fiddlers' Association "stated that it might be necessary for the fiddlers to go to one of the eastern studios to complete the film."[60] The outcome of this anticipated venture is not known.

After radio came to Atlanta in 1922 representative fiddlers from the conventions were frequently featured in studio broadcasts that carried their music to the far reaches of the country. On at least one occasion a segment of the convention was broadcast directly from the City Auditorium. During World War I, "representatives of the War Department's camp entertainment work held conferences with the [convention] management relative to presenting similar conventions in army camps in Virginia and Louisiana."[61]

The fiddlers' conventions even attracted the attention of the noted evangelist Billy Sunday. While her husband was holding a revival in Chattanooga, Tennessee, Mrs. Sunday attended the 1919 convention "to look over the fiddlers" before inviting some dozen "of the best known in Georgia up to Chattanooga next week to wield the bow and shake a foot at Billy Sunday's revival."[62]

Perhaps the most interesting result of the publicity received by the fiddlers' conventions followed the one held in 1924. That year a young man named Marcus Lowe Stokes of Cartersville won first prize in the contest that was held Saturday night, November 8. The next morning *Hearst's Sunday American* carried on page one a brief article announcing the fact and emphasizing the youth of

Stokes and the advanced years of his opponents. The headline gave his age as fourteen, while in the body of the article he was referred to as a "22-year-old." Later evidence suggests that he may have been twenty-four. Allegedly an account of Stokes's victory also appeared in the *New York Times*. In December 1924 the *Literary Digest* magazine, apparently inspired by the *New York Times* piece, carried a short article on the event. Referring to Stokes as a mere novice, the article reported that he "came down from the Blue Ridge foothills primed with all the Southern tunes that he had learned from his grandad, and full of the spirit of victory." In March 1925, a poem entitled "The Mountain Whippoorwill, or How Hill-Billy Jim Won the Great Fiddlers Prize" was published by the noted poet Stephen Vincent Benét. The poem tells the story of how Hill-Billy Jim, from "up in the mountains" where "it's lonesome for a child," took his fiddle to the "Georgia Fiddlers Show" to compete with a number of old-timers, including "Old Dan Wheeling" who had been "king-pin fiddler for nearly twenty years." After Hill-Billy Jim's performance "old man Dan" admitted defeat by placing his fiddle in the young man's hand. It is believed that Benét's poem was inspired by news stories of Stokes's performance in Atlanta.[63]

But all was not harmony—except, perhaps, in a musical sense—at the Georgia Old-Time Fiddlers' Conventions. Through the years disputes of various types arose among the contestants. A bone of contention at the 1913 contest was whether straw beating should be allowed in the contest. Straw beating, explained a *Journal* reporter for the benefit of "the city dweller, is the gentle art of keeping up an accompaniment to a fiddle. The fiddler handles the bow, while at his shoulder, keeping carefully out of the way of the bowing, stands the accompanist. His instrument is—or are—two slender wooden sticks, or straws, and with these he taps a continual accompaniment upon the violin strings near the neck of the instrument, very much as a xylophonist does his specialty in vaudeville."[64] The effect was described as something like a banjo accompaniment.

The straw-beating issue was of major concern to a delegation of enthusiasts of the art from Rabun Gap in north Georgia and a contingent of their Habersham County peers who held a different opinion as to the proper role of this particular talent. Said one contender from Rabun Gap, "I was raised to believe that straw beatin' was the most principal part of fiddlin'. Up my way the first thing they learn a youngster is fiddlin' and the next is straw beatin'. It takes a real sho-'nuff musician to beat a straw the right way." The folks from Habersham, however, perceived straw beating as "a mere side issue, not to be confounded with fiddling." The dispute terminated in a compromise in which the decision was made to permit straw beating in the exhibition numbers, but not in the tunes played directly in competition.[65]

The majority of Georgia's old-time fiddlers prided themselves on not being able to read music. In their attempt to create a primitive and rustic image of the old Georgia fiddler, the journalists who covered the annual conventions made much of the fact that the fiddlers played by ear. Any fiddler bold enough to admit to a knowledge of such erudite symbols and notation as key signatures, sharps, flats, rests, *poco animato, a tempo,* and *allargando al fine* could expect criticism from his peers. Such was the case in 1917 when the executive committee of the fiddlers' association met to consider the rules for the upcoming convention. At that time a dispute reportedly arose regarding the use of printed music by the performers. The controversy erupted, wrote a reporter for the *Georgian*, when "one Doc Wells, of Union County, declared his intention of playing a piece which recently became popular in his neck of the woods, entitled 'Memphis Blues.'" Since none of the other fiddlers had ever heard, or heard of, the tune, Wells was requested to acquaint them with the melody. When he was "so ill advised as to reach into his fiddle box and bring forth the printed music of the air," we are told that "two dozen fiddlers were on their feet in a moment, vigorously protesting against the introduction of any tune which ever had been printed and the admission of any fiddler who pretended to be able to look at a lot of black spots on a ladder and play them on a fiddle. But it appeared that several other musicians confessed to knowing something of printed tunes, and they boldly upheld their right to enter the state fiddling contest." After "considerable debate" it was reported that the issue had been resolved through adoption of a motion made by Professor Smart to the effect that no contestant would be allowed to play a printed tune except for exhibition purposes and that no page of sheet music would be permitted in the auditorium during the convention.[66]

Although a complete roster of state fiddling champions for the years 1913 through 1935 has not survived, we know who most of the winners were. In addition to J. B. Singley, who took first place in 1913, others who captured the championship title include Fiddlin' John Carson of Atlanta (1914, 1923, 1927); Wiley (Shorty) Harper from Monroe (1915, 1916); John Silvey of Floyd County (1917); A. A. Gray, Tallapoosa (1918, 1921, 1922, 1926, 1929, 1930, 1934); F. B. Coupland, Rome (1919); R. M. Stanley, Dacula (1920); Lowe Stokes, Rome (1924, 1925); Earl Johnson, Lawrenceville (1926); Gid Tanner, Gwinnett County (1929); Joe Collins, Stockbridge (1930); and Anita Sorrells Wheeler, Atlanta (1931, 1934).[67] In some years more than one "state contest" was held, but it is not always clear from contemporary accounts whether all were sanctioned by the Georgia Old-Time Fiddlers' Association. In any case, a "state champion" was named at each contest.

It seems that A. A. Gray, of Tallapoosa, Georgia, was the most frequent winner of the state title. At least he is most frequently mentioned as such by the newspapers. Ahaz Augustus Gray was born on September 7, 1881, in Carroll County, Georgia. Although his parents, Matt and Eliza Gray, were not musicians, Ahaz, as he was known to his friends, had an older brother who played the fiddle, and it was he who taught the younger brother the rudiments of the instrument. In 1934, Ahaz described his musical instruction to Willard Neal of the *Journal*'s Sunday magazine: "I guess I'm different from most of the fiddlers. Nearly all the others learned to play naturally, but I had to be taught. When I was seven years old my big brother started me off. He had to poke my fingers down on the strings and hold them there while I sawed with the bow. He taught me part of a piece, and then got mad because I couldn't learn any faster, and quit, but I kept trying 'till I picked out the whole tune. And I've been playing ever since."[68] Ahaz was apparently a faster learner than his brother realized since, according to family tradition, he played for his first dance when he was between seven and eight years old.[69]

At the age of twenty-five, Gray married Ida Clarinda Smith in a ceremony that took place in Buchanan, the seat of Haralson County. Sometime after their marriage, the Grays moved to a rural community near Tallapoosa, some eight miles southwest of Buchanan. They spent the remainder of their lives in and around Tallapoosa where Gray earned his and his family's living by farming and fiddling. They had three children, two boys and a girl.

Gray was popular among Haralson County residents as a square-dance fiddler and as a performer with Gray's String Band composed of Gray; Charlie Thompson, who played guitar; banjoist Henry West; and another fiddler, Fred Hill. An undated handbill (probably printed around 1925) announcing one of the band's forthcoming performances promised the audience good jokes, songs, buck-and-wing dancing, and "string music that will make you forget your troubles." Gray was constantly filling requests to play at square dances in his own and surrounding communities. As one lady who grew up with Gray's children once recalled, "The young people in the community kept an eye on where Mr. Gray went and followed him, because they knew wherever he went there'd be fun, music, and dancing."[70]

Saturday nights usually found the Gray family hosting a musical "get-together" in their home. Friends and neighbors would drop in to listen to Gray's fiddling as well as to the music of other members of the family. Mrs. Gray sang and played the guitar, as did their son Earl and their daughter, Gladys, who also played the organ.

Gray was remembered by his neighbors as a hard-working, serious-minded, devoted husband and father. Although his avocation inevitably brought him in contact with every level of social drinker, from those who liked only an occasional nip to those who would today be called alcohol abusers, Gray himself was a teetotaler. While his music inspired many an exhibition on the dance floor, he was not known for his dancing.

Gray's fiddling victories were not restricted to the state and regional contests, but included many local championships also. His children later recalled that he was a winner of at least one contest in Rome, as well as contests in other Georgia towns. In a 1934 interview Gray said, "Once I toured south Georgia with a big crowd, playing in a lot of conventions." In the same interview he also had something to say about his strategy for winning. "I find that the tune you play has a lot to do with winning prizes. A fellow just ahead of me [on the south Georgia tour] used 'Bully of the Town,' and that's a mighty good piece. He won four prizes in a row. Finally, I happened to think of 'Bucking Mule.' It's a hard piece, but it's snappy, and you do a lot of fancy work behind the bridge that makes the fiddle bray like a mule. I won so many prizes [with that tune] that the other fellows got to calling me 'Mule' Gray."[71]

Unlike most of the contestants at the fiddlers' conventions—
even the champions—Gray's fiddling has been preserved on phonograph records. The only solo record he made was "Bonaparte's
Retreat" backed by "Merry Widow Waltz," which was recorded
on the OKeh label. An OKeh advertising brochure dated June 5,
1924, states that

> Mr. A. A. Gray, hailing from Tallapoosa, Georgia, joins
> the ranks of Okeh's famous Southern hill-country musicians.
> His first record brings you his delightfully unique versions
> of the well-known BONAPARTE'S RETREAT and MERRY
> WIDOW WALTZ. Gray has a rare knack of playing two or
> three strings on his fiddle at the same time. It results in a com-
> bination of harmonies that are distinctly "up-country," and yet,
> charmingly "different" from anything you've probably ever
> heard before.

Other records on which Gray can be heard are "Streak-o-
lean, Streak-o-fat"/"Tallapoosa Bound," "Nigger Baby"/"The Old
Ark's a'Moving," "A Georgia Barbecue at Stone Mountain, Parts
1 and 2," and "A Fiddler's Tryout in Georgia, Parts 1 and 2," all
on the Vocalion label. The first two records feature Gray on fiddle,
and "Seven Foot Dilly" (John Dilleshaw) on guitar. "Streak-o-Lean,
Streak-o-Fat" and "Tallapoosa Bound" are instrumentals. Vocals
by Gray and Dilleshaw are heard on "Nigger Baby" and "The Old
Ark's a'Moving."

"A Fiddler's Tryout in Georgia" records a fake fiddling-contest
skit with "judges" and short solos by two supposedly competing fiddlers. The "contest" in this case was between Gray and Joe Brown,
a fiddler from Burnt Hickory, a rural community near Dallas, Georgia. Brown was also a frequent contestant at the real Georgia Old-
Time Fiddlers' Conventions. On the record Gray plays "Bucking
Mule" and "Sally Goodin'," Brown plays "Arkansas Traveler" and
"Blue Tail Fly," and the two together play "Leather Britches" and
"Katie Hill." "A Georgia Barbecue at Stone Mountain," another re-
corded skit, features the music of Gray, fiddle; Pink Lindsey, bass;
Shorty Lindsey, banjo and mandolin; and John Dilleshaw, guitar.

A. A. Gray died on June 21, 1939. He had been a member of
the Methodist church for more than thirty years when he died and
was remembered by those who knew him as a sober man and one
well-regarded in his community. The writer of his obituary stated

that "Mr. Gray was a good man and will be missed by his many friends."[72]

With few exceptions the performers at the Georgia Old-Time Fiddlers' Conventions were males. We read of the appearance on stage of an occasional female banjo-picker, singer, or dancer, and there were even a few women and girls over the years who were brave enough to enter the fiddling competition. In 1916 Louise Hall, a fourteen-year-old girl from Gilmer County, won the thirty-dollar second prize.[73] In 1920, a girl of fifteen named Anita Sorrells (the papers misspelled her name as Soers) played "Casey Jones" in competition and won second place.[74] Rosa Lee (also known as Moonshine Kate) Carson, daughter of Fiddlin' John Carson, was playing banjo at the conventions as early as 1924.[75]

It was not until 1929, apparently, that the old guard of Georgia's male fiddlers became concerned about the encroachment of women upon the field that they had dominated for so long. As the roaring twenties came to an end a presumably mature and serious woman fiddler registered as an entrant in the Georgia Old-Time Fiddlers' Convention. The applicant, a resident of Sumter County in south Georgia, was Miss Emilia Wells, who stated that she was a self-taught country fiddler.

Upon receipt of Miss Wells's application, Professor Aleck Smart, secretary of the fiddlers' association, announced, "Personally, I have no objections. . . . Looks like the women are running the men out of every kind of job, from driving cars to flying. But up in the mountain regions where most of our fiddlers come from they have always figured that the place for a woman is in the cabin, doing the cooking and looking after the children, with some plowing and hoeing in season. And they certainly are not used to women fiddlers. I reckon we'll have to take a vote on it."[76]

The outcome of Miss Wells's bid for a chance at the Georgia fiddling crown is not known, but it is likely that she was allowed to compete in the contest.

The following year, 1930, again saw a woman entrant. She was Mrs. Anita Wheeler of Powder Springs, the same Anita Sorrells who, in 1920, had won second place. Now married to J. P. Wheeler and the mother of two children, Mrs. Wheeler once more won second place which, that year, carried an award of twenty-five dollars. But this was not the last time the Georgia Old-Time Fiddlers' Association would hear from Mrs. Wheeler. She was back in 1931 to carry off the first prize and become Georgia's first and only woman fiddle champion. Also in 1931, Mrs. Wheeler entered the Interstate Fiddlers' Convention held in the Atlanta City Auditorium and again "sawed her way to victory." Willard Neal of the *Atlanta Journal Magazine* wrote, "Winning this contest means the championship of the United States, according to Professor Alex Smart, master of ceremonies, and that, of course, is the same as best fiddler in the world."[77] In 1934 Mrs. Wheeler returned to the annual state convention in Atlanta and for a second time was crowned champion fiddler of Georgia.

Anita Sorrells Wheeler was born on February 6, 1905, in Cobb County, on a farm near Lost Mountain, about five miles north of Powder Springs and twenty miles northwest of downtown Atlanta.[78] She was the first-born child of Dudley Maddox Sorrells and Annie Lena Estes Sorrells.

Mr. Sorrells barbered, farmed, and ran a chicken-peddling route. "He'd hitch up his mules and wagon and go out in the country and buy chickens and eggs and butter, and take them to town [and frequently to Atlanta] and sell them," the champion fiddler once explained. "He also bought and sold pigs," she added.

On the side, Mr. Sorrells made music. In fact, practically every member of the Sorrells family for several generations was a musician. Grandfather Sorrells, who was a fiddler, taught his children to play instruments, with his son Dudley concentrating on the fiddle. "They had their own band," said Anita years later. "Then when we kids came along we had our own band. We'd go play for miles around where anybody was having a get-together and wanted some music. We played in people's homes, at churches, and for square dances. We did it mainly for fun, except we got paid for playing at square dances. They'd take up so much [money] on the corner at the dances."

Anita began playing her father's fiddle when she was eight years old, and she played for her first square dance two years later. "I have played until daylight several times and never got very tired," she told a newspaper reporter in 1934.[79] The night in 1923 that she married J. P. Wheeler, Anita Sorrells was playing for a square dance at the hotel in Austell, Georgia. "During the break," she once explained, "we slipped away from the hotel and got married, and then came back and I finished playing the dance."

Anita was essentially a self-taught fiddler. "I just picked it up from my father. I learned the tunes and then did my own maneuvering." In 1931 she told the *Journal's* Willard Neal, "Fiddlers are never taught; they do their own learning. We figure that music comes from a person's soul. If you have it in you, you can play; and if you haven't, there is no use trying to learn. If a person taught you how to play a tune, you would simply be playing his music, and not your own." [80]

Anita's early fiddling career was not restricted to winning prizes at state and regional contests in Atlanta and performing with the Sorrells Family Band. For a while in 1925 she played the fiddle with the Dixie String Band, a group of Atlanta musicians that also included J. F. Mitchell, fiddle; C. S. Brook, guitar; and John Dilleshaw, guitar. This band numbered among its accomplishments several radio broadcasts over Atlanta's WSB.

After Anita's first husband died in 1933, she and her two children, a daughter and a son, continued to live in Atlanta, and in 1934 she was again being heard on Atlanta's WSB. This time she was performing with a group called the Tennessee Firecrackers.

In 1935 Anita joined an all-girl group called the Oklahoma Cowgirls with whom she performed for about a year. They played in theaters in Georgia, Alabama, Chicago, Ohio, and Indiana.

After the Oklahoma Cowgirls disbanded, Anita returned to Atlanta where she worked for a candy manufacturer and a bakery. She was married in 1937 to Bob Mathis with whom she moved to Houston, Texas, where she frequently played the fiddle at local square dances. In 1974, after her second husband's death, Mrs. Mathis returned to Atlanta where, in 1988, she was still living and occasionally playing the fiddle in public.

The twentieth century finally caught up with the Georgia Old-Time Fiddlers' Association, and the encounter appears to have been a lethal one for the yearly conventions. As early as 1926 Professor Aleck Smart found it necessary to announce that the annual event that year was "going to be a fiddlers' convention, and we want nobody but fiddlers to compete. We're going to have nothing but genuine, old fashioned music, with no notes. We're not going to have any printed music, and we won't have any of this crazy stuff they call jazz that is plumb ruining all the good fiddling in Georgia."[81] One journalist wrote that any young fiddler who had the nerve to try "to please the assemblage with a waltz tune or foxtrot, with a liberal jazz treatment, [was] frowned on, told to take his tunes elsewhere and given a lecture on his falling from grace. For not even the conductor of the Boston Symphony Orchestra could look with more contempt upon jazz than do Professor Alec Smart and his fellow fiddlers upon the profane melodies which have come out of New York's Tin Pan Alley to compete with the tunes their grandads played."[82]

In 1927, however, one Uncle Ebb Garston, a championship aspirant, shared with a *Constitution* reporter some gloomy opinions of the current status of fiddle tunes. "The good old tunes are passing away," he mourned. "These here phonografts and the radio air corruptin' our boys and gals worsen a circus or a stage show."[83] Capitulation came in 1930. A few days before the opening of that year's convention the *Journal* told its readers, "The phonograph and the radio, better roads and the flivver, and the advent of the picture show in the remote county seats of Georgia are beginning to crowd the old-fashioned tunes like 'The Bear Went Over the Mountain' into the discard." At last, readers were told, officers of the Georgia Old-Time Fiddlers' Association had "yielded to the change in popular musical tastes. They have thrown down the bars and opened the gates to any and every form of entertainment which contestants may desire to offer on the programs of the three sessions [of the convention]."[84]

There was at least one compromise between the old-timers and the moderns. The regulations which had governed the official contests from the beginning were to be maintained. "Nothing but old timey fiddle tunes may be played [in the competition]," the *Journal* explained, "no accompaniment is permitted, no jazz may be introduced. 'Straight fiddlin'' will be the only road to the championship," the paper added.[85]

As the date for the 1934 annual convention approached, Professor Aleck Smart was described as having been recently "scouting the highways and byways of Georgia and neighboring states in search of fiddlers of all kinds," to participate in the contest soon to be staged.[86] For, as Professor Smart explained, "fiddling [had] been in a kind of eclipse for the last year or so." [87] Smart's seemingly frantic pursuit of fiddlers stands in stark contrast to the situation that had existed only a few years earlier when he had bragged to reporters that "entries for the fiddling Championship of Georgia have been pouring in," and predicted that probably "an elimination contest [would] be necessary to weed out the weaker musicians." [88]

The following year Professor Smart "dropped in" at the office of a *Georgian* columnist to invite him to the 1935 edition of the fiddlers' convention "and to confess that finally he had surrendered to changing conditions and the new trend in musical taste. To the usual contest of veteran fiddlers, sawing away on 'Sugar in the Gourd' and 'Bonaparte's Retreat,' " Smart informed the *Georgian*'s writer that he had added "some half-dozen rival hill billy bands, banjoists, male quartets, and even a hog-calling contest open to men and women alike." Smart declared:

> Folks used to be satisfied with just straight fiddling. That's the way we started, . . . They didn't play any tunes that was ever writ down or printed. The fiddlers was most old fellers who come down from Fannin and Union counties. But the wiregrass country had some good ones too. Folks like that kind of fiddling, even city folks. They'd come from the country and had been raised on it.
>
> But times have changed. As far back as ten years ago you could hardly spend the night in a mountain cabin that didn't have a phonograph and a lot of records. Then come the radio, and that's up in the back country, too. The country folks ain't satisfied with the simple old fiddle tunes no more. They want this jazz band music. And I reckon we'll have to give it to them.[89]

Apparently the 1935 contest was the last one held in Atlanta under the auspices of the Georgia Old-Time Fiddlers' Association. One reads of an occasional fiddlers' contest held in the city after 1935, but they seem to have been casually conceived and appear to have lacked the old-time flavor that characterized the annual conventions of the 1913–35 era. Many Atlantans—and a lot of other Georgians, too, for that matter—by 1935 had become accustomed to getting their entertainment from the radio, especially from Atlanta's WSB which had gone on the air a dozen years earlier. Those who liked the sounds of the fiddle, the banjo, and the guitar could find ample fare to satisfy their musical palates by merely turning a dial.

In all likelihood the annual fiddlers' conventions were hardly missed. To some extent they were supplanted by hillbilly stage shows. By 1934 the hillbilly pickers and singers on radio were performing in live shows, not only on stages in Atlanta, but mainly on those of the schools and theaters in the numerous small towns of the state as well. Devotees of the fiddle and banjo who wanted to hear the music of these instruments, as well as see the performers in person, usually did not have to wait long for one of the hillbilly radio acts to appear in their locality.

As for the fiddlers who had been familiar sights at the annual conventions, their lives took many paths. Some had already embarked on recording and radio careers which they pursued with varying degrees of success after the conventions ended. Most of them, however, remained in their communities where they continued to make their living as farmers, mill hands, and followers of a variety of other vocations. We would like to think that for them the annual trips they had made to Atlanta to perform at the fiddlers' conventions provided a source of happy tales to be passed on to children and grandchildren, along with pointers on how to bow the notes just right on such tunes as "Soldiers' Joy" and "The Arkansas Traveler."

2

The Early Days of Radio, 1922–29

IT WAS THE "ROARING TWENTIES"—the decade in which the "cult of pleasure" helped shape national attitudes and behavior.[1] This was the decade that introduced the beauty pageant at Atlantic City[2] and witnessed the spread throughout the country of the Charleston, that vigorous dance with its energetic side kicks and other lively routines that made exhibitionists of old and young alike. It was the era in which parents were criticized for "trying to raise children with one hand and play cards or golf with the other."[3]

During this decade the United States celebrated its 150th birthday, and if the arbiters of fashion are to be believed, Miss and Mrs. America dressed for the occasion in attire designed to "show the knee, but hide the neck." The stylish lady, however, would not overdo things with respect to revealing the patellar region of her anatomy. The idea was for ladies to wear skirts that swayed and swished when they walked so that the knee was revealed only "occasionally in one's stride and then quickly concealed again on the back swish." This, the ladies were assured, gave "an alluring twinkle to the knee."[4] When it came to hiding the neck, there was no compromise. High stiff collars "absolutely must be worn," dictated one of the high priestesses of fashion in Paris.[5] The revealed knee and the hidden neck had to be slender ones if the owner were to achieve the height of fashion. We are told that females were starving themselves into sickness to get thin, and the superintendent of the Atlanta schools warned that "this 'straight line' fad for girls and women is going to be the ruination of the nation."[6]

The automobile, once the rich man's toy, was at last available for a price the average family could afford, especially when bought on the installment plan; and to satisfy demand the automotive industry each year turned out more and more vehicles. The number of passenger cars in service in the United States grew from 6,771,000 in 1919 to 23,121,000 in 1929.[7] As automobiles became more readily available and less expensive, roads were improved, and extended travel and local pleasure-driving, referred to as "joy-riding," increased in popularity. For one's driving convenience there was a wide variety of makes of car from which to choose, including Buick, Cadillac, Ford, Franklin, Locomobile, Maxwell, Olds, Packard, Peerless, Pierce-Arrow, and Studebaker. The popular songs of the decade reflected the nation's interest in mobility. Even those unable to make the trip could sing "Alabamy Bound," "Headin' for Louisville," "California, Here I Come," and "Show Me the Way to Go Home." To meet the needs of the new traveler plush hotels were opened all across the country: in Washington, the Mayflower; in Boston, the Parker House; in Chicago, the Palmer House and the Sherman; in Memphis, the Peabody; and in Miami, the Biltmore. In California the nation's first motel opened at San Luis Obispo in 1925. Located on one of the busiest motor routes in the country, it had accommodations for 160 guests.

This was the decade of Charles Lindbergh, Jack Dempsey, and Billy Mitchell; of the Scopes trial, the Teapot Dome scandal, and the stock market crash; of Harding, Coolidge, and Hoover.

Two monumental achievements in the field of communications occurred in the 1920s. In 1927, after a successful demonstration in which American Telephone and Telegraph Company president Walter S. Gifford in New York spoke with and saw Secretary of Commerce Herbert Hoover in his office in Washington, D.C., the first regularly scheduled television programming began on May 11, 1928, at station WGY in Schnectady, New York. It would be some twenty years, however, before commercial television would become widely available. At the beginning of the decade the world's first radio station had gone on the air with programs for the general public. The station was Westinghouse's KDKA in Pittsburgh, Pennsylvania, and the historic first broadcast occurred on November 2,

1920, when the presidential election returns were sent out through the facilities of a one-hundred-watt transmitter located in a tiny makeshift shack atop a Westinghouse manufacturing building.[8]

Radio came to Atlanta on March 15, 1922, when WSB, the South's first radio station, went on the air. An offspring of Atlanta's evening paper, the *Atlanta Journal*, WSB was also the first newspaper-owned radio station in the South. The *Journal*'s authorization to begin broadcasting was received by telegram from the United States Commerce Department on the afternoon of March 15. The message said, in part, "*The Journal* is authorized to temporarily broadcast weather reports on the wavelength of four hundred eighty-five meters. . . . If you desire to broadcast news entertainment and such matter this is permitted on wave length of three hundred sixty meters only." Shortly after the telegram was received WSB's initial broadcast took place. The next day's edition of the *Journal* was ecstatic with a front page story and banner headline announcing that the "*Atlanta Journal* Installs Big Radio Station." (It had a power of one hundred watts.) The writer of the lead article stated that "the fifth floor of the *Journal*'s building [home of WSB] is now being fitted out as a thoroughly modern receiving and sending radio station." Readers were assured that "the *Journal*'s radio broadcasting station will be operated purely for the benefit and enjoyment of the public, and there will be no commercial feature connected with it. By broadcasting weather and crop news it is hoped and believed that the *Journal* radio service may prove particularly helpful to farmers who are beyond the reach of telegraph and telephone."[9]

WSB's first newspaper radio log, published in the *Journal* on Saturday, March 18, 1922, showed the following schedule of programs:

Saturday's Program for *Journal* Radio
The following schedule is announced for Saturday by WSB, the *Atlanta Journal*'s Radio Station:
Noon—Weather forecast.
12:30 P.M.—Cotton closing and other
 market news.
6–7 P.M.—Late news flashes.
7–7:30 P.M.—Broadcasting of concert
 by Earl Fuller's Original
  New York Jazz Orchestra,

> which will play at the Metropolitan
> Theater next week.
> 7:30–9:00 P.M.—Quiet period under rules
>   of the Atlanta Radio Club
>   for listening to distant
>   concerts and other entertainment.
> 9:00 P.M. (Atlanta Time)—Receipt of
>   Astronomical time from
>   Arlington.[10]

The daily broadcast schedule was quite short—apparently a mere three or four hours. This would be the case for a long time. But people tuned the station in, gasping in awe and incredulity at every faint utterance that reached their ears. In Atlanta's living rooms "WSB's earliest listeners, equipped with crude earphones, bent over crystal sets manipulating 'cat whiskers,' as the [station] finders were called," searching amid the static for the ring of some musical instrument or the sound of a human voice.[11] Gatherings at the home of a neighbor who owned one of the primitive receivers quickly replaced the candy pull and the quilting bee as major social events. Barbers and storekeepers soon discovered that installing a radio was a sure way to attract a crowd—and perhaps customers. Shortly after WSB went on the air, a telegram arrived at the station from Lawrenceville, twenty miles away, to report that the "program was coming in fine. It went on to say that 'Forty of us are taking turns listening on the headphones at Hudgins Store.' "[12] But WSB's early signal reached farther than twenty miles. Before the end of the year the station would be heard off the coasts of England and Chile, in Hawaii, and all across the United States.

Within a few weeks of its birth WSB came under the care of a man named Lambdin Kay who was variously referred to as the station's manager, program director, chief announcer, radio editor, or whatever other title the occasion demanded. He began working for the *Journal* in 1918 and before transferring to WSB served the paper as reporter, feature writer, and tri-weekly editor.[13] Kay remained at WSB for almost twenty years, becoming one of the most popular personalities in local radio broadcasting.

In more ways than one, radio stations of the 1920s were quite different from those of the 1960s and later. Station managers believed, and correctly so, that their unseen audiences wanted to hear live talent, and thus one of Kay's primary tasks was to find sufficient and varied performers to fill WSB's daily broadcast schedule with fare that would capture and hold the attention of its listeners. Ernest Rogers, one of WSB's first announcers, entertainers, and jacks of all trade, later wrote that in those early days, "anybody who could sing, whistle, recite, play any kind of instrument, or merely breathe heavily was pushed in front of the WSB microphone. In a short time almost everybody in Atlanta who could ride, walk, or crawl to WSB had participated in a program. . . . None of the talent was paid for services rendered, but that made no difference. They trouped to WSB to perform, and Aunt Minnie stayed home to listen." [14]

Fortunately, there was no dearth of entertainers in the Atlanta area unwilling to keep their talents hidden under a bushel. During the next several weeks WSB treated its listeners to the performances of such diverse acts as mandolin and guitar clubs, steel guitar players, sacred-harp singers, yodelers, gospel singers, a chorus composed of state legislators, glee clubs, and the Howard Theater Orchestra.

Even Ernest Rogers, himself, got in the act. Bringing his guitar to the studio he treated listeners to his interpretation of such songs as "Willie the Weeper" and "Mythological Blues." He even did some composing and landed a recording contract with RCA Victor that resulted in the release of at least ten sides, including "Willie the Weeper," "Mythological Blues," "Waitin' for the Robert E. Lee," and "Steamboat Bill." One gets the impression that his approach to his music was tongue in cheek and that if he had been forced to label his musical style, he would have chosen the term "folk" rather than "hillbilly."

Not content to have its audience limited only to those who owned receiving sets, WSB, during the summer, sent trucks equipped with loudspeakers out into the city parks so that, as they picnicked, swam, played softball, and sunbathed, the crowds could hear the "Voice of the South." In the fall these "radio trucks" were dispatched to county fairs in such outlying areas as Newnan and LaGrange where additional thousands were entertained. And every day the *Journal* reminded its readers that "the public is invited to attend all broadcasting programs" at the studios on the fifth floor of the Journal Building.

It is greatly to the credit of WSB's early management that

among the artists allowed to perform on the infant station were some of Atlanta's and Georgia's most talented old-time musicians, many of whom had been performing for the past several years at the Georgia Old-Time Fiddlers' Conventions.

In 1922 Georgia's rural inhabitants were much like those of other southern states. About them and the advent of radio one writer has commented:

> Home-made music had developed among southern rural people to a far greater extent than anywhere else in the country, owing to a fortunate combination of community isolation from outside resources and just the right backwoods and small-town population density to promote singing and dancing socials. The result was a fund of amateur music of astonishing range and energy, a social accomplishment as widespread as hunting and farming. This fund was the source of most of the old time music of the 1920's.[15]

Furthermore, the sounds of the fiddle, the guitar, and the banjo appealed to the station management for another reason. As a writer for the *Journal* phrased it, "It is the belief of many that stringed instrumental music carries better over the radiophone than any other sort. . . ."[16]

Surviving records seem to indicate that Fiddlin' John Carson was the first of the area's old-time musicians to appear on the new radio station. Legend, weakly supported by statements of those who were there, has it that Carson's debut occurred on his fifty-fourth birthday, March 23, 1922, eight days after WSB had gone on the air. His efforts won for Fiddlin' John credit for being the first genuine old-time country musician to present genuine old-time country music over a radio station.

The numerous country music acts, or hillbillies as they came to be called, that appeared on WSB over the next several years can be classified into one of three categories: local (that is from Atlanta and the surrounding rural area) individuals and groups; acts, both local and from out of state, who, while in Atlanta to make commercial phonograph records, made appearances on the radio an added adventure; and professional entertainers who had come to Atlanta to appear on the stages of the city's theaters.

For the most part the local acts, in turn, appear to have been of two types. There were those who considered themselves to be, at least, semiprofessional musicians. They took advantage of every opportunity to use their talents to earn money. Although they did not get paid for appearing on the radio, the medium provided exposure and publicity that enhanced their ability to obtain other revenue-producing work as entertainers. These performers were heard, off and on, over extended periods of time, probably as often as the station would allow and their schedules would permit. The other category of local performers on the radio during its formative years consisted of those who considered themselves to be strictly amateurs. To many of these an appearance on the radio was a novelty, a lark, something to be tried once just for the fun of it, but not an event worth repeating. Many community bands and back-porch string orchestras were put together for the purpose of making a radio broadcast for the amusement and amazement not only of themselves, but of the friends and relatives back home who could be counted on to listen in.

On-the-air performances by the musicians who came to Atlanta to record in the temporary studios of the New York-based record companies benefitted all parties concerned. The radio station enjoyed the frequent availability of fresh talent, the performer gained additional exposure (perhaps, in most cases, of dubious value), and the record companies, no doubt, received free advertising. Although no radio scripts from the period seem to have survived—if, in fact, they ever existed at all—one can imagine an announcer introducing such-and-such a group as being "in Atlanta this week to record for the OKeh (or some other) company." Radio audiences even may have been told the approximate date when the records would be available in stores, as well as what songs were recorded.

The situation was similar with regard to the artists—mostly vaudeville acts—who, while in Atlanta to perform on stage, took advantage of the opportunity to appear on the radio: more fresh talent for WSB, exposure for the artists, and free publicity for the theaters.

With Fiddlin' John Carson cutting the trail, WSB was soon approached by other old-time musicians who wanted to sing and play on the air, and by 1930 more than one hundred different musical acts designed to appeal to a rural audience were given an opportunity to be heard. They included string bands, fiddlers, harmonica players, banjo pickers, old-time singers, novelty acts, guitar players, and even buck dancers.

One of the first acts with an appeal to the rural-oriented taste in music to appear on WSB consisted of H. W. "Pink" Lindsey and his son Raymond. The elder Lindsey, an accomplished musician on several string instruments, was well known and respected among the country-style musicians residing in Atlanta at the time. Prior to his WSB debut the *Journal* referred to him as a "guitar and man-dolin luminary." Raymond was billed as a boy soprano with "a remarkable voice" that "strikes the higher register with unerring accuracy." Pink Lindsey, who appeared with other musicians on WSB over the next several years can also be heard as featured artist and back-up musician on several phonograph records made in Atlanta in the 1920s and 1930s.

Lindsey was an employee of the Atlanta Fire Department, an organization which, in the 1920s, seems to have counted among its workers a number of other musicians. On several occasions these musical fire-fighters shared their talents with WSB listeners. The first of their radio programs was aired on Saturday night, January 20, 1923. According to the *Journal*, Lindsey and Claude Estes, "popular members of the [fire] department, engineered the program." Among those heard on the evening's bill was Raymond Lindsey, who sang "Call Me Back, Pal O'Mine" to a guitar and mandolin accompaniment provided by his father and his uncle, R. A. Lindsey. The Lindsey brothers presented "Fan Tan" as an instrumental duet.[17]

The firehouse musicians returned to WSB for another program on Tuesday night, February 6, 1923, at 10:45. Heard on this program were a string band, headed by Roy Thompson, playing "Waldemar," "The Messenger," and "Pert and Pretty"; a steel guitar solo by Russell Thompson; a square dance called by Jack Manning, who also sang "Homesick"; the "fire-proof trio" consisting of the Lindsey brothers and John Harper who presented "a fast and furious fusillade of old-time ditties"; and young Raymond Lindsey, who sang "Daddy Long Legs."[18] The musical fire-fighters were heard again on WSB in 1924.

During WSB's first few years on the air, string bands, proudly proclaiming their places of origin in their names, came from many of the communities and small towns of Georgia to perform before the microphone. Thus listeners were treated to the musical accomplishments of such groups as the Adairsville String Band (directed by Q. R. Hester), the Battle Hill String Band (Hal Edwards, fiddle; Charlie Connell, guitar; Apal Askew, guitar; George W. Walter, mandolin), the Braselton String Band (W. P. Hudgins, fiddle; R. L. Emmett, cello; Roy Emmett, guitar; Dewey Emmett, banjo; J. F. Smith, vocal; Bob Murphy), the Egan Park String Band, the Fife String Band (Wayman Luck, fiddle; J. T. Boyd, fiddle; Horace Lester, fiddle; Glen Harper, guitar; Edwin Ellington, guitar; Ralph Lewis, guitar; Ralph Ellington, guitar; Bryant Luck, banjo; William Boyd, banjo, ukelele, piano), the Hapeville String Band (Charlie Whitten, fiddle; Miles Whitten, guitar; W. L. Whitten, bass, guitar; J. B. Barron, guitar, bass; Ted Hawkins, banjo, mandolin; Riley Puckett, guitar, vocal; Boss Hawkins, guitar), the Hoschton String Band (Dewey Emmett, banjo; Roy Emmett, guitar; Oscar Aiken, fiddle; R. L. Emmett, cello), the Kirkwood Old-Time Fiddlin' Team (Mr. Wimberly, Johnny Jones, C. E. Waddell, H. R. Strickland), the LaGrange String Band, the Lawrenceville String Band, the Lithonia Old Time Fiddlin' Ramblers (W. J. Woodward, director), the Ludville Boys (May Wood, Jack Hilton), the Monticello String Quartet (S. G. Lynch, fiddle; Frank Huff, fiddle; F. C. Lynch, banjo; Doc Merritt, guitar), the Palmetto String Band (J. A. Moss, director; Johnny McMichael, guitar; Urian Blankenship, guitar; Claud Cooper, banjo; Cecil Cooper, banjo; Joe Northcutt, harmonica; Clarence Northcutt, harmonica; George Cochran, fiddle; B. T. Harrington, guitar; Louis Cochran, piano), the Paulding County String Band (Joe Brown, fiddle; Jim Shelton, fiddle; John Martin; John Dilleshaw, guitar; O. P. Cooper; Russell Mitchell; Bill Hammock), the Porterdale String Band (O. A. Finley; Eli Harp, guitar), the Rockmart String Band, and the Scottdale String Band.

Of all the groups to appear on WSB during this period, probably the most picturesque was the Mud Creek Symphony, of Pea Ridge in north Georgia's Habersham County. Presenting their program on Saturday evening, July 5, 1924, at 8 o'clock, this aggregation of mountaineers was described by the *Journal* as "one of the most unique combinations of musicians ever seen in Atlanta."[19]

Composing the orchestra were two pairs of brothers, the younger two nephews of the older two. The uncles, Newt and Ed Tench, sixty-four and sixty-one years of age, claimed to have been fiddling for forty-five years or more. They had fiddled together so long, said the paper, that "harmony between the two is merely a matter of second nature."[20] The younger Tenches played banjo and guitar.

We are told that Newt and Ed Tench held "an enviable reputation as musicians in the mountain districts of Georgia," with "Gettin' Up in the Cool," "Charleston Polka," "Secech," "Rickett's Hornpipe," and "The Downfall of Paris" listed as "some of their best selections."[21]

The story of the method employed by Newt Tench in learning "The Charleston Polka" attests not only to his ability as a musician, but to the native ingenuity of the north Georgia mountaineer as well.

"According to friends," wrote a *Journal* reporter, "Mr. Tench once heard another fiddler play the tune. Becoming interested in it, he requested that it be played again, and while it was being played he transcribed the melody on a piece of paper by a waving line, the high spots signifying the high notes and the low spots signifying the low ones. From this transcription, and knowing nothing of the regular musical scale, Mr. Tench learned the piece and taught it to the rest of the orchestra."[22]

Accompanying the Mud Creek Symphony to Atlanta were Ed Loudermilk, Hank Maxwell, and Ernest Holt, who "gave some old-time mountain songs as their part of the radio concert."[23]

In January 1925 the Lawrenceville Trio, whose "country melodies," said the *Journal*, "are now permanently recorded on OKeh records," gave a program of "ancient airs" that featured "Miss Roba Stanley, guitarist and vocalist; R. M. Stanley, fiddler and vocalist; and William Patterson, guitarist and harmonica [player]." The Stanleys and Patterson were on the air again in February and in June. On their June program they had as guest Henry Whitter, their fellow OKeh recording artist from Galax, Virginia. According to the *Journal* "their old-fashioned mountaineer tunes were warmly applauded."[24] This apparently was the last radio performance of Miss Stanley whose early appearance on WSB has led country music scholars to conclude that she was probably the first solo woman singer to perform country music on a radio station. For her efforts she has been called the first "Sweetheart of Country Music."[25]

It seems that novelty acts wishing to perform on the radio were almost always guaranteed a spot on WSB during those early years. C. S. Brook, whose performances on the broomaphone had delighted audiences at the annual fiddlers' conventions, was a regular performer. In addition the station aired appearances by hand-saw virtuosos, whistlers, and performers on spoons and washboards.

Among these novelty groups, perhaps the most memorable, perhaps the most traditional, and definitely the most important from a historical point of view was George Daniell's Hill Billies, a group first heard on WSB on Wednesday night February 18, 1925, at 10:45. The most significant feature of this band was its name—the Hill Billies. The group, who called Marietta and Cobb County home, may have been the first old-time string band to use the term "hill billies" as part of its name. It also may have been the first such group to introduce to a national audience the term "hill billies" while at the same time performing the type of music for which the term would become the label.

Country music historian Archie Green has written an extensive account of the source and meaning of the word "hillbilly," the name by which the ancestor of modern country music was known. In summary, he states that the word meant, as it still does, a poor white person.[26]

Understandably, through the years, many professionals who have played the kind of music to which the term once applied have been offended by "hillbilly" when applied to their craft. Numerous euphemisms have been tried—"mountain music," "folk music," "country-western," and now simply "country," a term that seems to have achieved a permanent place in the musical lexicon.

Green, in an attempt to establish the first use of the word "hillbilly" to refer to old-time string band music, tells the story of a recording session that took place in the New York studio of the OKeh record company on about January 15, 1925. On that date, according to Green, an unnamed string band whose members and leader, Al Hopkins, were from North Carolina and Virginia recorded two songs, "Silly Bill" and "Old Time Cinda." The tunes were subsequently released (Green speculates the following February) back-to-back on an OKeh record. When Ralph Peer, OKeh's man in charge of the recording session, asked for the band's name,

Hopkins is supposed to have replied, "We're nothing but a bunch of hillbillies from North Carolina and Virginia. Call us anything." When the disc was released the artists credit read "Vocal chorus by Al Hopkins/The Hill Billies."[27]

On the basis of these events Green christened Al Hopkins's Hill Billies "the band that named the music." Other evidence, however, indicates that this distinction belongs to George Daniell's Hill Billies. Prior to their WSB debut a *Journal* article described this group as "an ancient organization formed in the hills of Georgia some hundred years ago by Jerry Daniell, George's great-great grandpa." The article adds that "the name has been handed down from generation to generation until George, the present, fell heir to it, and George has kept its reputation unsullied."[28]

Perhaps we should allow for some journalistic or pride-of-ownership exaggeration and look to other sources for documentation of the name's longevity. A former member of the band, James W. Lee, stated in 1983 that the group was called George Daniell's Hill Billies when he started performing with it in 1924. It seems safe to assume, then, that the name George Daniell's Hill Billies preceded by several years the name The Hill Billies as applied to Al Hopkins's group. The matter of which group first reached a national audience is not so easily settled. George Daniell's group went on the air on February 18, 1925. Green assumes that the Al Hopkins record became available to the public "by February," basing his supposition on the fact that the OKeh catalog supplement for February 1925 carried an announcement of the Al Hopkins/Hill Billies record. If the record was on the market in February, the exact date appears to be unknown. Perhaps it was as late as February 28, ten days after George Daniell's Hill Billies appeared on WSB. Advertising for the record did not appear in the Atlanta newspapers until March 13, which may have been the date on which the record first appeared in Atlanta record stores.

In any event there appears to be no reason to doubt that the broadcast by George Daniell's Hill Billies reached a far larger national audience than did the Al Hopkins record. There seems to be no evidence that the record was a big seller even in an era when a record was considered a hit if it sold only sixty thousand copies in a year.[29] George Daniell's Hill Billies, on the other hand, may have been heard by more than two million people on the evening of February 18. At the time of the group's broadcast, WSB was "recognized as a favorite of long standing by millions of Americans and numbering close personal friends in every city and hamlet in the land."[30] Two years earlier the *Journal* had reported that WSB's advance programs were being mailed to newspapers every week in more than thirty states.[31] The 10:45 P.M. program on which Daniell's Hill Billies appeared was considered the station's "prime time," and as early as 1923, the size of the audience for this program was estimated at more than two million.[32] On the day after their radio appearance, the *Journal* reported, "as soon as the 'Hill Billies' concluded their first number in WSB's studio on their 10:45 program, messages began to pour in over the telegraph and telephone. Wires came from Florida, Texas, and Mississippi and numerous call[s] from Atlanta and vicinity clamoured for additional old-time 'chunes.'"[33] One would seem justified, then, in calling George Daniell's Hill Billies "the band that named the music."

Daniell's Hill Billies appears to have been a rather versatile band that over the years counted among its members a considerable number of local musicians. Those who performed with the band at one time or another included Charles E. Wilson, "figure caller par excellence"; T. W. Kee, bass fiddle player; Fred Becker, fiddler; John Burdine, "straw beater extraordinary"; Edwin H. Payne, saxophone player; Mrs. George Daniell, pianist; J. D. Collins, drummer; T. W. McGarrity, saxophone player; J. C. King, figure caller; Boag Richardson, fiddler; Bob Brown, "alto fiddler"; George Dunn, bass fiddle player; Buster Dunn, banjoist; Kem Wiley, guitarist; Henry Dunn, guitarist; Howard Scoggins, mandolinist; James W. (Bill) Lee, mandolinist; Herbert Wallace; Jake Groover, comedian and washboard player; Sherman Lee, guitarist; Cook James, blackface comedian; Robert McBrayer; Luke James, fiddler; Ewing Underwood; Edward Richardson; and Myrtle Richardson. Edward and Myrtle Richardson were the son and daughter of Boag Richardson. They performed with Daniell's band as children. Mrs. Daniell was a trained musician who taught her craft, and for several years she served as organist at the First Baptist Church of Marietta, Georgia. Her husband, according to a former member of the Hill Billies, referred to his wife's music as "longhair" music. But in referring to his own band he would say, "We're just a bunch of hillbillies." Mrs. Daniell, however, was no musical snob, and when needed she would join her husband's band on piano.

George Daniell, himself, played the autoharp and the harmonica "at one and the same time, and use[d] first his left and then his right foot as a baton while directing his other musicians."[34] The Hill Billies' repertoire and style were varied. According to the *Journal*, the band was "famous the country over for the characteristic country breakdown airs they feature[d]."[35] We are led to believe that these breakdowns, or fast fiddle tunes, included such fare as "Georgia Wagon," "Alabama Gals," "Turkey in the Straw," "Hog in the Canebrake," "Pop Goes the Weasel," "Billy in the Lowground," and "Honeysuckle."[36] Former Hill Billies band member Bill Lee later remembered playing most of those songs, as well as "Down Yonder," "Alabama Jubilee," and "Missouri Waltz."[37]

Howard Scoggins, who as a young man performed with Daniell's group from about 1925 to 1928, stated in 1983 that the band played whatever kind of music the occasion demanded, including sacred and popular music in addition to breakdowns. According to Scoggins, the band, which at any given time usually consisted of about fourteen members, played at churches, hotels, high-school commencement exercises, fairs, square dances, and other musical functions.[38]

George Daniell's Hill Billies were heard on WSB several more times during 1925. Following a broadcast in August the band received fan mail from Mobile, Alabama; Atlantic City, New Jersey; New York, New York; Ashland, Kentucky; and London, Tennessee. The listener from Tennessee wrote:

> Gentlemen:
>
> George Daniel's Marietta Hill Billies from the heart of Cobb County are hot shots. Close a 99-year lease on them soon as possible.
>
> We east Tennesseans revere the kind of music George Daniel [*sic*] gave us last evening. Daniel Boone and John Sevier brought this class of music into east Tennessee with them when they crossed the Blue Ridge to carve a civilization from the wilderness. It played an integral part in keeping up the courage of Tennessee's pioneers in their trying days.
>
> While some so-called high-class musicians look disdainfully

on this class of music, for real entertainment I prefer it to grand opera.

Gratefully yours,
I. O. Remine.[39]

George Daniell died on July 27, 1970, at the age of eighty-eight. He was never aware of the significance of his band's name and its February 18, 1925, broadcast over WSB. George had no children, so no one was left behind to bear the name and carry on the tradition inaugurated by Jerry Daniell "in the hills of Georgia" long before the Civil War.[40]

A number of other hillbilly musicians from Atlanta and the surrounding countryside made at least one appearance on WSB during the 1920s.

The Beehive Trio, a colorful group from out "beyond West End," was heard several times during 1924 and 1925. Consisting of Orris Jones, "Wild Bill" Thompson, and George Ivey, this threesome of "old-time instrumentalists" featured two guitars and a mandolin. Thompson, the mandolinist, was also a "honey grower and philosopher" who called Westhaven home. The group, sometimes referred to as the Westhaven Dance Orchestra and on occasion joined by Sam Little, included on its programs such "ancient airs" as "Just as the Sun Went Down," "Two Little Girls in Blue," "Sweet Bunch of Daisies," and square-dance tunes complete with a caller and "all the trimmings."[41]

During 1926 the Blue Ridge Entertainers from Tate performed on WSB on a number of occasions. The members of this act were Misses Amy and Vella Barrett, "talented pianists," and Fred Barrett, who accompanied them on the autoharp.[42]

In November 1926, J. A. Anderson and Lester Sullins of Dahlonega presented a program consisting of "old-time fiddlin' numbers" and "several exceptionally pleasing numbers, both as duets and solos, with their violins."[43]

Carl Daniel's String Band, from Griffin, was heard in March of 1927. This group was composed of Daniel, who played the fiddle; Mote Boggs, fiddler; Albert Battles and Will Porter, mandolinists; Robert Battles, guitarist; and Jesse Walker, who played tenor guitar.[44]

Jim King of New Holland brought his "old-time orchestra,"

which he called the Brown Mules, to WSB for broadcasts several times during 1927 and 1928. This group, "well-known throughout Hall and neighboring counties," numbered among its personnel Howard Coker, fiddle; Archer Chumbler, banjo-mandolin; Henry Thomas, tenor banjo; Howard Thomas, bass; and Elmo Chumbler and Harmon Canada, guitars.[45]

From time to time during the 1920s, WSB listeners were treated to a program of fiddle music presented by Blind Andy and his fiddle band. The leader of this group was Rev. Andrew Jenkins, a blind evangelist/musician who first played on WSB on August 14, 1922. Throughout the decade Jenkins and his two step-daughters, Irene Spain and Mary Lee Eskew, performed frequently on the station in programs of gospel and sentimental music. The trio also recorded a number of gospel songs, and Jenkins became well known as the composer of such popular tragedy songs as "The Death of Floyd Collins," "Ben Dewberry's Final Run," "The Wreck of the Royal Palm," and the gospel standard "God Put a Rainbow in the Cloud."[46]

Other local musicians who made the trip to the WSB studios for the purpose of sharing their talents with the great unseen audiences included old-time banjoist Bige Gibble (1924); harmonica soloist W. F. "Pistol Bill" Hobson of Cornelia (1924); Warren Sykes, who appeared on the station shortly after winning first place in a Lakewood Amusement Park harmonica-playing contest for children (1926); banjoist Joe Wages of Athens; the Davis Brothers, an old-time fiddling team from Blackwell (1927); and a string band headed by Canton resident Bill Green who provided listeners with a "varied program of folk songs and southern melodies" (1929).[47]

Performances by local hillbilly musicians were interspersed with programs featuring music by artists from other parts of the country. Sears, Roebuck and Company was instrumental in providing Atlanta radio listeners with opportunities to hear imported, as well as local, old-time musicians.

The summer of 1926 witnessed the opening in Atlanta of a new Sears, Roebuck and Company mail-order plant and retail store. Shoppers attending the new store's opening August 2 found silk dresses priced at $4.95, men's summer suits for $4.49, and broadcloth shirts and women's straw and felt hats for $1.19. The housewives of the day could take home an electric iron for $1.69 or a food grinder for 98 cents. Forty-five-pound mattresses were selling for $5.95.[48]

The coming of the Sears, Roebuck and Company operations to Atlanta proved to be of great significance to the development of country music in the city. On August 9 the Sears, Roebuck Agricultural Foundation began sponsoring on WSB a thrice-weekly noontime show called "Dinner Bell R.F.D.," the first program on the station to feature old-time music on a regularly scheduled basis. The star of the show was Dewey Burnett, "harmonicist and old-time fiddler," but other old-time musicians appeared on the program from time to time. An article in the *Journal* stated, "The R.F.D. Club, or Radio Farmers' Democracy, is being organized among radio listeners living on farms or who are interested in agriculture. Membership is secured by sending in a suggestion to the R.F.D. headquarters for some feature, type of music or type of farm information desired by the listener. . . . Each day the program will be opened by an appropriate symbol, such as a dinner-bell or a dinner-horn."[49]

Air time for the "Dinner Bell R.F.D." program was provided free by WSB. Sears paid a general director, a "homemakers' program director," and a small talent staff. While no commercials were aired, listeners were told that the program was sponsored by Sears.

The Sears, Roebuck and Company Agricultural Foundation had been chartered in 1923 "with the avowed objective of helping the farmer 'farm better, sell better, and live better.' " The foundation "was organized on a 'for-profit' basis and represented an attempt to mobilize the company's contacts and resources for the educational, social, and financial advancement of rural people."[50] Director of the foundation's radio operations in Atlanta was George C. Biggar, who came to the city from Sears's Chicago station, WLS (World's Largest Store), by way of WFAA in Dallas, Texas, where he had also produced a farm and home program for the Sears, Roebuck and Company Agricultural Foundation.[51]

In addition to the "Dinner Bell R.F.D." program, Sears, Roebuck and Company sponsored on WSB other programs of interest both to the farmer and to the devotee of old-time music. One such show was broadcast on Saturday evening, November 27, 1926, from 7:00 to 8:00. Participating in the presentation of the program, which was concerned with the problems of the cotton states, was the United States Department of Agriculture. The *Journal* reported that "practically every southern broadcasting station [would] co-operate . . . in presenting the special radio program" which featured the music of the Dixie Entertainers, "a prominent band of old-time players, in a typical 'breakdown' with a square dance expert to 'call' the dances."[52] Presumably the band heard that night was Earl Johnson's. As we shall see, this fiddler, who had gone to New York in 1925 to record for Paramount, recorded for OKeh in 1927 as Earl Johnson and His Dixie Entertainers.

During each morning of the 1926 Southeastern Fair at Lakewood Park, the foundation presented Earl Johnson and Arthur Tanner from the radio studio in programs that were heard on WSB. For these programs Johnson and Tanner were billed as the Fiddlin' Wampus Cats.[53]

The foundation was responsible for several special old-time music programs heard on WSB in 1927. On Monday evening, January 24, it presented a program entitled "Out at Uncle Henry's." This "picture production" depicted "a typical country home and a gathering of young and old folks presenting various forms of musical and vocational entertainment of days gone by."[54] Participants included an "old-time fiddlin' team" under the leadership of Dr. W. M. Powell, a fiddler who appeared frequently on WSB during the 1920s. The foundation sponsored another "Out at Uncle Henry's" program on the evening of March 21 from 8:00 to 9:00. This show featured "everything ranging from old-time fiddlin' selections to operatic excerpts" including "The Baggage Coach Ahead," "The Shooting of Dan McGrew," "That Old Gang of Mine," and "Bits from Operas."[55] Again, Dr. Powell and his band were among the performers.

On May 9 at 8 P.M. a program called "Ye Olde Tyme Barn Dance" was sponsored by Sears. The stars of this show were Benny Borg, "the Singing Soldier" with his "double barrelled" guitar and folk songs; Shorty Brown, a harmonica and autoharp player from Habersham County; the Hill Billy Trio from Pickens County; and the Milk Maids, a quartet composed of students from Agnes Scott College.[56]

Clayton McMichen's Melody Makers were heard on the foundation's July 4 program entitled "Celebratin' the Fourth at Uncle Hiram's." The program represented "a party at the home of Hiram and Mandy Doolittle [regulars on the 'Dinner Bell R.F.D.' program], with the old reed organ of the Sears, Roebuck and Company tower playing a prominent part in the offering." McMichen's group furnished square-dance music for the program.[57]

Taking advantage of the readily available talent of the musicians who had come to Atlanta for a fiddlers' convention, the Sears, Roebuck and Company Agricultural Foundation, on Friday, September 2, from 11:30 to 12 o'clock, presented WSB listeners with "a group of the south's foremost old-time fiddlers, recruited from the ranks of those gathered at the auditorium-armory." Among the participants on this special bill were Gid Tanner; Fiddlin' John Carson; Jep Tatum; the Slaughter sisters of Robbinsville, North Carolina; Roe and Charlie Young of Andrews, North Carolina; Allen Sisson of Frye, Georgia; and "Mrs. Barmgarner" [Bumgarner] of Sylva, North Carolina. Acccording to the *Journal*, "the old-timers gave an exceptionally fine program, vividly portraying to WSB's audience just what might be expected from the group of fifty or more fiddlers participating in the events at the auditorium." [58]

The Sears, Roebuck and Company Agricultural Foundation sponsored a special Thanksgiving program on Wednesday evening, November 23, at 7 o'clock, offering "olden songs, old-time fiddling, comic numbers and other variety" designed to convey "the spirit of an old-time Thanksgiving party." Among those heard on the program were the old-time fiddling team of John Dilleshaw and J. F. Mitchell, "rending the atmosphere with breakdown music" in an effort to give listeners "a glimpse of an old-time square dance." [59]

The local programming extravaganza of 1927 took place at WSB during the week of September 5 and featured generous amounts of old-time music. That was the week Edgar L. Bill, director and chief announcer at WLS, was in town to supervise "several unique radio productions distinctive of the Chicago broadcaster." [60] Set aside as the first anniversary observance of the Sears, Roebuck and Company Agricultural Foundation programs over WSB, the week was officially designated as "Sears-Roebuck's Atlanta Anniversary and WLS Review Week."

To assist him, Mr. Bill brought from WLS, Koby Sirinsky, staff violinist and director of "all the stringed instrumental units of the station," and "Chubby" Parker, old-time singer and banjoist.

A *Journal* article referred to Parker as "without doubt the premier old-time radio entertainer of the northern states. With banjo accompaniment, he sings in an inimitable way dozens of specialties, as well as numerous folk songs, ballads of the prairie, and negro melodies. From one WLS appearance last winter, he received over 2,800 applause cards and letters. Fame gained on the radio has brought him honors as a phonograph record artist and a theatrical performer."[61]

During the week, Parker appeared on the "Dinner Bell R.F.D." program, and Koby Sirinski "form[ed] an Atlanta WLS String Trio for the week, allying himself with a local cellist and pianist of exceptional ability."[62] And so, each evening during the week, WSB listeners were treated to an Atlanta version of at least one of the more popular WLS radio programs.

Monday night's program was four hours long, beginning at 8 o'clock and ending at midnight with the seventy-five minute "WLS Show Boat" program. An "Old Timers' fiddling team"; Dewey Burnett; and a harmonica- and guitar-playing regular on the "Dinner Bell" program, W. E. Jordan, were heard on the 8:00 to 8:35 segment of the broadcast.

On Tuesday night the 10:45 to 11:45 hour on WSB was given over to the "WLS Minstrel Show" which featured, among others, Chubby Parker and Koby Sirinsky.

After making two personal appearances—"arranged in answer to overwhelming demand from the radio audience"—at the Atlanta Sears, Roebuck and Company store earlier in the day, Edgar Bill and the other visitors from Chicago presented two shows from the WSB studios on Wednesday night. The "WLS Fantasy in the Old Neighborhood" program was heard from 8:30 to 9:30, while the "WLS Circus" show was beamed to listeners from 10:45 to midnight. Chubby Parker was among the artists heard on the circus program, which offered "all the flavor of the real show, with sideshows and scenes in the 'big tent.'"[63]

"Around the Campfire" was the title of the WLS program heard on Thursday night from 11:15 to 11:45. The program featured "old southern songs" rendered by Koby Sirinsky's String Trio and Chubby Parker.[64]

The week's broadcasting tour de force was brought to a close on Friday night with a two-hour presentation of the "WLS National Barn Dance," which, said the *Journal*, was "the most popular of the standing broadcast attractions from Sears-Roebuck's Chicago station." The star of the show was Chubby Parker, "supported by an array of old-time entertainers," including Fiddlin' John Carson; The Lost Three; "Red Neck" Jim Lawson and his son, Joe; W. E. Jordan; J. T. Waits, "harmonica wizard"; Dewey Burnett; the Foundation Four quartet; Paul and John, "the Disciples of Harmony"; and Marquis M. Smith, baritone and reader. Mr. Bill, the *Journal* promised, would "announce the feature with all the flurries, etc., used to make the National Barn Dance famous."[65]

WSB's affiliation with Sears, Roebuck and Company came to an end in October 1928. The last radio program broadcast under the auspices of the firm was presented at 9:30 P.M. on October 15. George C. Biggar, who had been in charge of the Sears-Roebuck Agricultural Foundation program at WSB, went to the newly organized KMBC in Kansas City to produce that station's farm and home service radio programs that were sponsored by Sears, Roebuck and Company's new Kansas City department store. Biggar later organized the popular country-western radio program "Boone County Jamboree" at WLW in Cincinnati. He returned to WLS in 1948 where for five years he served as director of the "WLS National Barn Dance."[66]

Among the other out-of-state purveyors of old-time and rural-oriented music to broadcast on WSB during the 1920s were Colonel William Hopkins, an itinerant fiddler; a couple of acts from the "Grand Ole Opry"—Obed Pickard and Dr. Humphrey Bates' Possum Hunters; the father of country music, Jimmie Rodgers; and a vaudeville act or two.

On Tuesday, January 4, 1927, WSB joined the National Broadcasting Company (NBC), a network that had made its initial broadcast the previous November on a twenty-two station linkup. WSB's first network program, aired from 8:00 to 9:00 P.M., was "The Eveready Hour"—"a splendid example of the 'variety' type of entertainment."[67] Those gathered around their radios that night heard the Eveready Orchestra directed by Nathaniel Shilkret; Betsy Ayers, soprano; Barbara Maurel, coloratura; and the Eveready Male Quartet.

With WSB now committed to scheduling network shows, less time would be available for programming local talent. Inevitably this would limit the opportunities of local old-time musicians to bring their kind of music to the radio audience. Too, affiliation with the network may have given WSB officials a sense of sophistication that they felt would have to be supported by local programming policies. The era in which a fiddler or banjo picker could drop by the station and go on the air on short notice had now ended.

3

Atlanta—A Regional Recording Center

THE TWO MOST IMPORTANT VEHICLES for the preservation, development, and dissemination of country music have been the phonograph and the radio. Although the phonograph became a popular instrument of entertainment in America long before the radio, the direct involvement of the two media in the commercialization of country music began at about the same time.

By 1895 magazines such as *Cosmopolitan*, *McClure's*, and *Harper's* carried prominent advertisements for parlor phonographs that could be bought for forty dollars. These early machines were small table models featuring a large external "morning-glory" horn to amplify the sound that came from a cylinder record. In 1897 the Columbia Phonograph Company introduced a machine selling for ten dollars which, it was promised, would bring into the home " 'all the pleasures of music, reproducing the performances of bands, orchestras, and operatic choruses, as well as of vocal and instrumental soloists.' "[1]

In 1917, as American soldiers crossed the Atlantic to take up positions in the trenches of World War I, they left behind a homeland in which records had become the most popular form of home entertainment. The phonograph industry had entered its golden age, and such recording artists as Enrico Caruso and John McCormack were getting rich from their royalties.[2]

Until 1923, however, the recording industry almost totally neglected the rural music—the folk music—of the South. There were a few earlier instances in which fiddle music and other rural-oriented performances had been recorded as novelty pieces, but for the most part the music available on records had consisted of vaudeville songs, classical works, jazz, and songs by such "popular" artists as Gene Austin, Henry Burr, Al Jolson, and Vernon Dalhart. String-band music such as had been heard at the Georgia Old-Time Fiddlers' Conventions since 1913 was not available. Recording-company executives, no doubt, considered the mountain singers and instrumentalists, with their unpolished style and delivery, unworthy of serious consideration as potential recording stars. Furthermore, they likely believed there would be little, if any, profit in recording such music.[3]

As we have seen, it was in Atlanta that authentic old-time music performed by an authentic old-time musician was first heard on radio when Fiddlin' John Carson stepped in front of the WSB microphone. It was also in Atlanta, and by the same performer, that the first real country music record was made. In 1923 Polk Brockman, director of the phonograph department of his grandfather's Atlanta furniture store, was aware of the popularity of Fiddlin' John Carson whose fiddle playing, singing, and comedy routines had, for years, been heard around Atlanta at fiddlers' conventions, political rallies, and more recently on the radio. Consequently, Carson came to mind when Brockman, while on a business trip to New York, visited a moving-picture theater and saw a newsreel of a Virginia fiddlers' contest. It occurred to Brockman that there would be a market for phonograph records by this most popular of Georgia fiddlers.[4] Subsequently an article in the *Journal* for June 15, 1923, informed readers that

> "Canned music" recorded by local musicians will be made for the first time in Atlanta by OKeh Company, of New York, it was announced Friday. . . .
>
> About thirty recordings will be made at the laboratory of the company on Nassau Street, including selections by the Morehouse College quartet of Negro singers, "Fiddlin'" John Carson, the Seven Aces, and other organizations.
>
> Manufacture of the records here is made possible by a recording machine recently invented by an engineer of the OKeh Company, which lowers the high cost of producing the records away from the home laboratories.[5]

Fiddlin' John, presumably encouraged by Brockman to do so, recorded two tunes during his first session: "The Little Old Log Cabin in the Lane" and "The Old Hen Cackled and the Rooster's Going to Crow."

In charge of this historic Atlanta recording session was Ralph Peer, the New York representative of OKeh, who, during the next several years, made frequent forays into the hinterlands to record local talent in its native habitat. The story has been told that Peer declared the efforts of Carson "pluperfect awful." Years later Peer was quoted as saying that the record was so bad "we didn't even put a serial number on the records, thinking that when the local dealer [Brockman] got his supply [an initial order of five hundred records], that would be the end of it."[6] Peer, however, greatly underestimated Carson's popularity. Within days, he recalls, OKeh was filling orders for fifteen thousand more copies of "The Little Old Log Cabin in the Lane" and its companion piece. "When the national sale got to 500,000," according to Peer, "we were so ashamed, we had Fiddlin' John come up to New York and do a re-recording of the numbers."[7]

OKeh also had field recording studios in Asheville, North Carolina; Bristol and Johnson City, Tennessee; St. Louis; and Dallas, Texas. "Of these locations, however," writes Bill C. Malone in his history of country music, "Atlanta with its wealth of folk talent was given top priority."[8] In fact, according to country music historian Charles K. Wolfe, "most of the genuine country music recorded in the 1920's came from Atlanta. It was the Nashville of the day," he continues, "and all the major record companies had studios there."[9] Thus it was that during the 1920s and the 1930s mountain singers, fiddlers, guitar players, and banjo pickers by the droves came to Atlanta from far and near seeking immortality in the grooves of an ebony disc.

Typically these field recording studios consisted of space rented on a short-term basis in some hotel or other building where a room or two of suitable size were available. The Kimball House hotel and the Woman's Club building were among the Atlanta sites in which the recording companies set up their temporary studios. Record company representatives, later called artists and repertoire (A & R) men, served as talent scouts. They made periodic trips to Atlanta and the other field recording cities accompanied by an engineer or two, with the necessary portable recording equipment and other materials of their trade in tow. Advertisements in local newspapers informed the public, including aspiring recording artists, of when and where auditions would be held. Performers who passed an audition were usually paid a flat sum, rather than royalties on subsequent sales of released records. Typical recording fees were in the twenty-five-dollar to fifty-dollar range for each song or "side" recorded. Many times performers who recorded were never heard by the public. For one reason or another—master discs could become damaged or lost, or company officials could have a change of mind regarding the commercial potential of an artist—their efforts were never released for sale. Others, who were lucky enough to have their recordings make it to record store counters, never, because of poor sales, had a second chance at putting out a hit. There were still others, one suspects, who considered a recording artist's life not worth the required time and inconvenience and, therefore, did not bother to return to the temporary studios, even when they had the chance to do so. According to Charles K. Wolfe, the average old-time release in the 1920s sold around five to ten thousand copies, with a thousand-seller being considered an accomplishment during the Depression.[10] Many sold fewer copies, while the "hits" of the day seldom sold more than one hundred thousand copies.[11]

Record-making techniques in 1923, when Fiddlin' John Carson first recorded, were primitive in comparison to present-day methods that involve magnetic tapes, stereophonic sound, and digital recording processes. In the 1920s the first step in the production of a record consisted of cutting grooves into the face of a blank three-quarter-inch-thick wax disc. This was accomplished by a machine whose action was the reverse of a phonograph: That is, instead of its needle following an existing groove, it cut its own groove in reaction to pressure from a transmitting diaphragm that pulsated in response to the sound waves generated by the voices and instruments of the performing artists. The wax discs containing the grooves of a successful "take" were transported to the record company's laboratory where, through an electrolytic process, a copper disc called the pressing matrix was created. Through the use of hydraulic presses the pressing matrix was used to mass produce, from a mixture of shellac, rottenstone, and lampblack, the 78 RPM records that eventually found their way to retail establishments.[12]

One would not expect warm wax to retain the precise imprint of a recording stylus; neither would one expect wax to remain cool and firm on a typical summer day in Atlanta. Those who recorded in the Atlanta studios later recalled that blocks of ice were sometimes brought in to keep the wax cool. In those days before air conditioning, performers themselves frequently sought relief from the heat by stripping to their underwear to record. (You can't open windows in a recording studio.) And to help keep artistic temperaments from becoming overheated, record company officials were known sometimes to make sure that an adequate supply of liquor was available. When the recording was done in a hotel room, the bathtub was a favorite repository for such refreshment.

The bands and individuals who went to Atlanta in the 1920s and 1930s to record hillbilly music can be divided into two groups: the locals—those who called Georgia home—and those from out of state. The former came primarily from Atlanta and north Georgia, while the latter came from adjacent states and even from as far away as Virginia, Kentucky, and Mississippi.

Of the local acts who recorded in Atlanta during the 1920s, those who became best known were Fiddlin' John Carson, Gid Tanner and the Skillet Lickers, Riley Puckett, and Clayton McMichen. But there were numerous other Georgians who found their way into the recording studios during that decade. Some enjoyed greater success than others.

A group that has been called "one of the most interesting and yet one of the more obscure of the Georgia [old-time] string bands" made their recording debut in Atlanta's OKeh studios on October 28, 1926.[13] They called themselves the Scottdale String Band in honor of Scottdale, the nearby mill village they called home. Their first session yielded two released numbers, "Aunt Hager's [*sic*, usually spelled Hagar's] Blues" backed by "Southern Blues." Between 1926 and 1932 they recorded an additional twenty-seven sides for OKeh and two sides for Paramount. Among the tunes they waxed were "Carolina Glide," "Chinese Breakdown," "Down Yonder," "Scottdale Stomp," "Sitting on Top of the World," and "Wang Wang Blues." Bill Rattray, in an article in *Old Time Music* magazine, speculates that their records sold "well, or at least fairly well." Rattray also states that "their instrumentation was profoundly different from that of the other, more well-known Georgia bands like the Skillet-Lickers, and gave their music a more sophisticated sound than that of the 'rough North Georgia' school." He notes that their recorded repertoire "shows a wider range of material including tunes used chiefly by the jazz bands," and that "the more traditional breakdowns, songs and ballads are hardly featured at all."[14] All of the group's records, except the two Paramount sides, were made in Atlanta.

The Scottdale String Band was one of that host of early Atlanta recording acts to appear also on the city's radio stations. In publicizing the initial appearance of the Scottdale group on WSB on January 29, 1927, the *Journal* did not mention the band's name. Readers were told that "old-time fiddlin' selections, presented by a quartet of two guitars and two mandolins [would] comprise WSB's headline offering to the twilight listeners Saturday afternoon from 5 to 6 o'clock."[15] *Journal* and WSB officials apparently considered it more important to identify the act as performers of fiddle music than to use the name under which the group recorded. Perhaps as a result of long contact with Fiddlin' John Carson and other local fiddlers the newspaper and radio station staffs seem to have equated hillbilly music in general with fiddle music. Composing the quartet, which the *Journal* referred to as "a new musical unit before WSB's microphone," were Marvin Head and Ed Freeman, mandolinists, and Eunice and Bonnie Pritchard, guitarists. "The quartet has been heard at gatherings, clubs and fraternity meetings in Atlanta," said the *Journal*, "and many of the selections which have proven so popular with their listeners will be repeated before the microphone for the invisible audience."[16] The *Journal*'s radio calendar for the day lists the act as "J. M. Head, old-time fiddler, and other entertainers."[17]

Three members of the J. M. Head group were back in the WSB studio on Saturday night, July 9, 1927, for an appearance on the 10:45 to 11:45 program. This time, using the name Scottdale String Band, the musicians were identified as Barney [Bonnie?] Pritchard, guitarist; Belvey [Ed?] Freeman, banjo-mandolinist; and Marvin Head, guitarist. Described as "OKeh recording artists of old-time and novelty numbers," the group was expected to play "Carbolic Rag" and "Italian [Carolina?] Glide" on their program.[18]

The Scottdale String Band continued to make occasional appearances on WSB through 1932. In addition to the persons already mentioned, Charlie Simmons, John Rody, and B. L. [Barney, Jr.] Pritchard also performed with the group. The band seems to have dissolved around 1940.

Atlanta's pioneer old-time country musicians were not unlike musicians of other genres, other times, and other places. While some of them are identified solely or primarily with one group in all facets of their careers—recording, radio broadcasting, and stage appearances—others at various times performed regularly with several groups. An Atlanta musician of the latter type was John Dilleshaw, one of the city's most noted country guitarists. He seems to have initiated his recording career in March 1929 with an OKeh pressing of four sides, two of which—"Spanish Fandango"/"Cotton Patch Rag"—were released. The following year, between March 19 and 24, he was involved in making several records for the Vocalion label. With fiddler Harry Kiker, tenor banjoist Shorty Lindsey, and bass player Pink Lindsey, he recorded a skit titled "The Square Dance Fight on Ball Top Mountain" which was released on both sides of one record. Another two-sided skit, "A Georgia Barbecue at Stone Mountain," featured A. A. Gray on fiddle, Shorty Lindsey on tenor banjo, John Dilleshaw playing guitar, Pink Lindsey on bass, and a speaking part by Bill Brown, an official with the record company. On yet another skit recorded during this period, "A Fiddler's Tryout in Georgia," one can hear Joe Brown and A. A. Gray playing fiddles, and the spoken voices of Archie Lee (William Archer Chumbler) and Hoke Rice. John Dilleshaw speaks on all three skits.

From these March sessions came the four sides featuring Dilleshaw on vocals and guitar and A. A. Gray playing the fiddle: "Tallapoosa Bound"/"Streak O' Lean-Streak O' Fat" and "Nigger Baby"/ "The Old Ark's a'Moving." Dilleshaw, the two Lindseys, and Harry Kiker recorded six sides under the artist credit Dilly [Dilleshaw] & His Dill Pickles, and Dilleshaw alone, speaking and playing his guitar, recorded two sides, "Farmer's Blues" and "Walkin' Blues."

In November 1929 Dilleshaw and various combinations of his fellow musicians, including Lowe Stokes, Harry Kiker, A. A. Gray, Pink Lindsey, Shorty Lindsey, Bill Brown, Dan Tucker, Archie Lee, and "Pops" Melvin, recorded ten sides for the Brunswick label. Only four of these sides, "Kennesaw Mountain Rag"/"Bibb County Hoe Down" and "A Bootlegger's Joint in Atlanta" (two sides), were released. All of Dilleshaw's recording activity took place in Atlanta.[19]

By the time he made his first record, John Dilleshaw had established an enviable reputation in the Atlanta area for his musical abilities, having been heard extensively on WSB. His first documented appearance on radio was in 1924 when a contingent of musicians from the Atlanta Fire Department (where Dilleshaw was employed) presented a program on the evening of Tuesday, June 3, over WSB. On this show Dilleshaw was billed as a "dare-devil guitarist."[20]

Two weeks later when Fiddlin' Joe Brown and his Paulding County String Band of Dallas, Georgia, presented a program on WSB, "two songs by Mr. Dilleshaw were a feature."[21]

By 1925 Dilleshaw was appearing on WSB as one of the Gibson Kings (with fellow guitarist and sometime broomaphonist C. S. Brook) and as a member of the Dixie String Band, which at one time or another was composed of a variety of Atlanta musicians, including J. F. Mitchell, fiddler and leader of the group; C. S. Brook; Anita Wheeler, future state and regional fiddling champion; Lowe Stokes; a Dr. W. M. Powell, who played fiddle; mandolinist F. G. Dearman; Walter Morris, fiddler, singer, and guitarist; fiddler Clayton McMichen; D. F. C. Linder, "an adept manipulator of the ivories"; A. M. Bean, tenor banjoist; and R. J. Bolton, banjoist.

The Gibson Kings and the Dixie String Band were both popular acts. Apparently named for the brand of instruments they played, the Gibson Kings, Dilleshaw and Brook, were said to be "unusually adept as guitarists, and their tuneful blending harmony brought many encores and requests from fans" when they appeared on radio.[22] In anticipation of one of their programs, listeners were promised that they would be "offering a number of new, catchy selections of their own composition which have never been given over the microphone."[23]

According to the *Journal*, the musicians in the Dixie String Band were "disciples of plain, old-fashioned country harmony."[24] Their musical selections included "barn dance tunes which made our grandmothers shuffle their feet," the latest Broadway hits, other new and popular numbers, as well as "original arrangements or compositions" that had "never before been broadcast."[25] The Dixie

String Band appears to have made its last WSB appearance in June 1930.

John Dilleshaw was born about 1896 on Pumpkinvine Creek, near the community of New Hope in northern Paulding County. When he was seventeen years old he injured his foot in a hunting accident and during his recuperation learned to play the guitar. His teacher was a neighbor, an older black man named Bill Turner. In 1918 Dilleshaw married another Paulding countian, Opal Kiker, and by 1922 the couple had moved to Atlanta where John found a job with the Atlanta Fire Department. Dilleshaw was a left-handed guitar player, and as an adult he was above average in height. Although not quite seven feet tall as some folks claimed, he was at least 6′ 7″ tall according to his brother-in-law, Harry Kiker.[26]

Unlike Dilleshaw, not all local recording artists recorded exclusively in Atlanta. Many journeyed to New York and other cities to have their music preserved. Earl Johnson, a fiddler on WSB as early as 1922 and a familiar figure at the Atlanta fiddlers' conventions between 1920 and 1934, first recorded in New York in 1925 for Paramount, but he made all of his many subsequent records in Atlanta. Among the tunes he recorded in New York were "Atlanta Special" and the then highly popular "Little Old Log Cabin in the Lane."

Johnson seems to have taken his music more seriously than many. He took a correspondence course in music and allegedly was as proficient on popular and classical numbers as he was on barn-dance breakdowns. It is reported that he was a favorite among record company officials because his group always came to the studio well-rehearsed and with their tunes timed to fit the constraints of the 78 RPM record. Such preparation contributed to an efficient recording session by eliminating time-consuming retakes and in-studio rehearsals.

Earl Johnson was born in 1886 in Gwinnett County, not far from Atlanta. His father, a farmer, was also an old-time fiddler. At an early age Earl and his two brothers had formed a band consisting of banjo, guitar, and Earl's fiddle. Following the deaths of his brothers, Earl performed and recorded with Fiddlin' John Carson before forming his own bands, the best known of which he called the Dixie Entertainers. Other members of the band included guitarist Lee Henderson of Blairsville, Georgia; banjoist Emmet Bankston of Atlanta; Byrd Moore, guitarist and barber from Norton, Virginia, who at one time lived in Atlanta; and J. T. Wright, left-handed fiddler from Marietta. Banjoist Fate Norris, better known for his work with Gid Tanner's Skillet Lickers, on occasion played with Johnson's group. The Dixie Entertainers (sometimes also called the Clodhoppers) recorded for OKeh, RCA Victor, and Columbia during a recording career that lasted until 1931 and produced more than fifty released sides, many of which were reissued on other labels. Johnson was a lifelong professional musician who traveled the southern and southeastern circuits to perform. He was crowned state fiddle champion in Atlanta in 1926, and in his later years he frequented many of the fiddlers' conventions held in the Southeast. He appeared at the Stone Mountain (Georgia) Fiddlers' Convention on Saturday before being confined to his bed with a heart attack on Monday, May 24, 1965. He died a week later, on May 31.[27]

Although most of the Atlanta recording artists stuck with one musical genre or one instrument, a few exhibited greater versatility. Such was the case with banjoist Bud Landress and fiddle player Bill Chitwood. This duo from Resaca in Gordon County, Georgia, about sixty miles north of Atlanta, was best known for its fiddle tunes, ballads, mother songs, and novelty tunes, but Landress and Chitwood also recorded a number of sacred songs as members of two gospel quartets. Their secular material was recorded under such artist titles as Bill Chitwood and Bud Landress, the Georgia Yellow Hammers, Bill Chitwood and His Georgia Mountaineers, and Uncle Bud Landress. In various combinations with Ernest Moody, Phil Reeve, Clyde Evans, J. M. Barnette, and Ira Mashburn, Landress and Chitwood joined the Turkey Mountain Singers and the Gordon County Quartet to record such gospel songs as "I Am Bound for the Promised Land," "Precious Memories," and "Walking in the King's Highway."

The Georgia Yellow Hammers' best-selling record was probably "The Picture on the Wall" backed by "My Carolina Girl." More than sixty thousand copies of this record were sold in 1928 alone, and it is estimated that, in all, more than twice that number were sold.

Landress and Chitwood made their first records in New York in 1925 for the Brunswick label. Their second recording session was for Victor and took place in February 1927 in Atlanta, where most of their other records were made. In August of that year Landress, accompanied by Ernest Moody, Phil Reeve, Clyde Evans, Andrew Baxter, and Jim Baxter (but not Bill Chitwood), went to Charlotte, North Carolina, to record as the Georgia Yellow Hammers. It was this session that yielded "The Picture on the Wall."

According to Charles Wolfe, the Baxters were of African–Cherokee Indian descent. The record on which Andrew Baxter performed with Bud Landress and other white musicians is one of the first old-time-music recording sessions known to have been integrated. The tune was "G Rag," recorded in 1927 at the Charlotte session.[28]

Landress and Chitwood, who made their last records together in 1930 in Atlanta, made several appearances on WSB during 1925 and 1926.

Bill Chitwood was born in Resaca in 1891. The first musical instrument he learned to play was a homemade fiddle belonging to his brother. Later he learned the other string instruments likely to be part of an old-time string band. Bud Landress, born in 1882 in Gwinnett County, settled, at the age of twenty-three, in Gordon County where, presumably, he met his musical partner, Bill Chitwood. Although Landress farmed for a living, music was his first love, and he spent a major portion of his spare time pursuing this avocation. He played in string bands, organized stage shows and fiddlers' contests, learned to read shape notes, sang bass in a quartet, served as an officer in the local singing conventions, and like Chitwood learned to play several string instruments. As late as the 1940s Landress, then about sixty years old, was doing stage shows and performing on a radio station in Rome, Georgia. He died in 1966.[29]

One of the most significant events in the history of country music occured at OKeh's August 1924 recording session in Atlanta. Roba Stanley, a fourteen-year-old girl from nearby rural Gwinnett County, recorded "Whoa Mule," "Devilish Mary," "Mister Chicken," "All Night Long," "Little Frankie," and "Railroad Bill," and, according to country music historians, became America's first recorded female country singer. Although two women, Eva Davis and Samantha Bumgarner, had recorded hillbilly tunes a few months earlier, they were primarily a fiddle and banjo team whose singing was incidental to their instrumental music. Roba Stanley, on the other hand, was "first and foremost a singer, and she used full, splendid texts of solid traditional songs and ballads."[30]

Miss Stanley was the daughter of R. M. "Rob" Stanley, the winner of the Georgia state fiddling championship in 1920. Born in 1910, she learned to play her brother's guitar at an early age, and it was not long until she was accompanying her father, whose fiddling was in demand at local square dances.

The Stanleys' recording session was brought about through the intervention of an Atlanta furniture dealer named Polk who heard them perform at a political rally. Like most furniture merchants of his day, Polk probably sold phonograph records in his store and consequently was acquainted with record company officials. At any rate he contacted the General Phonograph Company on behalf of the Stanleys and was successful in getting them recorded on the OKeh label. For their records, Roba and her father added the talents of a friend named William Patterson who played guitar and harmonica. At this initial Stanley session, four sides were recorded. The elder Stanley fiddled and sang "Nellie Gray," and Roba and her father sang "Whoa Mule" as a duet. The other two sides, "Devilish Mary" and "Mister Chicken," featured Roba's singing and Patterson's harmonica playing.

Miss Stanley recalled in later years that her records, especially "Devilish Mary," sold well in the local market. The group returned to the studio in December 1924 for additional recordings of which three were subsequently released.

Miss Stanley's voice at the time has been characterized as "strong and clear and deeper than many of the other women singers . . . who were trying to record during this time. It was ideally suited to the limitations of the acoustic sound of the time, and it had a pronounced North Georgia arch that no city singer could fake."[31]

As we have seen, the Stanleys and Patterson were heard together on WSB in 1925. Shortly after these radio appearances Miss Stanley met and married a young man from Miami, Florida. She gave up her career, moved to Miami, and slipped into obscurity. In the late 1970s she was found to be residing in Gainesville, Forida, unaware of the significance of her contributions to the history of country music. In 1984 she was belatedly recognized for her contribution to country music when her visit to a "Grand Ole Opry" performance was announced from the stage. Two of her songs, "Single Life" and "All Night Long," were reissued in 1979 by Rounder Records on an album, *Banjo Pickin' Girl*, that featured all female performers. Roba Stanley Baldwin died in 1986.

It was also in Atlanta, in November 1927, that Jimmie Tarlton and Tom Darby, who were living in Columbus, Georgia, at the time, recorded their hits, "Columbus Stockade Blues" and "Birmingham Jail," for Columbia. They received seventy-five dollars for recording the two songs that became famous around the world. Between 1927 and 1933, Tarlton, either alone or with Darby, recorded more than seventy-five songs for Columbia, Victor, and the American Record Corporation.[32] Darby and Tarlton's 1927 recordings, which featured Tarlton's steel guitar playing, were among the most influential of the early recordings of that instrument.[33]

Graham Wickham writes that "Darby and Tarlton helped solidify the more introspective guitar-accompanied blues and love song styles predominant today." He also notes that the duo's repertoire and style reflect a marked black influence.[34]

Georgia's supply of old-time musicians during the 1920s and 1930s must have seemed almost inexhaustible to record company officials who came to Atlanta to make records. Even a partial list of those who recorded includes an impressive array of talent.

Land Norris, singing to his own banjo accompaniment, recorded sixteen issued sides in Atlanta in 1925 and 1926, including his own composition, "Fox Chase in Georgia." In 1926, in New York, he recorded eight sides, of which only half were released.[35]

Fiddler George Walburn and guitarist Emmett Hethcox, of Hogansville, recorded in Atlanta for OKeh in 1925, 1926, and 1927. Their released sides included "K. C. Railroad," "Lee County Blues," "Wait for the Lights to Go Out," and two titles with a local slant, "Macon Georgia Bound" and "Decatur Street Rag." An originally unissued title, "Walburn Stomp," was released in the 1970s on the long-play album *Georgia Fiddle Bands, Volume 2* (County 544). George Walburn's Footscorchers, featuring Walburn on fiddle and now unknown accompanists on banjo and guitar, recorded two sides ("Halliawika March"/"Dixie Flyer") for Columbia in 1931. One critic detects some similarities between Walburn's fiddling and that of recorded black fiddler Eddie Anthony.[36] Walburn and Hethcox made several appearances on WSB during the 1920s.

Walter Morris, of Cartersville, singing and accompanying himself on guitar, was in Atlanta's Columbia studio on April 22, 1926, to record four sides: "Take Back Your Gold"/"The Railroad Tramp" and "Crazy Coon"/"Betsy Brown." He sang two more songs, "Crazy Cracker" and "Sweet Marie" (with guitar and fiddle accompaniment), for Columbia on November 4. Of these two only "Sweet Marie" was released. In 1927 he recorded four more sides for Columbia, but only two were released.[37]

Acworth native Thomas Lee "Uncle Tom" Collins, well-known in his home town as a dry-goods store proprietor and versatile musician, recorded eight sides on the OKeh label in 1927. His selections, of which six were released, included "Little Brown Jug" and "Every Day Will Be Sunday Bye and Bye."[38]

Kenneth M. "Mack" Compton, a fiddler from Paulding County, took a group he called Compton's Reelers to OKeh's Atlanta studios in 1928 where they recorded four sides, none of which was released. Compton, recalling his recording experiences in later years, said that one of his musicians, a fiddler, was probably responsible for the records' not being released. "They instructed us fully that I should play lead fiddle," Compton recalled, "and the other boy should play backup fiddle—not try to play the lead at all—and he broke in, in a place or two, and got in the lead, and they [the recording company officials] didn't like it. They let us know right then they didn't like it, and that might be the reason the records never came out."[39]

Novelty groups were not uncommon in the Atlanta area and possibly two such groups, but more likely one group (with perhaps varying personnel) under different names, succeeded in preserving their sound on wax. In November 1927 a group called the Spooney Five recorded "Chinese Rag" and "My Little Girl" for Columbia. A group presumably with the same name, though the *Journal* called them the Spoonery Five, had appeared on WSB during the previous February. The band making the radio broadcast consisted of Pat Patterson, mandolin; Bill Edwards, fiddle; Bill Chandler, guitar; Wallas Martin, harmonica; and J. H. Brown, director. The *Journal* reported that Brown "handles two ordinary table spoons, and a wash or scrub board, with symbols [*sic,* should be thimbles] attached to his fingers."[40] In 1928 and 1929 a group calling themselves Hershel Brown and His Washboard Band recorded eighteen songs that were released on the OKeh and Victor labels.[41] Presumably Hershel Brown of the washboard band and J. H. Brown of the Spooney (or Spoonery) Five were one and the same.

What has been called "one of the most famous and authentic Southern labor songs" was recorded by Victor in its Atlanta studios in 1928. Called "Cotton Mill Girl," it was later sung and recorded by a number of folk singers during the folk-music revival of the 1950s and 1960s. The Victor version was recorded by Lester Smallwood accompanying himself on banjo and harmonica. The song was backed by "I'm Satisfied," a variant of the song popularized in the Atlanta area by Gid Tanner. At his only recording session, Smallwood recorded two other songs, but they were not issued. Born at Gainesville, Georgia, in 1900, Smallwood began working in the nearby New Holland cotton mill at an early age. He was discovered by Ralph Peer who, Smallwood said, offered him a contract. The contract was rejected, however, and thus ended a recording career. Smallwood was rediscovered in the 1970s, and his singing and banjo playing were again heard at folk-music affairs in the Atlanta and Athens, Georgia, areas.[42]

Most of the old-time musicians of Georgia who came to Atlanta in the 1920s and 1930s to enter the fiddling contests, to play on the radio, and to record were from north Georgia. In 1928 fiddler Bill Helms of Thomaston, which is south of Atlanta, became one of the exceptions when he went to the city to record four sides for Victor: "Thomaston Breakdown," "Georgia Blues," "Roscoe Trillion," and "Alabama Jubilee." The other musicians heard on these records were Grady Owens, fiddler; John Hogan, banjo player and guitarist; and Ty Cobb Hogan, guitarist. In 1931 Helms recorded for Columbia with Riley Puckett and Gid Tanner as the Home Town Boys.[43]

Among the lesser-known north Georgia fiddlers who recorded in Atlanta in the 1920s was Bill Shores, a native Alabaman who spent most of his life in the Rome, Georgia, area. He first recorded with Riley Puckett in Atlanta in 1926. This endeavor yielded three issued sides, "Sally Goodwin," "Ida Red," and "Down in Arkansas." A year later Shores had formed his own band consisting of, besides himself as fiddler, Melvin Dupree, guitarist, and Fred Locklear, who played mandolin. On March 15, 1929, this group was in Atlanta where they recorded four sides ("Wedding Bells Waltz,"

"Underneath the Mellow Moon," "Cat Rag," "12th Street Blues") that were released on the OKeh label. Less than a month later, in early April, Shores took his band to Richmond, Indiana, where they recorded six sides for the Gennett company under the name Shores Southern Trio. Two issued tunes from this session were "Down Yonder" and "Backup and Push," a coupling of which by the Skillet Lickers five years later would be a best seller. In October Shores and Dupree were back in an Atlanta studio to record, as Bill Shores and Melvin Dupree, two sides for Columbia ("Wedding Bells"/"West Texas Breakdown").[44]

In March 1930 a group called the Carroll County Revelers recorded "Rome Georgia Bound" and "Georgia Wobble Blues" in Atlanta for release on the Vocalion label. Presumably this group was from the west Georgia county of Carroll and consisted of Jess Chamblie, fiddler; Henry Chamblie, guitarist and vocalist; and colorful Uncle John Patterson, banjoist and politician, whose musical career spanned six decades.[45] Patterson, who served in the Georgia legislature from 1968 to 1974, was also a composer specializing in topical songs. His "Watergate Blues" was inspired by the so-called Watergate scandal of Richard Nixon's presidential administration. Patterson wrote "Plains, Georgia Rock" and "First Lady Waltz" in honor of President and Mrs. Jimmy Carter, who, in 1977, became the first Georgians to make their home in the White House. His "Muddy Roads of Viet Nam" captured in music Patterson's reaction to the United States' involvement in the protracted conflict in southeast Asia during the 1960s and 1970s. In 1977, fourteen of Patterson's songs and tunes were released on a stereo long-play album on the Arhoolie label. Before his death in 1980, Patterson performed at the Georgia Grass Roots Festival in Atlanta and at the National Folk Festival at Wolf Trap Farm Park in Vienna, Virginia.[46]

The list of out-of-state hillbilly artists who came to Atlanta to record during the 1920s and 1930s reads like a who's who among early country musicians. There were perhaps multiple reasons for Atlanta's popularity as a regional recording center. As previously noted, it was relatively easily accessible by rail and automobile from all directions. Furthermore, the record company representatives probably enjoyed the big-city amenities that Georgia's capital city had to offer. The art form itself probably benefitted from the visits by out-of-state musicians, many of whom, while in Atlanta, were able to perform on the local radio stations. Meetings between the out-of-state and local musicians presented opportunities for exchanges of styles and repertoires. On occasion local musicians were called on to participate as backup performers on the records of the artists from out of state.

One of the first of the old-time musicians to cross the state line into Georgia to make records was Uncle Jimmy Thompson, the first person ever to perform on the "Grand Ole Opry." Thompson, a fiddler, was in Atlanta on November 1, 1926, to record two sides for Columbia, "Karo" and "Billy Wilson." [47]

Jimmie Rodgers recorded in Atlanta on two occasions. He waxed four sides for Victor in October of 1928: "My Carolina Sunshine Girl" and "Blue Yodel No. 4" on October 20, and "Waiting for a Train" and "I'm Lonely and Blue" on October 22. Arriving in Atlanta almost a week before he was due to record, Rodgers retained a room at the Robert Fulton Hotel. While making his rounds of the city's night spots, he encountered a small jazz combo with which he was so impressed that he persuaded its members to record with him. Subsequently the group, consisting of Dean Bryan, guitar; C. L. Hutchison, cornet; John Westbrook, steel guitar; James Rikard, clarinet; and George MacMillan, string bass, contributed to what have been called some of Rodger's best recordings. [48] Westbrook, who had come to Atlanta some five years earlier "as a star of the famous Vaughan's Virginians orchestra," was widely known in the city "as a teacher of steel instruments, as a master of fretted technique and as the originator of a system of instruction acknowledged by leading musicians to be extraordinary." [49] For several years Westbrook was a prominent figure on Atlanta's popular-music scene, not only with his teaching but also as a frequent performer on WSB.

Jimmie Rodgers was back in Atlanta in 1929, at which time he recorded eight songs for Victor over a period of four days, November 25–28. Also in Atlanta to record for Victor that week was the Carter Family of Scott County, Virginia. Rodgers and the Carters, Sara, A. P., and Maybelle, had recorded on the same day in August 1927 in Bristol, Virginia—a landmark event in the history of country music—but it was at this 1929 Atlanta session that the two groups became personally acquainted for the first time. [50] Among the Carter Family songs recorded on this visit were some of the trio's best known, including "Homestead on the Farm," "Wabash Cannon Ball," and "Jimmie Brown the Newsboy."[51] The Carter Family was in Atlanta again in February of 1932 for another Victor recording session. The eight songs etched in wax at this time included "Mid the Green Fields of Virginia," "Happiest Days of All," "Picture on the Wall," and "Where We'll Never Grow Old."[52]

Atlanta was the site of the recording debut of the Delmore Brothers, Alton and Rabon, on October 28, 1931. In his autobiography, Alton Delmore describes in detail the trip he and his brother made by automobile from their home in northern Alabama to make their first record. After sleeping in their car their first night in the Atlanta area, they made their way the next morning to the Columbia studios where they were somewhat overwhelmed by the galaxy of recording stars they found there—Clayton McMichen, Riley Puckett, Gid Tanner, Fiddlin' John Carson, and Andrew Jenkins. After securing an appointment for the next day, October 28, the Delmores again spent the night in the open, this time on a sawdust pile on the outskirts of the city. Between their 9 A.M. audition, which was successful, and the 5 P.M. appointment to cut their records, the brothers were befriended by Fiddlin' John Carson and Rev. Andrew Jenkins, who were at the studio. Carson asked the Delmores to sing and play for the other musicians congregated in the lobby outside the recording room. "We fired into 'Left My Gal in the Mountains,'" Alton later recalled, "and before we were half way through all those record stars were over there with us, singing along just like a choir."[53] Alton stated in his autobiography that this was one of the biggest thrills of his career. "I'll always have a warm place in my heart for those two old-timers, Fiddlin' John Carson and Rev. Andrew Jenkins," he wrote.[54]

When the Delmores returned to the studio that afternoon they recorded two songs that were subsequently released, "I've Got the Kansas City Blues" and "Alabama Lullaby." From this beginning the Delmore Brothers became one of the most popular and influential country music acts of the 1930s and 1940s. They subsequently recorded for the Bluebird, Decca, and King labels. They became regular members of the "Grand Ole Opry" and were heard on other important radio stations in the Southeast and Midwest. They later teamed up with Grandpa Jones, future star of television's "Hee

Haw" show, and guitarist/composer Merle Travis to form a popular gospel recording act called the Brown's Ferry Four.[55]

Ernest V. "Pop" Stoneman, from the Galax, Virginia, area, went to Atlanta in October of 1927 to make records for the Victor Company. The four sides from this session were narrative recordings by Uncle Eck Dunford with Stoneman providing banjo accompaniment. The titles of the pieces they recorded were "Sleeping Late," "My First Bicycle Ride," "The Taffy-Pulling Party," and "The Savingest Man on Earth."

Stoneman was one of the most prolific and most popular of the pioneer country music artists. He first recorded in 1924 when he introduced "The Titanic," a disaster song that would become a country and folk music classic. By 1929 he had recorded more than two hundred numbers for the OKeh, Victor, Edison, Gennett, Paramount, Plaza, and Pathé labels. Seven of his Victor releases were recorded in Atlanta in 1928.

Stoneman, who also helped popularize the autoharp, began a second recording career in the late 1950s as a performer with various combinations of his numerous children. Death at the age of seventy-five ended his musical career in 1968, but as late as 1989 some half-dozen of his children were still performing both as the Stoneman Family and as solo acts, with the bluegrass circuit as their primary venue.[56]

In March 1928, Dr. Humphrey Bate and His Possum Hunters, as we have seen, traveled from Nashville to Atlanta to record for Brunswick. At the time, Bate's group was enjoying considerable popoularity on WSM's fledgling "Grand Ole Opry." In fact, the Possum Hunters had been the first string band to perform on the show. Despite their popularity on the radio the group's Atlanta recording session was the only one of their career. An even dozen sides from the session were issued: ten on the Brunswick label and two on the Vocalion label.[57]

Other hillbilly artists from out of state who recorded in Atlanta during the city's reign as a regional recording center include Homer Christopher, accordion player from Greenville, South Carolina (1926 and 1927);[58] Richard D. Burnett and Leonard Rutherford, popular fiddle, banjo, and vocal duet from Kentucky (1926 and 1927);[59] the Allen Brothers of Chattanooga, Tennessee (1927, 1928,

1932);[60] Clarence Greene, a fiddler from North Carolina (1927, 1929);[61] the Leake County Revelers, a string band from Mississippi whose 1927 "Wednesday Night Waltz"/"Good Night Waltz" was one of the best selling pre-World War II country music records (1927, 1929);[62] G. B. Grayson and Henry Whitter, fiddle, guitar, and vocal duet from North Carolina and Virginia, respectively (1927);[63] in solo performances, vocalist and guitarist Henry Whitter of Galax, Virginia, a key figure in the development of the hillbilly recording industry who first recorded in 1923 (1925, 1927, 1928);[64] William Thomas Narmour and Shellie Walton Smith (known as Narmour and Smith), a guitar-fiddle duet from Mississippi whose recorded repertoire consisted of breakdowns, blues, Charlestons, ragtime tunes, shuffles, fox trots, and waltzes (1929, 1934);[65] the Roane County Ramblers, a string band from East Tennessee (1929);[66] Bascom Lamar Lunsford, folk singer, composer ("Mountain Dew"), and banjoist of Asheville, North Carolina (1924, 1930);[67] Grover Rann and Harry Ayers, a vocal duet from Chattanooga, Tennessee (1930);[68] and J. E. Mainer's Mountaineers from North Carolina (1935).[69] Wade Mainer, who had recorded with his brother J. E. at the 1935 Atlanta session, returned to the city in 1941 to record eight sides as Wade Mainer and Sons of the Mountaineers.[70]

Atlanta's role as a regional recording center peaked in the 1920s, began to erode in the 1930s, and came to an end in the 1940s. However, Atlanta continued to serve as a center for the dissemination of country music. A decade of important country-music radio shows and a half-decade of country music on television lay ahead.

4

Four Pioneers

OF THE NUMEROUS MUSICIANS who entertained audiences at the Georgia Old-Time Fiddlers' Conventions between 1913 and 1935, four rose to the top in the world of hillbilly music to become widely known and influential far beyond their native turf. They were Fiddlin' John Carson, Gid Tanner, Riley Puckett, and Clayton McMichen. Already famous locally as a result of their appearances at the fiddlers' conventions, these four musicians—three fiddlers and a vocalist/guitarist—acquired a national following when radio came along and record company executives discovered the market for hillbilly music.

Fiddlin' John Carson was present in 1913 at the first fiddlers' convention held under the auspices of the Georgia Old-Time Fiddlers' Association. The newspaper article announcing the opening of the convention informed readers that "John Carson of Blue Ridge, Georgia, known far and wide as 'Fiddlin'' John, the Champion of Fannin County," had come to Atlanta the previous Wednesday and had gone "straight from the train to the auditorium" to announce himself as an entrant in the upcoming contest.

Asked by Homer Weaver, auditorium custodian, if he could really play a violin, Carson is alleged to have replied, "I don't lay claim to playing the violin, but I certainly can rip the tunes out of a fiddle."

To demonstrate his prowess Carson "tenderly unwrapped a faded silk cloth from his instrument" and removed the fiddle from its case. It was described as "old and shiny with a generation or two of use, worn half through where the chins of his father and grand-father had rested, marred and scratched from mix-ups at country dances." Mr. Carson chose for his impromptu concert "Soldier's Joy," followed by "Arkansas Traveler" and "The Mockingbird." His efforts fell on appreciative ears, and the effect of his songs was ecstatically described by Mr. Weaver. "My, me, the music that man did make," the custodian is supposed to have remarked. "That's the kind of music that gets me. Talk about your orchestras and your operas. Why, Fiddling John just leaned back in that chair, rolled his eyes up to the ceiling, began to pat his foot against the floor and tore the real soul of music out of that fiddle until I couldn't keep still. . . . It took me clear out of this smoky old town and back to the farm." [1]

Newspaper accounts of the fiddlers' conventions, the perform-ers, and members of the audience were usually models of early twentieth-century journalism of the most colorful variety, and one suspects that the writers, caught up in the excitement of the events, were not always as careful with the facts as they could have been. Year after year, for example, John Carson is described as having freshly arrived from his home in Blue Ridge when, in fact, he had been making the Atlanta area his permanent residence since 1900. [2]

John Carson was, indeed, born near Blue Ridge in Fannin County, Georgia—on March 23, 1868, or perhaps a few years later. [3] When he was ten years old his grandfather presented him with a fiddle that had become a family heirloom. It had been brought from Ireland in a flour sack many years before. The fiddle, it has been said, was a reproduction of a Stradivarius bearing the date 1714. [4] Approximately a year later young Carson was playing his fiddle at a rural barbecue and political rally at Copperhill, Tennes-see, just across the state line from Blue Ridge, when he attracted the attention of Tennessee's governor, Bob Taylor, who was also an old-time fiddler. Taylor was so impressed with this north Geor-gia lad's fiddling that he not only gave him a new name—"Fiddlin' John"—but bought him a new suit (his first) and a new fiddle as well. [5] Perhaps the tune that caught Governor Taylor's attention was "Old Dan Tucker," which, according to Carson, was the first piece his grandfather taught him. [6]

While he was growing up in Fannin County—and afterwards —Carson's vocational experiences included a little farming, playing for dances, working as a railroad hand, jockeying race horses, working in a cotton mill, and painting houses. He was once quoted as saying, "I never went to school but two days. Went in my brother's place 'cause he was sick and Pa didn't want him to lose no time."[7] It was on the way to a dance that Carson met his future wife. She was in a field plowing with a team of steers at the time.[8]

Carson once told a newspaper reporter, "Gettin' in jail was the makin' of me." By way of explanation he stated that in 1899, as a result of some moonshining activity, he, along with his fiddle, had been put in the Atlanta jail. The sheriff, on hearing the incarcerated Carson play, and at about the same time learning of an upcoming fiddlers' contest, gave the musician permission to attend it. The sheriff further promised to set his peripatetic prisoner free if he won. Carson won the contest, his release from jail, and the official prize, a fifty-dollar gold piece. This allegedly was Carson's first fiddling championship, but it was not his last. He is credited with winning first prize for the next eight years.[9]

By 1913 Fiddlin' John Carson seems to have established a fairly widespread and especially favorable reputation as a fiddler. Although he didn't win first prize at the fiddlers' convention that year, he was, if a contemporary source can be believed, definitely the star of the show. "From the time [he] first unlimbered his awkward six feet of height on the platform," goes the report, "the crowd could not get enough of him. . . . he just naturally played with his mind, soul and every inch of his body to the tips of his eyebrows. He and his fiddle and the entire audience were one."[10]

From then on Carson was a permanent fixture at the annual Atlanta fiddlers' conventions, frequently emceeing the contests, greeting fellow fiddlers from out of town, and hamming it up for the local newsmen who never left a Carson interview without a picturesque quote or a colorful anecdote to report. He was conspicuous among the contestants at the 1914 fiddlers' convention when he was dubbed the "Kubelik of the Blue Ridge." He is reputed to have arrived at the auditorium that year with his fiddle under his arm, and in his hand a plow line, the other end of which was attached to Old Trail, "the sorriest looking hound that ever bayed the moon."

To demonstrate the quality of the canine in his company for the benefit of those who looked on in wonder, Carson uncased his fiddle and proceeded to deliver his usually moving rendition of "The Mockingbird." While he played, the dog "raised his voice in song," and as the duet progressed "his master's playing became gradually a mere obligato to his solo." Carson confided to the gathering, "If Old Trail will jes' sing that-a-way . . . when the fiddlers' convention opens, I've done got the prize won. But I don't know," he mused. "He's kinder shy of strangers, and I look for a crowd, but anyway I'll bring him along, if the plow line don't break on me."[11] If Carson was able to persuade his animal to exhibit its talents on stage, no record of the performance exists. It is known, however, that Fiddlin' John Carson won the state fiddling championship that year.[12]

Fiddlin' John Carson appears to have taken an interest in current events. Perhaps the biggest Atlanta news story of 1915 occurred on August 16, when vigilantes took Leo Frank, convicted of the 1913 murder of pencil factory employee Mary Phagan, from the state prison at Milledgeville and lynched him at Marietta. Among those found at the scene of this macabre event was Fiddlin' John Carson. According to a contemporary newspaper account:

> The hundreds of morbidly curious [following the removal of the corpse] congregated around "Fiddlin' John" Carson, who has turned up with his fiddle at every Frank development within a radius of thirty miles of Marietta since the day Mary Phagan's body was discovered, as he stood in front of the courthouse and fiddled a symphonic jubilee. . . .
>
> "Fiddlin' John" Carson swayed the crowds. . . . in his repertoire of folk songs, he has one that is adapted to a quaint, rural hymn, and has for its words a narrative of the murder of Mary Phagan "by Leo M. Frank, the president of the pencil factory."
>
> "Fiddlin' John" would fiddle and sing his song in a typical nasal twang, and he could be heard to the center of the square, around which were grouped hundreds of automobiles, buggies and mountain transports of the "schooner" variety, which were wagons covered with canvas over arched framework.
>
> The crowd would cheer and applaud him lustily, and, inspirited by this show of appreciation, he would repeat his song,

over and over again. Presently, when his hearers began to tire of the same tune, he deserted it, and replaced it with such well-known selections as "Little Old Log Cabin by the Lane," "Annie Laurie," "That Good Old-Time Religion" and "Mr. Shirley, the Furniture Man."

"Fiddlin' John," the troubadour of the mountains, basked in "reflected glory," and it was not until the courthouse crowds began to tire of his songs and fiddle that he departed, reluctantly.[13]

Earlier that year Carson had been in attendance at the 1915 fiddlers' convention. In fact it is said that he had "been on the grounds" several days prior to opening night, giving other early arrivers occasional samples of his fiddling skill. "Fiddlin' is like salvation—free and without price," he is quoted as saying. "If there is any man in Georgia who can out fiddle me, he's welcome to the championship. But he's got to fiddle some," Carson added with customary immodesty.[14]

Carson could be counted on to do his part in promoting the annual fiddlers' contests. Most Atlantans first learned of the impending 1920 convention following the visit, on Saturday, November 6, of Fiddlin' John to the office of the city editor of the *Georgian*. "I drapped in to let you folks know that the old fiddlers are a-coming' again," he told the newsman. "And I wish you'd put a piece in the paper about it, so they'll all get tuned up and set for the championship."[15]

Carson assured all who would listen that they could expect an impressive array of fiddling talent at the upcoming convention. "You see, I've been moving about considerable durin' the past year," he explained. "I've been playing for barn dances and hoedowns and such pleasantries from the Tennessee line clean down below Macon, and no matter where I've been at, I've spread the news about the big fiddling match here in Atlanta. And I'm free to remark, friends, that the fiddlers listened to my message, and they're coming, and coming strong."[16]

When WSB began broadcasting in 1922 John Carson did not wait for the talent scouts to come looking for him. He was not that kind of person. Instead, as Marion Brown, one of Carson's acquaintances of later years, recalled, "John was bold. He'd walk in anywhere and stutter out that he wanted anything." [17] Thus legend has it that on March 23, 1922, one week and one day after WSB went on the air, Fiddlin' John Carson paid the station a visit with the intention of performing before its microphone. The day happened also to be Carson's birthday. Ernest Rogers, writing in 1939, described the Carson of 1922 as "a slender man with an engaging smile and manner. . . . Under his arm was a fiddle case which showed it had been used . . . and frequently. With that same friendly manner that characterizes him now, the fiddler removed his hat and inquired if it would be all right for him to play and sing a song or two. . . ." Permission was granted and "as near as we can trace it down," Rogers continued, "the first tune John played and sang was a threnodic backwoods song called 'Little Old Log Cabin in the Lane.' He had a repertoire that apparently was limitless. He played and sang until, shall we say, exhaustion set in. But not before he had scored a signal triumph and the phones were jumping up and down with requests from listeners who liked this return to the old-time mountain music that John Carson had been playing and singing for years." [18]

Fiddlin' John Carson's next documented appearance date on WSB was Saturday evening, September 9, 1922. Appearing with him were his three "cronies," as the musicians who performed with him were called: T. M. Brewer, guitarist, of Knoxville, Tennessee; L. E. Akin, banjoist, of Hall County; and fiddler Earl Johnson, from Gwinnett County. Lambdin Kay later wrote that Carson was "the first old-time fiddler in the world to revive famous old songs . . . for a radio audience." [19] Other more sophisticated artists, perhaps, had sung some of the same old songs for the enjoyment and amusement of a similarly sophisticated audience far removed from the scenes and life-style the songs depicted. Carson, on the other hand, was an authentic mountaineer (hillbilly, if you will) whose performances appealed to a radio audience of his own kind. And the fact that he was the first to do this is what earned him his special place in the annals of commercial country music.

That Carson did indeed make a hit with the station's management and listeners alike is evidenced by the fact that he made thirteen additional appearances on WSB during the remaining sixteen weeks of 1922, frequently appearing on the same program with lyric sopranos, classical pianists, and vaudeville stars. He was a regular feature on WSB's 10:45 P.M. "Transcontinental" program where he created "a flurry of comment from sea to sea."[20]

Carson appeared regularly on WSB from 1922 into the early 1930s, and thereafter intermittently into the 1940s. It became a WSB tradition to have Carson perform on the station each year on or near his birthday. In early 1923 the *Journal* announced that "there can hardly be a hamlet in the Union where 'The Voice of the South' has not already spread Fiddlin' John's name and fame."[21]

Atlanta and Fiddlin' John Carson received additional national attention in 1925 when an article entitled "Radio Made 'Fiddlin' John Carson' Famous" appeared in the November 7 issue of *Radio Digest*. "Radio made me famous," Carson was quoted. "Until I began to play over WSB, more than two years ago, just a few people in and around Atlanta knew me, but now my wife thinks she's a widow most of the time because I stay away from home so much playing around over this part of the country." The biographical essay stated that Carson "is one of the most famous and one of the most popular radio entertainers in these United States."[22]

The most significant event of the year 1923—perhaps of the decade—in the history of country music, not only in Atlanta, but in the nation as a whole, took place on Thursday, June 14. It was on that date, as we have noted, that Fiddlin' John Carson made the world's first real country-music record produced explicitly for a rural-oriented audience.[23]

When the fiddlers of Georgia held a convention in Atlanta in July of 1923, Fiddlin' John's record had just been released, and always the opportunist, he proceeded to play it on a phonograph on the stage and to sell copies to members of the audience, thus initiating another custom that would become standard among future country-music recording artists.[24]

Carson early on proclaimed his achievement by having "OKeh Recording Artist" painted on the automobiles that transported him to an ever increasing number of schoolhouses, theaters, and fairs for personal appearances and perhaps new opportunities to sell his records.

As a frequent winner of the Georgia state fiddling championship, as the first real hillbilly to broadcast over the radio, as the first real country-music recording artist, as probably the first country musician to announce his show dates over the radio, and as the first to sell his records at his personal appearances, Fiddlin' John Carson can rightfully be called the father of commercial country music. As country music historian Bob Coltman has pointed out, "what began with Fiddlin' John Carson in Georgia in 1922 shortly became a musical revolution of explosive force that helped break the bonds of conventionality and create a commercial popular music."[25]

Much has been written about Carson—his repertoire, his style, the aesthetics of his performances, and his place in the history of country music. Norm Cohen, country music critic and historian, has pointed out that Carson "favored cross tunings, and used double stops and drones frequently," and that "on his better numbers, his rhythm and pitch were faultless." But to Cohen, "Carson's true artistry was in his singing; there is not another commercial hillbilly singer who could match his beautifully ornate, melismatic vocals."[26] Bob Coltman, on the other hand, finds Carson "careless of rhythm, rhyme or pitch . . . so that his music has a sprained, disorienting quality."[27]

But there was a host of Fiddlin' John's contemporaries who liked his music, and that's what mattered. They bought his records, and record company officials brought him back into their studios again and again to satisfy the demand for Fiddlin' John's brand of music. Mere weeks after that first session in Atlanta, Fiddlin' John once again found himself, on November 7 and 8, 1923, before the recording horn of the General Phonograph Company. This time the record making took place in New York City where Fiddlin' John proceeded to preserve twelve more songs and tunes on the OKeh label. His recording career would last another eleven years during which he would record some 150 sides for OKeh and about two dozen for RCA Victor.

Bob Coltman has catalogued the wide variety of musical material represented by Carson's recorded repertoire. There were the sentimental tunes—"When You and I Were Young, Maggie," for example; tragedy songs, such as "The Death of Floyd Collins"; what Coltman calls agrarian anthems—"The Farmer Is the Man" and "The Honest Farmer," for example; ballads, such as "The Boston Burglar"; breakdowns that included "Arkansas Traveler"; a category that Coltman calls local tunes and includes "Jimmie on the Railroad"; coon songs, represented by "I Got Mine"; and though not numerous, the sacred songs one would expect from a man of the rural South.[28] This latter category included "At the Cross" and "I Intend to Make Heaven My Home." Country music historian Gene Wiggins has made an exhaustive study of Carson's songs and has reported the results, along with both words and music to many of them, in his biography of Fiddlin' John.[29]

In September 1931, the *Journal* told its readers that Carson had just published "his first album of mountain ballads." The songbook, which contained a biographical sketch of Carson written by WSB's director, Lambdin Kay, was apparently advertised on a series of radio programs that Carson presented on WSB that fall.[30] Although the precedent of a hillbilly performer selling songbooks over the radio had been set earlier elsewhere—Bradley Kincaid, for example, sold his first songbook over WLS in 1928[31]—Carson's may have been the first such songbook sold through an Atlanta radio station.

By 1930 Carson's career was beginning to wane. His appearances on the radio became less frequent, and his last recording session took place in February 1934. But Carson, reluctant to throw in the towel, fell back on other resources. In 1932 his longtime friend Eugene Talmadge, who was running for governor of Georgia, needed a proven crowd-drawer and people-pleaser to help bring his message to the state's voters, especially the farmers and the working people. Fiddlin' John, who had a long history of involvement in political campaigns—for example, he and his five-year-old buck-dancing daughter, Rosa Lee, in 1914, helped Nat Harris become governor of Georgia[32]—was ready-made for the task.

Carson had used his musical talents in 1926 on behalf of Talmadge, who ran successfully for the job of state commissioner of agriculture,[33] and now in 1932 he had another chance to help advance the career of this ambitious politician. Eugene Talmadge's biographer describes Carson's role in the campaign:

> The Talmadge entourage, which by August was taking on the appearance of a traveling circus, and medicine show, brought on another attraction. Atlanta singer and composer Fiddlin' John Carson was a country singer who had seen better days, but he could set a foot to stomping with little effort. He and his daughter, Moonshine Kate, came on with the organization,

and it was their function to entertain the crowd before Gene arrived. They also set the tone for the speech, appearing as corny, redneck characters, a little down and out, but happy. . . .

Fiddlin' John Carson had even provided the campaign with a song. Probably the corniest piece of music ever to grace a political race, "The Three-Dollar Tag Song" was played at every speech by the strumming Carson and his daughter. It went:

> I gotta Eugene Dog, I gotta Eugene Cat
> I'm a Talmadge man from my shoes to my hat.

> Farmer in the corn field hollerin' whoa, gee, haw,
> Kain't put no thirty-dollar tag on a three-dollar car.[34]

In recognition of his contribution to the political successes of Gene Talmadge in 1932 and of Gene and his son, Herman, in later years, Carson was given a job as elevator operator in Georgia's capitol building. Here, where he spent the remaining years of his active life, he no doubt found ample time to reflect on his long and colorful career. Just as Fiddlin' John's first documented public appearance took place in a political setting, so did his last. Nine months before his death on December 11, 1949, at the age of eighty-one,[35] he played his fiddle in the Georgia senate chamber.[36]

Like Fiddlin' John Carson, Gid Tanner first attracted attention through his appearances at the Georgia Old-Time Fiddlers' Conventions in Atlanta. Although apparently he was not present at the first one, in 1913, he was on hand for the second.

"Perhaps the greatest novelty of the evening," said one reporter of the 1914 contest, "was Gid Tanner, a husky youth with tan face and shoes, roan hair, a mouth as flexible as a minstrel show coon's, and a voice which ranged from a high falsetto to a rumbling bass." (This habit of modulation was one of Tanner's trademarks.) He sang and fiddled "Everybody Works But Father" and gave a series of parodies in which the audience recognized a number of familiar "Decatur Street types" and at least one well-known public official. Tanner was so enthusiastically received that "it was with difficulty the performance was permitted to proceed."[37]

James Gideon Tanner was born on June 6, 1885, at Thomas Bridge, near Monroe, Georgia. When he was twenty-one years old he married a sixteen-year-old girl from Rockdale County. During the early years of their marriage they lived alternately in Gwinnett and Rockdale counties, finally settling permanently at Dacula in Gwinnett County where they farmed for a living. Tanner had learned to play the fiddle at the age of fourteen, using an instrument left to him in an uncle's will.[38]

Tanner was again present when the fiddlers of Georgia convened at the Atlanta City Auditorium in 1915. A reporter at that year's convention called him "Gwinnett County's 'Laughing Rufus,'" and when Tanner appeared on stage he "utilized his several voices to advantage in two or three songs he 'made up hisself.'" It is said that he got frequent encores for his fiddling and his imitations.[39]

Reporters at the 1915 convention began to play up a supposed rivalry between Fiddlin' John Carson and Tanner. It is difficult to determine from the newspaper accounts exactly how much of the alleged rivalry was real and how much was created on paper for the purpose of stirring up interest in the convention and attracting large crowds for the evening performances. Master showmen that they were, Carson and Tanner probably did their part to enhance the spirit of conflict, and although they no doubt were competitive by nature, the rivalry probably was not as intense as they, the reporters, and the convention promoters would have their fans believe. One reporter, after hearing them perform, stated that it was hard to "make first choice in popularity" between Carson and Tanner;[40] and, as the 1915 convention drew to a close, it was reported that betting was about even between the two. "They have been running a close race for popularity all week," said the report, "and that one of them will win the medal seems certain."[41] But when the contest was over neither of the two arch-rivals carried home the coveted first-place medal. A *Journal* reporter described what happened: "The judges had a tough time deciding third and fourth places between Fiddlin' John Carson and Gid Tanner, and after an hour and a half of deliberation brought the two favorites forward for a second try-out. Carson was awarded third place and Tanner fourth."[42]

When the 1918 Atlanta fiddlers' convention opened, Gid Tanner was there as usual making his fiddle "dance with the joy that's in it" and singing in his two voices. "Isn't [he]," someone wanted to know, "the original of all the jazz bands we hear so much of these days? If he isn't," the questioner answered himself, "he should be. But the imitators have left out the music because you can't play like these mountaineers unless the music is in you, as well as in your fiddle."[43] Almost fifty years later, Norm Cohen, after hearing the music that Gid Tanner and his band, the Skillet Lickers, recorded in the 1920s and 1930s, stated that they "are important not only because of their unusually rich traditional repertoire, but also because of their many attempts at recording 'popular' music and jazz." According to Cohen "the group [produced] some of the earliest recordings that combined hillbilly with popular music, and made a significant step in the development of a jazz-country music hybrid that is an important part of the modern country-western music scene."[44]

In 1924, a representative of the Columbia record company, no doubt motivated by John Carson's successful recordings, prevailed upon Gid Tanner to travel to New York to make the records that would allow Columbia to cash in on what was shaping up to be a lucrative hillbilly market.[45] Tanner invited fellow musician Riley Puckett to go with him, and on March 7 and 8 the two recorded a total of twelve released sides. Included were vocal solos by Puckett and such fiddle tunes by Tanner as "Buckin' Mule" and "Black Eyed Susie."[46] Puckett and Tanner returned to New York in September 1924 to make additional records for Columbia.

Among the most touted of the participants at the Georgia Old-Time Fiddlers' Convention of 1925 was Gid Tanner, "who," said the newspapers, "has carried Georgia's 'fiddling fame' to the far northern music marts where his numbers have been recorded on phonograph records."[47]

By far the most significant recording activity in Atlanta in 1926 took place on April 17, when Gid Tanner, Riley Puckett, Fate Norris (banjoist), and Clayton McMichen teamed up in Columbia's Atlanta studio to record eight sides. When these records were released artists' credits read, "Gid Tanner and His Skillet-Lickers with Riley Puckett." The output from this historic recording session makes for a rather unimpressive list of what even then were long-familiar tunes and songs: "Hand Me Down My Walking Cane," "Bully of the Town," "Pass Around the Bottle and We'll All Take a Drink," "Alabama Jubilee," "Watermelon on the Vine," "Don't You Hear Jerusalem Moan," "Ya Gotta Quit Kickin' My Dog Aroun'," and "Turkey in the Straw."[48]

Over the next eight years, various combinations of Atlanta-area musicians recorded under the name of the Skillet Lickers. In addition to Tanner, Puckett, Norris, and McMichen, they included Bert Layne, fiddle; Lowe Stokes, fiddle; Gid's son, Gordon, fiddle; and Ted Hawkins, mandolin. The Skillet Lickers, according to Norm Cohen, came to be regarded as "one of the finest and most popular of the hillbilly string bands to record during the twenties and thirties."[49]

Between 1926 and 1931 the Skillet Lickers recorded eighty-eight sides for Columbia of which eighty-two were released.

In addition to fiddle tunes, traditional ballads, and pop songs, the Skillet Lickers also recorded several skits or, as Norman Cohen describes them, "rural drama records" consisting of "humorous dialogue interspersed with snatches from songs and instrumentals that the group had recorded on other records."[50] Three such skits were "A Corn Licker Still in Georgia," "The Medicine Show," and "Kickapoo Joy Juice."

The Skillet Lickers made one of their rare appearances on WSB in November 1926. This appears to have been their first radio broadcast since assuming the name Skillet Lickers and achieving popularity as a result of their records. One of the unanswered questions in the history of country music in Atlanta is why the Skillet Lickers did not perform more frequently on WSB. Perhaps management felt that one famous fiddler—Fiddlin' John Carson—was enough for the station to help promote.

Another question regarding the Skillet Lickers that seems to have gone unanswered has to do with the group's name. Some have speculated that the band was named for a community called Lick Skillet allegedly located near Atlanta or, at least, somewhere in north Georgia. This does not seem to be the case, however. The only communities officially bearing the name Lick Skillet now known to have ever existed in Georgia were one in Fulton County near Atlanta and one in Harris County some eighty miles southwest of the capital city.

The Lick Skillet near Atlanta had had its name changed to Adamsville by 1881[51] and is now part of metropolitan Atlanta. The Lickskillet of Harris County, which received its name soon after the Civil War, still exists.[52] It does not seem likely, however, that this community provided the inspiration for naming the band, since no known members of the Skillet Lickers were from that part of the

state. A more plausible explanation is that the band was named for
an imaginary rather than an actual place. An authority on American place-names writes that Lickskillet is "a derogatorily humorous
appellation for a place so poor or boorish that people licked their
skillets."[53] Such poor-mouthing expressions were no doubt familiar
to and in common use by rural Georgians during the first quarter of this century. It is assumed that the name Skillet Lickers was
adapted from the name of the earlier band, the Lick Skillet Orchestra, that was frequently heard at the Georgia Old-Time Fiddlers'
Conventions.

In 1927 old-time music in Atlanta was again brought into the
national spotlight through the publication of a magazine article and
a songbook. In the December 1927 issue of *Holland's Magazine*,
Catherine Stewart Prosser told of a meeting between Gid Tanner
and folk song collector, singer, and dulcimer player Ethel Park
Richardson. Mrs. Richardson sought out Tanner for the purpose of
learning some of his songs. She allegedly won his confidence over
a dip of snuff. "Oh, I had to do it," Mrs. Richardson is quoted.
"There's real manners, you know, among mountain folk about re-
fusing snuff, so I dipped a good one while I was doing it, although
I sneezed for two days afterwards." Later at a concert when Mrs.
Richardson sang "Careless Love," a song she learned from Tanner,
she told her audience that she was singing the song as Tanner sang
it. In the then typically condescending and often inaccurate manner of journalists writing about mountain folks, the author of the
article stated that "Gid's fame has spread far beyond the confines
of his little whitewashed cabin, and he is now making records for
a talking-machine company."

According to the article, Mrs. Richardson, sometime after her
initial visit with Tanner, wrote to him that she would like to come
to see him again and bring a friend who wanted to write a story
about him. Mrs. Tanner, answering the letter for her husband, informed Mrs. Richardson that "I don't want no magazine [article]
writ about Gid, so there ain't no use in your comin'."[54]

Later in the year *American Mountain Songs*, a collection compiled by Mrs. Richardson, was published in New York. One of the
songs in the book, complete with words and music, was Gid Tanner's composition "I'm Satisfied." Another was "Howdy Bill," with
composer credit attributed to Bill Chitwood.[55]

Four Pioneers

In March 1934, after a two-and-one-half-year hiatus from recording, Tanner made his last records. The session was held in San Antonio, Texas, for the RCA Victor Company. The musicians, besides Tanner, who made up the Skillet Lickers for the endeavor were Gid's seventeen-year-old son, Gordon Tanner; Riley Puckett; and Ted Hawkins. The output from this venture included "Down Yonder," the Skillet Lickers' most famous recording and a top-five hillbilly hit of 1934.[56] Young Gordon Tanner was the featured fiddler on the record.

Gid Tanner spent the last years of his life in Gwinnett County where he farmed, played occasional show dates, and entered fiddling contests when the spirit moved him. The Skillet Lickers were heard on Atlanta's WJTL in 1935. In 1936, after the station's call letters were changed to WATL, we find the name Gid Tanner on the broadcast schedules for February, March, and April. In 1950 he, Gordon, and two local musicians, Red Bailey and Ray Coggins, had a program on an Athens radio station, and in the late 1950s Gid won his last fiddling contest at a convention held in Gainesville, Georgia.[57] He died on May 13, 1960.[58]

Tanner's longtime associate, George Riley Puckett, was born on May 7, 1894, some twenty-five miles northeast of Atlanta at Alpharetta. Through the misapplication of medicine for an eye ailment, he was blinded shortly after birth, and as a child he attended the Georgia Academy for the Blind at Macon where he studied piano. He later moved with his parents to Atlanta and there, as a teenager, taught himself to play the banjo.[59]

Perhaps because he was not a fiddler, Puckett is not often mentioned in newspaper accounts of the Atlanta fiddlers' conventions, although he must have been regularly in attendance. His name in connection with these events first appears in print in 1916 when we read in the *Journal* the brief statement that "the blind banjoist" was "ready for the big doings" at the fourth annual Georgia Old-Time Fiddlers' Convention.[60] We are later told that on opening night he played "Tipperary" for an encore.[61]

His presence at the 1917 fiddlers' convention prompted one newspaper reporter to write that "no description of a fiddlers' convention would be complete without reference to Riley Puckett, the blind banjo player, whose flying fingers picked a rhythmic accompaniment to any tune that might be offered, no matter whence it came or how often it switched its key."[62] On opening night he "played and sang 'When You and I Were Young, Maggie,' by request."[63] Puckett was at the fiddlers' convention held in Atlanta in July 1923, and he appeared in company with "several of the prize fiddlers" on WSB in a prelude broadcast to the opening of the contest.[64] Professor Aleck Smart, who was in charge of the radio program, "contributed a yodeling and vocal duet" with Puckett, who by now was being "dubbed by his admirers" as "The Bald Mountain Caruso." Their joint renditions consisted of a medley and "Sleep, Baby, Sleep." Puckett also presented a novelty song, "Thompson's Old Grey Mule."[65] Puckett's last documented appearance at an Atlanta fiddlers' convention was the one held in March 1934 when he won first prize in the banjo contest.[66]

On September 28, 1922, Puckett made what was apparently his radio debut on the six-month-old WSB. He appeared with the Home Town Boys String Band headed by Clayton McMichen. Their program was presented on the 10:45 P.M. "Transcontinental" concert, which was heard not only in the Southeast, but as far away as the Pacific Coast and the Rocky Mountain country.[67] Listeners heard Riley's rendition of "the 'Old Cabin' song, a wonderful yodeling solo," and the *Journal* opined that "the Hometown outfit scored a knockout by introducing Mr. Puckett as one of their stars."[68]

Puckett appeared with the Home Town Boys on WSB through 1923. He and Ted Hawkins were frequently featured as a duet on WSB and were heard in this capacity as late as 1927. Puckett and Gid Tanner also occasionally teamed up for a WSB broadcast. A writer for the *Journal* noted in November 1922 that Puckett's "tenor voice carries with a silver clearness that compels attention and admiration."[69] Riley's "extraordinary yodeling proclivities" and guitar playing also impressed his listeners. One journalist wrote that "the blind musician's peculiar method of handling his guitar perhaps has something to do with the unusually . . . fine harmony he gets from it."[70] Puckett's radio repertoire consisted of such songs as "Dapper Dan," "Ring Waltz," "Little Old Log Cabin in the Lane," "Sleep, Baby, Sleep," "St. Louis Blues," and "Lonesome Mama Blues."

Although those early hillbilly performers on WSB were not paid by the station, radio exposure had its fringe benefits. Listeners longed to see, as well as hear, their favorite radio entertainers. By the end of 1922, Puckett and his cohorts were "heavily in demand for affairs in Atlanta and this part of the southeast," and allegedly were "scoring as heavily when appearing in person as when before the microphone."[71] Radio exposure, however, was not limited to the local area. Following an October 1923 WSB broadcast by Puckett and the Home Town Boys the station was flooded by an "immense amount of mail" from such places as Herndon, Iowa; Madison, Wisconsin; Oakland, Florida; Geneva, Nebraska; Cleburn, Texas; Victor, West Virginia; and Canada.[72]

As we have seen, Riley Puckett accompanied Gid Tanner to New York in March 1924 to record for Columbia and to become the first hillbilly artists to be heard on discs bearing that company's label. At these sessions, held on March 7 and 8, Puckett recorded six solo numbers with only his guitar as accompaniment. These songs, which became the first released recordings by Puckett, were "Little Old Log Cabin in the Lane," "Old Joe Clark," "Casey Jones," "Steamboat Bill," "Strawberries," and "Rock All Our Babies to Sleep."[73] The latter song, which became one of the top-five hillbilly songs that year, featured Puckett's yodeling and established him as probably the first recorded hillbilly artist to employ that vocal device.[74] This was about three years before Jimmie Rodgers became famous as America's "blue yodeler."

In September 1924, on his second trip with Tanner to New York to record (again for Columbia), Puckett took along his banjo, and on five of the resulting releases ("Sourwood Mountain," "Cripple Creek," "Georgia Railroad," "Oh! Susanna," and "Cumberland Gap") we hear examples of his rarely recorded banjo work.[75] Puckett's records met with tremendous success, and he soon became, after Fiddlin' John Carson, the most frequently recorded southern singer.[76] By the end of 1925 orders for pressings of Puckett's records were exceeded in number among Columbia's artists only by those of pop singer Vernon Dalhart.[77]

Puckett was a member of the Skillet Lickers when they recorded their first numbers for Columbia in 1926. The value of his name on a record label is attested by the fact that artist credit for the first Skillet Lickers' releases read "Gid Tanner and His Skillet-Lickers With Riley Puckett." Clayton McMichen's name was added on later releases. Years later McMichen gave Puckett credit for the popularity of the Skillet Lickers' records. "Well, Riley Puckett proved the people wanted to hear singin'," he said. "And if he didn't sing, the records, why, they didn't sell, much."[78]

Puckett continued to record, both alone and with others, into the early 1940s, leaving behind more than two hundred solo records on such labels as Columbia, Decca, and Bluebird.[79] Puckett's vocal repertoire revealed a decided eclecticism. Among his recorded output we find novelty songs, religious songs, traditional folk songs, cowboy songs, and composed pieces spanning the time period from the Victorian era to his own. Puckett's interpretation of this material likewise reflects a diversity of influences, including the folk tradition, commercial hillbilly, ragtime, and blues.

In February 1925 Puckett was severly injured in an automobile accident while riding in a car driven by Ted Hawkins. The nurse who attended Puckett during his lengthy convalescence was a young widow with whom he fell in love. They were later married and had one child, a daughter, who, like her mother, was named Blanche.[80]

Puckett spent much of the 1930s traveling around the country performing on various radio stations and making personal appearances. He was heard on stations in Covington, Kentucky; Columbus and Cleveland, Ohio; Memphis, Tennessee; Huntington, West Virginia; Gary, Indiana; and Chicago, Illinois.[81] For a time he had his own tent show with which he traveled throughout the South and as far west as Texas and Oklahoma.[82]

During periodic visits back home Puckett would appear on radio stations in Atlanta. From February through May 1934, he was on WSB with his own bands variously called the Sand Sifters, the Georgia Red Hots, and the Georgia Hot Shots. Newspaper radio logs for WJTL carry the name Riley Puckett during November 1935. (It is possible that these programs featured his records rather than live performances.) In June and July of 1939 he was in Atlanta again appearing on WGST with Daddy John Love, a former member of Mainer's Mountaineers, the popular North Carolina radio and recording act. In 1941 Puckett was heard on Atlanta's WAGA with a group that included singer Dwight Butcher and fiddler Ernie Hodges.[83] Around 1945 Puckett was a member of the Tennessee Barn Dance troupe broadcasting over WNOX in Knoxville, Tennessee, where he shared billing with such well-known groups as the Delmore Brothers, Grady and Hazel Cole, Lost John and the Allied

Kentuckians, Chet Atkins, Sam and Kirk McGee, and Wally Fowler and His Georgia Clodhoppers.[84]

Puckett's last radio job was at WGAA in Cedartown where he was working when he had to be hospitalized for treatment of a boil on his neck. He never returned to his home in the Atlanta suburb of College Park, as death struck on July 13, 1946, while he was still in the hospital. Among the pallbearers at his funeral were Gid Tanner, the man with whom Puckett had made his first record, and Gordon Tanner, who, along with his father, had participated in Puckett's last recording session as a Skillet Licker.[85]

Another member of the Skillet Lickers, Clayton McMichen, first attracted the attention of newspaper reporters in 1915. That year's edition of the Georgia Old-Time Fiddlers' Convention was held during the first week of February, and an audience of 4,500 at the Friday night festivities[86] helped confirm declarations that this was the "biggest and best" fiddlers' convention to which Atlanta had ever played host.[87] The following evening, the appointed time for the selection of the state champion, the judges were confronted by an array of seventy-five contestants. The next morning the *Journal* reported that the winner of eighth place had been Clayton McMichael, aged fourteen.[88] The *Constitution*, in its report of the contest, agreed with the youngster's age but gave his name as Clayton Micher.[89] Both newspapers, apparently, were wrong on both counts, for, no doubt, the youthful contender, who received five dollars for his efforts, was Clayton McMichen, who had turned fifteen less than two weeks before.

McMichen was born on January 26, 1900, at Allatoona, Georgia, a village located about forty miles northeast of Atlanta.[90] The McMichens, Clayton said in an interview later in life, had come from Scotland, perhaps around the turn of the nineteenth century, eventually settling in Paulding County, Georgia.[91] At the age of eleven, Clayton, whose father was a fiddle player and whose grandmother played a fretless banjo, began to take an interest in the fiddle. From his father he learned many of the tunes that would later make him famous. Country dances, at which his father provided the fiddle music and his mother beat straws, were a significant part of McMichen's early social life, and he never forgot how farmers in the neighborhood would move all the furniture out of one

room of their houses to create a space for the square dancing that
would continue until midnight or later.[92] In 1913, the McMichens
moved to Atlanta, where thirteen-year-old Clayton took a job as an
automobile mechanic.[93]

McMichen's name appears less frequently in newspaper coverage of the Atlanta fiddlers' conventions than one would expect.
No doubt, however, he was present at these events more often than
such accounts indicate. In 1922 he was in attendance and won the
second-place prize of thirty dollars for his rendition of "Arkansas
Traveler."[94] Presumably the name "Mac Miken" listed in the *Constitution's* roster of fiddlers appearing on the Friday evening program of the 1924 convention is evidence that Clayton McMichen
was present.[95] Bands whose leaders are identified only as McMichen are mentioned briefly in connection with conventions held in
1929 and 1931.[96]

Approximately six months after WSB went on the air a string
band bearing the name Home Town Boys became the first such
musical group to appear on the new radio station. The leader of the
band was Clayton McMichen, and their first program was broadcast on Monday, September 18, 1922. The next day, the *Journal*, in
its customary review of the previous evening's programs, reported
that the Home Town Boys had "qualified as a combination of talent that appealed hugely to auditors both in and out of Atlanta,"
and that "they made a tremendously impressive showing."[97]

WSB received numerous telephone calls and letters praising the
music of the Home Town Boys and "calling on [them] for special
numbers."[98] They soon became one of the most frequently programmed acts on the station. Although the frequency of their appearances diminished with time, the group was heard on the station
intermittently through June 1926. At one time or another, the Home
Town Boys band included Charles Whitten; Miles Whitten, guitar; Boss Hawkins, guitar; Ted Hawkins, mandolin; Riley Puckett,
vocalist, guitarist, and banjo player; Robert Stephens, saxophone;
and Lowe Stokes, fiddle. Their programs, featuring such instrumental numbers as "St. Louis Blues," "Wabash Blues," "Old Pal, Why
Don't You Answer Me," "Three O'Clock," "Lonesome Mama,"
and "Dixie," were somewhat more uptown than those of Fiddlin'
John Carson and his cronies who stuck mainly to old-time fare. The

Journal repeatedly commented on the group's ability to alternate between "break-down ditties" and "popular airs," and maintained that they had "introduced America to the famous break-down tunes of north Georgia mountaineers, as well as putting a new twist on the popular jazz numbers of the day." [99]

In August 1923, McMichen and other members of the Home Town Boys band "descended upon a fiddlers' convention at Macon ... and literally stampeded the assemblage." [100] McMichen won first place in the fiddle competition, Riley Puckett took first place and Miles Whitten second place in the guitar category, Ted Hawkins was declared top banjoist, and Charlie Whitten placed third with his fiddle. [101] McMichen "carried away also a new nickname of 'The North-Georgia Wildcat' bestowed upon him by Macon listeners." [102] Presumably this nickname formed the basis for the name of one of McMichen's later bands, the Georgia Wildcats.

Although the Home Town Boys' music was recorded, their records were never as popular as those of the Skillet Lickers with whom McMichen recorded from 1926 to 1930.

McMichen's association with the Skillet Lickers was not always pleasant because of personality clashes and differing musical tastes. He once said that "two or three in there [the Skillet Lickers band] couldn't play" [103] and that he didn't like playing with Gid Tanner and Fate Norris "because they just was about 30 years behind us, or 40, in the music business." [104]

By the time the original Skillet Lickers disbanded, McMichen had already organized another group (perhaps more) which was much more to his liking. His new band, called Clayton McMichen and His Melody Men, made several appearances on WSB in 1930. One of their programs, which was broadcast in February, was advertised as "the *Journal's* first big 'Radio Barn Dance.'" [105] Apparently this was also its last radio barn dance—at least for several years. McMichen and Riley Puckett were heard in May on a one-hour program on WSB during the station's 11 P.M. to midnight "Transcontinental Hour" presentation. In pre-broadcast publicity for this program we are told that the two had "returned to Atlanta recently following an extensive tour of the west" where they had appeared "in programs over leading southern and western stations," including Saturday-night barn dances at KTHS, Hot

Springs, Arkansas.[106] McMichen and His Melody Men were heard on thirty-minute programs on three consecutive Friday nights in July and August and every Tuesday night in December.

McMichen's Melody Men made two broadcasts on WSB in January 1931. The last one, heard on January 13, seems to have been McMichen's final appearance on an Atlanta radio station. He apparently left Atlanta at about this time to work on radio stations in various parts of the country including KDKA, Pittsburgh; WSM, and the "Grand Ole Opry," in Nashville; WWVA, Wheeling, West Virginia; KMOX, St. Louis; WLW and WCKY in Cincinnati; WLS and the "National Barn Dance" in Chicago; and WHAS and WAVE in Louisville, Kentucky. He continued to front a band, his famous Georgia Wildcats; to record; and to win numerous fiddling contests. During the period 1945–55 McMichen converted his string band to a Dixieland jazz band that was heard daily over Louisville's WAVE. He retired from the music business in 1955, but enjoyed a comeback in the 1960s when his discovery by folk music and bluegrass enthusiasts led to several appearances on college campuses and at bluegrass and folk music festivals.[107]

During his career McMichen was credited with writing or co-writing a number of songs, including "My Carolina Home," "Dear Old Dixie," "Peach Pickin' Time in Georgia," and "Dreamy Georgiana Moon." McMichen died on January 3, 1970, in Battletown, Kentucky.[108]

5

Radio in the Early 1930s

THE 1930S, IN THE MINDS of most Americans, are synony-
mous with "the Great Depression." One of the most written-about
periods in American history, the decade has been called "A Time to
Remember,"[1] "The Anxious Years,"[2] "The Desperate Years,"[3] and
"Years of Protest."[4] It was, as one writer put it, the era that left an
"invisible scar."[5]

The 1930s—these were the days of a rising national suicide
rate, of bank failures, and of mobs of unemployed men demon-
strating and attacking city halls across the country. These were the
days of street-corner apple vendors, bread lines, and food riots;
of Hoovervilles, bonus armies, and presidential fireside chats. It
was in the 1930s that, at a single point, perhaps seventeen million
Americans were unemployed, more than six million were on state
and municipal relief rolls, and forty-five million were living in dire
poverty.

These were the days when millions of men, women, and children took to the highways and railways of the country in search
of jobs; when the federal government paid a million cotton farmers more than one hundred million dollars to plow up their cotton
crops; when the American public was first forced to decipher a
bewildering array of such bureaucratic alphabetic codes as CCC,
NYA, NRA, WPA, and RFC.[6]

What effect then did the Depression have on the course of
country music? Chroniclers of the period are not in complete agree-

ment. Although an official of the RCA Manufacturing Company has reported that, in general, "record sales suffered severely,"[7] and another writer has stated that "record sales slumped by 94% and phonograph sales by 96%,"[8] the country music segment of the recording industry seems not to have been so drastically affected—if other writers are to be believed.

According to Ralph Peer and one-time Columbia Records president Goddard Lieberson, hillbilly records continued to sell well during the Depression.[9] An *Atlanta Journal* columnist writing about Fiddlin' John Carson in 1931 stated that "his hill-billy discs are apparently the only ones with a sure-fire sale today. Big-time songsters, once scornful of Fiddlin' John and his kind, are falling over each other to make the sort of records he originated."[10] On the other hand, country-music historian Bob Coltman writes:

> Recording activity of course did not cease with the Crash, and the industry continued to function at a gradually diminishing rate until economic ruin brought it to its knees in 1932. But more and more recordings remained unissued, for those that were issued did not sell well. People were frightened, holding on to their money, waiting to see how the economic crisis would turn out. As a result fewer people heard new country records after 1930, and the influence of recordings on the further development of country style fell toward zero.[11]

Although the precise effect of the Depression on country music within the recording industry may be clouded, one thing about the period is clear: radio emerged as the dominant factor in the dissemination of the genre. Whereas the phonograph industry had been instrumental in shaping the history of country music in the 1920s, radio was the primary force in the progress of the art form during the 1930s. Census takers in 1930 found radio sets in more than twelve million American homes, making for a potential listening audience of fifty million persons.[12] Radio captured the imagination and loyalty of the public in a way that the phonograph never had. While the phonograph was viewed as a passive instrument of entertainment and very much the machine that it was, the radio was perceived as a vibrant, living thing—almost as another member of the family. A phonograph record was a historical document; a radio broadcast was the here-and-now. Radio performers communicated not only through their music, but through conversation as well.

Listeners could write—were, in fact, encouraged to write—to their favorite entertainers, and in return they could hear their names read on the air. What fan has ever heard a singer call his or her name on a phonograph record? The radio, once turned on, would play without interruptions, allowing listeners to perform the chores of the household, shop, or farm while being entertained and informed. On the other hand, a person listening to the phonograph for any length of time had to be available to perform the inconvenient and annoying task of changing records about every three minutes. The radio also provided more than music. It gave the listener news, weather forecasts, comedy, and drama tailored to every age and taste.

By 1930 one would have been hard-pressed to find a phonograph advertised in the daily newspaper, but advertisements for radios were in abundance, conveying a message that life without radio was all but unbearable. The few newspaper ads for phonographs were small and unobtrusive, as compared to the lavish and frequently full-page ads for radios.[13] As the 1929 Christmas season approached, Atlanta radio dealers ran a full-page ad in a Sunday issue of the *Journal* in which readers were told that "no gift is more comprehensive than that of a beautiful new and up-to-date radio, with its message of music, of eloquence, of fun for not only one individual, but for all the family and friends. Such a gift at Christmas time is indeed worth almost any sacrifice needed for its accomplishment."[14]

And what a variety of models and makes of radios from which the buyer could choose. There were table models, consoles, and "uprights." Among the brand names available were Philco, Atwater Kent, Stewart-Warner, Victor, Spartan, Crosley, Musette, Clarion, Gloritone, Stromberg-Carlson, Silver-Marshall, Echophone, Zenith, Majestic, Fada, Temple, RCA, Eveready, Apex, Brunswick, Graybar, and Earl. One would not be surprised, then, to find that when a family had the money to buy either a radio or a phonograph, they bought a radio. No wonder that in the 1930s, as Bob Coltman has noted, "the brash young medium of radio became America's single most popular form of entertainment, with its intimacy, its dreamglow, its knack of getting inside the head."[15] Bill C. Malone, in his book *Country Music, U.S.A.*, concurs, writing that "the real source of entertainment for the country-music fan during the early period . . . was the radio."[16]

Pickin' on Peachtree

While radio was replacing the phonograph as the dominant home-entertainment medium a change was also occurring in the nature of the performer. "The early 1930's witnessed a definite turning point in country-music history," writes Malone. "Thereafter, the performers tended to be more polished and self-conscious about their commercial status."[17] Bob Coltman states, "A wholly new kind of country music ensued," as "amateurs gave way to professionals, as country music ceased to be a casual avocation pursued for its own sake and began to be a commercial industry."[18]

One suspects that many hillbilly musicians who might otherwise have remained amateurs decided, because of the Depression, to turn professional. What did they have to lose? Other jobs were hard to find, and the life of a commercial entertainer, though it may not always have been one blessed with wealth, was a happy alternative to life in a soup line, on a relief roll, or in a hobo camp.

Nationally, new opportunities for employment became available to country music entertainers in the early 1930s with the birth and expansion of several Saturday night barn-dance radio shows. Midwest listeners could tune in the "Iowa Barn Dance Frolic" at WHO in Des Moines beginning in 1932. The "Wheeling (West Virginia) Jamboree" began broadcasting over WWVA in 1933, and in 1934 WBT in Charlotte, North Carolina, became the radio home of the "Crazy Barn Dance." The NBC network began broadcasting a segment of the well-established "WLS Barn Dance" in 1933. That same year, the Delmore Brothers joined the "Grand Ole Opry," which was well on its way to becoming the premiere attraction of its type. In 1934 Gene Autry moved to Hollywood where he assumed a leading role in popularizing western music and the singing cowboy. The previous year found Bob Wills organizing the Texas Playboys, a group that would set the standard in a musical genre that would become known as western swing. It was during the early 1930s that the jukebox became a favorite attraction among café, roadhouse, and speakeasy habitués. The top-selling phonograph records during these early Depression years included those of the Carter Family ("Lulu Wall," "Sweet Fern," "Worried Man Blues"), Jimmie Rodgers, who died in 1933 ("Peach Pickin' Time in Georgia," "Muleskinner Blues," "Mother, the Queen of My Heart"), Gene Autry ("That Silver Haired Daddy of Mine," "Yellow Rose of Texas"), the Delmore Brothers ("Brown's Ferry Blues"), Karl and

· 112 ·

Harty ("I'm Here to Get My Baby Out of Jail"), and Patsy Montana ("I Want to Be a Cowboy's Sweetheart").

As we shall see, the evolution in country music and the country music performer that occurred in the nation as a whole during the 1930s occurred in microcosm in Atlanta. We shall witness the demise of the Georgia Old-Time Fiddlers' Conventions as they became symbols of the archaic styles and amateurish performances that the modern country-music artist, striving for the credentials of professionalism, wished to avoid. We shall see the establishment at WSB of a booking agent, one of the symbols of the professional entertainer, and the importing of out-of-state performers, those professional artists who moved from radio station to radio station as the personal-appearance potential at the old location was exhausted.

For the most part the hillbilly musicians heard on Atlanta radio stations in the 1930s were full-time musicians. Steady radio work was essential to their survival as performers. Playing on the radio was not the once-in-a-while, just-for-the-fun-of-it indulgence it had so often been in the 1920s. Radio exposure was necessary for the cultivation of audiences for personal appearances from which the bulk of the artists' income was derived.

Atlanta's greater metropolitan area entered the decade of the thirties with a population of more than 350,000, making the city second in size in the South (New Orleans was first) and twenty-second in the nation.

As Atlanta grew, so did its major radio voice. Throughout the 1920s WSB, among Atlanta's few radio stations, had been the primary source of hillbilly music. During the next two decades it would be the Atlanta radio station reaching the largest audience for that kind of music. The programs that WSB presented after February 8, 1930, could be heard for greater distances than ever before. On that date the station's power was boosted to five thousand watts. Having started broadcasting with a power of one hundred watts in March 1922, the station had increased its power to five hundred watts three months later and then to a thousand watts in 1925.[19] In 1933 WSB increased its transmitting power to fifty thousand watts, becoming as powerful as the law would allow any station to be.[20] Each increase in power, of course, was accompanied by an increase in listeners.

WSB audiences in the early 1930s were hearing a radio station more sophisticated than it had been in the decade before. It was about this time, for example, that the station began airing commercials with any great regularity.[21] In 1929 WSB had begun offering listeners a full day of continuous broadcasting. The first such day was Monday, November 4, when the station initiated a broadcasting schedule that ran continuously from 7 A.M. to midnight.[22]

Two important advances in radio entertainment—advances that would have an effect on the dissemination of hillbilly music —were announced in 1931. An article in the *Journal* for February 22 noted that "Philco engineers have just introduced the Philco Transitone—a full size radio receiver—which provides motorists with melody as they pass along crowded boulevards or over winding highways." According to the *Journal* the new invention was designed to be "attached to the dashboard and a twist of the dial brings in music from distant and local stations, the purr of the motor being completely subdued by melody and spoken entertainment."[23]

Later in the year *Journal* readers were informed:

> A new invention, of especial interest to radio listeners, is the new long-playing record that has just been brought on the market. It is capable of reproducing an entire symphony, a complete vaudeville act or musical program lasting a full half-hour. Called "program transcriptions," the record does not require automatic changing instruments. The long playing feature is obtained by slowing down the turn table speed and by doubling the number of grooves on the playing surface. The discs are made of a new semiflexible composition that makes practicable the finer grooves, reduces noises by at least half and will not break when dropped. Makers of the new transcription prophesy that it will soon replace the present-day recordings in use at broadcasting studios.[24]

Electrical transcriptions were widely used in the 1930s and 1940s by country musicians. Performers on radio stations usually depended on personal appearances as their main, if not sole, source of income. It was difficult for them to maintain a regularly scheduled radio program while filling personal appearance dates in small towns and rural areas located at great distances from the station. The use of transcriptions provided a solution to the problem. Radio performers with an evening show date so far from the station that they could not get back in time to make the next day's program (which frequently was on in the early morning) could transcribe their program before leaving for the personal appearance. The transcription could then be played at the program's regularly scheduled time. It was not unusual for groups to listen to themselves on their car radios while returning from personal appearance dates.

The use of transcriptions provided some groups exposure far beyond their local base of operation. Transcription companies contracted with artists who prepared transcribed programs that were then leased to radio stations for air play at the stations' convenience. A transcription company might have leasing arrangements with several hundred radio stations around the country. Through the use of transcriptions a local group could gain popularity throughout the country.[25]

Programming at WSB by 1930 had become less casual than it had been in the past. Network affiliation, a longer broadcast day, and the selling of radio time to commercial sponsors made advanced planning necessary. The radio logs of the early 1930s show a decided trend toward the scheduling of the same performers at the same times on the same days of the week. Listeners could organize their activities in a way that would allow them to be near their radios at the times their favorite programs were scheduled for broadcast. Sponsors knew when their products were being advertised, and the station, no doubt, derived numerous benefits from a more structured programming format.

On Tuesday, January 7, 1930, WSB presented what may have been its first sponsored country-music program. Broadcast at 6:15 P.M., it was "a program of typical southern melodies presented by a group of old-time fiddlers and singers . . . broadcast under the auspices of the J. W. Miller Company, manufacturers of poultry farm equipment."[26] The fifteen-minute program was heard every Tuesday afternoon through March 18, 1930. The only other clues we have regarding the content of this offering are brief notes that appeared occasionally in the *Journal*'s radio logs: "Miller String Band," "Old-time Southern melodies and plantation lullabies," "A company of typical old-time fiddlers, playing characteristic Southern melodies and folk songs," "string band . . . with another of its popular old-time fiddlin' concerts," and "old-time tunes."

There were at least two commercially sponsored hillbilly acts on WSB in 1931. Beginning on April 16 Hank Keene and His Hill Billies, "rural instrumentalists," were heard in a weekly fifteen-minute show through July 20. Their programs of "songs and patter" were sponsored by Tom Huston, Inc., of Columbus, Georgia, southern distributors of Chocco Yeast, "the new health confection."[27] Atlanta seems to have been just one stop in the career of Hank Keene. Sometime during his career, he recorded at least two songs for Bluebird, "Yodeling Blues" and "I've Got a Girl in the Mountains,"[28] and in 1940 Hank Keene's Tent Show brought country music to audiences in New England.[29]

Also making their first WSB appearance in April (on the twentieth) were Hiram and Henry, "two Kansas farmer boys who won fame and fortune by 'actin' natcheral' before a microphone." They were sponsored by the Kraft-Phenix Cheese Corporation, a firm that boasted a "large and modernly equipped cheese factory" recently constructed in Atlanta. While in Atlanta, Hiram and Henry were heard simultaneously over ten southern stations.[30] Billed as "hill-billy musicians," the duo had been heard on a Topeka, Kansas, radio station and on WLS in Chicago prior to their WSB debut. They had been known to WLS listeners as "the Barnyard songsters from Kansas" whose "old time and humorous melodies and jokes never fail[ed] to please."[31] After playing on WSB in the late afternoon on Wednesdays, Thursdays, and Fridays, Hiram and Henry made their farewell appearance on July 17, 1930.

Not all the hillbilly acts heard on WSB in the early 1930s were sponsored. Many probably performed on the station just for the fun of it, while others perhaps used the station to publicize personal appearance dates. One of the more persistent of the unsponsored groups was the North Georgia Buggy Riders. From their residences in northern Dekalb and Fulton counties and southern Gwinnett County, some fifteen miles northeast of downtown Atlanta, the performers in this band made their way to the WSB studios each Saturday afternoon, almost without fail, between January 17 and May 16, 1931. They presented for their listeners' enjoyment a fifteen-minute sampling of the string-band music for which they were famous among the square-dance enthusiasts of the area they called home. The group consisted of guitarist Jimmy Maloney; Harvey "Red" Carpenter, who played banjo and guitar; and a fiddler named Dewey Stringer. It was Maloney who years later recalled that they did not have a sponsor at WSB and that they were not paid by the station.[32]

During the 1930s and 1940s, early morning was a prime time for the presentation of radio programs appealing to a rural audience. Rare was the southern radio station of that era that did not have its pre-dawn hillbilly program. WSB's first such early-morning program began on October 4, 1933. The featured act was the Tweedy Brothers, whose shows were first heard from 6:30 to 7 A.M. Later in the month they moved to the 7:15 to 7:30 A.M. spot under the sponsorship of the manufacturers of Crazy Water Crystals.

The Tweedy Brothers group at WSB consisted of brothers Harry and Charles Tweedy and Jack Lee, a "singer and dancer." Harry Tweedy was described as "a fiddler of great vigor and variety," while Charles was said to have played the piano "in his own characteristic manner."[33] Described as "exponents of hill billy and mountain music,"[34] the Tweedy Brothers' act, in addition to being heard on the early morning program, also appeared on a Saturday night "Georgia Jamboree" show that was broadcast for a while on WSB. When, on Saturday, December 30, 1933, from 2 to 4 A.M., WSB presented a DX (distant listeners) program, the Tweedy Brothers were among the featured acts. The "Big Show," as it was called, was "designed for listeners all over the world" and was expected to be heard "many thousands of miles from the point of origin."[35]

The Tweedy Brothers were born in Wheeling, West Virginia, Charles in 1902, and Harry in 1906. Harry, the fiddler, was called "Little Red," and Charles went by the name of "Big Red." At WSB they were referred to as the "Red-Headed Music Makers." With an older brother, George, the Tweedys, in 1922 or 1923, left their home in Wheeling to begin a show business career to which they would devote most of the rest of their lives. Over the years they performed extensively in the Midwest, as far south as Georgia and Texas, and westward to California. During the early years of their career they performed on showboats, working such rivers as the Ohio, the Kanawha, and the Tennessee.[36]

The Tweedy Brothers remained at WSB through the middle of March 1934. They returned to Atlanta in the fall of that year and appeared on WGST from October 1 through November 9.

It appears that the Tweedy Brothers act was the first on WSB to be sponsored by the Crazy Water Crystals Company, a firm which, during the 1930s and 1940s, sponsored numerous hillbilly radio programs around the country. Crazy Water Crystals were "the minerals . . . taken from natural crazy water from wells at Mineral Wells and Thorndale, Texas, by simply evaporating the water away."[37] Crazy Water Crystals was just one of many patent medicines that helped keep hundreds of hillbilly musicians employed during the Depression and World War II. Advertising copy for these patent medicines was written to appeal to rural listeners accustomed to treating their physical ailments with home remedies and over-the-counter drugs rather than with medicines prescribed by a doctor. The following commercial, transcribed from an actual radio program of this era, not only serves to provide information about the nature of the product, but also reminds us of what the early radio listener had to endure in order to be entertained:

> Now I wonder if you're going to be interested in what I have to say during the next few seconds. I know that if you have arthritis, you'll certainly be interested in these words of a well-known physician and medical author: "Arthritis is caused by some source of infection inside the body." Check up to find the cause. Then it should be removed. You can't get well without removing the cause. Faulty elimination is widely regarded as a chief and primary cause of arthritis. It always aggravates this disorder, as well as all other diseases. And other serious ailments are usually associated with faulty elimination, too. Some of them are neuritis; sore muscles and stiff, painful joints, commonly called rheumatism; backache; extreme nervousness; and disturbed conditions of the stomach. And as this noted doctor said, you can't expect to conquer your ailment until you've removed the cause. Now if you are troubled with faulty elimination, if it is caused or if it aggravates your suffering from those painful disorders, here's an easy practical way for you to get at the cause of your troubles. It simply consists of drinking—that's all—just drinking plain ordinary drinking water to which you've added Crazy Water Crystals. This helps to cleanse your system in the very way that nature would have done—with water. It washes away the body's impurities likely to produce the poisons that favor disease. When you use Crazy Water Crystals, you make, right at home, a mild, pleasant-tasting mineral water such as has been successfully used for

over fifty-four years in the treatment of diseases associated with faulty elimination—a mineral water used by millions of people throughout America today. It's simple and a natural thing to do —just drinking Crazy Mineral Water made from Crazy Water Crystals—yet people everywhere tell us every day how very much it's helped them. Won't you give it a chance to help you? Thank you.[38]

Other acts on WSB in the early 1930s were sponsored by Crazy Water Crystals. In 1934 a novelty group called the Hickory Nuts "attracted wide attention by their WSB broadcasts."[39] The act consisted of Dave "Specs" Robertson, Willie "Red" Newman, George "Blackie" Herman, and Jack Guillet [*sic*, presumably Gillette]. When they were heard on WSB they had been together for seven years and had played "all the major Vaudeville circuits in this country and six months in Europe."[40]

Another show sponsored by Crazy Water Crystals began on WSB on February 14, 1935. Dick Hartman and His Crazy Tennessee Ramblers provided the music on this show which was aired daily, except Sunday, at 12:30 P.M. According to the *Journal* "Hartman and his associates [were] hill-billy musicians pure and simple."[41] The act featured a fiddle, two guitars, a banjo, and a piano. In addition to their midday show they were sometimes heard on "Sunrise Serenade," an early-morning variety program that also featured WSB's other hillbilly artists. At the time of his affiliation with WSB, Hartman had been associated for two years with the Crazy Water Crystals Company, for which he had made appearances on other radio stations around the country. Sometime during his career Hartman also recorded several sides for the Bluebird label. Hubert Fincher, manager of the Crazy Water Crystals operations in Atlanta, served as master of ceremonies on Hartman's WSB programs.

November 28, 1931, is a notable date in the history of country music programming at WSB. On that date a group called the Carolina Tarheels was heard on the station for the first time. Except for a twelve-week absence during which they were on a personal appearance tour, the Tarheels were daily features on WSB for a little over two years, the longest tenure on the station of any hillbilly group between 1930 and 1936.

While at WSB the Carolina Tarheels set a performance pattern that hillbilly groups followed there and at other Atlanta radio stations for the next two decades. It was a pattern that was becoming the standard among hillbilly acts at radio stations in other parts of the country. In addition to their daily radio program the Tarheels made personal appearances around the state in the evenings and on weekends. These personal appearances were probably announced on the air and may have been booked through the Georgia Artists Bureau, the booking agency which at the time was directed by entertainment entrepreneur Billy Beard.[42] Later, for several years, the booking agency was directed by Mrs. Lambdin Kay, wife of WSB's general manager.

We do not know if the Tarheel's radio programs were sponsored. They may have performed on the station free in exchange for the privilege of announcing their show dates on the air. During their stay at WSB the Carolina Tarheels received extensive publicity in the pages of the *Journal*. The morning after their first appearance the paper described them as "a new battalion of mountain minstrels . . . fresh from successful appearances before the microphone and on the stages of Carolina theaters."[43] Within a week after going on the air the Tarheels, billed as "progressive exponents of old-time music mixing highly modern rhythms, yodeling and other fancy trimmings with their ancient ballads of the Blue Ridge," were booked for a personal appearance at Atlanta's Toyland Theater on Marietta Street.[44]

The *Journal* did not divulge the individual identities of the Carolina Tarheels until November 20, 1932, almost exactly a year after their first performance. At that time readers learned that the group then consisted of Claude Davis, guitarist, violinist, and vocalist; Hoke Rice, tenor banjoist; Carolina Clyde (presumably Clyde Kiser), guitarist and harmonica artist; Rudle Kiser, yodeler; Chuck Rogers, blackface comedian; Louie Bailey, rube comedian; and Esther Mae Davis, "the Carolina Sunshine Girl. Others who appeared on WSB as members of the group included Archie Ward, Curly Fox, and Walter Propst."[45]

Claude Davis, the leader of the Carolina Tarheels, was born Claude Dennis (Davis was a professional name) in Salisbury, North Carolina, on February 25, 1895, and died in Charlotte, North Carolina, on May 25, 1961.[46] He spent a considerable amount of time "during the dawn of country music" in the Chattanooga, Tennessee, area where he helped promote fiddlers' conventions and stage shows.[47] Davis was frequently in Atlanta and other cities between 1928 and 1931 to record for various labels both as an accompanist for other artists, and as featured vocalist.[48] Records released under his name include "Standing by the Highway," and "I Don't Want Your Gold or Silver," recorded for Columbia in 1931,[49] and "Over in the Hills of Carolina"/"When Flowers Bloom in Springtime," for the Brunswick label.[50]

Judging from the *Journal's* coverage of their activities, one must conclude that the Carolina Tarheels were extremely popular with WSB listeners. Columnist Ernest Rogers once wrote that their fan mail was "immense"[51] and "would make big timers in the east turn red, white, and blue with envy."[52] They drew letters from as far away as Chicago, and, according to the *Journal* of May 2, 1932, a letter they received from Jasper, Georgia, requesting that their daily radio program be extended from fifteen to thirty minutes, contained the signatures of 150 of that city's citizens.

The Tarheels apparently had no trouble obtaining personal appearance bookings in churches, schools, and theaters around the state. On Thursday night, April 28, 1932, they scheduled an appearance at the City Auditorium in Atlanta. According to the *Journal*, the show was "a good benefit affair, with the good ladies of the Theodore Roosevelt Auxiliary No. 2, Spanish War Veterans, as the sponsors."[53] Ticket holders were promised a show that would be filled with musical numbers, stunts, comedy, and "a rousing feature" in the form of "a duel between Gid Tanner, famous Georgia old-time fiddler, and the mysterious Tarheel fiddler." Readers were told that "Gid will spend several days riding the streets of Atlanta on an old gray mule looking for his opponent, eventually running him down at the auditorium."[54]

On Saturday night, May 7, 1932, WSB presented the Carolina Tarheels in a "broom dance" program from 11:30 to midnight. The broom dance apparently was the same as a barn dance. As one old-timer has recalled, before you could have a barn dance you had to take a broom and sweep out the barn.[55] The broom dance was a regular Saturday night feature on the station for the remainder of 1932 and through May 6 of the following year.

After their Saturday night show was taken off the air, the Tarheels were frequent guests on the Georgia Jamboree, a Saturday night variety show that originated from the stages of various Atlanta theaters. A portion of the show, which ran from September 1933 through March 1934, was broadcast over WSB.

When the Tarheels returned to WSB in August 1933, following a personal appearance tour of several weeks duration that had taken them to Pennsylvania, West Virginia, and Ohio, their daily radio show was moved from a midafternoon slot to a spot near noon, usually 12:30 P.M.

Moving the station's top hillbilly act to the middle of the day may be an indication that WSB's management was becoming aware of the need to match a program's content to the type of listening audience it attracted. The majority of the Tarheels' listeners were probably farmers and their families. Typically, during the 1930s, farm families, especially the male members, had an early breakfast and were soon out of the house attending to the business of fold, field, and farmyard. They returned to the house at noon to eat their midday meal and rest a while before returning to the duties of the farm that kept them occupied until time for the evening meal. This routine especially was followed during the planting and harvesting seasons. The noon hour, then, was a logical time for a radio station to present programs that appealed to the tastes and interests of farmers.

The Carolina Tarheels played their last show over WSB on March 1, 1934. As we shall see, Louie Bailey and Curly Fox were not off the station for long, and Hoke Rice was to return a few years later.

Just over a week after the Carolina Tarheels' departure from WSB another group made its debut on the station. Called the Tennessee Firecrackers, this act consisted of Louie "Slim" Bailey, announcer and blackface comedian; Arnim "Curly" Fox, fiddler and yodeler; Ira Green, guitar and banjo player; Tweet Roark, left-handed guitar player; and Jimmie Brown, buck-and-tap dancer.[56] Louie Bailey had been the Tarheels' blackface comedian, and Curly Fox, who also had been a member of that group,[57] would become the Firecrackers' most famous member. After leaving Atlanta he became one of the country's best-known fiddlers, and with his wife, Texas Ruby, was one of the leading acts on the "Grand Ole Opry" during the 1940s.[58]

Later in 1934 the Tennessee Firecrackers apparently underwent some personnel changes. As we have seen, state fiddle champion Anita Wheeler performed with them at one time, and in September 1934 Roy Anderson, Paul Weber, and Bubber Floyd were listed as performers with the group when they appeared on a WSB broadcast originating from Atlanta's Southeastern Fair. The Tennessee Firecrackers were last heard on WSB in December 1934.

Atlanta during the early 1930s was a favorite stop on the itinerary of hillbilly station-hoppers—acts that performed on a local radio station and made personal appearances within the station's reception area until audiences, through nonattendance, indicated that they were ready to see and hear new talent. The more powerful the radio station the greater were the opportunities for booking personal appearance dates. Landing a job at WSB with its fifty thousand watts was a major coup by a hillbilly act during that period.

Cowboy Roy Lykes, the Yodeling Fence Rider, joined WSB's roster of stars in January 1934. Described as a "real cowboy"[59] who sometimes sang in Spanish[60] and habitually wore "regulation cowboy shoes to get him in the proper mood,"[61] Cowboy Roy may have been the first cowboy singer to appear regularly on the station. He left Atlanta in May 1934 to return to his home in Laredo, Texas.[62]

Also signing on at WSB in January 1934 were the Ozark Mountaineers, who featured "rural rhythms such as have thrilled many a backwoods fandangle."[63] In March the group performed on stage with Amos 'n' Andy during an engagement by the nationally known radio comedy team at the Georgia Theater.[64] In a picture appearing in the *Journal*, members of the Mountaineers were identified as Grandpappy (banjo), Hiram (guitar), Uncle Ezry (fiddle), Mirandy (fiddle), and Shep (guitar). They were all males, including Mirandy, and all looked to be in their mid-twenties, including Grandpappy.[65] Before leaving WSB in August 1934, the Ozark mountaineers "added new ten-gallon hats to their wardrobes for personal appearances."[66] After all, this was the year that Gene Autry established the singing cowboy as a staple of American entertainment.[67]

Perhaps making capital of the developing mania for things western, WSB, in 1934, gave its listeners a Christmas present of the sounds of Doc Schneider and His Yodeling Cowboys. "Fresh from stage triumphs in the Carolinas, this famous organization" was heard twice daily on WSB from December 24 through 31.[68] The music performed by this troupe of entertainers was " 'cowboy' not hill billy," a fact *Journal* columnist Ernest Rogers emphasized. The group consisted of "Doc" Schneider, "expert rifle shot"; May Lewis, "Texas recording Yodeler"; "Vic" Scheider, "the Red-Haired Comic"; "Toby" Durnal, "the Cowboy Master of Ceremonies"; Whit Gorsuck, "wizard of the banjo and guitar"; Jess Scoby, "bull fiddler and mandolinist"; and Otis Clements, "the Lonesome Cowboy."[69] The Yodeling Cowboys were originally scheduled for only a week of "snappy, happy entertainment" on WSB, but because of "tremendous mail response" and personal appearances that "pleased listeners in many north Georgia towns and cities" they were held over through January 15, 1935. The band, which was said to have played theaters in forty-three states, returned to WSB in April 1935 for a three-day stint of broadcasts. As late as 1941 the peripatetic Doc Schneider could be heard on station WRDW in Augusta, Georgia.[70]

Also making their first WSB appearance on December 24, 1934, were the Kentucky Coon Hunters, a group that "combine[d] hill-billy music with comedy and other radio entertainment."[71] Like the Yodeling Cowboys they had just completed a series of "triumphant stage and radio engagements in the Carolinas" and were "widely known" for their appearances on WJAX in Jacksonville, Florida; WHAS in Louisville, Kentucky; and "other important broadcasting stations throughout the nation."[72] We are told that their stage shows were "amplified . . . with a group of feminine dancers and other features that have appealed strongly to hundreds of audiences."[73] The similarity in their recent activities and the fact that the two groups came to WSB at the same time suggest that the Kentucky Coon Hunters and Doc Schneider's Yodeling Cowboys may have been traveling together when they arrived in Atlanta. The Coon Hunters were last heard by WSB listeners on January 5, 1935.

Two groups chose October 1935 to begin broadcasting over WSB. One was Bob Atcher and His Kentucky Mountain Minstrels; the other was the Blue Ridge Music Makers, headed by fiddler Charlie Bowman. Both groups had performed at WHAS in Louisville prior to coming to Atlanta.

Bob Atcher was twenty-one years old when he went to Atlanta, having been born in Hardin County, Kentucky, in 1914.[74] With a grandfather and father who were fiddlers and a mother who played piano and organ, young Atcher was exposed to the music of the Kentucky mountaineers from birth, and began to play the guitar at the age of six.

Shortly after arriving in Atlanta, Atcher told a *Journal* reporter that his aim was the elevation of the songs of his childhood. "We are not hill billies in the sense in which the term is used," he said of himself and the musicians performing with him. "We play mountain music as it should be played, without distortion. We inject musicianship into the presentations. And I think that makes a difference."[75] The band members Atcher took to Atlanta were all native Kentuckians and included his brother, Francis Atcher, who played bass and mandolin; Joe Blair, Dobro player; Jack Calloway, rhythm guitarist; fiddler Paul Wood Greer; and female vocalist Loeta Applegate. Miss Applegate was one of several female singers who, over the years, performed with Atcher under the stage name Bonnie Blue Eyes.

Joe Blair may have been the first country music artist to play the Dobro over WSB, since, at the time, the instrument was relatively new. The Dobro, a guitar with a built-in resonator, was developed and manufactured by a group of brothers by the name of Dopyera in response to the need for a guitar with more volume than was provided by the acoustic guitars of the time. The name comes from the first two syllables of "*Do*pyera *bro*thers." When played, the Dobro is usually held in the horizontal position like a Hawaiian guitar. Noting is done with a metal bar. Now popular in bluegrass bands, the Dobro yielded its role in country music to the electric steel guitar.

A feature attraction of Charlie Bowman's Blue Ridge Music Makers was a vocal duet consisting of Pep, a thirteen-year-old girl whose real name was Clara Louise George, and Rhythm, a guitarist whose further identity is unknown. Other members of the group were Walter "Sparky" Hughes, guitarist; Ferril "Red" Lambert, banjo player and dancer; and Hal Armstrong.

Charlie Bowman, a native Tennessean, was a well-known fiddler who, either as head of his own band or as a member of someone else's band, performed widely throughout the Southeast in the 1920s and 1930s. The Blue Ridge Music Makers were heard on WSB through the middle of May 1936.

Other hillbilly artists who performed on WSB during the early 1930s included Lew Childre, the Chumbler Family, Bill Green's Midnight Ramblers, Harmonica Sam and His Gang, Earl Johnson, Pink Lindsey, Poslo Bill's Razor Backs (fiddlers), Sherman Sutton's String Band, Warren Sykes, Joe Wages, "Rustic" Waters, Slim White's Oklahoma Cowboys, and the Woodstock Bearcats.

The Home Town Boys. Left to right: Clayton McMichen, Robert "Punk" Stephens, Bob Stephens, Lowe Stokes. (Ca. mid-1920s) Source: Juanita McMichen Lynch.

George Daniell's Hill Billies. Left to right, back row: Boag Richardson, Howard Scoggins, Kem Wiley, Luke James, Bill Lee, Jake Groover, George Dunn; seated: George Daniell, Robert McBrayer, Edward Richardson, Myrtle Richardson, Ewing Underwood; seated on floor: Cook James. (Ca. mid-1920s) Source: Howard Scoggins.

Riley Puckett. Source: Juanita
McMichen Lynch.

Anita Sorrells Wheeler Mathis.
(Ca. late 1920s) Source:
Anita Mathis.

Fiddlin' John Carson. Source: Gene Wiggins.

A. A. Gray's String Band. Left to right: Charlie Thompson, A. A. Gray, Fred Hill, Henry West. (Ca. 1925) Source: Gladys Gray Langley.

Gid Tanner. Source:
Gordon Tanner.

The Hidden Valley Ramblers. Left to right: Jimmy Maloney, Slim (Collus) Maddox, Gene Mitchell, Carl "Cowboy Jack" Talton. (Ca. 1935) Source: Carl Talton.

The Carolina Tarheels. Left to right, front row: Rudle Kiser, Claude Davis, Esther Goodman McClain (The Carolina Sunshine Girl); back row: Slim Bailey, Clyde Kiser, Red Freeze. (Ca. early 1930s) Source: Katherine G. Smith.

Bill Gatins's Jug Band. Clockwise from top left: Louis Poss, Ben Ferrell, Carl Poss, Nick (last name unknown), Bill Gatins. (Ca. early 1930s) Source: Mrs. Bill Gatins, Sr.

The Blue Sky Boys. Left to right: Earl Bolick, Bill Bolick, Red Hicks. Source: Bartow Henry.

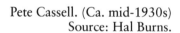
Pete Cassell. (Ca. mid-1930s)
Source: Hal Burns.

Red and Raymond and the Boys from Old Kaintuck. Clockwise from top left: Red Anderson, Raymond Anderson, Doug Dalton, Milton Estes, Ernie Hodges. (Ca. mid-1930s) Source: L. E. "Red" Anderson.

The Dixie Roamers. Left to right: Bud Mote, Paul Bennett, Clarence Pope. (Ca. 1940s) Source: Bartow Henry.

Grady (left) and Hazel Cole. Source:
Carl Talton.

Pop Eckler and All the Young'uns. Left to right: Ruey "Curley" Collins, Tex
Forman, Kay Woods, Garner "Pop" Eckler, Red Murphy. (Ca. 1936) Source:
Bartow Henry.

Pop Eckler's Jamboree. Left to right, seated: Tex Forman, Unidentified, Cicero Merneigh; center, standing at microphone: Pop Eckler; first row: Kay Woods, Unidentified, Marion Reindhardt, Mary Grace Treadwell, Leon Smith, Carolyn Treadwell, Curley Collins, Rex Griffin, Boudleaux Bryant, Pete Cassell, Casa Nell Coleman; second row: Unidentified, Unidentified, Unidentified, Unidentified, Unidentified, Unidentified, Unidentified, Slim Hutcheson, Marvin Taylor, Doug Spivey, Unidentified, Unidentified, Red Murphy, Uncle Ned (Gene Stripling); third row: Unidentified, Unidentified. (Ca. 1938) Source: Doug Spivey.

Uncle Ned and His Texas Wranglers. Casa Nell Coleman, Uncle Ned (Gene Stripling), Chick Stripling, Slim Hutcheson, Sammy Forsmark. Source: Tex Forman.

The "WSB Barn Dance" Cast: Left to right: Aunt Hattie (Ricca Hughes), Glen Hughes, Warren Sykes, Casa Nell Coleman, Chick Stripling, Red Murphy, Harpo Kidwell, Marvin Taylor, Doug Spivey, Boudleaux Bryant, Dwight Butcher, Martha (Irene Amburgey), Mattie (Opal Amburgey), Minnie (Bertha Amburgey), Hank Penny, Louise Elders, Louis Dumont, Jenny Rogers. (1940) Source: Harpo Kidwell.

The Hoot Owl Hollow Girls. Left to right: Mattie (Opal Amburgey), Esther (Violet) Koehler, Martha (Irene Amburgey Roberts) Carson. Source: Tex Forman.

James and Martha (Roberts) Carson. Source: Eugene Akers.

The Sunshine Boys. Left to right: A. L. (Smitty) Smith, Milt (Ace) Richman, J. O. (Tennessee) Smith, Ed Wallace. (Ca. mid-1940s) Source: Ed Wallace.

Tommy Trent and His Dixie Fun Barn Gang. Left to right: Nat Richardson, Marion Sumner, Tommy Trent, Bartow Henry, Dixie Lee. (Ca. mid-1940s) Source: Bartow Henry.

The Swanee River Boys. Clockwise from left: George Hughes, Merle Abner, Bill Carrier, Buford Abner. Source: Harpo Kidwell.

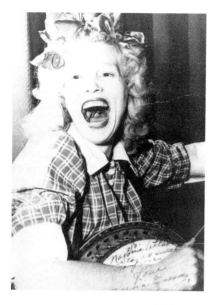

Cousin Emmy. (Ca. mid-1940s)
Source: Navonia Atcheson.

The T.V. Wranglers. Left to right, front row: J. O. "Tennessee" Smith, A. L. "Smitty" Smith; back row: Pat Patterson, Cotton Carrier, Boots Woodall, Paul Rice. Source: Boots Woodall.

The Swingbillies. Left to right: Harry Chumbler; Ruel Parker; Paul Lunsford; Ray McCay, emcee, vocals, and staff announcer at WLW-A-TV; Junebug Thomas; Randy Jones. Source: Ruel Parker.

The Peachtree Cowboys. Top to bottom: Jimmy Smith, Marvin Wilson, Bobby Atcheson, Mac Atcheson, Cotton Carrier, Ivy "Herman Horsehair Buggfuzz" Peterson. Source: Jane Atcheson.

The Cherokees. Left to right, front row: Shorty Boyd, Len Miller; back row, Carl Leming, Speedy Price, Jack Greene, Lem Bryant. "Dixie Jubilee" staff band, East Point (ca. early 1960s). Source: Carl Leming.

Brush Fire. Clockwise from left: Jay Richardson, Ted Lolley, Eddie Turner, Joe Partridge, Mike Fleming. Source: Mike Fleming.

Bill Lowery. Source: The Lowery Group of Music Publishing Companies.

CHAPTER

6

The "Cross Roads Follies,"
1936–40

As THE 1930S MARCHED inexorably toward the 1940s, the Depression continued to be a matter of overriding concern to the nation's leaders. In 1936 Franklin D. Roosevelt, in a landslide election, won a mandate from the people to continue for another four years efforts to pull the nation out of that economic morass. The year before he had seen his New Deal program strengthened by the birth of the Works Progress Administration (WPA), a government agency designed to provide work for the unemployed, and passage of the Social Security Act creating a pension plan to provide for old age. Atlanta, meanwhile, made international headlines with the publication in 1936 of *Gone With the Wind*, Margaret Mitchell's tome about the Civil War. The book sold a million copies during the first six months of its life and won a Pulitzer Prize for its author in 1937. In 1939 frequency modulation (FM) radio reception was invented, and nylon stockings made their first appearance in ladies' wear sections of department stores across the country. On September 1 of that year German armies invaded Poland, and two days later Great Britain and France declared war on Germany. World War II had officially begun.

A number of significant events transpired in the world of country music during the last half of the 1930s. Joining the "Grand Ole Opry" cast during this period were Pee Wee King (1937), Roy Acuff (1938), and Bill Monroe (1939). In 1937 John Lair and Red Foley unveiled their "Renfro Valley Barn Dance" in Cincinnati, Ohio.

Two years later they would take it home to a real barn in Renfro Valley, Kentucky, where it would enjoy a long run on the CBS radio network. In 1938 the Carter Family packed their bags and set off from their home in Maces Spring, Virginia, for Del Rio, Texas, where for a year they would be heard on XERA, one of several powerful radio stations with transmitters, located across the Rio Grande River in Mexico, set to blanket all of North America with hillbilly music, evangelistic preaching, "quacks, yodelers, pitchmen, psychics, and other amazing broadcasters."[1]

Among the country music hits turned out by the record studios between 1935 and 1940 were "Maple on the Hill" (J. E. Mainer's Mountaineers), "San Antonio Rose" (Bob Wills), "Wabash Cannon Ball" (Roy Acuff), "Back in the Saddle Again" (Gene Autry), and "It Makes No Difference Now" (Jimmie Davis).

The most widely listened to and most popular country music radio program broadcast from Atlanta during the 1930s was WSB's "Cross Roads Follies." The first show was aired on Monday, February 3, 1936, and featured three acts that were then currently performing on WSB. The "Cross Roads Follies" appears to have been the station's first country music program to bring together more than one act on the same show. Prior to the launching of the "Cross Roads Follies" WSB's hillbilly acts had each had its own individual program. The Saturday night "Georgia Jamboree," which had been heard in 1933 and 1934, and the early morning "Sunrise Serenade" apparently had presented more than one hillbilly act on the same show, but the "Jamboree" was not a strictly hillbilly show. It was a variety show whose performers were mostly pop artists, and the "Sunrise Serenade" apparently was similar in format. Whereas the programs of the individual hillbilly acts had been, for the most part, fifteen minutes long, the "Cross Roads Follies" in the beginning lasted for thirty and sometimes forty-five minutes. It was later expanded to an hour-long show. One suspects that management at WSB was discovering the greater appeal of the longer show to listening audiences. George Biggar, former WSB program producer and "National Barn Dance" director, once wrote, "People want to hear the same type of program for several hours without turning the dials. Very few folk [hillbilly] musical programs of 15 to 30 minutes duration—spotted between other types of radio shows—have ever been successful. A minimum of one hour seems essential for building sizeable [and profitable] audiences for this type of program."[2]

The "Cross Roads Follies" was generally heard daily, Monday through Friday during the middle of the day, with the first show being broadcast from 1:00 to 1:30 P.M. Subsequent time slots for the program varied, with starting times as early as 11:15 A.M. and as late as 1:30 P.M. The "Follies" was also heard on Saturdays, but then usually in the middle of the morning.

The three acts heard on the first broadcast of the "Cross Roads Follies" were the Blue Ridge Music Makers with Pep and Rhythm, who, as we have seen, had been at WSB since October 1935, and two other groups of fairly long tenure at the station, Bill Gatins' Jug Band, and Red and Raymond with Ernie Hodges.

William S. (Bill) Gatins was born in Atlanta on June 26, 1909, a second-generation American whose grandparents emigrated to this country from Donegal, Ireland. At an early age Gatins exhibited a decidedly independent nature, as well as an interest in music and things mechanical, such as automobile repair and crystal radio construction.[3]

Sometime in the late 1920s or early 1930s Gatins, according to his onetime music partner, Marion Brown, began his musical career by entering a talent contest sponsored by the Madison Theater, located on Flat Shoals Avenue in southeast Atlanta. Brown later recalled that "for his act Bill played a tenor banjo and sang 'I'm in the Jailhouse Now,' that old Jimmie Rodgers number. And that was the beginning of his career."[4]

Brown and another Atlanta musician, Cliff Vaughn, entered the same contest playing guitars and singing comedy songs. "That's where we met Bill Gatins," Brown once related, as he explained how, after the contest, the three of them (Gatins, Brown, and Vaughn) decided to pool their talents to form an act. Calling themselves Bill Gatins' Band, they played at dances, schools, theaters, and anywhere else they could get a booking. Soon after landing a radio job at one of Atlanta's smaller stations they were pressured by the station's management to diversify their act. Inspired by a black jug-band they had heard on a Louisville, Kentucky, radio station, Gatins and his cohorts decided to add a jug to their arsenal of instruments. It was also at about this time that Skinny Anglin, a local harmonica player, joined the group to complete what Brown called the original edition of Bill Gatins and His Jug Band. It consisted of Gatins on jug and tenor banjo; Marion Brown playing rhythm guitar; Cliff Vaughn, lead guitarist; and Skinny Anglin on harmonica. Their programs featured vocal solos by Bill Gatins and Marion Brown, as well as instrumental tunes by the whole group. Their repertoire consisted of Jimmie Rodgers songs, comedy numbers, sentimental ballads, rags, marches, and breakdowns. The jug served both as a novelty feature and as a bass fiddle substitute.

Over the next ten years Bill Gatins became one of the best known hillbilly personalities of the Atlanta area. He and his jug bands moved back and forth among the various Atlanta radio stations and, at one time or another, played on all of the city's pre–World War II stations except, possibly, WDBE. The jug band changed personnel frequently and counted among its alumni numerous Atlanta-area musicians.

Marion Brown left Gatins in the mid-1930s to perform in other bands and to head up his own. In 1935 he and Cliff Vaughn joined Pink Lindsey, who played fiddle, and Raymond Lindsey, tenor banjoist, to record, as the Novelty Four, two tunes ("Twelfth Street Rag"/"The Story of Adam") for the Bluebird label. Earlier Brown had gone to Camden, New Jersey, where he played guitar accompaniment on some Fiddlin' John Carson records. Brown's bands were heard on various Atlanta radio stations, off and on, into the 1940s. After retiring, Brown continued to sing and play guitar with a group that included his children and grandchildren. They were performing publicly as late as 1988.

Bill Gatins was first heard on WSB in 1931, appearing intermittently on Saturday afternoons from May through September. He then moved to another Atlanta station where he was heard regularly until his return to WSB in November of 1934. He was performing there when the "Cross Roads Follies" was organized.

In July 1935 Gatins took his jug band, then consisting of himself; Marion Orr, fiddler; Skinny Anglin, harmonica player; banjoist Bill Power; and Walter Kite, guitarist, to New York where, on July 10 and 11, they recorded sixteen sides for Decca. Two sides, "Talkin' Blues" and "I Don't Work for a Living," were released as solos by Gatins (the record company erroneously printed his name as Gatin). Of the remaining songs, eight were released, for some now unknown reason, under the name Cherokee Ramblers. Two sides featured Gatins singing "Bully of the Town" and "My Little Girl." The remainder consisted of five breakdowns, "Alabama Jubilee," "Goin' Down the Road Feelin' Bad," "Back Up and Push," "Home Brew Rag," "Short'nin' Bread," and one slow tune, "Magnolia Waltz."

Gatins continued to perform as a member of the "Cross Roads Follies" until January 1938 when he switched to Atlanta's WGST. After a year there and a stint at another Atlanta station, WATL, Gatins moved to Norfolk, Virginia, where he worked as a painter at the nearby shipyards by day and as a musician at night and on weekends. For approximately twenty years he made personal appearances and entertained on radio and television stations in the Norfolk-Portsmouth area. In 1960 Gatins returned to Atlanta where he worked as a painter while playing an occasional nightclub gig or other small job. He died on June 15, 1973.[5]

Besides those already mentioned, the Atlanta-area musicians who performed with Gatins at one time or another included Jack Bell, fiddle; Curly Harris, guitar; Ed Smith, harmonica; Toots Hodge, electric guitar; Reidy Reed, fiddle; Joe Scott, bass; Freddy Hayes, piano; Tom Bennett; J. W. "Slimbo" Smith, fiddle; Louis Poss, bass; Carl Poss, steel guitar; Vernon Whiddon, saxophone; Charlie Power, guitar; Wiley Kite, fiddle; Cecil Gilham, vocal; Jack Lee, comedian; "Shorty" Steed, fiddle; "Bud" Mote, fiddle; and Johnny Street, fiddle.

Kentucky native Red Anderson and his son Raymond came to Atlanta in September 1934, the first of numerous hillbilly acts from the Blue Grass State who performed on WSB during the next twenty years.

Red was born Lonnie E. Anderson on June 12, 1899, in Litchfield, Kentucky.[6] His parents sang a lot around the house and at church, and when he was sixteen years old Red learned to play the guitar. It was not long before he was exhibiting his musical skills at community parties and square dances.

In 1931, while recuperating from an accident, Red heard an announcer on WSMK in Dayton, Ohio, invite listeners to come to the station to audition. Red decided to give it a try, passed the audition, and was immediately hired by the station.[7] Judging from a songbook that Red published sometime later to sell to radio listeners, his repertoire consisted mainly of the then popular hillbilly songs that other artists were recording and singing on the radio. The song book contains the words to such songs as "Put My Little Shoes Away," "Floyd Collins," "The Picture on the Wall," "Yellow Rose of Texas," "The Blind Child," "Pearl Bryan," and "That Silver Haired Daddy of Mine."

In 1933 Red took his five-year-old son, Raymond (born December 10, 1928), to WCKY in Covington, Kentucky, to begin a father-son act that during the next decade became familiar to listeners of several radio stations in the Southeast.

Red decided to go to Atlanta in 1934 when a physician advised him to seek a warmer climate for his older son, who suffered from asthma. Red and Raymond began their affiliation with WSB in September. The *Journal* announced that their second program on WSB, scheduled for broadcast at 4:45 P.M. on Saturday, September 8, 1934, would include "Just a Message from Home"; "Careless Love," a solo by Raymond; and "Home on the Range" and "If I Could Hear My Mother Pray Again" sung by the two of them.[8]

On the air Red was called the Red-Headed Briar Hopper, Raymond was billed as "the little feller with the big voice," and the entire ensemble, which included several other musicians, was called the Boys from Old Kaintuck. Over the years while at WSB, the group included fiddlers Ernie Hodges and Slim Clere; Douglas Dalton; Milton "Bozo" Estes; multi-instrumentalist Glenn Hughes; bass fiddle player Paul Penn; Bill Miller; a female vocalist who performed as Kentucky Evelyn; "Happy" Wilson; and Red's brother, Check Anderson, who sang and played guitar. According to the *Journal* they "yodel[ed] and they [made] old time music in a manner that pleas[ed] many thousands of listeners," and by the end of 1934 they were "among the most popular attractions at WSB."[9] In February 1935 Raymond received more than three hundred valentines from devoted fans.[10]

Red and Raymond were heard on WSB through January 1938, their tour of duty there occasionally interrupted by brief forays into other radio markets in search of larger audiences for their personal appearances. After leaving WSB for the last time they worked at WBRC, Birmingham, Alabama; WCHS in Charleston, West Virginia; and WSAZ in Huntington, West Virginia. The group disbanded in the early 1940s never again to perform together professionally. Red spent his final working years as a bus driver and security guard in Louisville, Kentucky. Raymond married, had two children, and in the 1980s was also living in Louisville where he drove a furniture truck.

One of the most significant events in the history of country music in Atlanta occurred in July 1936 when another act consisting of mostly Kentucky musicians joined the "Cross Roads Follies" on WSB. They called themselves Pop Eckler and His Barn Dance Gang, and according to the *Journal*'s radio log they made their premiere broadcast on the "Follies" on Monday, July 6. A picture in the *Journal* the day before shows that, besides Eckler, the band was composed of Curley Collins, "who plays instruments, sings and dances"; Red Murphy, "the dancing demon from Lee County, Kentucky, also a trick harmonica manipulator"; Tex Forman, "the pride of Paragon, Ky., chief comedian and all-round cut-up"; Reidy Reed, "old-time fiddler deluxe"; and Katherine (Kay) Woods, "the Belle of the Blue Grass." [11] This group, which was later called Pop Eckler and His Young'uns, remained at WSB for four years. During this time they were the main attraction on the "Cross Roads Follies," helping make it Atlanta's top-ranking hillbilly radio show.

Garner "Pop" Eckler was born around 1906, in Dry Ridge, Kentucky.[12] During the early part of his career he sang and played guitar with Bert Layne and His Mountaineer Fiddlers in the Cincinnati, Ohio, area. He and another singer/guitarist named Roland Gaines performed as a duet, calling themselves the Yodeling Twins. According to Bert Layne, "They were about the first to come out with that harmony yodeling. They were good and that Garner," Layne recalled, "was full of fun and jokes too." [13]

Mrs. Lambdin Kay, then director of the Georgia Artists Bureau, invited Pop Eckler and his troupe to come to Atlanta after Charlie Bowman and the Blue Ridge Entertainers left WSB in May 1936, and Red and Raymond departed in June on one of their periodic pilgrimages to other stations. According to Curley Collins, Mrs. Kay was familiar with Eckler's group through their broadcasts from WLW in Cincinnati where they were working at the time.

Eckler's group was a self-contained unit with sufficient talent and diversity to provide a full evening of entertainment at the theaters, court houses, and school auditoriums in which they booked their personal appearances. Tex sang songs made famous by Jimmie Rodgers, yodeled, and furnished the comedy, playing the part of a country rube. Red Murphy did a buck-and-wing dance routine and played harmonica, Reidy Reed played old-time fiddle tunes, and Kay Woods sang solos. Pop performed the master of ceremonies duties, played guitar, and sang. His most requested number at WSB was "Too Many Parties and Too Many Pals." Tex and Curley sang duets, and with Kay performed trio numbers, specializing in songs that included harmony yodeling, like those popularized by the Sons of the Pioneers. For gospel songs Pop would join Kay, Tex, and Curley to form a quartet. One such sacred song that they sang frequently was "You've Got to Walk that Lonesome Valley." They sang other gospel songs from a Stamps-Baxter type of songbook that they kept on hand.

An article appearing in a newspaper serving Temple, one of the small Georgia towns in which Pop Eckler and his entourage once appeared, provides insight into what one of their stage shows was like. The show mentioned in the article took place after the group had undergone some personnel changes.

> Outstanding in record-breaking attendance was the second appearance of Pop Eckler and all the Young'uns, popular and far-famed radio attractions of WSB and WAGA Cross Road Follies, at the high school auditorium here, Friday night. A capacity crowd filled the auditorium to overflowing, and this act has the distinction of netting the largest sum of money to be taken in at any single performance in Temple in several years.
>
> Garner "Pop" Eckler very capably acted as master of ceremonies for the act and with his ready wit and jokes, along with Tex Forman, radio's funniest comedian, kept the crowd laughing. Adding to the enjoyment of the program were the vocal and fiddle tunes of the little handyman, Curley Collins, former national champion hillbilly fiddler, and the songs of Kay Woods whose sweet, golden voice was heard in solos, duets and trios, with Tex Forman, national champion yodeler, and Curley Collins. The young and very talented dancer, Leon Smith, gave an excellent rendition of fancy buck and wing dancing. Other sparkling radio personalities featured on the program were the famous Pine Ridge Boys, Marvin Taylor and Doug Spivey, heard each weekday morning over Charlie Smithgall's Morning Merry-Go-Round, whose voices were harmonized in both popular and hillbilly singing and yodeling. The

combined talents of the troupe contributed [to] an evening of enjoyability, hilarity, and diversity, for both the young and old, and those who failed to attend missed a rare treat.

A neat sum of $77.85 was realized, the proceeds of which were used to increase the senior class funds for a trip to Washington, D.C., in the spring. The public is anxiously awaiting a return engagement of these popular radio favorites and hope to have the privilege of hearing them again in the near future.[14]

While in Atlanta, Eckler, the consummate showman, developed into something of a show-business entrepreneur. Not content with a daily radio show and stage appearances in the small towns surrounding Atlanta, he soon set about organizing a Saturday night barn-dance show cut on the pattern of the "Grand Ole Opry." Originating from the stages of various Atlanta theaters, a segment of the show was broadcast over WSB from July 1938 through February 1940. Extant printed programs reveal that the show, called "Pop Eckler's Radio Jamboree," sometimes featured as many as fourteen acts including, in addition to the Young'uns and other musical and comedy acts, tap dancers, "Major, the Educated Dog with a human mind," and an "old Fashion Kentucky Square Dance Set."

The programs carried advertisements for cafes, garages, service stations, hardware stores, plumbing companies, and Pop Eckler's Majik Foot Powder for the relief of "athlete foot, ringworm, itching, tired, burning, acheing, perspiring feet." The foot powder, which was said to be cooling, refreshing, and a stopper of odors, was allegedly "sold at all good druggists" for sixty cents or could be ordered by mail from WSB.[15]

Eckler's venture into the field of journalism was heralded by a *Journal* columnist on November 9, 1939. "Nobody thought, when Pop Eckler stepped up to the microphone, that he'd turn into an editor," the columnist wrote, "but such is the case." [16] According to the *Journal* the new publication, called *Fiddler's Gazzette*, was "a nonprofit publication for the sole purpose of furnishing Jamboree patrons with news items of their favorite radio stars." [17] The one copy of Eckler's paper known to exist is a four-page, letter-size publication containing jokes, gossip about the various "Jamboree" performers, lists of acts scheduled to appear on the "Jamboree" on November 4 and 11, 1939, advertisements similar to those appearing in the "Jamboree" programs, and "Pop Eckler's Diary," a feature that sheds some light on the nature of the day-to-day life of a hillbilly radio performer in the late 1930s.[18]

On the side Eckler promoted fiddlers' contests and brought out-of-town hillbilly artists to Atlanta stages. One of his fiddlers' contests was held on Saturday, June 18, 1938. Touted as the National Fiddlers' Contest, it was held in the City Auditorium, former home of the Georgia Old-Time Fiddlers' Conventions. A matinee at 2:30 P.M. and an evening show at 8:00 featured an extensive lineup of local hillbilly entertainers that included Pop Eckler and All the Young'uns; Uncle Ned and the Texas Wranglers; Bill Gatins and His Jug Band; Bill Chitwood and band; Joe Harvey, "Yodeling Cowboy"; Freeman Turner and band; the Blue Sky Boys; the Drifting Hillbillies; Tew Manning and band; the Patterson Brothers; the Freeman Brothers; the McClendon Brothers; the Richardson Brothers; the Georgia Ramblers; Orbie and Bobbie Barfield; Buell Martin and the Alpharetta Hillbillies; Ernest and Curtis Martin; the Dixie Rhythm Makers; Ben Stewart and the Georgia Hillbillies; the Hoosier Playboys; Lloyd Jenkins and the Happy Hollow Hillbillies; the Turkey Mountain Cowboys; the West Sisters; Tommy Dukes and the Wanderers of the Wastelands; Riley Puckett; Anderson Wakefield; the Steel-Driving Devils; and Theron Hale.[19] The prizes, donated by Atlanta merchants, were a nine-tube Philco cabinet radio for the best fiddler, an innerspring mattress for the winner of the yodeling contest, a silver loving-cup for the first-place dancer, and a total of 110 gallons of gasoline, a complete lubrication, car wash, and oil change, and two automobile tires for winner of the band competition.[20]

As a booking agent Eckler brought to Atlanta such "Grand Ole Opry" stars as Roy Acuff and Uncle Dave Macon. Acuff, who appeared in concert at the Atlanta Theater on Sunday, December 17, 1939, was also a guest on Eckler's "Jamboree" on the preceding Saturday night, a commitment, said the *Journal*, that would necessitate Acuff's absence from his usual spot on NBC's "Grand Ole Opry" broadcast.[21]

Pop Eckler left WSB in 1940, but he remained in Atlanta several years working at smaller radio stations and making personal appearances with a band called the Radio Cowboys. Part of the time after leaving WSB he worked as a disc jockey.[22]

Eckler, who had recorded extensively with Roland Gaines and Guy Blakeman during his Cincinnati days, later recorded for King. His "Money, Marbles, and Chalk" on that label was a considerable success.[23]

Eckler retired from the music business in 1950 and took a job as a fireman with the Louisville and Nashville Railroad. On March 21, 1970, at the age of sixty-four, he was hit and killed by an automobile near his home in Covington, Kentucky.[24]

The musicians Eckler brought with him to Atlanta were more than mere "sidemen." Each was allowed to exploit his or her own special talent and to develop an individual identity with the radio audience. Tex Forman, Curley Collins, and Kay Woods, in particular, endeared themselves to radio listeners with, respectively, their comedy, fiddle playing, and singing.

Tex Forman was born on September 13, 1915, in Paragon, Kentucky. He learned to play guitar at the age of twelve, and when he was sixteen he had his own radio program on WMAN in Mansfield, Ohio. Billed as "The Sixteen-Year-Old Hillbilly," he sang such songs as "Red River Valley," "The Wreck of the Old Ninety-Seven," and "Casey Jones," and played harmonica to his own guitar accompaniment. Tex soon met Reidy Reed who was from Parkersburg, West Virginia, and the two of them decided to put together an act and go on the road. After spending a summer traveling with a medicine show and playing in bars, Tex and Reed joined Curley Collins and fiddle player Slim Clere in an act called the Prairie Pals. They performed approximately a year and a half on WCMI in Ashland, Kentucky, before Tex, Reed, and Collins left the Prairie Pals to join Pop Eckler's group in Cincinnati.

Forman once said he would never forget those first few weeks after he came to Atlanta with Eckler's troupe. "We were all staying in about three rooms at a house on Peachtree Street," he reminisced. "I think we had to pay about $2.50 a week, apiece, for the rooms. The first show date we had was down at Carrollton, Georgia, at the Carroll Theater." After that first personal appearance, things began to pick up for the group. "We had one of the hottest booking acts in the area," Forman recalled. "We worked six days a week, and a lot of times we worked seven days a week when we had to work on a Sunday fiddlers' contest. Sometimes we made around thirty-five or forty dollars a week"—after Eckler deducted expenses from gross receipts. In addition to their work on WSB and their personal appearances resulting from that exposure, Eckler looked elsewhere for other sources of income for the band. According to Forman, "We had a Crazy Water Crystal show on WGST. We couldn't use our right names there, because we were already on WSB. I forget what we called ourselves."[25]

As a singer Tex's rendition of "Rattle Snakin' Daddy" was a favorite among "Cross Roads Follies" listeners. Tex was also the comedian with Eckler's act. His rube routines were featured on all the group's stage shows.

After leaving Atlanta around 1940, Tex returned to Mansfield, Ohio, where he worked in the home construction business by day and played in a country band at night and on weekends. His years after the "Cross Roads Follies" also included a hitch in the army and a stint as a country-music disc jockey on WMAN in Mansfield. Tex and his family returned to the Atlanta area in 1966, where, until his retirement later, he continued to pursue his home building trade and his musical interests. As late as 1979 he conducted a live country-music program on WDGL in the Atlanta suburb of Douglasville. Following the demise of his radio program Tex continued to be musically active.

Kentucky native Ruey "Curley" Collins was born in Catlettsburg on July 28, 1915. Both his parents were musicians, and Curley, having learned to play the five-string banjo at the age of ten, spent most of his youth performing with his father and friends at local barn dances, picnics, and private parties. His first professional job was with a group called the Mountain Melody Boys under the direction of Catlettsburg police chief Dolpha Skaggs. Curley played the guitar with the group, which had a program on WSAZ in nearby Huntington, West Virginia.

It was not until 1937 that Curley learned to play the fiddle, which became his primary instrument. Under Pop Eckler's supervision he gained sufficient skill to win several fiddlers' contests, including the one held in Atlanta in June 1938.

Curley left Atlanta in the early 1940s for West Virginia, where he performed on radio stations in Wheeling (WWVA) and Charleston (WCHS) before taking a defense job in Pittsburgh, Pennsylvania. Following a tour of duty in the army he moved to Richmond, Virginia, where he continued his musical career, performing on the

"Old Dominion Barn Dance" heard on WRVA. When the show folded around 1955, Curley took a job with the General Telephone Company, from which he retired in 1979.[26] Collins continued to live in Richmond and play his fiddle at various public establishments catering to a country-music clientele until his death in 1986.

Kay Woods was a native of Knoxville, Tennessee, where she was born September 8, 1913. When her father died, she moved with her mother to Cincinnati to be near relatives. For her first radio work Kay teamed up with Eula Ware to perform as the Southern Sisters on WCKY, then located in Covington, Kentucky, across the Ohio River from Cincinnati. The two also toured briefly with a theatrical road show performing in a musical adaptation of "Uncle Tom's Cabin" and at the Century of Progress Exposition held in Chicago in 1933 and 1934. Kay joined Pop Eckler's act in 1935, and when she came to Atlanta with him a year later, she became the first featured hillbilly female vocalist to have an extended career on an Atlanta radio station.

At WSB Kay, billed as the "Soap Box Soprano," was well received by "Cross Roads Follies" listeners and stage show audiences who watched her perform in her white cowgirl outfit complete with boots and fringed skirt. Her most requested solo numbers were "When the White Azaleas Are Blooming"; the Patsy Montana hit, "I Want to Be a Cowboy's Sweetheart"; a tearjerker titled "Finger Prints on the Window Pane"; and "Hills of Old Wyoming."

Kay left show business in 1939 to have more time to spend with her young son. She did office work and attended evening school to improve her business skills. When her second husband retired they moved to a home on Lake Hartwell near Lavonia, Georgia.[27] After her husband's death she continued to make her home there, where, until her death in 1986, she led an active life that included extensive involvement in the activities of her church.

The roster of "Cross Roads Follies" entertainers was constantly changing as various groups and individuals joined the show for short periods of time before moving on to other stations and what they hoped would be greener pastures in the form of larger showdate audiences, perhaps a commercially sponsored radio program, and maybe the break that would catapult them into the ranks of the big-time artists such as Gene Autry, Jimmie Davis, Roy Acuff, Lulu Belle and Scotty, Bob Wills, and the legendary Jimmie

Rodgers. In 1937 alone, at least four acts made their debut on the show. In January the Rice Brothers Gang became the first new act to join the "Follies" after the arrival of Pop Eckler's group. (Red and Raymond had rejoined the "Follies" in August 1936.)

The Rice Brothers, Hoke and Paul, born around 1909 and in 1913, respectively, were two of the most seasoned hillbilly entertainers ever to broadcast on any radio station. Their step-father was "Uncle Bud" Silvey, old-time fiddler and show business impresario, and their mother was a five-string-banjo player. They grew up making music, and each became proficient on several instruments.[28] Hoke developed into an accomplished guitar player and by the time he was twenty years old was recording extensively in Atlanta both as a sideman with other hillbilly artists and under his own name. He recorded, for the QRS label's race series, a couple of instrumental duets ("New Sweet Petunia"/"I Just Can't Wait") with Atlanta's white blues singer/pianist Catherine Boswell. Early songs and tunes recorded under his own name include "Chinese Breakdown"/"Macon, Georgia Breakdown" (Hoke Rice and His Southern String Band, QRS), "Waiting For a Train"/"Lullaby Yodel" (Hoke Rice, vocal with guitar accompaniment, QRS), and "Put on Your Old Gray Bonnet"/"Wabash Blues" (Hoke Rice and His Hoky Poky Boys, Brunswick).[29] In 1929 Hoke played guitar accompaniment on two Gennett sides ("You Lied About that Woman," Part I and Part II) by blues singer Mary Jones.[30]

As we have seen, Hoke had been a member of the Carolina Tarheels heard on WSB a few years earlier. His radio work before the "Cross Roads Follies" also included brief periods on Atlanta's WJTL where he performed both alone and with Raymond Lindsey.

Hoke, described as a "singer and rollicking entertainer," and Paul, referred to as "guitarist and man-about-town," brought three other musicians with them to WSB—Johnny Gorman, who played saxophone; a fiddler named Clinton Collins; and a girl, identified only as Mary Ann, who "entertain[ed] energetically."[31] Others who played in the Rice Brothers band during the "Cross Roads Follies" days included Mack Eargle, bass, and Warren Sykes, harmonica.

The inclusion of a horn in their band provides a clue to the musical style and repertoire of the Rice Brothers Gang. They always took pride in the fact that their music was more sophisticated than that of the typical hillbilly band of the 1930s and 1940s. "When me and Hoke teamed up together," Paul recalled after he had retired from the music business, "I mean to actually stay together and do it as the Rice Brothers, we didn't go in for what we called dyed-in-the-wool hillbilly. . . ."[32] On another occasion he explained, "We didn't stick to just hillbilly, we [played] popular stuff."[33] Rice described the music of one of the more popular traditional hillbilly acts with whom they worked as "real corny stuff."[34]

The centerpiece of the Rice Brothers act was the brothers' vocal duet. "We had what was rated one of the top harmony teams," Paul reminisced in later years.[35] "We tried to do it in good harmony without our voices being harsh and broke up," he elaborated. "We'd do it smooth. At least, that's the way we tried to do it."[36] According to Paul, a newspaper writer once referred to the Rice Brothers as "two boys with two guitars from away down South in Georgia with two voices that blend as one."[37]

The Rice Brothers left WSB in 1938. Both before and after their tour on the "Cross Roads Follies" they played on several other radio stations in various parts of the country, including a long stay at KWKH in Shreveport, Louisiana, in the late thirties and early forties. Between 1938 and 1941 they recorded more than fifty songs for Decca.[38] Their recorded output reflects their efforts to throw off the stereotypical hillbilly image and includes such pop songs and tunes as "On the Sunny Side of the Street," "Mood Indigo," "You've Got to See Daddy Every Night," and "Yes! We Have No Bananas." On the other hand, they recorded a couple of gospel songs ("I Love My Savior" and "On the Jericho Road"), tunes that nearly any hillbilly band of the period would have been likely to record ("Down Yonder," "The Railroad Boomer," "Alabama Jubilee"), and cowboy songs ("Below the Rio Grande," "Ridin' Down the Canyon").

Soon after World War II Hoke gave up his music career and went to work for an appliance firm in Shreveport, where he was living at the time of his death. Paul returned to Atlanta where, during the 1950s, he performed on local television with a western-swing band. He was living in retirement in the Atlanta suburb of Mableton at the time of his death in 1988.

Uncle Ned and His Texas Wranglers joined the "Cross Roads Follies" cast in August 1937, coming to Atlanta from Macon, Georgia. In addition to the leader, Uncle Ned, who played piano, guitar, and bass, the band consisted of Marvin "Texas" Taylor, singer and guitar player; Sam Hutcheson; Slim Hutcheson, singer and banjo player; and Pete Arnold.

Macon native Uncle Ned, whose real name was Gene Stripling, once explained how he acquired the radio/stage name that he had used since his first public performance. "The family pride was such that I didn't want to do anything to disgrace it," he related. "If I appeared under another name, and the debut was a flop, my folks wouldn't be any wiser, and there wouldn't be any embarrassment to anybody but myself."[39]

Despite the name Texas Wranglers, none of the band members were from the Lone Star State. We are told that the band's name "expresse[d] the admiration they [the band members] feel for the cowboys and their life."[40] To further enhance their cowboy image, the Texas Wranglers dressed in western outfits, including boots, chaps, guns, and ten-gallon hats.

As was (and is) typical of musician groups, the Texas Wranglers underwent a number of personnel changes during its stay at WSB. Others who performed for Uncle Ned included Pete Cassell, singer, pianist, and guitarist; Chick Stripling (no relation to Gene), fiddler and buck-and-wing dancer; Cicero (Ray) Merneigh, instrumental virtuoso and comedian; steel guitarist Sammy Forsmark; Leon Smith, buck-and-wing dancer; fiddle player Boudleaux Bryant; Eddie Evans; Sy Raines, steel guitarist; Buck Wilson; and Cassie Nelle Coleman, a female singer and bass player who married Chick Stripling on October 29, 1939.[41]

After the "Cross Roads Follies" went off the air in 1940, Uncle Ned returned to Macon where he continued his musical career on radio stations in that city. Some of the other members of the band remained at WSB or later returned to work at the station, and we shall have more to say about them later.

Also casting their lot with the "Cross Roads Follies" troupe in August 1937 were Roy Cross and His Bust O'Dawn Boys. Members of the group, besides Cross, were Eddie "Zeb" Grishaw, Connie Parsons, Eddie Walker, and Harold Compton. Later additions and replacements included Billy Basel and Jimmy De Meo. *Journal* radio columnist Ernie Rogers once wrote that the Bust O'Dawn Boys "have a swell lick. It might be called the evolution of the hillbilly.

These boys cling to some of the mountain music, but their style is definitely toward the modern manner. And it helps."[42]

A November 29, 1937, addition to the "Cross Roads Follies" cast was Uncle Walt and His Sante Fe Trailers, described as "gaily garbed gentlemen" who did "songs of all kinds including novelties, hillbilly tunes, modern and western ballads, and even light classical music."[43]

Although the origin of this group is not known, it was apparently western, not only in name, but in appearance and repertoire as well. We are told that before coming to WSB, these musicians had "sounded their wares over many radio stations."[44]

The Sante Fe Trailers was composed of six musicians whose true identities, unfortunately, remain hidden behind their nicknames. Uncle Walt, the leader of the group, was "a musician and entertainer of the old school" who was "a master of violin, harmonica, and harp." The featured star of the troupe, allegedly a former member of Fred Waring's orchestra who answered to the name Piccolo Pete, played saxophone, clarinet, piccolo, and drums, sang, and served as comedian. Sam played the accordion, sang both bass and baritone, and sometimes directed the band. Shorty, described as a "hefty fellow," played "bass jug" and sang tenor. Cactus, said to have been from the Far West, played violin and mandolin and sang baritone. All we know of the other member of the band is that he was called Smoky. What happened to these musicians after they left Atlanta remains as much a mystery as where they had come from.

Two new acts joined the "Cross Roads Follies" cast in 1938. First came Hank and Slim with the Two Nitwits, Bob and Jack, who arrived on the scene in the spring, "fresh from triumphs with WHKC, Columbus, Ohio, and the Mutual and National Broadcasting Company networks."[45] The quartet, consisting of comedian Jack Lee and brothers Hank, Slim, and Bob Newman, had, it was said, "what it takes in the way of song and comedy."[46]

Although the Newman brothers had been born and reared south of Macon, Georgia, they spent most of their professional careers in the Columbus, Ohio, area and in California. Usually performing under the name Georgia Crackers, the Newmans' band featured a western-swing sound while the three brothers specialized in the close-harmony vocal stylings of the Sons of the Pioneers. They recorded for such labels as Vocalion, Victor, Mastertone, Black and White, and King, and appeared in several western movies. By the late 1970s they had retired from the music business and were living in Arizona.[47]

Biff Ware's Swingsters, a "new aggregation" of musicians, played on the "Follies" beginning in the summer of 1938. The group consisted of Ware, who played saxophone; pianist Jimmie Bryant; saxophonist Noel Walker; fiddler J. W. "Slimbo" Smith; and guitarist Wallace Lancaster.

The last full year during which the "Cross Roads Follies" was heard on WSB was 1939. It also seems to have been the year in which the most new acts joined the show's cast. No less than eight groups were heard on the program for the first time in 1939.

In March the newest act on the show was the Hidden Valley Ramblers which, unlike most of the groups on the show, was composed entirely of local musicians. They were "Butch" Cannon, Bartow Henry, Jimmy Woody, Shorty Steed, and Henry's wife, Hilda, known to radio listeners as Montana Anne.

The Hidden Valley Ramblers had been heard on Atlanta's WATL and WGST before they joined the "Follies" cast. Various combinations of the band members sang duets and trios. Montana Anne sang western songs and the then popular sentimental love ballads such as "Montana Annie," "Singing in the Saddle," and "I'm Sorry, That's All I Can Say." Prior to her marriage to Bartow Henry she had traveled with Charlie Bowman's band.

Country music artists performing on the radio in Atlanta, like their colleagues on other radio stations in other parts of the country, received fan mail. For many fans, writing to their favorite artists was a way of reaching out to a radio "friend" that they would probably never see in person. Others wrote to have a performer dedicate a song to a friend or loved one. Montana Anne, unlike most such artists, saved some of her fan mail. One such letter that she still had fifty years after having received it was from a male listener in Sunnyside, Georgia, and was dated February 19, 1938. "Dear Friend," it began. "I listen to your program and enjoy your songs very much. I would like for you to do a number for me soon. I would also like to have a picture of you, so won't you please send me one. I'll be looking for an answer soon." Preceding the signature were the words, "Your friend." Also unlike many radio performers, Montana Anne answered her admirer's letter and sent him her picture. About a month later she received a note of thanks and a request for a song dedication.

Bartow Henry, who grew up in a rural area a few miles to the northwest of Atlanta, once spoke of the events that got him interested in music. "What inspired me really was just a country band—just a bunch of cotton pickers [who would] get together on Saturday night at different houses. We didn't have any entertainment other than just whatever people provided locally, and these people—the Davis family of Cobb County—played fiddle, banjo, guitar, and, I believe, two fiddles." Bartow was just a child at the time, but as soon as he was able, he acquired a guitar and started entertaining himself.

For Bartow Henry, landing a job on the "Cross Roads Follies" was a dream come true. "In those days," he said years later, "the 'Cross Roads Follies' was like Nashville is now. It was the most popular thing in Atlanta. Pop Eckler was the big dog then, and he inspired a lot of musicians to get started."

After about a year the Hidden Valley Ramblers disbanded, and Bartow joined one of the other "Follies" groups. He later left the program to pursue various other musical activities including jobs at other radio stations.[48]

Once again the state of Kentucky was represented on the "Follies" when, in April 1939, Glenn Hughes brought his Roundup Gang to WSB. With previous experience in Ohio and Kentucky, this group consisted initially of Hughes; Little Joe Isbell, Swiss yodeler and bass player; Harpo Kidwell, guitarist and harmonica player; Jean (Mrs. Glenn) Hughes, who played mandolin; and fiddle player Red Herron. Later additions to the act included Lost John Miller and brothers "Curly" and "Ducky" Woodruff.

One of the most interesting groups to be heard on the "Follies" was Lulu Belle's Maw and Paw and Brother Pete with their National Drifters, who joined the show in July 1939. Maw and Paw were Mr. and Mrs. John Cooper, parents of Lulu Belle who, with her husband Scotty Wiseman, had become one of the country's most popular hillbilly acts through records, movies, and appearances on the "WLS National Barn Dance." Brother Pete was Lulu Belle's younger brother. Other members of this troupe, which was at

WSB for only a short while, were Milton Borden, Edward Borden, and Floyd Kirby.

Signing on with the "Follies" in August 1939 were the Wyoming Rangers under the leadership of Atlanta native Jimmy Smith, a singer and guitar player. The other members of the band were steel guitarist Jesse Carpenter, fiddler Lawrence Wakefield, bass player Herschel Hall, accordionist Lang Howe, guitarist Harry Hampton, and Hank Turner.

Jimmy Smith, who got his start doing stage shows at Atlanta's Fairview Theater on Memorial Drive, became one of the more familiar country music figures in Atlanta. In addition to performing on other radio stations in the city after leaving the "Cross Roads Follies," he returned to the station in the 1940s to serve as master of ceremonies and featured vocalist on the "WSB Barn Dance." He also recorded for RCA Victor, and, as we shall see, during the 1950s, was a member of the Peachtree Cowboys, a country-music TV and nightclub act. In 1963 Jimmy retired from show business and moved to Florida to pursue a second career in real estate.

The way in which Jimmy Smith, whose early idols were Jimmie Rodgers and Gene Autry, broke into show business provides a lesson in audacity, ingenuity, and perseverence. "I heard of a theater out on Memorial Drive," he once recalled, "that played all the 'Cross Roads Follies' acts. So I knew my band wasn't good enough to get on the 'Cross Roads Follies.'" Jimmy thought that if he could get together some good musicians and get booked into the theater that featured the "Cross Roads Follies" acts he might be able to finagle a spot on that popular radio show. With this in mind he obtained the name of the theater manager, John Elder, and paid him a visit. "So on this particular Sunday," Smith continued, "I go out to the old Fairview Theater, and I asked, was this John Elder, and he told me that he was. And I told him who I was—I was Jimmy Smith, and I had a band and I wanted to book them in that theater. He says, 'What's the name of your act?' Well, right off the top of my head I says, 'The Wyoming Rangers.' He says, 'What radio stations have you been working on?' And I told him we hadn't been on a radio station. He says, 'Have you made any records?' I said, 'No, we haven't made any records.' He said, 'Well, without publicity you wouldn't do me any good here.' I said, 'Well, you play Hank Penny in here, and I'm as good as Hank Penny.' Now Hank Penny had one of the best shows in the country, and when I told him this, he laughed and said, 'I'll tell you what I'll do. You come down after the show closes and put me on a show. If I like it, I'll book you in.' "

Smith did as he was told, but halfway through the demonstration show Elder interrupted to inform the aspiring musicians, "That's the stinkingest thing I ever saw in my life." To everyone's surprise, Jimmy Smith retorted, "If you know so much about it, get up here and show us how to do it." For whatever reason, the theater manager did just that, and after coaching the band through several trial runs, agreed to book the act at the theater. As a result of a few more similarly bold acts Smith, within a few months, was able to get his Wyoming Rangers a coveted spot as regular performers on the "Cross Roads Follies."[49]

A group called the Tennessee Ramblers came to the "Follies" for a brief stint in September 1939. This band, composed of bass player Tex Martin, "Horse Thief" Harry Blair, Montana Jack Gillette, who played fiddle, and banjoist Cecil (Curly) Campbell, was heard on several other radio stations, over the years, including WBT in Charlotte, North Carolina. Cecil Campbell had assumed leadership of the group following the retirement of Dick Hartman, who had been heard on WSB in the early 1930s. The Tennessee Ramblers became fairly widely known through their records and Campbell's Hawaiian-guitar playing.[50]

Hank Penny, a native of neighboring Alabama, brought his Radio Cowboys to the "Cross Roads Follies" in September 1939 to begin an association with WSB which, off and on, would last for several years. The Radio Cowboys, when first heard on the "Follies," consisted of Penny; banjo player Louis Dumont; Sammy Forsmark, electric steel guitarist; Sheldon Bennett, fiddler; and another fiddler, Boudleaux Bryant, a former member of Uncle Ned's Texas Wranglers. Carl Stewart later added his bass fiddle artistry to the group's instrumentation.

Yet another Kentuckian, Cynthia May Carver, better known as Cousin Emmy, brought her hillbilly band to the "Cross Roads Follies" in October 1939. Known as Cousin Emmy and Her Kin Folks, the group included Emmy, who played numerous instruments, mainly the five-string banjo; Bud Kissinger, who played guitar; Bud's brother, Benny Kissinger; and fiddle player Tiny Stewart, who later assumed the name Redd and helped Pee Wee King write "Tennessee Waltz."

What apparently was the last act to affiliate with the "Cross Roads Follies" in 1939 was a group referred to as "one of the nation's 'really great' square-dance bands." Known as the Broncho Busters, this act, prior to signing on at WSB, had performed on radio stations in New York, Massachusetts, and South Carolina, and had made guest appearances on several network programs, including the "National Barn Dance." The group consisted of Ken Waite, guitar; Mel Nellis, guitar; Putch [sic, Butch?] Morley, banjo; Will Waite, bass; and Lyman Meade, fiddle. A special feature of this act was the three Singing Callers.[51]

One of the most popular and successful of the acts heard on the "Cross Roads Follies" was created by Pop Eckler. Dubbed the Pine Ridge Boys, it was a vocal duet composed of Marvin Taylor, who had come to WSB as one of Uncle Ned's Texas Wranglers, and W. L. "Doug" Spivey, a Copperhill, Tennessee, native, who grew up in Atlanta.

At the age of ten Doug was taught to play guitar by one-time Skillet Licker Ted Hawkins. The young musician was soon entertaining family, friends, and neighbors with his newly learned guitar skills and vocal versions of the songs made famous by his early idols, Jimmie Rodgers, Vernon Dalhart, Red Foley, and Riley Puckett. Doug was introduced to Pop Eckler by Bill Gatins, who was performing on WGST at the time. Eckler, who was impressed with Doug's singing and yodeling, offered him a job on the "Cross Roads Follies." When Eckler discovered that Doug's voice blended nicely with Marvin Taylor's, he began to feature them on the program as a duet. "We hit it off real good," Doug recalled later. "We both pronounced our words with the same southern accent, and our voices were practically on the same level or pitch. We could switch parts and nobody ever knew it. I could sing tenor, and Marvin could sing lead. Or I'd sing lead [which he usually did] and Marvin would sing tenor."[52]

A few months after their introduction as a duet, Marvin and Doug recorded six songs for the Victor label in temporary studios in Atlanta's old Kimball House Hotel at 30 Pryor Street. At this session, which took place on August 22, 1939, under the direction of Frank B. Walker and Victor's local representative, Dan Hornsby, the Pine Ridge Boys recorded "You Are My Sunshine," "Farther Along," "The Convict and the Rose," "Where the Old Red River Flows," "When Mother Prayed for Me," and "The Clouds Will Soon Roll By." They recorded an additional eighteen sides for Victor in two later sessions, one each in 1940 and 1941.[53]

According to existing documents the Pine Ridge Boys were the first act to record "You Are My Sunshine," a song destined to become one of the most popular country songs of all time and one of the earliest of the cross-over hits. It was recorded by popular country-music artist Jimmie Davis on February 5, 1940,[54] and was one of the top five country music records that year.[55] Gene Autry's recording of the song was a top-five country record and reached number twenty-three on the pop charts in 1941. Other recordings of "You Are My Sunshine" that made the pop charts in 1941 were those by Bing Crosby (no. 19) and Wayne King (no. 20).[56] It is from Jimmie Davis's recording that most country music fans remember the song.

The identity of the composer of "You Are My Sunshine" has, to some extent, been cloaked in mystery and controversy. Doug Spivey once explained how he and Marvin Taylor acquired the song: "We first got it from a young lady that played guitar and sang from South Carolina that got it from some fellow there. . . . She gave us the song because we were a duet. . . . She said it would sound good as a duet. She said, 'Take the song. Do with it what you want to,' and we mentioned about recording it. She said, 'Take it. Get it copyrighted. It will be yours.'" Unfortunately they failed to heed her advice to have the song copyrighted. After the passage of many years Doug did not remember the girl's name. "We met her in the studios of WGST by going up and visiting somebody else there [Marvin and Doug were performing on WSB at the time], . . . I think it was to see Dan Hornsby, . . . and we happened to meet her, and she was singing this song for us. She came from South Carolina there with a show. They were putting on a stage show of some sort at one of the theaters, . . . and she stayed in Atlanta . . . a short while with one of the bands, and I forget exactly what band it was. . . . She played guitar with them and did some singing. . . . And I remember she was slightly red-headed."[57]

In 1956, an article about "You Are My Sunshine" appeared

in the *Shreveport* (Louisiana) *Times*.[58] The story stated that Paul Rice, who with his brother Hoke once performed on Shreveport's KWKH, was the original composer of the song. The newspaper article related that "on a day in 1939—no one seems to remember the exact date—Charlie Mitchell and Jimmie Davis . . . called at the station [KWKH] to see Paul Rice. Paul's wife was in the hospital at the time and needed cash for her bills. He sold 'Sunshine' to Davis and Mitchell for $35. Each put in $17.50." The article went on to say, "On January 30, 1940, 'You Are My Sunshine,' with 'words and music by Jimmie Davis and Charles Mitchell,' was published by Southern Music Publishing Company, Incorporated, of New York.

"But in the meantime, Charlie had sold out his half interest in the song to Jimmie, . . . but not the right to have his name listed as co-composer."

The Rice Brothers recorded "You Are My Sunshine" on September 13, 1939.[59] In 1980, Paul Rice stated that he wrote "You Are My Sunshine" in 1937. "Where I got the idea for it," he explained, "a girl over in South Carolina wrote me this long letter. . . . It was long, about seventeen pages. And she was talking about I was her sunshine, and I got the idea for the song [and] put a tune to it."[60]

According to Paul Rice, "there's at least twenty people 'wrote' 'You Are My Sunshine.' I had a gal write me from California that she wrote it."[61] One writer has stated that the song "first occurred to Jimmie [Davis] while he was fishing one sunny afternoon."[62] In her book *Sing Your Heart Out, Country Boy*, Dorothy Horstman has compiled statements, usually by composers, of how popular country songs came to be written. In a statement regarding "You Are My Sunshine" that he made for the book, Jimmie Davis does not claim authorship of the song as its sheet music proclaims. He merely recites its remarkable history of popularity.[63]

Another country music artist who recorded "You Are My Sunshine" ahead of Jimmie Davis was Bob Atcher, who etched the song on wax for Columbia on January 17, 1940.[64] As Atcher later recalled, "Art Satherley, then A & R [representative] in charge of the catalog I was in, brought me a manuscript copy of ['You Are My Sunshine'] to record. He had picked it up in Charlotte, North Carolina, while he was there for a session. As I remember, he said that he got the song from a boy named Taylor, a singer with the Pine

Ridge Boys. They were working at WSB and told Art that a little girl in Atlanta had written the song and had given it to them. We, Bonnie Blue Eyes and I, [recorded] the song, but when Columbia sent me the release for my signature the name of the composer had been put in to be Jimmie Davis." [65]

So like some of the works ascribed to Shakespeare, the authorship of "You Are My Sunshine" probably will never be decided to everyone's satisfaction.

CHAPTER

7

Hillbilly Music on Atlanta's Smaller Radio Stations, 1925–50

ALTHOUGH IT WAS THE MOST powerful and the most widely heard, WSB was not the only radio station in Atlanta during the decades of the twenties, thirties, and forties. Twenty-four hours after the *Journal* put WSB on the air, its rival, the *Constitution*, gave the public another radio station, WGM.[1] Programming at WGM was, from the start, purely educational, and it was not long before the *Constitution* presented the station as a gift to Georgia Tech, the state-supported engineering school located in Atlanta. On January 13, 1924, the station began broadcasting with new call letters, WBBF.[2] Georgia Tech operated the station as an educational facility until 1930, when, with the call letters WGST (standing for Georgia School of Technology), it went commercial and became a CBS affiliate.[3]

Another Atlanta radio station, WDBE, went on the air in May 1924. Owned first by the Gilham-Schoen Electric Company,[4] WDBE changed hands at least twice before finally giving up the ghost toward the end of the 1920s. Other owners of the station were the Ludden and Bates Company[5] and the J. M. High Department Store.[6]

It was not until 1931 that Atlanta radio listeners could again tune in more than two hometown stations. Thornwell Jacobs, then president of Atlanta's Oglethorpe University, conceived the idea of establishing a radio station in the area for the purpose of "broadcasting certain lectures from the classrooms which would especially

appeal to the general public and the sum total of which would fur-
nish a reasonably complete college education absolutely without
charge, the first time in the history of radio."[7] Shortly after the
hundred-watt station, WJTL, went on the air "courses were inaugurated in such subjects as Spanish, French, German, English
literature, History, and Appreciation of Music, Modern Economic
Problems and many others and . . . this station immediately won a
place in [Atlanta's] civic life as 'a college of the air,'. . . ."[8]

In 1935 WJTL's call letters were changed to WATL when a
private organization bought the station, closed the studios at Oglethorpe, and reopened in the Shrine Mosque. The station's facilities
were later housed in the Henry Grady Hotel on Peachtree Street.
Although much of its broadcast schedule served educational purposes, WJTL, from the beginning, also presented programs designed for the entertainment, rather than the education, of its listeners. Many of these programs featured live performers, but the
majority of the noneducational programming prior to 1940 was
delivered via electrical transcriptions. In addition, an arrangement
had been worked out that allowed the Atlanta station to broadcast
programs originating in the studios of such more powerful stations
as WLW in Cincinnati, WLS in Chicago, and WSM in Nashville.
WATL became an affiliate of the Mutual Broadcasting System in
1940.[9]

After 1931 Atlantans had to be content with three radio
stations (WSB, WGST, and WATL), until August 1, 1937, when
WAGA, another *Journal*-owned station, went on the air. Before the
Journal acquired the station's license, WAGA had been broadcasting as WTFI from studios in Athens, Georgia. The *Journal* brought
the station to Atlanta so listeners in the area could hear programs
offered by both of NBC's networks, the Red, devoted to entertainment, and the Blue, which was "culturally oriented."[10] Until the
Journal sold the station in 1940, it featured the same hillbilly acts
that were heard on WSB. The "Cross Roads Follies" performers,
for example, would present their program on WSB, then rush across
town to give another show on WAGA.

In 1947 three positions on the radio dial were alloted to three
new Atlanta stations—WBGE, WEAS, and WCON. Licenses were
granted to WQXI and WERD in 1948 and to WGLS in 1949.
WTJH in East Point went on the air in December 1949 to bring

to eleven the total number of radio stations broadcasting in the Atlanta area prior to 1950.[11]

Besides WSB, then, the only radio station in Atlanta to offer its listeners hillbilly music during the 1920s was WDBE. One of the first acts with an appeal to a rural-oriented audience to be heard on this station was the Cofer Brothers band which made an appearance on Saturday evening, October 31, 1925. In addition to the Cofers, consisting of Paul, who played fiddle, and L. J. (Leon), who played banjo, the group for this broadcast also included guitarist Ben Evans and mandolinist Homer Barnett.

Born in Jackson County in 1899 and 1901, respectively, Leon and Paul Cofer came by their music honestly. Their father, in addition to being a Methodist minister, was an organist, songwriter, and singing-school teacher who taught his children to read shape-note musical notation. The music of the younger Cofers, who learned to play various string instruments early in life, reflected a strong influence of the rural black musicians they had known in Hancock County where they grew up.

In 1927 and 1929 the Cofer Brothers recorded for the OKeh label in Atlanta during a total of three sessions that yielded twelve released sides including such titles as "The Great Ship Went Down," "The Georgia Hobo," "The Georgia Black Bottom," and "Keno, the Rent Man." Artist credits on half their records are listed as the Georgia Crackers and on the other half as the Cofer Brothers.

Having moved to Atlanta in the early 1920s, Paul and Leon did some performing in clubs and lodges around the city and perhaps made an occasional radio appearance in the early 1930s on WGST while pursuing full-time jobs. Paul was a sheet metal worker and Leon tuned pianos, a skill he had learned at the Georgia School for the Blind, which he attended after a childhood accident left him sightless. Paul Cofer died in 1967 and Leon in 1968.[12]

Other hillbilly acts appearing on WDBE included several who were already familiar to WSB listeners—Bud Landress and Bill Chitwood, broomaphone expert C. S. Brook, and the Dixie String Band. One group whose only radio experience seems to have been on WDBE was Hamlett's Melody Three, which broadcast several times in 1926. The band was composed of the personnel of Hamlett's Automatic Valve Grinding Company and consisted of S. B. Hamlett, who played steel guitar and mandolin and served as the group's leader; Pep Holmes, guitarist; and H. L. Chastine, who played guitar.

An abundance of hillbilly music could be heard on WGST during the 1930s and 1940s. Some artists, such as Bill Gatins, moved back and forth among WGST, WSB, and WJTL. Many of the acts consisted of local musicians, but others were from out of state and included Atlanta on an itinerary that carried them from city to city in search of show-date audiences sufficiently large to keep food on the table.

By far the most popular hillbilly group to appear on WGST was the Blue Sky Boys. The nucleus of this act, which usually included a third musician, consisted of brothers Bill (born October 29, 1917) and Earl (born November 16, 1919) Bolick, natives of Hickory, North Carolina. The professional career of the Bolick brothers began in 1935 on radio station WWNC in Asheville, North Carolina, when Bill and Earl were seventeen and fifteen years old, respectively. Appearing with them on their programs, which were sponsored by JFG Coffee, was a fiddle player named Homer Sherrill. To their radio audiences the three were John, Frank, and George—names suggested by the initials in their sponsor's name.[13]

Bill and Earl first came to Atlanta in March 1936 for a three-month stay on WGST where, known as the Blue Ridge Hillbillies, their programs were sponsored by Crazy Water Crystals. The Blue Sky Boys' subsequent periods of employment at WGST were February–July 1937; January 1938–December 1939; and March 1946–February 1948. Between and after jobs in Atlanta, Bill and Earl appeared on radio stations in other parts of the Southeast. During World War II both brothers served with distinction in the armed forces of the United States.

With Bill playing mandolin and Earl playing guitar, the Bolicks were noted for their close vocal harmony on a wide variety of songs, including those of a religious nature, sentimental tunes of the late nineteenth century, and British and American folk songs. A typical fifteen-minute Blue Sky Boys radio program was the one presented over WGST on October 26, 1939. It consisted of "Where We'll Never Grow Old," "You Are My Sunshine," "Song of the Saddle" (solo by Red Hicks), and "Cripple Creek," the latter probably a mandolin tune by Bill or a mandolin duet by Bill and Red Hicks.[14]

The sources of the Blue Sky Boys' material were similar to

those of other hillbilly artists of their era. "I learned the tunes of a few songs from my maternal grandmother," recalled Bill in later years. The brothers also learned songs and tunes from their mother and father, who frequently sang around the house. "Especially on Sunday mornings we'd wake up hearing him [their father] singing hymns," Earl once related. "We definitely learned a lot of our hymns from him," said Bill in a 1980 interview. Some of the songs in the Blue Sky Boys' repertoire were learned from neighbors and acquaintances.

Like A. P. Carter and other musicians who served as links between folk music traditions and early commercial country music, the Bolick brothers did not feel constrained to transmit an exact copy of the songs and tunes they learned from others. "Sometimes we would rewrite old songs, making up a little here and there, and maybe adding a verse when we knew only part of a song," Earl once explained. "Many of the old-timers sang a song exactly as it sounded to them," Bill elaborated. "There were many times a lot of the words just didn't make sense. When this happened I always tried to rewrite it enough to make it understandable."

Bill Bolick once explained how he and Earl developed their musical style:

> Both of us realized from the very beginning that in order to produce good, clear harmony, one had to sing at a moderate pace in order to be understood, and softly if your voices were to blend. From the first, we strove to keep the harmony and lead separate. Many of the early duets did what we termed 'ran together.' In other words, they sang identical notes instead of lead and harmony. This is one thing we were very careful about. If you will listen to any song we ever recorded, I don't think you will find one where we sang portions of a song without clearly separating the lead and harmony.
>
> We always tried to sing in our natural God-given voices. We never attempted to copy anyone's style, or sound like them. We didn't try to see how high we could sing, or how loud we could sing. We tried to sing in a key that we felt would suit our voices best, without yelling or straining. We didn't play our instruments loud. When it was necessary that the harmony reach a high pitch, I learned to reach these notes without increasing the volume of my voice so the sound that I attained wouldn't be any louder than Earl's lower-pitched voice.[15]

On their personal appearances Earl performed as a comedian, assuming the role of Uncle Josh, "an old man who thought he knew everything, but didn't know anything." [16] For his routine Uncle Josh wore baggy trousers tentatively held up by a giant safety pin and untrustworthy-looking suspenders, a floppy felt hat, and oversized shoes. A corncob pipe, wire-rimmed spectacles perched low on his nose, and a rumpled coat and tie completed his costume.

Homer Sherrill, who had been with the Bolicks in Atlanta in 1936 and 1937 and who left them to join another group, was replaced by Richard "Red" Hicks, also a native of North Carolina. Red was a member of the group throughout their last pre-war period at WGST. "When Red joined us," Bill later recalled, "we immediately started working on the trios and usually included at least one on each program." Hicks sang lead with Bill carrying the tenor part and Earl singing bass. Besides playing guitar, Hicks also sang solos and played mandolin, sometimes joining Bill for a mandolin duet. His vocal repertoire embraced the then popular western songs such as "Riding Down the Canyon" and "There's an Empty Cot in the Bunk House Tonight"; tear-jerkers that included "Don't Make Me Go to Bed and I'll be Good" and "The Letter Edged in Black"; and such love ballads as "I Wonder If You Feel the Way I Do" and "You're the Only Star in My Blue Heaven."

When Hicks left the Blue Sky Boys in October of 1940, he was replaced by Gilmer County native Samuel "Curley" Parker, a fiddle player who also helped out with the trio numbers. He stayed with the Bolicks until they were separated by the war. He rejoined them after the war and remained a part of the act, except for one brief period, until January 1948. Joe Tyson, a fiddler from Carroll County, Georgia, took Parker's place temporarily. The last musician to perform with the Blue Sky Boys before their breakup in 1951 was Leslie Keith, a fiddler and bullwhip artist, who became known as the originator of the fiddle tune "Black Mountain Rag." [17]

The Blue Sky Boys were widely recorded between 1936 and 1950 by RCA Victor. It was at their first session in 1936 that Victor executive Eli Oberstein and the Bolicks came up with the name Blue Sky Boys, which was inspired by the term "Land of the Sky" used to describe the Blue Ridge Mountain area around the Bolicks' original home. Of the many songs recorded by the Blue Sky Boys, such as "Sunny Side of Life," "Are You from Dixie?" (their radio theme song), and "The Sweetest Gift, a Mother's Smile," their biggest hit was "Kentucky," a song composed by Karl Davis and Harty Taylor. The Bolicks recorded the song on May 7, 1947, in Victor's New York City studios.

After disbanding in 1951, Bill and Earl Bolick went their separate ways. Earl took a job with the Lockheed-Georgia company in Marietta, Georgia, while making his home in the Atlanta suburb of Tucker with his wife and three sons. Bill returned to the Hickory, North Carolina, area where he attended Lenoir Rhyne College and worked for the United States Postal Service. After his retirement he continued to live with his wife near Hickory.

The Blue Sky Boys were among the many old-time country acts rediscovered by the folk music revivalists of the 1960s and the bluegrass festival promoters of the 1970s. They subsequently performed intermittently on a few college compuses and at Carnegie Hall. They also recorded four long-play record albums between 1963 and 1975—two for Starday, one for Rounder, and one for Capitol that was reissued by the John Edwards Memorial Foundation.

In the early 1940s—while the Blue Sky Boys were in the service —WGST listeners were rewarded with the songs of another duet, Grady and Hazel Cole, a husband and wife team who had come to Atlanta from station WRGA in Rome, Georgia. Grady, who had been born near La Fayette on August 26, 1909, and Hazel, a native of Fannin County, Georgia, met in a Rome textile mill where they both worked.[18]

By the time the Coles, who had married on August 18, 1930, came to WGST they had established a large following through their broadcasts over WRGA and their personal appearances in the Rome area. Grady had written more than thirty-five songs, published several popular songbooks, and written and marketed a mail-order guitar instruction course. He and Hazel were veterans of a successful recording session for the Bluebird label that had taken place in Atlanta in 1939. Among the songs they had recorded were "You Can Be a Millionaire with Me," "I'm on My Way to a Holy Land," "Shattered Love," "What a Change One Day Can Make," and "The Tramp on the Street." The latter was destined to become one of the most popular of country music songs, one that would be recorded by more than twenty artists, including such diverse stylists as Molly

O'Day; Joan Baez; the Lewis Family; Patsy Montana; Peter, Paul and Mary; the Staple Singers; and Hank Williams.[19]

At WGST, where they performed not only under the name Grady and Hazel Cole, but also as the Country Cousins, the Coles found themselves to be just as popular as they had been at Rome. Shortly after their move to Atlanta Grady reported that they were averaging 75 cards and letters per day. On one day alone they received 115 pieces of mail. They heard not only from listeners in Georgia but from fans in Alabama, North and South Carolina, Tennessee, Florida, and "quite a scattering from other states," according to Grady.[20]

Grady and Hazel featured their young son, Jackie, on their radio programs and stage shows while they were working at WGST. Jackie, who had been born in 1933, began performing with his parents when he was three-and-a-half years old. He endeared himself to listeners with the singing of such songs as "Fly Birdie Fly" and "Beautiful Morning Glory." When World War II came along Grady and Hazel, like most musical acts of the period, added patriotic songs to their broadcast and personal appearance repertoires. Jackie, especially, was called on to help out with this type of song. According to Grady, he made quite a hit with such war songs as "You Won't Know Tokyo When We Get Through," "Hitler's Last Roundup," and "The Devil and Mr. Hitler."[21] As Jackie grew older he frequently joined his parents to form a trio in which he sang lead, Hazel sang alto, and Grady sang baritone and played the guitar.

While at WGST, the Coles shared personal appearance dates with other Atlanta-area country music acts. For a while they appeared every Saturday on the stage of Atlanta's Joy Theater with Riley Puckett, Gid Tanner, and a group called the Blue Ridge Mountain Boys that was appearing on another Atlanta radio station. Grady reported in 1944 that they played to "a packed house on every show."[22] Another Atlanta-area country music artist who joined the Coles on personal appearances was Pete Cassell.

As had been the case while they were broadcasting in Rome, the Coles seem to have encountered no problems securing sponsors for their programs on WGST. Among the firms for whom they broadcast were the *Southern Agriculturist*, a regional magazine for farmers; the Retonga Medicine Company; and the Allied Drug Company.

WGST's managers once stated that while the Coles were at their station they drew "more fan mail than any other group ever featured over this station over such a period of time." [23] During their last year at WGST the Coles were paid a weekly sustaining fee of thirty dollars. [24]

After the Coles left WGST in the mid-1940s they appeared on several other radio stations in the Southeast, including WNOX in Knoxville, where they were a feature of the "Tennessee Barn Dance." For a while they performed with Lost John Miller and the Allied Kentuckians on a program that was heard over more than 144 radio stations in the United States and Canada. [25]

In the late 1940s the Coles returned to Georgia, where they made their home in the Atlanta suburb of East Point. A final recording session, which, according to Jack, took place in 1950, resulted in the release of several sides on the Gilt Edge label. After returning to Georgia the Coles engaged in church and evangelistic work, singing with a local evangelist who conducted street meetings and preached from courthouse squares on Saturday afternoons in the small towns surrounding Atlanta.

By 1950 Jackie had stopped performing with his parents. He enrolled in a vocational school, and later took a job as billing clerk with a trucking firm. He married in 1951, and in 1957 was called to the ministry. In the 1980s he was pastor of a Baptist church in Rome where he had served for several years. In the early 1950s the Coles stopped performing. Hazel worked in an Atlanta textile mill and later as a welfare case worker for the city of Atlanta. Grady continued to teach music and write songs. He died in 1981. In the mid-1980s Hazel was living near her son, Jack.

Like WSB, Atlanta's WGST also featured hillbilly performers from the state of Kentucky. The best known of these was Pappy Slats, who called his group the Kentucky Mountaineers. Slats, whose real name was Melvin Bethel, was from Muhlenberg County, Kentucky. Before coming to WGST in 1940, Slats had performed with other groups including E. E. Hack's String Band, a popular group in western Kentucky during the 1920s and 1930s. Among the many musicians who performed in Pappy Slats's band while he was at WGST were Hoyt Pruitt, Marvin Taylor, Doug Spivey, Bobby Atcheson, Cicero (Ray) Merneigh, Paul and Leaford Lunsford, Cassinelle Coleman, Eddie Smith, Bud Mote, Bobby Staples,

Al Gillig, and Randy Barnet. Slats left WGST around 1942. He died in 1972.

The many other hillbilly acts heard on WGST during the 1930s and 1940s included Johnny Barfield (1936); the Bucka-roos, composed of Bartow Henry, Butch Cannon, Andy Thomas, Marion Sumner, and Mac Atcheson (1949); Herschel Brown and his Washboard Band (1932); the Corn Dodgers with Paul Rice (1946); the Corn Huskers featuring Eddie Smith (1948–50); John Dilleshaw and His Dill Pickles (1930); the Dixie String Band featuring, presumably, some of the individuals who had performed with the band on WSB in the 1920s (1930, 1932); Ted Hawkins and His Atlanta Ramblers (1931); Jack Holden and the Georgia Boys (1948); the Hoosier Playboys, with Bobby, Hubert, Tom, Shirley, and Guy Atcheson, Andy Thomas, and possibly Leon Smith (1938); Lang Howe (1940); the Hudson Brothers (1932); Pink Lindsey (1936); the Logan Sisters (1949); Daddy John Love and Riley Puckett (1937); the Milo Twins (1938); the Monroe Brothers, Bill and Charlie (February 27–March 3, 1936); Elmer McMichen's String Band (1930); Jim Pritchett and His 'Possum Hunters (1932); and Biff Ware's Swingsters (1940).

Elmer McMichen is of interest not only as a musician in his own right, but also because he and Clayton McMichen were cousins, according to several of his contemporaries, including Hoyt "Slim" Bryant. Bryant also stated that Elmer McMichen was a fiddler who recorded for the OKeh label with a group called McMichen's Harmony Boys. Other members of the group were Hoyt Newton, a fiddler; a banjoist whose last name was Woods; and Bryant, who played guitar. Of the songs recorded by the group, Bryant in later years could recall only "Sweetheart Days," which he composed, "Down by the Old Mill Stream," and "Ain't She Sweet."[26]

A native Atlantan, Slim Bryant began making music after graduating from high school in 1926. Through Elmer McMichen he met Clayton McMichen, with whom he had an extensive professional association. The two left Atlanta together in the early 1930s to work on radio stations in Cincinnati, Pittsburgh, and other eastern cities. In 1939, while working at radio station WRVA in Richmond, Virginia, Bryant and McMichen decided to pursue their musical careers as separate acts. McMichen went to Louisville, Kentucky, while Bryant remained in Richmond to perform on the Old Dominion Barn Dance. In 1940, Bryant, who had established an enviable reputation as an outstanding guitarist, returned to KDKA in Pittsburgh where he and his band performed for the next nineteen years. Billed as Slim Bryant and His Wildcats, Bryant's group made the transition to television when that medium of entertainment came to the Steel City. Their run on TV lasted for ten years. During his days at KDKA Bryant was the featured artist on a series of transcriptions that were heard on radio stations around the country. In the late 1980s Bryant was still living in semi-retirement in Pittsburgh, while teaching guitar and occasionally performing.[27]

Among the early hillbilly performers on WJTL were Fiddlin' John Carson and Moonshine Kate (1934), Bill Childers and His String Band (1932), George Daniell's Hill Billies (1933), the Dixie String Band (1932), Ted Hawkins's Mountaineers (1932), Wiley Kite's Playboys (1931), the North Georgia Buggy Riders (1931), John Patterson (1932), Riley Puckett (1935), the Skillet Lickers (1935), and the Stripped Gears with Marion Brown, Cliff Vaughn, Skinny Anglin, and (possibly) Pink Lindsey (1931). All of these acts were on the station for very short periods of time, many apparently making only one appearance.

The hillbilly performer with the longest tenure on WJTL (WATL) was Carl Talton, who appeared on the station, off and on, over a period of more than ten years.[28] Talton began his association with WJTL in the early 1930s while still in his teens. Billed as the Day and Night Cowboy in deference to his sponsor, the Day and Night Dentists (so called because, presumably, they were open day and night), Talton presented a daily fifteen-minute program of cowboy songs and Jimmie Rodgers hits to his own guitar accompaniment. "I was making a dollar a day," Talton later reminisced. "I had another job, too," he recalled, "working in a factory that made springs for automobile seats."

Talton decided to try for a spot on the air after having been laid off from work because of a strike. "I put my old guitar in a pillow case—I couldn't afford a guitar case—" he recalled some fifty years after the fact, "and got out on the highway and hitched a ride to Atlanta." He went to the WJTL studios where he managed to obtain an audition before the station manager. Talton recalled that his audition number was a Gene Autry song.

In 1936 Talton changed his radio name to Cowboy Jack. He later organized a band he called the Hidden Valley Ramblers—a name adopted (with Talton's concurrence) by Bartow Henry and Butch Cannon for the group they took to the "Cross Roads Follies" in 1939. Groups that Talton organized later were called Cowboy Jack's Roving Cowboys, Cowboy Jack and the Southern Drifters, and Cowboy Jack and His Roundup Gang. In later years Talton recalled that the musicians who played in his bands included Collus Maddox, Gene Mitchell, Marion Orr, Jimmy Myers, Bill Dopson, Herman Hall, Dill Ross, Lydia Brand, and Doug Wheelis.

After serving in the armed services during World War II Talton returned to Atlanta where he continued to make music on a part-time basis while working full time at other jobs. For several years he owned and operated a restaurant in suburban Decatur. His musical activities during this time included appearances on radio stations WSB, WGST, WERD, WGLS, and WEAS. In 1949 and 1950 Talton, billed as Cowboy Jack, appeared regularly on the "Georgia Jamboree," a program on WGST that featured a number of other Atlanta country music artists. On this program, which was fed to the Mutual Broadcasting System network and broadcast on Armed Forces Radio, Talton sang such songs as "Shenandoah Waltz," "When the Work's All Done this Fall," "Blue Eyes Crying in the Rain," and "Echoes from the Hills."

In 1955 Talton's band won an award as the best hillbilly band of the year at a contest held in Gainesville, Georgia. Talton died in 1984.

The American public has never been able to resist the charm of a talented child performer. In the 1920s and 1930s the movies gave us Jackie Coogan, Jackie Cooper, and Shirley Temple. In the world of country music the 1930s witnessed the popularity of Georgie Goebel of the "National Barn Dance" and Little Jimmy Sizemore who captured the hearts of thousands of fans who heard him on several radio stations around the country including WSM and the "Grand Ole Opry." Not to be outdone, the Atlanta country-music scene in the 1930s, as we have noted, included two youngsters at WSB—Pep, of Pep and Rhythm, and Raymond Anderson. A little later WGST had Jackie Cole.

In 1939 those who tuned in WATL could hear yet another child singer, little Lorene Pierce. Her specialties, which she sang on a program called "Lorene, Ma, and Pa," were western songs such as "I Want to Be a Cowboy's Sweetheart" and sentimental ballads that included "The Old Spinning Wheel." The Ma and Pa on the program were Lorene's parents, Johnny and Stella Pierce, veterans of several years of radio broadcasting when they added to their act Lorene, who was born in 1929.[29]

Johnny was born in Speedwell, Tennessee, in 1907, and first performed on WNOX in Knoxville, Tennessee, in 1931. Stella, whom he married in 1927, was born in Adairsville, Georgia. The Pierces had worked at WRGA in Rome and at Atlanta's WGST before switching to WATL. They sang mostly gospel songs and popular love songs including many composed by their friend Grady Cole. The Pierces' singing, accompanied by Johnny's guitar playing, was a regular Saturday morning feature on WATL during most of 1939.

Like many of the old-time hillbilly radio artists, Johnny composed a special theme song that brought him and his wife and daughter on and took them off the air. When the man in the control room gave them the high sign on Saturday mornings the Pierces greeted their listeners with

Good Morning, everybody;
Good Morning, how do you do?
We come to WATL
To sing a song for you.
So if you'll just be patient
With what we have to say,
We'll start you off in happiness
And smiling on your way.
  (Hum)
If you want a dedication,
It's not against the law
To write a little scratch or two
To Lorene, Ma, and Pa.

When their allotted time (usually fifteen minutes) was up, they went off the air singing:

Although we hate to leave you,
I guess we'd better go
Before you start to pull your hair
And bust your radio.

If you think you can stand it,
And your nerves are very tough,
Tune in again next Saturday
If you ain't got enough.
  (Hum)
If you want a dedication
It's not against the law
To write a little scratch or two
To Lorene, Ma, and Pa.

In the mid-1940s the Pierces moved to Knoxville. There they were heard on WROL and on WNOX where, according to Johnny, they were members of the "Mid-Day Merry-Go-Round." Returning to the Atlanta area around 1950 the Pierces rejoined fiddler Bud Mote and singer-guitarist Paul Bennett with whom they had performed before going to Knoxville. Billing themselves as the Stone Mountain Gang, this group performed on several Atlanta-area radio stations including WTJH in East Point.

According to Pierce, he and Stella shared the stage with Gid Tanner on the last show that he played. "Me and Stella and Paul Bennett played with him at the courthouse in Summerville [Georgia]," Johnny related. "He died just a few weeks after that and we went to his funeral out at Dacula." At the courthouse show, Johnny recalled, "We just almost had to help Gid out on to the stage, but he could fiddle up a storm when you'd get him out there. He'd get his balance, and he would just tear that thing up. He had that spark in him. He was quite a showman."

During their years as performers music was a part-time job for the Pierces. In Atlanta and Rome Johnny worked in textile mills, and in Knoxville he worked in a grocery store owned by country music entrepreneur Cas Walker. By 1984 Johnny and Stella Pierce had retired and were living at Kennesaw, Georgia, near Atlanta.

It was on WJTL that a young fellow, destined to become one of the most familiar and enduring figures to grace the Atlanta country music scene, made his radio debut. He was Hall County native George "Sleepy" Head who, by his own account, first broadcast on the station in 1935.[30] It was a few years later, however, in 1939 and 1940, that he had his first big show on the station. Called the "Fulton County Jamboree," this barn-dance program was usually heard on Saturday nights, although it moved to a Sunday-night spot during October, November, and December of 1939. Several Atlanta-area hillbilly performers got their start on the "Fulton County Jamboree" including Dobroist Hoyt Pruitt and singer/guitarist Mickey Barner.

With a harmonica-playing father and a mother who picked the banjo, George Head was exposed to hillbilly music from the day of his birth in 1914. He liked to sing, and by the time he was fifteen or sixteen years old, he and two guitar-picking friends, Loy Stewman and Elmo Oswald, were hitchhiking to south Georgia to perform at tobacco auctions for the nickels and dimes the farmers would drop in the musicians' hat.

Most of the many hillbilly bands that George organized over the years had the term "Blue Ridge" as part of their names, and they used "Blue Ridge Mountain Blues" for their theme song. There were the Blue Ridge Mountaineers, the Blue Ridge Boys, and the Blue Ridge Mountain Boys. One of his first bands, in addition to himself, was composed of Hermes Harris, guitarist; Loy Stewman, who played guitar; Hoyt Pruitt, who played Dobro; and banjoist, Steve Stewman. Others who played in Head's bands over the years included Glenn "Junebug" Thomas, electric guitarist; Richard "Sonny" Albright; Ernest Harris; Dallas Burrell; Lisodos Bennett; Dewey Parker; Eddie Shaw; Clem Brooks; N. J. "Slim" DeFoor; James Peacock; Vernon Brinkley; and Romeo Brinkley.

In addition to WJTL (WATL) Head's bands were heard on other Atlanta-area radio stations including WAGA, WGST, WEAS, WERD, and probably WQXI. In the early 1950s Head moved to Birmingham, Alabama, where he was seen and heard on WBRC-TV. His Birmingham band, which he called the Bunkhouse Gang, included Hoyt Pruitt, Dewey Parker, Gene Holcombe, and Eddie Shaw.

Head once recalled that during his radio career his sponsors had included Light Crust flour, Kay Jewelers of Atlanta, and Standard Feed and Milling Company. "A lot of times," Head once stated, "we were sponsored by a manufacturer of women's hosiery. We were paid on a p.i. [per inquiry] basis by them," he recalled. "Listeners would send in money to the station for the hosiery. We could tell how much we were making by the amount of mail we were receiving."

George Head acquired the nickname "Sleepy" while working an early-morning radio program on WAGA. "Charles Smithgall was the manager of WAGA and [emcee of] one of those 4:30 A.M. morning programs. I got up just a little bit early—we opened the station at 4:30—one morning. I was sitting in the floor [waiting for the program to begin] nodding, and he [Smithgall] said, 'George Sleepy Head.' And the name stuck with me."

According to Hoyt Pruitt, some of Head's most requested songs were "You Can't Break My Heart," "Have I Told You Lately that I Love You," "Pocket Full of Dreams," and "Jealous Heart."

Head had a small part in the 1951 movie, *I'd Climb the Highest Mountain*, which was filmed in Georgia and starred Susan Hayward. George Head died on December 4, 1981.

WATL was the radio home of several other hillbilly performers during the 1940s. They included the Arkansas Travelers (1941) and the Dixie Playboys with Hoyt Pruitt, Dobro; Willard Cohran, guitar; Ernest Dunahoo, harmonica; and fiddler Bill Brown (1942). Others were the Dixie Roamers, with Bud Mote, Paul Bennett, Dewey Parker, Mary Englett, and Clarence Pope (1947–49, intermittently); Tiny Fuller and the Georgia Playboys (1949); the Georgia Kids with Clarence Pope, Hoyt Pruitt, Jim Carroll, and Ernest Dunahoo (1942); Jane and Bob Atcheson (1942); Lost John Miller and the Kentuckians (June 1942–January 1943, 1944); and the Rainbow Ramblers with Marion Brown, E. O. Bennett, Blackie Summers, Carl Barber, Marvin "Cotton Top" Brown, Harry Hampton, Bill Dobson, and Charles Stephens (1948–50).

Some twenty-three years after the *Constitution* divested itself of its first radio station, Atlanta's morning newspaper once again decided to try its hand in the broadcasting business. The *Constitution*-owned WCON went on the air on December 15, 1947, with a power of five thousand watts. Although the station did not program a great amount of hillbilly music, it did provide Tommy Trent with a radio outlet for a few months in 1949.

Born into a musical family on August 3, 1924, at Strawberry Plains, Tennesse, Tommy Trent, guitarist, bass player, and singer, got his start as a professional musician on WNOX in Knoxville, Tennessee, in 1943.[31] He was heard on the popular "Mid-Day Merry-Go-Round" program as a member of Mel Foree's Victory Boys, and in 1944 he performed for about three months on the "Grand Ole Opry" with Paul Howard's Arkansas Cotton Pickers.

In September 1946 Trent brought his "Dixie Fun Barn" show to Atlanta's WAGA, where it became one of the area's top country-music programs. The show had been heard first on WPDQ in Jacksonville, Florida, where it was sponsored by Co-Go cold medicine, a product that also sponsored the program on WAGA.

The "Dixie Fun Barn" was heard in the early morning, during the middle of the day, and, for most of 1947, on Saturday nights. Besides serving as the show's producer and emcee, Trent was a featured performer specializing in the current country-music favorites including those made famous by such stars as Eddy Arnold, Cowboy Copas, Roy Acuff, and Red Foley. "Dixie Fun Barn" listeners also heard the music of Hoyt Pruitt, Dewey Parker, Bartow Henry, Don West, Curley Harris, Calvin Bragg, Garr Moss, Dixie Lee, Bobby Atcheson, and Lang Howe.

The "Dixie Fun Barn" was last broadcast on WAGA in December 1948. Following a brief stint at WQAM in Miami, Florida, Trent brought the show back to Atlanta where it was heard on WGST from October 1949 to January 1950. After leaving Atlanta for good in 1950, Tommy Trent was heard on the "Louisiana Hayride" at KWKH in Shreveport, and on radio and TV stations in Little Rock, Arkansas, until his retirement from show business in 1970. In the 1980s Trent was serving as president of a publishing firm in Little Rock, where he also lived.

From the time it began broadcasting in 1947 WEAS devoted a considerable amount of its programming time to hillbilly music. Among the acts to be heard during the 1940s were Johnny Johnson and the Carolina Sunshine Girls (1948); the Dixie Roamers (1947–48); Jack Holden and the Dixie Home Folks (1948–50); the Log Cabin Boys (Ramblers) with fiddler Speedro Patterson (1947–49); Red and Check Anderson (1949); the Stone Mountain Boys with Bud Mote, Elden Hooper, and Paul Bennett (1948–49), and Andy Thomas (1949).

A native of Pickens County, Georgia, Jack Holden came to WEAS in 1948 with a considerable amount of country music experience and relatively widespread popularity.[32] Jack, whose real name was Milton Jackson, took the name Holden for professional purposes after forming a duet with Fairley Holden, a native of Gilmer County, Georgia, to perform as the Holden Brothers. Jack (born in 1915) and Fairley (born in 1916) met while both were serving in the Civilian Conservation Corps (CCC), one of Franklin D. Roosevelt's Depression-fighting organizations. They were stationed at Ft. McPherson, Georgia, just outside of Atlanta, and after a few weeks of singing and playing their guitars together in the barracks, they decided to see if George Head, who was then performing on WATL, would give them a spot on his program. George, after hearing their try-out number, decided they were good enough and allowed them to go on the air. Fairley later recalled that they wound up with a regular program on WATL that lasted for about six months during which time they favored their listeners with such songs as "No Drunkards Shall Enter," "Southern Moon," "Going Back to Alabama," and "Don't that Road Look Rough and Rocky."

Following their discharge from the CCC, Fairley and Jack hitchhiked to Akron, Ohio, where they found jobs working in a steel mill at nearby Barberton. They continued to make music together in their spare time, performing at area night spots and over a local radio station. After six or eight months in Akron the Holdens decided to go into the music business full time, and subsequently performed on radio stations in Charleston and Bluefield, West Virginia; Bristol, Tennessee; Raleigh, North Carolina, and Dallas, Texas. The Holdens were joined in Charleston by fellow Georgian Curley Parker, who played fiddle for them as he did later for the Blue Sky Boys.

In the early 1940s the Holden Brothers experienced the biggest break of their career when they were hired by John Lair to perform on the "Renfro Valley Barn Dance" and the "Sunday Mornin' Gatherin'," two programs then heard on the CBS network. According to Jack the first song they sang on the barn dance was "There's a Star-Spangled Banner Waving Somewhere," which the audience enjoyed enough to call the boys back for four encores.

The Holdens' career, at its peak in Renfro Valley, was interrupted by World War II. Jack was drafted into the army, and Fairley did a tour of duty in the navy. After the war they returned to Renfro Valley, but after a short time they broke up and each went his separate way. Jack organized a new band called the Georgia Boys that he took to Bluefield, West Virginia; Dayton, Ohio; and Topeka, Kansas. Fairley rejoined Jack in Topeka and while there, according to Jack, they recorded two songs, "Dust on the Bible" and "Mother's Not Dead, She's Only Sleeping," for the White

Church label. At about the same time Jack Holden and the Georgia Boys recorded four sides for the Red Barn label—"Black Mountain Blues," "Mama I'm Sick," "Mocking Bird," and "New Drifting and Dreaming."

It was shortly after the Holden Brothers' final separation that Jack and his wife, whom he had met in Bluefield, West Virginia, came to Atlanta to perform on WEAS as members of the Dixie Home Folks. Mrs. Holden performed under the name Frances Kay. Other members of the Dixie Home Folks cast, at one time or another, included Tip Sharp, Wayne Midkiff, James Padgett, Johnny Crider, Eldon Hooper, and Paul Bennett.

While at WEAS Jack and his wife, using the names Jack Holden and Frances Kay, recorded several songs for RCA, including "Empty Tomb," "When the Hell Bomb Falls," "Standing by His Side," "No Wars in Heaven," "With a Ring in My Pocket," "Jesus and Me," and "They Locked God Outside the Iron Curtain."

Jack eventually stopped performing professionally to become a disc jockey and sales-and-service representative for the Dee Rivers radio station chain, a job that he held for approximately fifteen years. The 1980s found Jack affiliated with WLAW in Lawrenceville, Georgia, just outside of Atlanta. Mrs. Holden at the time was the station's bookkeeper and traffic manager.

Fairley, the other member of the Holden Brothers duo, left Topeka, Kansas, to resume his career as a solo performer, specializing in novelty songs that included "When Grandma Got Her Teeth in Upside Down." He worked in such cities as Knoxville, where he appeared on the WNOX "Mid-Day Merry-Go-Round" with Lonnie Glosson and Homer and Jethro; Detroit, where he played in the same nightclub with Moon Mullican; and Atlanta, where he became a member of the "WSB Barn Dance" troupe. In 1952 Fairley joined Ernie Lee and other stars from Cincinnati's WLW in an overseas USO show that carried them to Germany and France.

After becoming a solo performer, Fairley landed a recording contract with King. Among the sides he recorded were such novelty songs as "Don't Monkey 'Round My Widder when I'm Gone," "Coo-See-Coo," "The Intoxicated Rat," "Port to Portal Pay," "Graveyard Light," and "Keep Them Cold Icy Fingers Off of Me," which was his best known.

Fairley's last work as a professional musician was in Detroit for Casey Clark on WJR's "Big Barn Frolic." In the 1950s he left show business and took a job with an Atlanta trucking firm from which he later retired to make his home in Atlanta with his wife. Fairley died in 1987.

The sharing of hillbilly talent between WSB and WAGA ceased after the *Journal* sold the latter station in 1940. The hillbilly acts heard on WAGA after the change included Micky Barner (1947); Dwight Butcher (1941); Pete Cassell (1943–45); Lew Childre (1943–44); the Cripple Creek Gang with Uncle Billy Woods, Eddie Smith, Hoyt Pruitt, the Woody Sisters (May and Mary), Dewey Ford, Jake Pitts, Tex Martin, Kitty Jackson, Bobby Atcheson, and Billie Brown (1943); the Kentucky Mountaineers (1940); the Light Crust Doughboys, composed of Smitty and Tennessee Smith, Ace Richman, and Eddie Wallace (1943–45); Lost John Miller and the Kentuckians (1943, 1947); the Pine Mountain Valley Boys with Eddie Smith, Tommy Harris, Hoyt Pruitt, Red Murphy, and Vivian Watson (1943–44); the Red River Rangers, composed of Ace Richman, Pat Patterson, and Tennessee and Smitty Smith (1942); Mattie and Salty Holmes (1949); and the Sunshine Boys, a gospel quartet whose personnel was the same as that of the Light Crust Doughboys (1943–46).

During the 1930s and 1940s, according to radio station logs, many other hillbilly groups appeared on Atlanta's radio stations. The identities of the individual members of these groups, however, are forever lost in such program titles as "Hillbilly Band," "Hillbilly Jamboree," "Variety Program," and "Barn Dance."

CHAPTER

8

The "WSB Barn Dance,"
1940–50

THE PERIOD FROM 1940 TO 1950 will long be known to
Americans as the decade in which their country became involved
in "the greatest, the most widespread, the most destructive, and
the most costly war in history" up to that time.[1] No facet of life
escaped the impact of World War II. Those who lived through the
three years and nine months during which this country was engaged
in actual combat recall the newspaper stories and radio dispatches
from such previously unheard-of places as Corregidor, El Alamein,
and Palermo. They remember ration stamps needed for the purchase
of gasoline, automobile tires, shoes, coffee, sugar, canned goods,
and other foodstuffs; sons, husbands, boy friends, brothers, and
fathers going off to fight in the Army, the Navy, the Coast Guard,
and the Marines; daughters and sisters also going off to serve in
the WACs (Army), the WAVES (Navy), the SPARS (Coast Guard),
and the WASPs (Army Air Force); the patriotic songs—"Praise the
Lord and Pass the Ammunition," "This Is the Army Mr. Jones,"
"Comin' in on a Wing and a Prayer," and "There's a Star-Spangled
Banner Waving Somewhere"; the death of President Franklin D.
Roosevelt; the first atomic bomb; and, finally, VE-Day and VJ-Day.
   Then came the GI Bill of Rights that sent millions of ex-
servicemen to college; the Cold War that produced fears of another
global confrontation; flying saucers that triggered a major national
controversy; and television that helped take people's minds off the
Cold War and flying saucers.

Those keeping up with goings-on in country music circles in the 1940s learned of the breakup of the original Carter Family and their last recording session (1941); the "Grand Ole Opry's" move to the Ryman Auditorium (1941); the formation of the Acuff-Rose music-publishing company, the first country music publisher in Nashville, by Opry star Roy Acuff and songwriter Fred Rose (1943); the election of Jimmie Davis as governor of Louisiana (1944); the marriage of Dale Evans and Roy Rogers (1947); and the formation of the Foggy Mountain Boys by Lester Flatt and Earl Scruggs, who left Bill Monroe's Blue Grass Boys to front their own bluegrass band (1948). Those who regularly tuned their radio dials to 650 on Saturday nights to hear the "Grand Ole Opry," or tuned in the show on an NBC affiliate, witnessed during the 1950s the debut of a number of new members of what had become the nation's premiere showcase of country music talent. They included Minnie Pearl (1941); Ernest Tubb and the Bailes Brothers (1943); Bradley Kincaid (1944); and Hank Williams (1949).

Among the top country music records of the decade were "New San Antonio Rose" (Bob Wills, 1940), "I'm Walking the Floor Over You" (Ernest Tubb, 1941), "Wreck on the Highway"/ "Fireball Mail" (Roy Acuff, 1942), "Pistol Packin' Mama" (Al Dexter, 1943), "Smoke On the Water" (Red Foley, 1944), "Shame on You" (Spade Cooley, 1945), "Divorce Me C.O.D." (Merle Travis, 1946), "Smoke! Smoke! Smoke! (That Cigarette)" (Tex Williams, 1947), "Bouquet of Roses" (Eddy Arnold, 1948), and "Lovesick Blues" (Hank Williams, 1949).

By 1940 more people were listening to live hillbilly music on the radio than ever before. There were 765 radio stations on the air nationwide and 81 percent of American families owned receiving sets. At the end of the decade there would be 2,867 radio stations (781 of which were FM) and 94.7 percent of the families would own receiving sets.[2] " 'Hillbillies' are in radio in a big way," wrote George C. Biggar, then program director at WLW in Cincinnati, in a 1940 article in *Billboard* magazine.[3] They "are ringing the cash registers for scores of stations in the sale of time and personal appearances," he continued, noting that "hillbillies have changed former non-revenue-producing early morning hours of radio stations into money-making hours" and "have also changed Saturday night from 'bath night' to *jamboree* and *barn dance* night for millions of lovers of home-folks entertainment."[4] Whereas, according to Biggar, "Saturday night was once radio's dead night, . . . the success of old-time performers was largely responsible for opening up the sale of Saturday-night air time."[5]

Biggar could have been describing the hillbilly scene in Atlanta in 1940, especially what was taking place at WSB, by then a fifty-thousand-watt clear channel station, the most powerful radio voice in a thriving metropolis of more than three hundred thousand souls. In December 1939, the Cox enterprises of Ohio purchased WSB and its parent, the *Atlanta Journal*,[6] and within a year new management had completely redesigned WSB's hillbilly programming. Pop Eckler and most of the other hillbilly performers at WSB moved to other radio stations in Atlanta and other cities, and John Lair of Renfro Valley, Kentucky, who had more than a decade of experience in promoting radio hillbilly shows, was employed as a consultant to bring in new talent and to facilitate the changes.[7] When Lair had completed his job WSB was providing its listeners with hillbilly music on an early morning program (variously labeled), two usually mid-morning shows ("Cracker Barrel" and the "Little Country Church House"), a mid-day program ("Georgia Jubilee"), a thirty-minute broadcast on Friday nights ("Hayride"), and the "WSB Barn Dance" heard for thirty minutes on Saturday nights. WSB's hillbilly artists also provided entertainment on the station's early morning (begun in 1940) and mid-day (begun in 1941) "Dixie Farm and Home Hour" programs which were "produced with the idea of giving listeners in the South localized farm and home information that is easily adaptable to Southern conditions."[8]

The early and mid-morning programs featured small groups of entertainers all of whom came together for full-cast productions at noon and on Friday and Saturday nights. The "Barn Dance" joined the ranks of such other shows as the "WLS National Barn Dance" (started in 1924), the "Grand Ole Opry" (1925), the "Renfro Valley Barn Dance" (started in 1937 over WLW, Cincinnati, later switching to WHAS, Louisville, Kentucky), and the "WWVA Jamboree" in Wheeling, West Virginia (1926).[9] The Saturday-night show continued uninterrupted for almost ten years. It soon gained a reputation as one of the largest barn dances in the South,[10] and the May-September 1941 Hooper ratings showed that it had the highest rating of any program—network or local—on any Atlanta radio station.[11]

Broadcasting before an audience in the station's main studios on the top floor of Atlanta's Biltmore Hotel, the "WSB Barn Dance" was heard for the first time at 10:30 on Saturday night, November 16, 1940. Demand for tickets exceeded the availability of seats for spectators, but fans who had to be turned away were promised tickets to future performances. The roster of entertainers for the initial broadcast included guest star Judy Dell of the "Renfro Valley Barn Dance" and regular WSB personalities Dwight Butcher, the Pine Ridge Boys, Hank Penny, Harpo Kidwell, Louis Dumont, Boudleaux Bryant, and Warren Sykes.[12]

Unfortunately, the *Journal* did not publish a list of the songs and tunes presented on the "Barn Dance's" first broadcast, but we do have a record of the program that was planned for the following Saturday night's show. Dwight Butcher, who served as master of ceremonies, introduced the following line-up on November 23, 1940:

> "Down Yonder"—Boudleaux Bryant, fiddler
> "Careless Love"—Harpo Kidwell, harmonica
> "Back in the Old Sunday School"—Judy Dell
> "Darktown Strutter's Ball"—Warren Sykes on spoons
> "Where the Old Red River Flows"—The Pine Ridge Boys
> "Black-Eyed Susie"—Whole Gang
> "When I'm Gone You'll Soon Forget Me"—Dwight Butcher
> "Sowing on the Mountain"—Coon Hunter's Quartet
> "The Old Folks at Home"—Glenn Hughes on the banjo
> "Talking Blues"—Hank Penny
> "Chicken Reel"—Red Murphy, tap dancer.[13]

Beginning on January 4, 1941, the "Barn Dance" broadcast from the stage of the Atlanta Woman's Club Auditorium at the corner of Peachtree Street and Fourteenth Street in order "to accommodate the hundreds of persons anxious to see and hear the show."[14] Further evidence of the popularity of the "Barn Dance" is the fact that during its tenure at the Woman's Club two stage shows were presented each Saturday evening, one at 7:30 and another at 9:30.

In celebration of the move to new quarters, two broadcasts

were scheduled from the stage on opening night, but on succeeding Saturdays only one segment of the show was broadcast, usually from 10:30 to 11:00 P.M. Tickets for each show cost forty cents for adults and twenty cents for children.

The "Barn Dance" was presented regularly at the Woman's Club Auditorium until May 23, 1942, when the show moved to the stage of the Erlanger Theater also located on Peachtree Street. Although the Woman's Club Auditorium and the Erlanger Theater housed the "Barn Dance" on a regular basis, the show, especially in the summertime, frequently originated from the stages of theaters and school auditoriums in other cities throughout Georgia and in neighboring states. Toward the end of the decade the "Barn Dance" was presented on, more or less, a regular basis from the College Park Auditorium, the Forest Park High School Auditorium, and the Hapeville City Auditorium. Among the sponsors of the "Barn Dance" broadcast over the years were the makers of Wildroot Cream-Oil hair tonic and the Mason Pecan Cocoanut Candy Company.

While the full complement of entertainers got together for the Saturday night "Barn Dance" and the short-lived Friday night "Hayride" show, personnel of the smaller performing units—the "Barnyard Jamboree," the "Cracker Barrel," and the "Little Country Church House"—generally performed separately during the week, filling show dates in different cities around the state. The shortage and rationing of gasoline and tires during the war years hampered the personal appearance activities of the artists. James (Carson) Roberts, who used his car to transport himself and his fellow entertainers to and from show dates, has estimated that they could have done twice the personal appearance work if tires and gasoline had been readily available.[15]

Like most Americans during the war, the "Barn Dance" cast found plenty of opportunities to engage in acts of patriotism and to further the cause of their country. They sold war bonds from the stage, entertained patients at the local veterans' hospital, performed for army personnel at nearby Fort McPherson, and helped relieve the labor shortage by assisting the state's farmers in gathering their crops. In October 1942, about twenty-five members of the "Barn Dance" troupe journeyed to Rome, where they spent a day picking cotton for a farmer there. The performers presented the mid-day "Georgia Jubilee" broadcast that day directly from the cotton field.

Over the years, a number of different people served as master of ceremonies on the "Barn Dance." Some of the performers, as well as members of WSB's announcing staff, filled this position at various times. As we have seen, Dwight Butcher was master of ceremonies on the second "Barn Dance" broadcast, and he probably announced the first broadcast as well. Others who performed this duty, at one time or another, were George Hughes; Dudley McCaskill; Chick Kimball; Bill Spencer; Jimmy Smith; Ivy Peterson, known to fans as Herman Horsehair Buggfuzz; and Cotton Carrier.

Joseph A. "Cotton" Carrier came to WSB from WPAD in Paducah, Kentucky, where he was a performer and emcee with a hillbilly group called Goober and His Kentuckians.[16] Cotton went to work at WSB on Monday, September 1, 1941, and emceed his first "Barn Dance" broadcast the following Saturday night from the stage of the Albany Theater in Albany, Georgia. His opening words were:

> Well, howdy everybody, *everywhere* from Portland, Maine to Portland, Oregon and from Canada to the Gulf of Mexico. Its WSB, the Voice of the South in Atlanta, Georgia, bringing you another thirty minutes of home folk entertainment done up in that good old country style. Yes Sirree, bobtail, its the WSB Barn Dance. And tonight we're broadcasting from the stage of the Albany Theatre *way down South* in Albany, Georgia. And to get things started here are the Hoot Owl Hollow Girls with a coupla spasms of "Lonesome Road Blues." [17]

Following the Hoot Owl Hollow Girls' number, steel guitarist Jimmie Colvard played "Steel Guitar Rag," Jimmy Carson sang "Precious Jewel," Chick Stripling played "Ida Red" on the fiddle, Harpo Kidwell played his harmonica and sang "How Many Biscuits Can You Eat," the entire cast sang and played "Take Me Back to Tulsa," Pete Cassell sang "Wabash Cannon Ball," comedienne Aunt Sarrie did a routine, and the Swanee River Boys sang "Rockin' On the Waves." Cotton closed the broadcast with these words: "Its about time for us to get off the wind now, but we've had a fine time at your house tonight, and we hope that you'll let us visit with you next Saturday night at the same time, 9:30 P.M., when we'll be broadcasting from the High School Auditorium in Covington, Georgia. The 'WSB Barn Dance' is a regular Saturday-night feature of WSB, the Voice of The South, Atlanta, Georgia." [18]

Born into a musical family on a farm near Arthur, Kentucky, Cotton learned to play guitar, mandolin, and fiddle at an early age, and by the time he was sixteen had decided to become a professional musician. Before joining Goober and His Kentuckians in 1940, Cotton had organized a band that played for square dances in the state of Washington where he lived for a while.

In June 1942, less than a year after coming to WSB, Cotton was drafted into the army and subsequently served in Europe and the Philippines. Upon the completion of his military service, which included a battlefield commission in Germany, Cotton returned to WSB in March 1946 and remained with the "Barn Dance" until its demise in 1950.

In addition to his emcee duties, Cotton, as a member of the "WSB Barn Dance" cast, also played fiddle and sang, both the popular hits of the day and his own compositions. One of his original songs, "Why Should I Worry Now," was especially popular with his radio audience.

From 1940 until around 1948, according to Cotton, country music performers at WSB had been paid a salary by the station. Beginning in 1948, he explained, "They quit hiring us on salary and allowed a few of us leaders of the groups to form our own bands. We could form a band, hire our own musicians, and pay them any way we wanted to. We would have certain time [slots] on WSB that were sponsored. The sponsors paid us. That's when I formed my band, the Plantation Gang." In addition to Cotton, the original members of the Plantation Gang were Dink Embry, bass; Dean Bence, mandolin; Chuck Franklin, electric steel; and Lee Roy Blanchard, fiddle. Others who, at one time or another, were members of the Plantation Gang included Arlie Wade, bass; Willis Hogsed, five-string banjo; and Calvin Bragg, steel guitar and fiddle. When Bragg played fiddle rather than steel guitar, the Plantation Gang had the typical instrumental composition of a bluegrass band, and, Cotton recalled later, the group's "styling was slanted a little toward bluegrass. The reason I formed that type of band [was] I'd been around Georgia long enough, and been around hillbilly music in Kentucky and wherever to feel that [with that type of band] I could please people, draw crowds, and earn a living. I didn't really think of myself as forming a bluegrass band at that time, but that's what we had." One of the sponsors of the Plantation Gang's radio programs was Tube Rose snuff.

In 1947 Cotton Carrier became WSB's first country-music disc jockey, hosting early morning and late Saturday-night record shows. In 1957, following a stint on local TV, Cotton took a job as record promoter with the Lowery Music Company, an Atlanta music-publishing firm with which he was still employed in 1988.

The "WSB Barn Dance" featured a wide variety of musical styles and vocal and instrumental combinations while staying within the bounds of the hillbilly genre. In format, the "Barn Dance" was much like the "Grand Ole Opry." Listeners to the show heard fiddlers, harmonica players, accordion players, steel guitarists, banjoists, and male and female vocalists—soloists, duets, trios, and quartets. The "Barn Dance," with its life span encompassing that of World War II, provided a laboratory for innovative utilization of country music talent as the program's management sought to cope with the manpower shortage. With so many men off at war, female performers probably had a greater opportunity to become feature attractions. They were well represented on the show during its lifetime. For the same reason, some male musicians who otherwise might have been doomed to the role of "member of the band" may also have had a better shot at becoming a solo vocalist or instrumentalist.

Among the fiddlers heard on the "Barn Dance" were Cotton Carrier, Chick Stripling, Bertha Amburgey, Viola Turner, Shorty Steed, Blackie Hastings, Mattie O'Neal (Opal Amburgey), Boudleaux Bryant, and Bobby Atcheson.

The fiddling of Bobby Atcheson was a familiar sound to "WSB Barn Dance" listeners from 1944 to 1946.[19] He had previously performed on WSB and other Atlanta radio stations with such groups as Bill Gatins's Jug Band, the Hoosier Playboys, Pappy Slats's Kentucky Mountaineers, Pop Eckler's Young'uns, Lost John Miller and the Kentuckians, Uncle Billy Woods's Arkansas Travelers, and a band headed by Pete Cassell. In addition, he and his wife, Jane, had performed in 1942 as a singing duet on their own program on WATL. On the "Barn Dance" Bobby played such fiddle breakdowns as "Devil's Dream," "Fire on the Mountain," and "Back Up and Push."

After leaving the "Barn Dance" Bobby continued to perform with hillbilly bands in Atlanta, Kentucky, Tennessee, and Florida. For several years during the 1950s he was a member of the Peachtree Cowboys, a group that gained wide popularity through their appearances on WSB-TV and at the Covered Wagon, an Atlanta country-music night spot owned by Bobby, his brother Mac, and friend and fellow Peachtree Cowboy Ivy (Herman Horsehair Buggfuzz) Peterson.

Bobby, who was born on April 1, 1920, at Dallas, Georgia, was not only a talented musician, but a practitioner of the visual arts as well. He specialized in still lifes and landscapes and was equally proficient with pencil, watercolors, and oils. His artistic abilities enabled him in 1962 to accept a position in the art department at WSB-TV. This was the last job he held before his death in 1978 from complications arising from a congenital heart defect.

Although Boudleaux Bryant, another "Barn Dance" fiddler, began his country music career as an instrumentalist, it was for writing songs that he became best known.[20] A native of Shellman, Georgia (born February 13, 1920), Boudleaux, whose father gave him the name of a Frenchman who saved the elder Bryant's life during World War I, was trained from the age of six to be a classical violinist. At the same time he absorbed the ryhthms and melodies of old-time fiddling, gospel singing, and hillbilly music that abounded in the rural Georgia area in which he grew up.

In further pursuit of a career in classical music Boudleaux went to Atlanta after finishing high school. In 1938, a chance meeting with Uncle Ned led to Boudleaux's becoming a member of the Texas Wranglers band and a job on the "Cross Roads Follies." After a few months with the Wranglers he joined the Radio Cowboys under the leadership of Hank Penny, who had just brought the group to WSB. Boudleaux's tour with Penny took him to jobs at radio stations in Birmingham, Alabama; Chattanooga, Tennessee; and Greenville, South Carolina, before the group returned to Atlanta to perform again on the "Barn Dance."

After leaving the "Barn Dance" in the early 1940s, Boudleaux performed with mostly jazz and pop bands working nightclubs around the country, including jobs in such cities as Washington,

D.C., Detroit, Chicago, Memphis, and Milwaukee. It was while in Milwaukee that he met his future wife, singer Felice Scaduto.

In 1950 the Bryants moved to Nashville where they opened a music-publishing company called House of Bryant. From this firm and the pens of the Bryants came some of country music's biggest hits, including "Country Boy," recorded by Little Jimmy Dickens; "Hey Joe," a top-ten hit for Carl Smith in 1953; "Bye Bye Love," recorded by Webb Pierce; and the all-time bluegrass favorite, "Rocky Top," recorded by the Osborne Brothers in 1967. The Bryants were still turning out hits at the time of Boudleaux's death in 1987.

The harmonica has always had a place in country music, from Henry Whitter's 1923 recording of "Wreck of the Old 97" to "Hee Haw's" Charlie McCoy. This instrument was featured regularly on the "Barn Dance." Warren Sykes played a harmonica on the first broadcast, and mouth organists Eddie Smith, Buck Glosson, and Lonnie Glosson were heard on some of the last "Barn Dance" shows.

The dean of the "Barn Dance" harmonica players, however, was Harpo Kidwell, whose extended association with WSB made him perhaps the best known performer on that instrument in the Atlanta area.[21] Another of the many Kentuckians who brought their brand of hillbilly music to Atlanta, Harpo, as we have seen, made his initial WSB appearance on the "Cross Roads Follies" as a member of Glenn Hughes's Roundup Gang. Prior to that he had performed on radio stations in Dayton, Columbus, and Cincinnati, Ohio. Except for two brief interludes, Harpo was with WSB for more than twelve years. In addition to playing breakdowns, waltzes, and other types of tunes on his harmonica, Harpo also sang such songs as "How Many Biscuits Can You Eat," "Just Because," and "Boo-Hoo Blues," a song he wrote. Two of his most requested harmonica tunes were "The Fox Chase" and another of his own compositions that he called "Harpo's Waltz."

It was at the WSB studios that Harpo met his future wife, Clestelle "Tink" Jones. A native of the nearby Atlanta suburb of Smyrna, Miss Jones, like many country music fans at the time, would sometimes visit WSB to watch the broadcasts. "Somebody made me acquainted with her," Harpo later recalled, "and we started dating and then got married."

After the "Barn Dance" folded, Harpo Kidwell stayed at the

station for approximately another year to front his own band on a program at one time sponsored by Tube Rose snuff. In the early 1950s he moved back to Cincinnati to take a job on the "Midwestern Hayride" and other programs heard simultaneously on WLW radio and TV. When Harpo retired from the music business he returned to the Atlanta area to make his permanent home. There, as of 1988, he could still be prevailed upon to play the harmonica for special occasions.

Accordions were not as common among hillbilly performers in the South as they were in other parts of the country. Early on, however, the "Barn Dance" featured a performer on that instrument named Kid Clark. He was succeeded by Jane Logan. Other accordion players on the show included Dottie Castleberry and Lang Howe.

Jane Logan was the stage name of Mrs. Cotton Carrier, who accompanied her husband to Atlanta in September 1941.[22] She and Cotton met when he joined Goober and the Kentuckians, a band with which Jane was already performing. A native of Simpson County, Kentucky, Jane early in life learned to play an accordion she ordered from Sears, Roebuck. Her first professional experience was with a WLS (Chicago) road show that played dates in the Midwest. She later joined Goober and the Kentuckians with whom she played on WDZ in Tuscola, Illinois, and WDOD in Chattanooga, Tennessee. When Goober's group disbanded in Chattanooga, Jane joined an act called the Radio Rangers headed by Roy Cross. Her job with Cross also included comedy routines. When a man named Ken Hackley brought an all-girl troupe called the Hollywood Cowgirls through Chattanooga, Jane joined the act and traveled the Tennessee-Kentucky-Virginia circuit with them, putting on stage shows in movie theaters. She later rejoined Goober, who had organized a new Kentuckians band that was playing on WIBC in Indianapolis, Indiana. From there she went with them to WHOP in Hopkinsville, Kentucky, where they were performing when Cotton joined the group.

When the Carriers went to Atlanta Jane took a job at WGST where she was a member of an all-girl band headed by Aunt Hattie, who previously had been at WSB. Chick Kimball, head man at the "Barn Dance" at the time, did not approve of Jane's working with the competition and offered her a job. Consequently Jane moved over to WSB and joined her husband on the "Barn Dance" and other country music programs on the station. After Cotton was drafted, Jane stayed with the "Barn Dance" until she was able to join him at his permanent assignment. Jane was remembered by "Barn Dance" listeners for her spirited accordion renditions of tunes such as "Under the Double Eagle," "The Washington and Lee Swing," and "Golden Slippers." When Cotton was discharged from the service Jane, rather than returning to her career as an entertainer, elected to stay home and look after their son and two daughters. When the children were older she went back to work as a market researcher. In 1976 she took a job at the Northside Shepherd's Senior Citizens Center sponsored by Atlanta's Tenth Street United Methodist Church where she remained for more than ten years. Drawing on her show business experience Jane organized a senior citizens washboard band that soon found itself in considerable demand to provide entertainment at nursing homes, church socials, civic meetings, fairs, and festivals.

The unique sound of the steel guitar, an instrument inspired by the Hawaiian music that reached a peak of popularity in this country around the time of World War I, had, by 1940, become familiar to hillbilly-music enthusiasts.[23] By then electrified and made popular by such virtuosos as Leon McAuliffe, who played the instrument in Bob Wills's Texas Playboys band, the steel guitar seems always to have been featured on the "Barn Dance." Among the many steel guitarists who played on the show were Eddie Ross, Billy Strickland, Jesse Carpenter, Little George Tanner, Jimmy Colvard, Dewey Aderhold, and Boots Woodall.

Dennis "Boots" Woodall, born October 9, 1921, in Paulding County, Georgia, grew up in Buckhead, a community located in what was then considered the northern outskirts of Atlanta.[24] He learned to play straight guitar when he was about ten or eleven years old, but later switched, first to the Hawaiian, and then to the steel guitar. Boots made his first radio appearance as a teenager on "Uncle Harry's Variety Show" heard on WAGA. This was followed in 1939 by a job in Bill Gatins's Jug Band which was then playing on WATL. His next move was to WSB and a job on the "Cross Roads Follies," where he became a member of Uncle Ned's Texas Wranglers. When the "Cross Roads Follies" folded, Boots went to Macon with Uncle Ned to do radio work there. After a few months in Macon, Boots and the Lunsford brothers, Lee and Paul, went north where they worked in a WLS road show out of Chicago and on radio station KMMJ in Grand Island, Nebraska. While in Nebraska, Boots was offered a job on the "WSB Barn Dance," and in November 1941 his name began appearing on "Barn Dance" rosters published in the *Journal*. Woodall's interpretations of such popular tunes as "Blue Steel Blues," "Steel Guitar Rag," and "Hilo March" provided a touch of instrumental variety to "Barn Dance" programs.

Boots's music career was interrupted in 1942 when he joined the U.S. Air Force. Upon his discharge in 1945 he returned to the "Barn Dance" for a short while before organizing his own band, the Radio Wranglers, the original members of which were Woodall, steel guitar; Bobby Atcheson, fiddle; Bob Stoddard, piano; Marvin Taylor, guitar; Lee Lunsford, bass; and Doug Chandler, fiddle. The Radio Wranglers were heard on WGST from which, for a while during 1949 and 1950, their program was fed to the Mutual Broadcasting System chain of radio stations. These network shows were also transcribed for the United States Armed Forces Radio Service. Released under the program name "Georgia Jamboree," these transcribed shows featured other artists including "June Bug" Thomas; Ruel Parker; Betty and Christine, the Logan Sisters; Fairley Holden; Jack Jackson; Calvin Bragg; Cowboy Jack (Talton); Eddie Smith; Buck Glosson; Paul and Lee Lunsford; Harold Dunn; the Le Fevre Trio; and Johnny Atkinson.

The "Georgia Jamboree" radio shows were written and produced for the Mutual Broadcasting System by Don Naylor, a longtime announcer, writer, and producer at WGST. The announcers on the programs were Howard Turner and Ken Wilson. The introduction to the February 27, 1950, broadcast was typical. "From Atlanta, G.A., the Mutual Broadcasting System presents the Georgia Jamboree," were Ken Wilson's opening words. Following a few bars of the show's theme music, Wilson continued:

> Well, howdy! Whatcha doin'? Anything important? Then, how's about settin' a spell and takin' in th' Georgia Jamboree, a Monday through Friday presentation on th' coast-to-coast network of th' Mutual Broadcasting system, from Atlanta, Georgia. And for annoyment—I mean enjoyment today—we have th' pickin' and singin' of a whole passel of folks. Welcome

back to th' famous LeFevre Trio and Johnnie Atkinson, who've been entertainin' thousands of folks up in North Carolina th' past 10 days. Boots Woodall and his Radio Wranglers are here, too—Paul Rice and Marvin Taylor, and Ruel Parker's Rhythm Ranchers, Junebug Thomas, Chuck Miller, and th' Atcheson boys, Bobby and Mac. Yessir, and here's Tommy Trent and th' Dixie Fun Barn Gang. Dixie Lee is here, too, and so is ol' lover-boy, Andy Thomas, and accordeen squeezer Lang Howe, so how's about settin' a spell like we said and takin' in th' Georgia Jamboree![25]

After listening to tapes of the Armed Forces Radio versions of the "Georgia Jamboree" programs, Don Naylor stated that "all of the music was a direct lift from our shows. But what they had done was put their own announcer on it because our announcer's words were too local for overseas use."[26]

In 1947 Boots and his band recorded for the King label in Cincinnati, both as a backup band for other artists and as a featured band. Four songs that he recorded on the King label were "Do You Ever Worry," "I Wonder," "Rattle Snakin' Daddy," and "Since You've Been gone." Boots also wrote some songs during his career, including "If I Could Send You Roses" and "Dog House Boogie," the latter, he said, recorded by Hawkshaw Hawkins.

Around 1950 the Radio Wranglers changed their name to the TV-Wranglers, landed a job on WAGA-TV's channel 5, and became one of the station's major attractions. In addition to their TV show, the Wranglers, as we have seen, provided entertainment and dance music at the Atlanta Sports Arena. In 1963 Boots retired from the music business to pursue a career in real estate. He died on January 27, 1988, in Atlanta, where he had continued to make his home after retiring from the music business.

By the 1940s the five-string banjo had become almost extinct among hillbilly entertainers. Popular in the 1920s as a complement to the fiddle and guitar, the role of the banjo seems later to have been supplanted by the steel guitar, the mandolin, and other instruments. Before becoming the essential instrument of bluegrass bands, the five-string banjo was looked upon primarily as a novelty instrument to be played, usually in the frailing style, by comic performers such as "Grand Ole Opry" stars Uncle Dave Macon, Bashful Brother Oswald, and Grandpa Jones. Of the few featured banjoists on the

"Barn Dance," one, Louis Dumont, was a tenor banjo player, and two, Mattie O'Neal and Cousin Emmy, were women.

As we have seen, Cousin Emmy was a member of the "Cross Roads Follies" cast in 1939. Before then this native Kentuckian, who played fifteen musical instruments, had worked at several radio stations around the country, including WHB, Kansas City; WHAS, Louisville, Kentucky; and WWVA, Wheeling, West Virginia. One of her fellow performers in Wheeling was Grandpa Jones who, at that time, played guitar when he sang. He was so impressed by Cousin Emmy's banjo picking that he persuaded her to teach him to play the instrument that has since become his trademark.[27]

After leaving the "Cross Roads Follies," Cousin Emmy was again heard on WHAS in Louisville and on WNOX in Knoxville, Tennessee. In 1941 she took her act to St. Louis, where she reached the peak of her career on the powerful KMOX. While there she was written up in *Time* magazine[28] and analyzed by a university folklorist.[29]

It was in the fall of 1945 that Cousin Emmy paid a return visit to Atlanta to become, for several months, a regular on the "Barn Dance." The songs that Cousin Emmy sang and played on the program were typical of her repertoire and included "John Henry," "Rabbit Soup," "Ain't It Hard to Love," "Ground Hog," "Foggy Mountain Top," "Milk Cow Blues," "Ruby," "Free Little Bird," "Lonesome Road Blues," and "I Wish I Was Single Again."

From Atlanta Cousin Emmy returned to KMOX where she worked for another season. Sometime later she moved to the West Coast where, in 1961, she was "discovered" by the New Lost City Ramblers, a folk music group then consisting of Mike Seeger, John Cohen, and Tom Paley. When she met Seeger's group Emmy was performing at Disneyland, where she was one of several West Coast country music acts presenting a program for the amusement park's Country and Western Night attraction. Under the guidance of the New Lost City Ramblers, she enjoyed something of a comeback, performing at the Newport Folk Festival, appearing with folk singer Pete Seeger on television, and touring Europe.

Although Cousin Emmy made her name primarily through radio appearances, she did achieve some measure of success with records and movies. In 1947, under the direction of folklorist Alan Lomax, she recorded for Decca an album of 78s called *Kentucky*

Mountain Ballads. Her biggest hit, however, recorded at about the same time, was "Ruby," a Decca 78 RPM single (backed by "The Broken Hearted One You Left Alone"). Through the efforts of John Cohen, Mike Seeger, Peter Bartok, and Tracy Schwarz, Folkways Records, in 1968, released a long-play album by Cousin Emmy called *The New Lost City Ramblers with Cousin Emmy*. Cousin Emmy's movie credits include roles in *Swing in the Saddle* (Columbia Pictures, 1944) and *The Second Greatest Sex* (Universal Pictures, 1955). Cousin Emmy died on April 11, 1980, at Sherman Oaks, California.

A native Georgian named Mac Atcheson was in Cousin Emmy's entourage when she returned to Atlanta in 1945. He had joined her band earlier in St. Louis and performed with her in Louisville before coming to Atlanta.[30]

The younger brother of fiddler Bobby Atcheson, Mac began his music career at the age of twelve as a mandolin player in a band that also included Bobby and another brother, Guy. They commuted from their home in Roswell, just north of Atlanta, to make Saturday appearances on radio station WGAU in Athens. Mac also played in Pete Cassell's band at WDOD in Chattanooga, Tennessee, before joining Cousin Emmy's troupe.

Although he later became one of Atlanta's best-known steel guitar players, Mac, during the early part of his career, sang and played the straight guitar and bass, chores that he performed as a member of Cousin Emmy's band. Mac later remembered that Cousin Emmy could draw a crowd. "When she'd do a show she'd pack the house twice every night, practically, at these little school houses. She was a showman that wouldn't wait. She played banjo and sang 'Ruby' and all these songs like that. Then she'd play fiddle. She always drove a new Cadillac," he added.

Mac would also never forget the traveling by automobile that came with the job of being a country music radio entertainer in the 1940s. "You rode all the time," he once lamented. "The roads seemed about four feet wide in places. A good many of them were dirt."

There were no air conditioned busses and equipment trucks for the comfort and convenience of these pioneer country-music artists. "We loaded in one car, usually five to six people in a unit," Mac Atcheson reminisced as he talked about his life as an entertainer. "We'd put all the instruments in the trunk, the bass fiddle on the top, and everybody would get in the car and drive one car to a show date."

Every survivor of those days on the road has a memorable experience to recount, and Mac Atcheson was no exception. "Mattie O'Neal [Opal Amburgey] liked to have wrecked us one night," Mac related. "We were coming back from a show date and Mattie was [sitting in the front seat] in the middle, and something happened to the ball joints of the car and it started shaking. It scared Mattie and she woke up and slammed her foot against the gas pedal," sending the car forward at a rapid rate. The fact that they were on one of those little-traveled rural roads may have kept them from having a serious accident.

When Cousin Emmy left Atlanta to go north, Mac went south to Florida and a job at WHOO in Orlando. It was here that he started playing the steel guitar. After a couple of years in Florida Mac returned to Atlanta where he helped operate the Covered Wagon restaurant and performed on television with the Peachtree Cowboys. Like his brother Bobby, Mac was artistically inclined, and in 1951 he went to work in the art department at WSB-TV, where he was still employed in the 1980s. He ended his music career around 1960.

As on other hillbilly radio shows around the country in the 1940s, male vocalists abounded on the "Barn Dance." Male soloists on the show included Dwight Butcher, Hank Penny, James (Carson) Roberts, Mac Wiseman, Fairley Holden, Cotton Carrier, Pete Cassell, Louis Innis, Harold Dunn, Jimmy Smith, and Little Joe Isbell.

Dwight Butcher was born in Oakdale, Tennessee, on August 6, 1911.[31] He learned to play the guitar at an early age, and while still in his teens did medicine-show work and performed on WNOX in Knoxville. Around 1932, in quest of a career as a recording artist, he went to New York City, where he met with some success. By the time he left New York in the mid-1930s, he had recorded for the Crown, Victor, and Decca labels (under his own name as well as the pseudonyms Slim Oakdale, Slim Butcher, Hank Hall, Slim Tex, Tex Slim, and Joe Smith). While in New York he also had some fifteen of his original songs published by Southern Music Company; had several of his songs (notably "Old Love Letters") recorded by Jimmie Rodgers; and performed as a member of Ray Whitley's band, the Range Ramblers, on radio station WMCA.

Through Victor executive Ralph Peer, Dwight met Jimmie Rodgers, and at one time was considered a likely replacement for the blue yodeler in the even more likely event of the latter's untimely death. When Rodgers did pass away on May 26, 1933, Dwight, with Lou Herscher, quickly composed the song "When Jimmie Rodgers Said Goodby," which was recorded by Gene Autry.

From New York, Dwight went to Philadelphia to begin a career in radio that took him to Des Moines, Iowa; Kansas; Cincinnati; and eventually to Atlanta. In Cincinnati, and later in Renfro Valley, Kentucky, he worked for John Lair, who was responsible for his "WSB Barn Dance" assignment.

Butcher was remembered by "Barn Dance" listeners for such songs as "When I'm Gone You'll Soon Forget Me," "Shy Little Ann from Cheyenne," and "Molly Darling."

After about a year on the "Barn Dance," Dwight moved over to WAGA where for a while he had his own group that included Riley Puckett. In the early 1940s he went to WBAP in Fort Worth, Texas, later moving to Southern California where he acted in stage plays before retiring from show business. Dwight died on November 11, 1978.[32]

Prior to his coming to Atlanta in 1939 to work on the "Cross Roads Follies," Hank Penny had appeared on radio station WAPI, Birmingham, Alabama; WWL, New Orleans; and WDOD, in Chattanooga, Tennessee.[33] Herbert Clayton "Hank" Penny, who was born on September 18, 1918, near Birmingham, Alabama, began, at the age of fifteen, an entertainment career that would eventually include singing, guitar playing, comedy, radio announcing, disc jockey work, nightclub ownership, and leading a western-swing band. He would entertain audiences through radio and television broadcasts, on phonograph records, on movie screens, and from every kind of stage that ever was home to a hillbilly performer.

While a member of the "WSB Barn Dance" cast Penny sang, played guitar, did comedy, and part of the time served as emcee of the show. He was the headliner on the "Cracker Barrel" program heard daily on WSB during the mid-morning time slot.

At WSB, Hank once explained, "Me and the Radio Cowboys were trying to do something similar to Bob Wills. We were the only ones in the Southeast that were doing this. Hoke and Paul [Rice] had kind of an idea, but they didn't have the idea as well as we had it. They sounded like they were New York oriented, and they didn't swing free like me and the Cowboys did. We were different because most of the others were playing strictly hillbilly music, and I, for one, never liked hillbilly music, per se. I liked good country music. When we did a hillbilly song, we would make it swing."

Hank's "Barn Dance" repertoire was rather eclectic, covering such musical ground as "Standin' Neath the Old Pine Tree," "Sweet-Talking Mama," "Worried Mind," "I Love Molasses," "El Rancho Grande," "Riding Down the Canyon," "You're My Darling," "I'm Walking the Floor Over You," and "The Talking Blues." Hank has several original songs to his credit, a good number of which he recorded. While at WSB he wrote a song called "The Army Blues" that was popular with listeners who were concerned with the war that was in progress at the time. As a tribute to his onetime home state, Hank penned a song titled "Tell Me All About Georgia" that he recorded on the King (Dee Jay Special) label.

Although Hank appears to have done well financially later in his career, he would be the first to admit that he saw some lean times when he first went to Atlanta to work. "I remember playing one date where we slept in the automobile," he once said. "We went to play a date in south Georgia. Nobody showed. Aw, there were five or six people. We did three or four numbers and gave them their price of admission and took off. Well there we are [in] south Georgia and not a dime. We slept in the automobile all night. Just slid down in the seat and went to sleep. When I woke up in the morning all the doors of the automobile were open, and I was freezing. You know how those Georgia [spring] mornings can be. I looked and there were all the guys down to the side of the road picking blackberries. At first I didn't understand it. It didn't take me long to put it together. Friend, that was breakfast. So we helped ourselves to a good amount of blackberries, and then I took off and went into town and found the theater manager. We were going to play a theater in the town that day, and I got an advance from him. Then we bought some food. I'll never forget that."

When Hank left Atlanta around 1943, he joined the "Boone County Jamboree" at WLW in Cincinnati. From there, in the mid-

1940s, he moved to the Los Angeles area where he spent most of the remainder of his career. On the West Coast Hank established himself as one of the area's foremost purveyors of western swing.

The highlights of the West Coast phase of Hank's career included some highly successful nightclub work, a spot as comedian on Spade Cooley's TV show, and his own television program called "The Hank Penny Show."

From 1938 to 1980, Hank recorded extensively for several labels including Conqueror, Vocalion, OKeh, Columbia, King, Victor, and Decca. Among his most popular records were "Get Yourself a Redhead," "Bloodshot Eyes," and "Missouri." In the 1980s Hank was still living and performing on the West Coast.

The history of country music in Atlanta has been influenced by three blind men, the Rev. Andrew Jenkins, Riley Puckett, and Pete Cassell. As we have seen, Pete Cassell was first heard on WSB in the 1930s as a member of the "Cross Roads Follies" cast. It was in the 1940s, however, that he reached the peak of his popularity with Atlanta audiences. Born on August 27, 1917, in Cobb County, Georgia, Pete Webster Cassell, like Riley Puckett, was blinded as an infant through the misapplication of medicine to his eyes.[34] He grew up in Atlanta where, until the age of twelve, he attended the public schools as a member of a special class for blind pupils. He later attended the Georgia Academy for the Blind at Macon, lacking one year of graduating from high school. With a grandfather on his mother's side who was a Baptist preacher, and a mother who taught Sunday school, Pete was exposed to religious influences during his formative years. According to Pete's mother he had absolute pitch, and early in life displayed an above-average talent and interest in music. Hillbilly and religious songs were his favorites, and before embarking on his professional career, he frequently sang in church. Although he accompanied himself on guitar when he sang on stage and radio, the first instrument he learned to play (before he was twelve years old) was the piano. He had some training in music while attending the school for the blind.

During the 1940s Pete was in and out of Atlanta several times, performing on both WSB and WAGA, between trips around the country to work on other radio stations. At one time or another during his career he was heard on WDOD, Chattanooga; WWVA,

Wheeling, West Virginia; WEEV, Reading, Pennsylvania; WROM, Rome, Georgia; WARL and WFAM, Arlington, Virginia, and on stations in Milwaukee, Wisconsin, and Springfield, Missouri.[35]

Pete's most popular songs among Atlanta audiences included "Freight Train Blues," "Where the Old Red River Flows," and the sacred song "One Step More."

In 1941 Pete lent his songwriting talents to the composition of a theme song for the "WSB Barn Dance." For a time afterwards, listeners to the show were greeted with the cast's rendition of

> Howdy Friends and neighbors
> Both near and far away,
> The WSB Barn Dance
> Will drive your cares away.
>
> We always wear a great big smile
> And never shed a tear.
> We try to spread some sunshine
> With songs you like to hear.
>
> So, won't you come and join us
> And spend a little while;
> We'll try to make you happy
> In good old country style.
>
> So, come on to the Southland
> Way down here in Dixie
> For you're always welcome
> To the WSB Barn Dance party.[36]

As a recording artist for the Decca and Majestic labels, Pete's recorded output includes "St. Louis Blues," "I know What It Means to Be Lonesome," "Why Don't You Come Back to Me," "One Step More," and "I Can't Feel at Home in this World Any More."

Pete married Ruth Hamlin in 1941. They had a son and a daughter. Pete died in Key West, Florida, on July 29, 1954, at the age of thirty-seven.

Female vocalists played a prominent role in establishing and maintaining the popularity of the "WSB Barn Dance." As we have seen, the premiere broadcast of the show had a female vocalist as special guest. She paved the way for other "Barn Dance" female solo vocalists such as Mattie O'Neal (Opal Amburgey), who specialized in Jimmie Rodgers's blue yodels and other blues and yodel numbers; Willie Mae Thomas (known to listeners as Ne-Hi because her short stature necessitated her standing on a box to reach the microphone), who sang western songs; and Dottie Castleberry, whose specialty was singing the popular love songs of the day. Other female soloists who sang on the "Barn Dance" were Mildred Fredericks, Millie Jackson, Evelyn Head, Ruby Katherine "Kitty" Wells (not the Kitty Wells of the "Grand Ole Opry"), Jenny Rogers, Elizabeth (Connie) Coleman, Nell Coleman, and one known only as Linda Lou.

While the pop music of the day had the Andrews, the De Marco, and the King sisters, the "Barn Dance," too, had its sister acts. There were Joyce and Juanita Oxner; Ruth and Ruby Helgerson; Betty and Christine Buice, known as the Logan Sisters; Judie and Julie, who came to WSB from West Virginia; Betty and Ann Hefner from Missouri; and Mary and Margie Humes from Illinois, who were billed as the Prairie Song Birds.

The first sister act to perform on the "Barn Dance" was a trio, consisting of the Amburgey sisters, Bertha, Irene, and Opal. They made their initial "Barn Dance" appearance on Saturday night, December 7, 1940, as Minnie (Bertha), Mattie (Opal), and Martha (Irene), the Hoot Owl Hollow Girls. On the 10:30 broadcast over WSB that night they sang "Single Girl, Single Girl." In the trio Minnie played fiddle and sang tenor, Mattie played five-string banjo and sang lead, and Martha was the guitarist and alto singer.

The Amburgey sisters were born and reared in southeastern Kentucky near the town of Jenkins, daughters of a man who made his living as a farmer and coal miner.[37] Their mother played piano and organ, their father played five-string banjo, and both were singers. The girls were exposed to music early in life by attending singing conventions and by listening to records and the radio. Bertha, Irene, and Opal soon became accomplished singers and instrumentalists.

Bertha got her first fiddle when she was sixteen years old. When she saw it in a store window with an eight-dollar price tag attached she reduced the family chicken yard by eight fat hens which she sold for a dollar each to buy the coveted instrument. One month later she won a fiddling contest at nearby Pound, Virginia. Irene and Opal had already acquired their instruments. Their father used the money from the sale of some of his tools to buy Opal a banjo, and Irene sold a calf to get the money to buy her guitar.

According to Bertha, it was around 1938 when the girls took a job at WHIS in Bluefield, West Virginia, where they performed for about two years as the Sunshine Sisters. When John Lair heard the Amburgeys on the Bluefield station he invited them to Renfro Valley, Kentucky, where they performed on the "Renfro Valley Barn Dance" as members of the Coon Creek Girls, an all-girl band headed by Lily May Ledford. When Lair became involved in developing the "WSB Barn Dance" the Amburgey sisters formed one of the acts he brought to Atlanta, and it was there that they became the Hoot Owl Hollow Girls. The songs the girls chose to sing on the "Barn Dance" covered a wide range of genres that had an appeal to lovers of country-oriented music. They sang traditional songs like "My Horses Aint Hungry" and "Free Little Bird"; novelty songs such as "Watermelon Smiling on the Vine" and "Old Dan Tucker"; spirituals like "Swing Low, Sweet Chariot"; gospel songs, including "Turn Your Radio On"; and hillbilly fare of then recent vintage such as "Fire Ball Mail" and the topical "I'll Be Back in a Year, Little Darling."

In 1941 Bertha (Minnie) married Charles "Ducky" Woodruff, who with his brother, Curly, was working at WAGA as the Woodruff Brothers. Bertha and the Woodruff brothers left Atlanta in 1942 for Cincinnati, Ohio, where Ducky and Curley took jobs unrelated to music. Bertha continued to perform, working at radio station WKRC in Cincinnati. Opal (Mattie), who married Salty Holmes, onetime member of the Prairie Ramblers, also later went to Cincinnati to work with Bertha on WKRC. Opal later returned to the "Barn Dance" as Mattie O'Neal, a featured vocalist and fiddler. She and Salty also performed together in a partnership that included recording on the King label, television appearances, and a short stint on Atlanta's WAGA in 1949. Opal later moved to Nashville where, using the name Jean Chappel, she became known as a writer of country songs.

In the late 1940s or early 1950s the Amburgey sisters recorded for King as Mattie, Martha, and Minnie. Among the songs they waxed was "You Can't Live with 'Em (And You Can't Live without 'Em)," which was written by Bertha.

Irene (Martha) remained in Atlanta through the 1940s. After Bertha (Minnie) and Opal (Mattie) left, their places in the Hoot

Owl Hollow Girls act were filled by various female singers who happened to be on the "Barn Dance" at the time, including Jane Logan and Nell Coleman.

Brother duets were fashionable in the world of hillbilly music during the 1930s and 1940s. The Delmore Brothers, the Bolick Brothers (the Blue Sky Boys), the Bailes Brothers, the Monroe Brothers, and the Shelton Brothers were among the many such acts that achieved widespread popularity through their phonograph records and radio broadcasts. Although they weren't brothers, the Pine Ridge Boys, consisting of Marvin Taylor and Doug Spivey, were a male duet whose style, sound, and repertoire gave the "Barn Dance" the additional variety that a brother act would have provided. Brought to the "Barn Dance" stage by John Lair, who no doubt realized the potential drawing power of an act of the brother duet type, the Pine Ridge Boys were present for the show's first broadcast. For them it was a homecoming, since, as we have seen, they earlier had been members of the "Cross Roads Follies" cast. After having left that program, Marvin and Doug had been hired by Lair to work on his various Renfro Valley, Kentucky, radio programs that included the Saturday night "Renfro Valley Barn Dance," an early morning show, and the "Renfro Valley Folks" program heard on NBC.

To further showcase the talents of the Pine Ridge Boys at WSB, Lair initiated the "Little Country Church House" program that was allotted a fifteen-minute mid-morning slot on the station's daily schedule. The show, which featured old-time hymns sung by Marvin and Doug to the accompaniment of their two guitars, was hosted by Dwight Butcher. The program became immediately popular with listeners, and within two months *Journal* columnist Ernest Rogers was able to report that hundreds of people were writing to the Pine Ridge Boys each week requesting their favorite songs.[38]

"John Lair was a very smart man," Doug noted while discussing the "Little Country Church House" program. "He would walk downtown and stand on the streets and listen to the different people talk. He always listened out for what he thought would appeal to the people. At that particular time the world was coming close to World War II and people were becoming more religious-minded than they had been before, so he decided that this would be a good time to start the 'Little Country Church [House]' program with Dwight Butcher as the emcee. His speaking voice was real good for radio work."

When the Pine Ridge Boys learned that they were to have a program of religious music, they had to get busy and quickly learn some material for the show. "Boudleaux Bryant," Doug later noted, "was responsible for that because [he] read music. He used to teach us the songs and the tunes of the songs. We'd try this one and try that one. He would go over [them] with the violin, and we would listen, and the ones that appealed to us the most were the ones that we would pick. We got [the songs] out of the hymnbooks out of the churches."

In the spring of 1941 the Pine Ridge Boys moved from WSB to WAGA, where they had a regular program with Dwight Butcher. Before World War II finally dissolved the partnership permanently, they worked at WGST and in Chicago, where they performed in nightclubs and on road shows booked out of that city.

During the war Doug was a ship fitter and steelworker, a field of employment in which he was engaged for many years. After getting out of the music business he entered the Church of God ministry, and for several years served the denomination as an evangelist and pastor of a number of churches in Georgia, before retiring from that calling. He died on January 13, 1987.

Following the Chicago stint Marvin worked with Jack Gillette and the Tennessee Ramblers at WRVA in Richmond, Virginia, and with Boots Woodall and the Radio Wranglers at WGST in Atlanta. Following a recording session for the King label as featured vocalist with Woodall's band, Marvin retired from show business to take a job at Warner Robins Air Force Base near Macon. He, too, was later called to preach and studied for the Baptist ministry. He pastored churches in Georgia and South Carolina before his death in 1973.

Beginning in the late 1920s with Mac (Lester MacFarland) and Bob (Gardner), who, respectively, played mandolin and guitar on records and radio (including the WLS "National Barn Dance"), the combination of those two instruments became one of the most popular hillbilly sounds of the 1930s and 1940s. This instrumental blend was featured during the period by many other well-known hillbilly acts including Karl and Harty, Bill and Charlie Monroe, the Blue Sky Boys, and the Bailes Brothers.

On the "WSB Barn Dance" the mandolin-guitar sound was provided by a husband and wife, James and Martha Carson. Martha, who played guitar, was the former Irene Amburgey, one of the original Hoot Owl Hollow Girls. James, the mandolin player, was born James Roberts on February 10, 1918, in Madison County, Kentucky.[39] The son of Fiddlin' Doc Roberts who, mostly with guitarist Asa Martin, recorded extensively in the 1920s and 1930s, James was a seasoned performer by the time he reached adolescence. He can be heard, as a boy of ten, singing on his father's early records. Radio work soon followed with jobs at WAAN, Omaha, Nebraska; WHO, Des Moines, Iowa; WOC, Davenport, Iowa; and WLAP in Lexington, Kentucky. It was while in Lexington that James met Irene Amburgey who, with Bertha and Opal, was performing at WLAP as one of the Sunshine Sisters. James and Irene were married in Lexington on June 8, 1939. James accompanied his new wife and her sisters as they moved first from Lexington to Bluefield, West Virginia; then to Renfro Valley, Kentucky; and eventually to Atlanta.

While the three sisters appeared on WSB as the Hoot Owl Hollow Girls, James, at first, was not allowed to work on the station because of a policy that prevented both a husband and wife from being on the payroll. Not to be without a job, James worked personal-appearance dates with various acts in the Atlanta area, including those heard on other radio stations.

Eventually WSB gave James a job, but, as he recalled, he had to use an assumed name, and the one he chose was James (sometimes Jimmy) Carson. The *Journal* for Saturday, April 12, 1941, reported that a newcomer on the "Barn Dance" that evening would be Jimmy Carson, "singer of sentimental ballads."[40] At first James performed as a soloist, singing such songs as "The Great Speckled Bird," "The Letter Edged in Black," and "A Distant Land to Roam." Then one morning, as James later recalled, while they were performing on the "Dixie Farm and Home Hour" program, Martha joined him in singing "Keep on the Sunny Side." Listener response was so favorable that they began singing together regularly and were soon given top billing on the "Barn Dance" and other WSB programs as James and

Martha Carson, the Barn Dance Sweethearts, "the most promising singing duet of 'home folk' songs in radio."[41] Thus was launched the career of what became, with the possible exception of the Blue Sky Boys, the most popular country-music act ever heard regularly on local Atlanta radio. James and Martha specialized in old-time gospel songs and spirituals such as "When the Saints Go Marching In" and "Farther Along," as well as sentimental love songs that included "The Precious Jewel," "Maple on the Hill," and "When It's Time for the Whippoorwills to Sing." In addition, James frequently was featured as mandolin soloist on such tunes as "Rolling Stone Blues," "Under the Double Eagle," and "Farewell Blues."

In the mid-1940s James and Martha entered Lee Roy Abernathy's recording studio in Canton, Georgia, to record eight songs for the White Church label. They included "The Sweetest Gift, a Mother's Smile," "He Will Set Your Fields on Fire," and some of James's original compositions, such as "There's an Open Door Waiting for Me," "The Man of Galilee," and "When He Heard My Plea." Five sessions for Capitol in 1949 and 1950 yielded several recordings of the songs for which James and Martha are best remembered—"Looking for a City," "When God Dips His Pen of Love in My Heart," "I'll Fly Away," and James's composition, "Budded on Earth to Bloom in Heaven."

In early 1950 James and Martha left Atlanta for a job on the "Mid-Day Merry-Go-Round" at WNOX in Knoxville, Tennessee. Shortly after this move they separated, both professionally and as man and wife. Martha embarked on a solo career as a gospel singer, gaining considerable success with such recorded hits as "Satisfied" and "Jesus Is the Rock," and as a star of the "Grand Ole Opry." For the next ten years James worked as vocalist and instrumentalist with various groups including Wilma Lee and Stoney Cooper, the Masters Family, and the Lonesome Pine Fiddlers. He also worked as staff musician at WWVA in Wheeling, West Virginia, and on various radio, television, and stage shows promoted by Cas Walker of Knoxville. In 1960 James ceased to perform on a full-time basis. Thereafter he worked in a non-music-related field, only occasionally appearing publicly as an entertainer. Both of the onetime Barn Dance Sweethearts remarried. Martha made her home in Nashville, Tennessee, and James established residence in Lexington, Kentucky. In the late 1980s James returned to Renfro Valley, Kentucky, to work briefly as staff guitarist on the "Renfro Valley Barn Dance." Some fifty years earlier he had worked as a parking-lot attendant there while Martha and her sisters performed on the show.

Developing side by side with hillbilly music and interrelated with it was gospel music.[42] Many of the pioneer hillbilly recording artists such as the Carter Family preserved both secular and sacred material on early 78 RPM discs. Hillbilly radio performers of the 1930s and 1940s made a point of including a "song of hope and inspiration" on every program. The large hillbilly variety shows and barn dances heard on radio frequently featured at least one act, sometimes a quartet, whose specialty was gospel and spiritual songs. For several years during the 1940s, for example, the "Grand Ole Opry" featured the John Daniel Quartet. The Brown's Ferry Four was a popular attraction at WLW in Cincinnati, and from Shreveport's KWKH the gospel-singing Frank Stamps Quartet and the Rice Brothers, who featured love songs, fiddle tunes, and comedy, shared dual billing on personal appearances.

The "WSB Barn Dance" cast included a quartet throughout most of its tenure on radio. First came the Swanee River Boys, who made their "Barn Dance" debut on March 22, 1941.[43] When the group went to Atlanta it consisted of Buford Abner, lead singer; Billy Carrier, baritone singer and guitarist; Merle Abner, bass singer; and George Hughes, tenor.[44]

Born on June 16, 1913, near Arthur, Kentucky, Billy Carrier was a brother to Cotton Carrier who, as we have seen, later joined the "Barn Dance" staff as master of ceremonies. Prior to embarking on a career as a singer, Billy had studied music at the James D. Vaughan School of Music in Lawrenceburg, Tennessee, and taught singing schools in Kentucky.

The Abner brothers, Buford and Merle, were born (on November 10, 1917, and April 25, 1913, respectively) and reared near Wedowee, Alabama. They met Billy Carrier through their uncle, Stacy Abner, who was a graduate of the Vaughan school. In 1938, Billy Carrier and Stacy Abner formed a quartet called the Vaughan Four which soon included Buford and Merle. They performed on WNOX in Knoxville, Tennessee, and made personal appearances in the area. In 1940, they changed their name to the Swanee River Boys, moved to radio station WDOD in Chattanooga, Tennessee, and added George Hughes (born March 1, 1911, in Texarkana,

Arkansas), who replaced Stacy Abner. It was while they were at WDOD that the Swanee River Boys attracted the attention of John Lair, who persuaded them to cast their lot with WSB's hillbilly troupe. In addition to appearing on the "Barn Dance" and the "Georgia Jubilee," the Swanee River Boys became the featured artists on the "Little Country Church House," the program that had orginally spotlighted the Pine Ridge Boys. The Swanee River Boys' repertoire consisted not only of gospel and spiritual songs, but included folk, western, and pop songs as well. Among the songs they sang on the "Barn Dance" were "Home on the Range," "Steal Away," "Carry Me Back to Old Virginny," "Jes' a-Settin' in My Ol' Cabin Door," "Rock of Ages," and "My Old Kentucky Home." Their most popular number while at WSB was the gospel song "I Found a Hiding Place."

The Swanee River Boys were forced to disband in late 1942 when Merle and Buford Abner entered military service. During part of the Abners' absence they were replaced by Lee Roy Abernathy and Bill Lyles. The original members were reunited at WSB in 1946. Two years later they left WSB for a job at WLW in Cincinnati. During their career the Swanee River Boys also worked at WBT in Charlotte, performed on the NBC radio network, and recorded for the King, Skylite, and Zondervan labels. Following their retirement from show business, the Swanee River Boys settled in various parts of the country: Billy Carrier in the Atlanta suburb of Smyrna; Buford Abner in Indianapolis, Indiana; Merle Abner in Wedowee, Alabama; and George Huges in Texarkana, Arkansas.

When the Swanee River Boys left WSB in October 1942 they were replaced by the Sunshine Boys, another male quartet, consisting of Atlanta native Eddie Wallace, piano player and baritone singer; John O. "Tennessee" Smith, tenor; A. L. "Smitty" Smith, lead singer; and Ace Richman, bass.[45]

The Smith brothers, born in Oneida, Tennessee, met Cincinnati native Ace Richman while working on radio stations in that city in the late 1930s. The three formed a country music team called the Red River Rangers which was heard on WCHS in Charleston, West Virginia, WMAZ in Macon, Georgia, and on WAGA in Atlanta. From WAGA they moved over to WSB as the Sunshine Boys after adding Eddie Wallace (replacing Pat Patterson, who entered military service) as the fourth member of the quartet. The Sunshine

Boys' most popular songs with Atlanta radio listeners were "Lead Me to that Rock," "Danger Zone," and "He'll Understand and Say Well Done." After about a year on the "Barn Dance" they returned to WAGA where, for several months, they performed both as the Sunshine Boys gospel quartet and as the Light Crust Doughboys, a western band whose styling and repertoire were after the manner of the Sons of the Pioneers and western-swing innovator Bob Wills. The Light Crust Doughboys were equally comfortable harmonizing on a western ballad or treating listeners to their western-swing-oriented interpretation of an instrumental tune. The Sunshine Boys' radio programs were sponsored by the makers of such products as Vicks VapoRub and 4-Way Cold Tablets.

The Sunshine Boys were heard again on WSB in the late 1940s, but in 1949 the original quartet split. A new Sunshine Boys composed of Richman, Wallace, Fred Daniel, and J. D. Sumner took a job at WWVA in Wheeling, West Virginia, while the Smith brothers remained at WSB to work as the Smith Brothers duet with the Carroll Family, a local gospel group. The Sunshine Boys were heard again on WSB between 1951 and 1955, after which they moved to the Las Vegas-Lake Tahoe area where they worked the nightclub circuit until 1968. The Smith brothers spent most of the 1950s in Atlanta as members (with Boots Woodall, Cotton Carrier, Pat Patterson, and Paul Rice) of the TV-Wranglers band appearing on the popular daily "TV-Ranch" show on WAGA-TV.

The Sunshine Boys' career was not limited to radio. In the late 1940s they appeared on Atlanta television, and between 1945 and 1952 they appeared in several western movies with Eddie Dean, Charles Starrett, and Smiley Burnette. The Sunshine Boys also recorded extensively for several labels including Bullet, Decca, Dot, and Starday. After withdrawing from the quartet, the Smith brothers recorded for the Mercury, King, and Capitol labels not only as the main artists, but as backup musicians and featured vocalists with such other artists as James and Martha Carson and Boots Woodall. In 1988 Richman, Wallace, and the Smith brothers, all retired from full-time entertaining, were living in the Atlanta area.

From the very beginning the commercial hillbilly music entrée was served up with spicy side dishes of humor—jokes, skits, blackface routines, and country rube acts—all descended from the medicine shows and vaudeville troupes of earlier days. At first there were the skit records of the 1920s and early 1930s that featured members of the pioneer string-band recording artists engaged in comic dialogues centered around moonshine stills, barbecues, and juke joints. When radio came along these comedy routines were transferred to the air waves and stage shows. In the thirties and forties a hillbilly radio or stage show without a comedian would have been almost as unusual and unpopular as one without fiddles and guitars. Thus it was that the public's need to laugh helped make stars of such entertainers as Minnie Pearl, the Duke of Paducah, and Grandpa Jones.

Comedy was not forgotten by John Lair, Chick Kimball, and the others responsible for the content of the "WSB Barn Dance." The first purveyor of comedy on the show was a woman, Ricca Hughes, known to listeners as Aunt Hattie. She appeared on the initial broadcast of the "Barn Dance" and for several months thereafter played the role of the hayseed mother of the Hoot Owl Hollow Girls.

Other comedians who made "Barn Dance" fans laugh included Aunt Sarrie; Hank Penny; Oscar McGooney, whose real name was Jack Baggett; Hot Shot Elmer (Bill Carlisle); and Herman Horsehair Buggfuzz.

Ivy Peterson, who perfected the Buggfuzz role, was born in Birmingham, Alabama, where he gained his first musical experience playing upright bass with various pop bands.[46] Peterson's introduction to hillbilly entertaining occurred when he took a job with Curly Fox. Out of necessity he took up comedy when Fox's regular comedian left the group.

When he was offered a job at WSB in 1941, Peterson was working with a western-swing band, the Ranch Boys, at radio station WREC in Memphis, Tennessee. After the original "WSB Barn Dance" folded he became a member of the Peachtree Cowboys, performing with them on WSB-TV and at the Covered Wagon nightclub. He spent his last working years as a prop man at WSB-TV before retiring to a life of leisure. The 1980s found him dividing his time between the mountains of north Georgia, the suburbs of Atlanta, and the Florida beaches.

The following typical comedy skit featuring Buggfuzz and emcee Cotton Carrier took place on the "Barn Dance" broadcast of September 20, 1947:

HERMAN: Bonus noches, monsewers and signeritas!

COTTON: Herman . . . Herman, what are you bouncing up and down like that for?

HERMAN: Oh I took me some medicine just now and forgot to shake the bottle!

COTTON: Well what's the matter, Herman, are you sick?

HERMAN: I shore am, Cotton. I couldn't eat more than six or eight helpings of chitlings right now if I had to!

COTTON: You must be sick all right. What seems to be the trouble?

HERMAN: Well, you see, ever' time I bend way down, stretch my arms out, and then lift up my leg, I get a pain in my chest.

COTTON: But what do you want to do all that for anyway?

HERMAN: 'Cause it's the only way I can put my britches on.

COTTON: Oh Herman, I don't think you're very sick.

HERMAN: You don't, huh?

COTTON: No. Your face looks kinda' green, but I wouldn't worry about that.

HERMAN: You wouldn't huh?

COTTON: Of course not.

HERMAN: Well if *your* face was green *I* wouldn't worry about it either!

COTTON: Herman, why do you keep looking down? Have you lost something?

HERMAN: Huh?

COTTON: I say, have you lost something?

HERMAN: No, the doctor just told me to watch my stomach.

COTTON: So you went to see a doctor?

HERMAN: Yep, I shore did. And you know what? He gave me some pills, and he told me to take three of 'em ever' day.

COTTON: And have you been doing that?

HERMAN: Not for the past three days.

COTTON: Why not?

HERMAN: Cause I took twelve of 'em the first day.

COTTON: But Herman, you shouldn't have done that . . . It's too much medicine at one time.

HERMAN: Aw no it ain't, because he gave me some other medicine and I didn't take it at all.

COTTON: He gave you some medicine and you didn't take it?

HERMAN: Naw, I couldn't take it.

COTTON: But why not?

HERMAN: 'Cause it said right on the bottle to keep the cork in tight . . . so I couldn't take it.
COTTON: But Herman, don't you know that unless you take your medicine you might have to have an operation.
HERMAN: Oh I ain't worried about that. I had one of them there operations once, and I laughed all the way through it.
COTTON: Herman, you laughed all the way through an operation?
HERMAN: I shore did! (*CHUCKLE*) That doctor had me in stitches!
COTTON: Oh Herman, I wish you'd stay away from here. Every time I start talking to you I get a headache.
HERMAN: Don't worry about a headache, Cotton, I can cure a headache.
COTTON: You can?
HERMAN: Shore . . . I cured a headache for my cousin Blub once.
COTTON: Well how did you do it?
HERMAN: I just gave him two quarts of turpentine.
COTTON: Two quarts of turpentine! Why that would kill me!
HERMAN: I know! It killed my cousin Blub! So long, Cotton![47]

The original "WSB Barn Dance," which had begun in 1940, was heard for the last time on Saturday evening, February 18, 1950. Its demise marked the end of an era in country music in Atlanta. Although, as we shall see, a Saturday evening show called the "WSB Barn Dance" was initiated on the station a year or so later, it achieved neither the large audience nor the longevity of the original "Barn Dance." Nashville had emerged as the capital of country music with the "Grand Ole Opry" boasting a cast of some 120 performers,[48] including most of the biggest names in the business. Radio station managers had learned that it was cheaper to play records than to keep live performers on the payroll, and income from personal appearances melted away as potential audiences stayed home to watch that new wonder, television.

CHAPTER
9

The Demise of Live Radio, the Birth of Television, and Beyond, 1948–

IN 1950 THERE WERE 331,314 people living within the city limits of Atlanta. By 1980 the population of the city had grown to 425,022, an increase of 28 percent. These figures, however, do not adequately reflect the impact of population growth on Atlanta after World War II. For a better understanding of the effect of postwar population dynamics on the city, we must look not only at what happened within the confines of the city boundaries, but at what took place in the surrounding area as well. The population of the greater metropolitan Atlanta area went from 671,797 in 1950 to 2,138,231 in 1980, an increase of 218 percent. Atlanta, like many places in the United States, experienced a phenomenon that came to be known as urban sprawl. In the process Georgia's largest city became a major convention center, continued to grow as a major transportation hub, became the southeastern headquarters for some seventy governmental agencies and numerous businesses, received national recognition in the areas of professional sports, arts, and entertainment, constructed a model mass-transit system, and achieved the distinction of having the world's second busiest airport and the nation's largest airport terminal complex.

By 1950, 45 percent of Georgia's three-and-a-half million residents were urban dwellers, 27 percent were nonfarmers living in rural areas, and 28 percent were farmers.[1] But the rural dwellers and their urban cousins had become more alike than ever before, as those living in rural areas became more cosmopolitan—a result of improved and increased mass media communication and transportation. Widespread public-school consolidation, for example, "helped diffuse urban education and values to rural areas."[2] The trend toward homogenization of urban and rural practices, ideas, and attitudes continued unabated into the 1980s, not only in Georgia, but throughout the nation.

Since social change influences the cultural expressions and activities of society members, it is not surprising to find that the social changes that took place in Georgia and Atlanta after World War II had a drastic effect on country music in the state capital. And what took place in Atlanta was also taking place in other parts of the country.

If, in the 1950s, there were fewer farmers in the rural areas and newly urbanized areas around Atlanta to support the city's country music business, their places had been filled by farmers turned office workers, insurance salesmen, and factory hands. In 1945 Atlanta had been described as a "white-collar town, full of office workers."[3] The city boasted 900 factories of varying sizes, the largest in the area being an aircraft plant in suburban Marietta that had 28,000 employees on its payroll.[4] Two automobile assembly plants on the outskirts of the city had a combined payroll of 3,000 by 1950.[5] At mid-decade Atlanta could be portrayed as the "distribution and sales capital of the Southeast, fifth insurance center of the nation, . . . transportation and communication center of the Southeast with one of the ten top expressway systems in the country, [a] billion-dollar banking city, [a] big textile center, and heart of the Southeast for universities, hospitals, pipelines, office buildings, and auto and aircraft assembly."[6] Many of the Atlanta residents shuttling back and forth between home and work in their automobiles were among the legendary country-music-loving commuters aspiring to sophistication who turned down their radios when they stopped at traffic lights so fellow commuters in neighboring autos wouldn't know they were listening to country music.

The role of radio in the dissemination of country music was changing in the early 1950s from that of purveyor of live music to that of promoter of recorded music. As country musicians in Atlanta encountered fewer and less attractive jobs in radio they turned elsewhere in search of opportunities to perform. For some, the new television stations provided jobs for a few years. Others found work in the country music nightclubs that bloomed and faded with predictable regularity in the city. Some musicians moved to other cities where radio shows were still available. A fair number even made the roster of the "Grand Ole Opry" and otherwise achieved success as a part of Nashville's country music empire. Several performers assumed an "if you can't beat 'em, join 'em" attitude and became radio disc jockeys. Many younger country-oriented musicians who came along later, and who would have been radio performers a decade or so earlier, were able to find an outlet for their talents in the field of bluegrass music. Many other musicians who had been heard on the "Cross Roads Follies," the "WSB Barn Dance," and other local radio programs gave up their entertainment careers altogether and took jobs unrelated to music.

Live country music on Atlanta radio died a slow death. Although, as we have seen, the original "WSB Barn Dance" went off the air in February 1950, a new version of the program debuted on Saturday night, January 5, 1952, at 8:00. This attempt to re-create the ambience of live radio of the past was part of a larger scheme on the part of WSB's management to breathe new life into the medium, to hold onto those listeners who had not totally abandoned radio for television, and perhaps to lure some of the old listeners away from those new contraptions that were showing up in every American living room.[7]

The premiere cast of the new "WSB Barn Dance" included the Peachtree Cowboys, consisting of Cotton Carrier, Marvin Willis, Jimmy Smith, Mac Atcheson, Bobby Atcheson, and Ivy Peterson (Herman Horsehair Buggfuzz); and the Carroll Family. Most of the Peachtree Cowboys, as we have seen, had appeared as solo acts on the original "Barn Dance." The Carroll Family, who originally came to WSB from WFOM in Marietta where they had a regular show, were also former "Barn Dance" performers. In 1952 this family act, whose specialty was gospel music, consisted of Johnny Carroll, guitarist and baritone singer; Johnny's wife, Margie, who sang alto; and their fourteen-year-old son and lead singer, Don, who had been performing professionally with the family for four years. In the late 1940s Johnny had arranged for the Sunshine Boys to listen to Don sing backstage at a Saturday night "WSB Barn Dance" show at the College Park City Auditorium. Producer Chick Kimball was sufficiently impressed that he put the ten-year-old boy on stage that night as a solo performer with backup provided by the Sunshine Boys. Don later recalled that he was well received by the audience and was asked to return for performances on subsequent Saturday nights. At about this time the Sunshine Boys were breaking up, and Smitty Smith asked Don and his parents to join him and Tennessee to form an act to be known as the Smith Brothers and the Carroll Family. The new group was given a featured spot on the "WSB Barn Dance," performed on the station daily, and made personal appearances throughout Georgia and in surrounding states during the week. The combination of Smiths and Carrolls made possible several vocal groupings that brought considerable variety to their radio and stage programs. The Carroll Family sang together as a trio, the Smith Brothers and Johnny and Don Carroll performed as a male quartet, and for some numbers all five formed an ensemble whose offerings were reminiscent of the Chuck Wagon Gang, a then highly popular gospel group headquartered in Texas. James and Martha Carson frequently joined the Smiths and Carrolls on personal appearances, and in 1949 and 1950, when the Carsons recorded for Capitol Records, the Smith Brothers and the Carroll Family joined in on choruses and provided hand clapping on some of the cuts to create a camp-meeting revival effect. The biggest hit from these sessions was a gospel song, "Looking for a City," recorded in the WGST studios.

Between the demise of the original and the birth of the new "WSB Barn Dance," the Carroll Family was heard on the relatively new WEAS in Decatur.

The Carrolls left the "Barn Dance" around 1954 in a move that also marked the family group's retirement from show business except for some personal appearances with Harpo Kidwell. Johnny returned to his job as a wholesale grocery salesman and Margie resumed her duties as housewife and mother, but Don, after graduating from high school in 1955, continued to pursue a music career in the pop field. With the help of local music publisher Bill Lowery, Don landed a contract with Capitol Records that yielded four sides, none of which caught the public's fancy to any great extent. Subsequent recording stints with the MGM and Cadence labels met with a similar fate. In the 1960s he worked as a record promoter for the Warner Brothers and Mercury labels. Don later was an independent record producer, and in 1983, went into full-time music evangelism, a career in which he was actively involved in the late 1980s. Margie died in 1967 at the age of forty-six. Johnny was sixty-one when he passed away in 1974.[8]

Other acts heard on the new "WSB Barn Dance" included Cowboy Jack (Talton) and His Roundup Gang, Red Estes and the Fescue Boys, the Log Cabin Ramblers, the Golden Tones, and Smoky Harper and the Starlight Valley Boys.

The new "WSB Barn Dance" usually was presented before a small audience in the WSB studios to which admission was free. In the summer of 1953 the show moved downtown to the larger, air-conditioned Roxy Theater from which a portion of the stage show was broadcast over WSB. The large audiences the theater management had hoped for did not materialize, and not long afterwards the "Barn Dance" left the Roxy and went off the air as a live show. Jerry Vandeventer, a WSB announcer who had produced the program, continued the "Barn Dance" as a Saturday-night record show until March 1957.

Another barn-dance type of show that provided work for Atlanta-area country musicians during the fifties was the "Georgia Jubilee" (later called the "Dixie Jubilee"), which for most of its tenure was held at the City Auditorium in Hapeville, one of Atlanta's southern suburbs. Under the direction of Jim Davenport, manager of East Point's WTJH, the show was presented to a paying audience each Saturday night, recorded, and played back over WTJH the following Saturday afternoon. Originally the show incorporated a talent contest in which weekly winners vied for a monthly prize. Ray Kinnamon, who had worked at radio stations in Cartersville and Atlanta, served as master of ceremonies, and Archie Campbell was hired to produce the show and serve as comedian. The Cherokees, a house band directed by Jack Greene, provided backup music for the amateur talent and opened for the "Grand Ole Opry" stars and other well-known artists who were spotlighted each week. In addition to Greene, who sang and played guitar and drums, the Cherokees, at one time or another, also included Shorty Boyd on steel guitar; Lem Bryant on bass; lead guitarists Rodney Attaway and Jerry Shook; and Carl Leming, who played fiddle. According to Kinnamon, the show featured such other local talent as Jerry Reed, Ray Stevens, Joe South, and Bill Anderson.[9] Before the 1950s had come to an end the show had folded, but some of the local talent that had performed there went on to become nationally and internationally known country music stars.

Jack Greene, one of the graduates of the "Georgia Jubilee," was born in Maryville, Tennessee, in 1930. He came to Atlanta in the late 1940s and immediately became involved in the country music scene. Back home in Tennessee he had been a regular listener to the "WSB Barn Dance" and other country music programs on the Voice of the South. The science of radio transmission is such that he was able to get a better signal from WSB than from WSM in Nashville. Greene especially admired the singing of "Barn Dance" star Pete Cassell whom he often heard sing "The Last Letter," the song that would one day elevate Greene himself to country music stardom. Greene played guitar and sang as one-third of a trio that also included Lem Bryant on bass and fiddler Speedy Price. Later he joined the Rhythm Ranch Boys, a group that was heard on WATL, WBGE, and WTJH in the early 1950s.

Greene's music career was interrupted by a stint in the army during the Korean War. Returning to Atlanta in 1952, he resumed musical activities that included a lengthy association with the Peachtree Cowboys. In 1962 he joined Ernest Tubb's Texas Troubadours, a move that provided valuable exposure through Tubb's extensive personal-appearance tours, a chance to appear on the "Grand Ole Opry," and an opportunity to record with Tubb on Decca. When Greene's vocal solo, "The Last Letter," a single from the album *Ernest Tubb Presents the Texas Troubadours*, made the country charts in the mid-1960s, he was well on his way to stardom. A string of hit singles followed, including "There Goes My Everything," a number-one hit that was named song of the year in 1967. That same year Greene was named male vocalist of the year, and the album containing his hit song was named best album of the year. In December 1967 he was made a regular member of the "Grand Ole Opry" as a solo artist.[10]

Of the local musicians who performed on the "Georgia Jubilee," probably the one destined to become best known was Bill Anderson. Born in Columbia, South Carolina, on November 1, 1937, Anderson, when he was about ten years old, moved with his parents to the Atlanta suburb of Decatur where his father earned a living as a business executive. At an early age, Bill exhibited an interest in country music that was wholly out of character with the urban, middle-class life-style of his parents, who did not share their son's musical taste. Nevertheless, Bill pursued with diligence his passion for the sounds that had made Hank Williams, Roy Acuff, and Ernest Tubb household words in many homes, if not his own. He learned to play the guitar and, while a student at Avondale High School, he organized his own band, the Avondale Playboys. After graduating from high school Anderson entered the University of Georgia at Athens where he continued to front a band that played at fraternity parties and other local gatherings. On weekends he returned to Atlanta to appear on the "Georgia Jubilee" and at other places where country music was featured.

During his university days, Bill worked as a disc jockey at radio stations in Athens and nearby Commerce, Georgia. His country-music radio show at WJJC in Commerce earned him recognition as a "Mr. D.J. U.S.A." in 1958. It was also during his tenure at WJJC that his efforts as a song writer first bore fruit. His "City Lights," written one night atop a two-story building in Commerce, was recorded by Ray Price, who turned it into an all-time country hit.

Anderson's rise to superstardom was rapid and steady. Along the way he found exposure in every medium of the business and picked up most of the accolades that are a part of the dreams of all country pickers and singers. He became a regular member of the "Grand Ole Opry" in 1961, was the star of a widely syndicated television program, performed in several motion pictures, and served as host of a television game show. He had numerous hit records, both singles and albums, and his country music awards include top male vocalist of the year (several times), record of the year, top songwriter of the year (several times), and top duet of the year (with female country artist, Jan Howard). In addition to "City Lights," the best known of the songs Anderson recorded and/or composed include "Po' Folks," "Still," "The Tip of My Fingers," "I Love You Drops," "Where Have All the Heroes Gone," and "Southern Fried." Well into the 1980s Bill Anderson still maintained a high profile as a country music personality.[11]

Country music historian Bill Malone has observed that although nationwide, "radio performances preserved their potency up into the fifties, the trend toward the playing of phonograph recordings proved irresistible." He noted further that "disc jockeys proliferated during the fifties and many of them proved to be as popular as the musicians whose records they played," adding parenthetically that "many of them, of course, were musicians."[12] Radio programming in Atlanta was no exception—in fact, radio stations in that city may have set the trend as popular local country-music personalities overnight turned into hillbilly disc jockeys.

Cotton Carrier became a disc jockey on Saturday, November 8, 1947, when his "Hillbilly Record Roundup" program premiered on WSB at 11:30 P.M. The fact that the program was listed in the newspaper radio logs as "Cotton Carrier," rather than under some other more descriptive title, suggests that station management considered Carrier's name as big a drawing card as the artists whose records he would be playing. In subsequent advertisements for the program Carrier's name was prominently featured. For the next five years Cotton spun records (at first 78's and later 45's) and interviewed such stars as Cowboy Copas and Red Foley on various record programs on WSB.

In the early 1950s Jack Holden, while performing with his country band at Decatur's WEAS, a station owned by E. D. Rivers, Jr., was persuaded by the station's management to become a hillbilly disc jockey. Again, the radio log's listing of the program as "Jack Holden's Hillbilly Record Show" emphasized the name of the disc jockey, a name familiar to listeners who liked country music. Subsequently he worked as country disc jockey, assistant manager, and general manager at Rivers-owned stations in Savannah, Georgia, and Memphis, Tennessee. While at the station in Memphis, Jack was named "Mr. D.J. U.S.A." by Nashville's WSM.

Another Atlanta hillbilly musician who became a disc jockey was Cowboy Jack Talton. For several years during the fifties he played hillbilly records on Atlanta-area stations WEAS, WGLS, and WERD.

While the local radio stations were deleting live hillbilly acts from their daily formats the television stations began to add some of them to their program schedules.

Commercial television first came to Atlanta in 1948, when WSB-TV, the South's first TV station, went on the air on September 29. As far as can be determined, the Sunshine Boys were the first group familiar to country music fans to have a regular spot on the new television outlet. Within a month of the station's debut, their program, produced by Elmo Ellis and Brad Crandall, was seen and heard every Tuesday at 7:45 P.M. Viewers who had learned to expect mostly gospel music from the Sunshine Boys may have been surprised when they heard the group singing the latest fare from the hit parade. On November 11, 1948, a reporter for the *Atlanta Journal* wrote:

> Whether singin' about the sidewalks of New York or the prairies of Wyoming, WSB-TV's Sunshine Boys are smooth performers. Their acts are always varied so as to be unpredictable. The eternal question among their audience is "What next?" But there's one thing you can say for their performances that is consistently true: They're good.
>
> Tuesday evening the boys had more treats in store than seemed possible for a brief ten minutes.
>
> First they were city slickers in gray flannels to the tune of "Easter Bonnet" and "Buttons and Bows." Then came a quick change (who knows where or how?) to Western costume and Western scenery: bright plaid shirts, cowboy hats and high-heeled boots against a backdrop of mountains and the lone prairie.[13]

At about the same time, another writer stated, "One reason the Sunshine Boys' shows go over so big is that they've got plenty of enthusiasm. They have as good a time singing as the audience has seeing and hearing them."[14]

The Sunshine Boys, which at the time consisted of Ace Richman, Eddie Wallace, and Tennessee and Smitty Smith, were not on the station for long, however. In 1949 Richman and Wallace hired replacements for the Smith Brothers and went to Wheeling, West Virginia, to continue their careers as the Sunshine Boys, while the Smith Brothers remained in Atlanta where they continued to be heard on radio and later seen on television.

In 1951 all three of the television stations then in Atlanta introduced a regularly scheduled country music program to their viewers. The first of these to go on the air, and the one destined to last the longest, was "TV Ranch" which made its debut on WAGA-TV on Monday, January 15, at 12:15 P.M. This program, which stayed on the air until the latter part of 1957, featured the TV Wranglers, formerly known to Atlanta-area country music fans as the Radio Wranglers. The original members of the group were Boots Woodall, steel guitarist; bass player Paul Rice; Tennessee Smith, who played fiddle, and Smitty Smith, guitarist. Later additions to the show were Pat Patterson, accordionist/pianist, and Cotton Carrier, who played guitar and sang.

Making regular guest appearances on the program was Conyers, Georgia, resident Brenda Mae Tarpley, who billed herself as Brenda Lee. Still in elementary school at the time, "Little Miss Dynamite," as she came to be known, captured the hearts of Atlanta TV viewers as she belted out the popular songs of the day with a delivery that would have made an opera diva envious. Brenda soon left Atlanta, headed down a career path that would soon place her in the company of popular music's superstars. A Decca recording contract at the age of eleven eventually led to a dozen gold records, more than thirty top-rated albums, and such awards as Britain's top female vocalist (three consecutive years), *Billboard* magazine's "Most Programmed Female Vocalist" (five consecutive years), and *Cashbox* magazine's "Most Programmed Female Vocalist" (three consecutive years). By the mid-1980s Brenda Lee, who had crossed from country to rock and back to country again, was still drawing large crowds at her personal appearances, but by choice she had cut her work schedule back to about six or seven days a month.[15]

The second Atlanta television station to add a live country show to its local programming schedule was WSB-TV, which added the Peachtree Cowboys as a daily feature on Monday, October 8, 1951, at 11:30 A.M. The Peachtree Cowboys featured "homey ballads, fast break-downs, and Western cowboy tunes, plus sentimental songs and old hymns that tug[ged] at the heart-strings."[16] In addition, comedy was provided by Herman Horsehair Buggfuzz, who also played bass fiddle and guitar, and sang. Other members of the troupe, at one time or another, were Jimmy Smith, Bobby Atcheson, Mac Atcheson, guitarist-singer Park Hall, fiddle player Ray Kelly, accordionist Lang Howe, and Dude King, who also played guitar and sang. The Peachtree Cowboys appear to have gone off the air during the latter part of 1953.

A mere two months after the Peachtree Cowboys first appeared on television, WLTV (later WLW-A-TV) made its contribution to country music entertainment by signing a group called the Swingbillies. Making their debut on Tuesday, December 4, 1951, at 6 P.M., the charter members of the group were Ruel Parker, fiddle, mandolin, and vocals; Paul Lunsford, rhythm guitar and vocals; "Junebug" Thomas, lead guitar and steel guitar; Lang Howe, accordion; and Bartow Henry, bass and vocals. Viewers were promised a program that would feature "western swing, pop tunes, mountain melodies and cowboy songs." [17] Although aurally this group had the same name (except for spelling) and perhaps a similar musical style as another band, there was no connection between the Atlanta Swingbillies and a North Carolina group called the Swing Billies headed by Charlie Poole, Jr., a decade earlier.

The Swingbillies' program was produced by Ray McCay, a native of McCaysville, Georgia, who was billed as the singing emcee. Randy Jones, pianist and accordionist from New Holland, Georgia, was also seen and heard on the show before it went off the air around mid-decade.

On July 23, 1951, WAGA-TV introduced a second program bound to attract viewers who liked country music. The stars of this show were the Logan Sisters, who may have been the first female country-music artists to have their own TV show. Born Betty and Christine Buice in Atlanta, the girls had been performing as a country music act since they were preschoolers. They got their start by winning a talent contest in which, with their cousin, Katherine Wells, they were billed as the Three Little Maids. With Christine singing mostly lead and playing bass fiddle and Betty singing primarily alto and playing the guitar, the Buices performed regularly under the name Betty and Christine on several Atlanta radio stations and made personal appearances with many of the local country-music acts during the 1930s and 1940s. For a while they were heard on radio stations in Knoxville, Tennessee, and Cincinnati, Ohio. It was when they joined the "WSB Barn Dance" in the late 1940s that they became known as the Logan Sisters, a name given them by "Barn Dance" promoter Chick Kimball.

Their TV program occupied an early-evening time slot, and according to Christine, they enjoyed a high audience rating and drew a large amount of fan mail. Initially appearing before the television cameras in matching evening gowns, but later switching to street-length dresses, Betty and Christine sang, not only the country hits of the day, but many pop songs as well. The Logan Sisters last performed on TV in the spring of 1953 just before they left show business to get married and raise families. Betty moved to Marietta, Georgia, while Christine made her home in Jonesboro, an Atlanta suburb on the southside.[18]

Although there were other locally produced television programs on Atlanta stations between 1948 and the mid-1980s none of them enjoyed the longevity or popularity of those that featured the TV Wranglers, the Peachtree Cowboys, the Swingbillies, and the Logan Sisters.

For many years country music had been heard in Atlanta nightclubs where "round and square" dancing flourished, but these places of entertainment assumed greater importance for both artist and audience as live performances were dropped by radio and television stations. As early as 1950 a band fronted by Ruel Parker was appearing regularly at Joe Cotton's Rhythm Ranch, located on Baker Street in downtown Atlanta. The group provided the music for round and square dancing on Wednesday, Friday, and Saturday nights. At the same time Parker and his band, known as the Rhythm Ranchers, could be heard daily over WEAS radio. For several years the club remained a mecca for country music fans, especially those who liked western swing. On several occasions, portions of the club's Friday- and Saturday-night stage shows were broadcast live over WAGA and other Atlanta-area radio stations. Jimmy Smith at one point bought part interest in Rhythm Ranch, and the Peachtree Cowboys became regular performers there.

In addition to local talent, Rhythm Ranch also featured out-of-town guests, some of whom enjoyed extended engagements. Among the artists and groups performing at the club during the 1950s were Leon Beavers and the Las Vegas Seven, Texas Bill Strength, and Bigg Bennett and His Western Stars.

Destined to become the best-known performer at Rhythm Ranch was Billy Walker who, with his band, the Texans, was the featured artist for a long engagement during 1951. Walker, a native Texan who had acquired a following in the Southwest and had been a member of the "Big D Jamboree" barn-dance show in Dallas, was later a member of Shreveport's "Louisiana Hayride" and the "Ozark Jubilee" television show that originated in Springfield, Missouri. In 1960 Walker became a regular member of the "Grand Ole Opry" and subsequently turned out a long string of singles and albums, including "Charlie's Shoes," a number-one country hit in 1962.[19]

From the late 1950s to the early 1960s Jimmy Smith owned and operated another country-music club, the Longhorn Ranch, located at the corner of Marietta and Spring streets. Years later Atlanta fiddler Dallas Burrell recalled the days when he was a member of the house band, the Longhorn Ranch Boys. "The Longhorn Ranch was probably the biggest dance around in this period," Burrell once wrote, "and we had many well-known entertainers visit us here from time to time."[20] Other members of the Longhorn Ranch Boys band included Jimmy Smith, who sang and played guitar; steel guitarist Vern Kendrick; bass player Lem Bryant; and lead guitar player Jimmy Dempsey.

Another popular country-music night spot of the 1950s was the Covered Wagon which opened in March 1953. Located on Marietta Street just off Spring, the Covered Wagon was owned and operated by Ivy Peterson (Herman Horsehair Buggfuzz) and Mac and Bobby Atcheson. When the club opened, Peterson and the Atchesons were appearing daily on WSB-TV as the Peachtree Cowboys. It was this band that provided the music at the Covered Wagon.

While welcoming TV viewers to visit the Covered Wagon, Ivy Peterson stated that the club was open to "our friends and their friends and no roughnecks or trouble-makers" invited.[21] The decor of the Covered Wagon was decidedly country and western. The booths were in the shape of bass fiddles, the menus were burned into the table tops, and guests were invited to carve their initials into the tables. A rail fence divided the establishment's floor into two parts, booth space and floor space, while wagon-wheel chandeliers provided the lighting. Fourteen wall murals and the plate-glass front depicted scenes from the old West, all painted by artist/musician Bobby Atcheson.

In the 1960s Atlanta's best known country-music nightclub was the Playroom located on Peachtree Street at Tenth Street. Formerly a rock-and-roll gathering place, the Playroom changed to a country music format in November 1966. Two house bands, the Swinging Gentlemen and the Cherokees, played on alternate nights, while big-name country artists from Nashville made regular guest appearances. The first star attraction at the Playroom after its switch to country was George Hamilton IV. Others who appeared in subsequent years included Charley Pride, Ferlin Husky, Conway Twitty, Billy Walker, David Houston, George Jones, Dottie West, and Roy Drusky. The Playroom was frequently referrred to as "Nashville on Peachtree."

The genial hostess at the Playroom during much of its heyday was Mama Wynette Mitchem, who became a legend to Atlanta's country music enthusiasts and a favorite among the stars she introduced to Atlanta audiences. Many, notably Charley Pride, have publicly acknowledged her help in furthering their careers. After leaving the Playroom at the end of 1970, Mama Wynette became associated with other Atlanta-area country-music night spots, including the Golden Nugget, Picker's Alley, the Big Frontier, Mama's Country Showcase, Mama's East, and Mama Wynette's West.[22]

In the 1980s those in search of live country music to which they might drink and dance could find it at several clubs, most of which were located in the suburbs. The Buckboard in Smyrna, Lithonia's East Texas Music Club, Harlow's in Stone Mountain, Hoss and Saddle in Doraville, the Silver Saddle Club in Decatur, the West Texas Music Club on Cleveland Avenue in southwest Atlanta, and Miss Kitty's, located in Marietta, offered patrons a choice among several local bands as well as top-name acts from Nashville. Among the local bands that either performed regularly as house bands or moved around from club to club were A. Jaye and Swampcreek, Paul Peek and the Generals Band, Ben Dover and Tennessee Tucker, the Trash of the South, Chuck and the Woodchucks, John Tice and the West Texas Music Company, and Atlanta, a group that enjoyed a brief flirtation with national recognition after several of their records made the charts in the early 1980s.

While many of the local artists who played in the clubs remained in Atlanta, frequently making music at night while pursuing other primary occupations, some moved on to other places, especially Nashville, where they pursued music as a full-time career. One of these, Jack Greene, has already been mentioned. Two other veterans of the Atlanta club scene who later gained widespread recognition were Roy Drusky and Pete Drake.

Roy Drusky was born in Atlanta on June 22, 1930, and although his mother was a church pianist, Drusky showed no unusual interest in music while growing up in his native city. Baseball was what attracted his attention, and after an outstanding high-school showing in the sport, he spent a few days at the Cleveland Indians' minor-league spring camp at Waycross, Georgia. Convinced by that brief experience that he did not want to be a professional baseball player after all, Drusky joined the navy, a move that proved to be pivotal in his life. An on-board hillbilly band, which he heard as part of a captive audience while doing sea duty, kindled his interest in country music. While on shore leave in Seattle, Washington, he bought an inexpensive guitar which he taught himself to play.

Back home in Atlanta following his discharge from the navy, Roy's preoccupation with country music remained at a high level, and he soon attracted a coterie of fellow enthusiasts who met regularly to pick and sing. When WEAS in Decatur sponsored a talent contest, Roy and his friends entered and won. Since the prize was a regular spot on the station, the group suddenly discovered they were radio stars performing as the Southern Ranch Boys. Their popularity on radio led to feature billing on WLW-A television and to personal appearances in the city and surrounding area. Local nightclub work followed, including appearances at the King of Clubs and the Circle H Ranch located on Memorial Drive.

Drusky soon expanded his musical activities to include song writing. After Faron Young's recording of his composition "Alone with You" reached the top ten on the country music charts, Drusky became a regular member of the "Grand Ole Opry" cast. His own recordings and his compositions recorded by other artists were well received during the following year. His "Another" and "Anymore" were top-ten songs in 1961. His recording of "Second-Hand Rose," which made the scene in 1963, was a big hit for him, as was "Peel Me a Nanner," written for Bill Anderson. In 1965, "Yes, Mr. Peters," which Drusky co-wrote, became his first number-one hit.

While following an active schedule of recording, writing, and personal appearances, Roy found time to appear in such movies as *White Lightning Express*, *Forty Acre Feud*, and *The Golden Guitar*. With numerous albums behind him, Drusky was still attracting large crowds at his personal appearances well into the 1980s.[23]

Noted steel guitarist Pete Drake appears not only to have played in most of Atlanta's country music clubs during the 1950s, but likely performed with every local country musician who played for the public during that time. Born in Augusta, Georgia, in 1932, Pete grew up in Atlanta where he developed a passion for the steel guitar. With the help of a pawn-shop instrument for which he paid $33, a four-neck pedal steel guitar of his own construction, and a batch of phonograph records by which he taught himself to play, Drake soon became one of Atlanta's most respected steel guitarists.

The first band Drake organized included Jerry Reed, Joe South, Doug Kershaw, Roger Miller, and Jack Greene. That was before he took the advice of nightclub owner Kathleen Jackson and moved to Nashville in 1959.

Appreciation of Drake's artistry by Nashville's stars and record producers led to the placing of his distinctive steel guitar sound on countless singles and albums, not only in the country idiom, but in the folk, rock, and pop fields as well. His performance on records was not restricted to that of a sideman. His solo work included "For Pete's Sake" for Starday; "Forever" on the Mercury label; and several albums, including *Talking Steel Guitar* (Smash), *Fabulous Steel Guitar* (Starday), and *Pete Drake Show* (Stop Records).[24] Drake died in 1988.

Among the artists who, in the late 1980s, gave evidence of a commitment to entertaining Atlantans rather than seeking greener pastures in Nashville, Gordon Dee was one of the best known on the city's country-music club circuit. He came to Atlanta from Savannah, Georgia, where he had replaced Billy Joe Royal as nightclub personality in that coastal city. Vocalist, pianist, and leader of the Pure Ivory Band, Dee made his Atlanta debut at a place called the Steak and Trumpet. His longest run in an Atlanta club was at Mama's Country Showcase where he worked for three-and-a-half years. Born Gordon Dillingham in Asheville, North Carolina, Dee has stated, "My first musical inspiration was a guy named Fred Moody, a brother to [former "Grand Ole Opry" star] Clyde Moody. He was the first person I ever heard sing and play the guitar." Dee was still a preteenager at the time. He later came under the influence of Elvis Presley and Jerry Lee Lewis. While working the Atlanta clubs on a regular basis, Dee took time out to travel to other cities to open for some of the big stars such as Hank Williams, Jr. Although, according to Dee, some of his records, notably "Cuttin' Right of Way," have shown up in some of the charts, "it was," he emphasized, "my videos that gave me the greatest exposure." Two of these, "Nothing Left Between Us But Alabama" and "Paradise Knife and Gun Club," he noted had been shown frequently on television by the late 1980s. At that time he could look back on a long and rewarding career in Atlanta. "I'm satisfied doing what I do very well—writing and performing," he confessed. But a note of frustration and disappointment could be detected as he added, "Very few songs from this area go to the big-time artists. You must be part of the Nashville community [to reap substantial rewards in the field of country music]." [25]

At least one mainstay of the Atlanta club milieu of the 1980s decided to try his luck in Nashville without completely severing his ties to the city where his country music career had taken root and blossomed. In 1987 Jimmy Smart moved his base of operations to Music City, but continued to commute to Atlanta each weekend to fill a Saturday-night engagement at the VFW Club in the suburb of Conyers. A native of Terrell, Texas, Smart moved to the Atlanta area in 1955 to work at the Lockheed-Georgia aircraft plant in Marietta. In 1960 he took a job with Delta Air Lines from which he retired in 1986. A vocalist, guitarist, and fiddle player, Smart began the Atlanta phase of his musical career around 1958. "I won a talent contest in 1958 at the 'Georgia Jubilee' [stage and radio show in East Point]," he reminisced thirty years later. "After that I formed my own band and started cutting records and doing show dates." Over the ensuing years, while holding down a day job, he spent his evenings and weekends playing at square dances, working in nightclubs, providing warm-up music for touring country-music acts visiting Atlanta, and performing on local radio stations. "I also had a TV show on Channel 17 that ran for a year in 1967 and '68," he added. "It was an hour show on Sunday evenings. I was the host, producer, and featured vocalist. Also on the program was David Rogers, a male vocalist, and two female vocalists, Carolyn Carl and Patty Powell." According to Smart, between 1961 and 1970, two of his records, "Shorty" (Plaid) and "A Broken Dream" (All Star), made the *Billboard* charts, and two, "Tell Me What to Do About Today" (Chancellor) and "Forget You" (Jed), were charted by *Record World*. In 1988 Jimmy Smart, a member of the Country Music Association, was looking forward to achieving significant career goals as a Nashville artist, writer, and publisher. [26]

Beginning in the mid-1950s as rock and roll began to influence

Pickin' on Peachtree

performance styles, as electrified instruments supplanted acoustic instruments in country music bands, and as the country music available on records began to sound more and more like the pop music of the 1940s and 1950s, many Atlanta musicians—professional, semi-professional, and amateur alike—became disillusioned, not by the paucity of opportunities to perform, but rather by the sound they would have to produce in order to be considered "country." Many turned to bluegrass music in search of a sound and a musical philosophy more in keeping with their backgrounds and tastes. Bluegrass music, like country music in general, was derived from the string-band styles of the 1920s and 1930s. As a definable genre it had first been played by Bill Monroe and His Blue Grass Boys (and hence the name of the music) in the mid-1940s. The bluegrass instrumental style was characterized by an acoustical ensemble sound produced by guitar, banjo, fiddle, bass, mandolin, and sometimes the Dobro. The interplay of instruments in which primarily the mandolin, the fiddle, and the banjo alternately took a lead role against a rhythmic background provided by the guitar and bass was reminiscent of jazz. The banjo was played in a three-finger style with picks, which produced a vastly different sound from that produced by frailing, the method of playing (without the use of picks) that was usually heard in the early string bands. Bluegrass solo singers tended to have high-pitched voices that came to be called the "high lonesome" sound. Harmony singing heard on religious songs and the choruses of secular songs owed an obvious debt to the shape-note singing schools that flourished in the South prior to World War II.

As the Nashville sound became more and more unpalatable to some country music fans the popularity of bluegrass music rose in direct proportion. In 1965 a music entrepreneur in Virginia staged an event featuring bluegrass performers in a format that became the basic pattern of future such events that were called bluegrass festivals. The idea caught on, and similar festivals began to be held all over the country, usually outdoors. The festival season in most areas of the country was from the first of May to the middle of October. At first the typical bluegrass festival started around 7:00 P.M. on Friday and ended late Sunday afternoon. Later on, most festivals dropped the Sunday show, with some adding a Thursday show.

Amateur and professional bands took turns performing on stage in sets that varied in length from fifteen minutes to an hour, depending on the number of bands engaged to perform. Friday night and Saturday night shows frequently lasted until after midnight. Fans began arriving on Friday, and most did not leave until the last note was sounded on Sunday. Festivals were touted as family affairs and all ages attended, while the adjacent campgrounds—a must at any festival—were filled with all styles and sizes of tents, pickup campers, vans, and motor homes. Before, during, and after the stage entertainment, amateur musicians gathered in small groups around the parking lots and campgrounds for impromptu jam sessions.

The first bluegrass festival in Georgia was held in 1968, and others followed in increasing numbers each year. By the mid 1980s more than twenty festivals were being held in Georgia each year. With increased opportunities to perform, bluegrass bands sprang up in almost every community as former back-porch and living-room pickers joined forces to share their talents with larger audiences.

An Atlanta musician who made the transition from country to bluegrass was fiddler Carl Leming. It was in 1951 that Carl, a native of Kentucky, went to Atlanta, which was home base for his job as a pilot with Delta Airlines. Carl learned to play the fiddle from his father who, like many Kentuckians, was an accomplished old-time fiddler. While Carl was still in grade school the elder Leming organized a band that included Carl on fiddle, another young son who played guitar, and two of Carl's playmates who played guitar and harmonica. Known as the Barnyard Banties, this group of youngsters, who played what Carl later called hillbilly string music, became quite popular locally, providing entertainment for family reunions, school events, ice cream socials, and square dances. The band also performed on the "Liberty Theater Barn Dance" broadcast over WCKY in Covington, Kentucky. After five or six years the Barnyard Banties disbanded as the boys grew older and other interests began to compete for their time.

After moving to Atlanta Carl made contact with other local country musicians and was soon performing with various bands as his job permitted. As previously noted, he was a member of the house band at the "Georgia Jubilee" in East Point. In the mid-1960s he performed with a country group called the Dixie Playboys that also included Vernon Kendrick, pedal steel; Carl's wife, Buzzy, bass; the Lemings' son, Mark, drums; and a brother team, Jimmy and Bobby Williams.

In 1969, Carl and Buzzy organized a bluegrass band and attended their first festival. Carl in later years described the move as getting back to their roots. "We like the natural sound of un-amplified instruments," he explained. Joining Carl and Buzzy early were a local guitar virtuoso, John Farley, and his wife, Debbie, who brought to the group a strong, clear voice capable of both lead and harmony singing. First David Dougherty and later Mark Bramlett provided the necessary five-string banjo sound. Others who played in the band at one time or another were lead guitarist Billy Scroggs and Candy Bramlett, who played rhythm guitar and sang harmony. Calling themselves the Dixie Hoedowners, Carl and his troupe became favorites of bluegrass audiences throughout the Southeast. In the 1980s the band, by then called Nu Dixie, was still performing regularly at bluegrass festivals.[27]

For proof that bluegrass musicians were not all older people seeking an alternative to the Nashville sound, one had only to note the number of young boys and girls performing on festival stages. Bluegrass bands composed entirely, or almost entirely, of children and adolescents were not uncommon.

When Brush Fire, an Atlanta-area group, was organized in 1977, all but one of the members were in their twenties, with three of the five in their early twenties. The diversity of musical backgrounds of the members of this band illustrates another phenomenon of bluegrass music—it could appeal to people with a wide variety of previously formed tastes. Mike Fleming, lead singer and guitarist with Brush Fire, was attracted to the folk music that was popular during his formative years. He liked the sounds of acoustic instruments better than the amplified ones used in rock and country performances. Like many another youth of his generation he bought a guitar and learned the basic chords that allowed him to be more than a mere spectator in the music scene that was dominated by such acts as the Kingston Trio, Joan Baez, and Bob Dylan. Eddie Turner, the tenor and sometime lead singer of the group who also played mandolin, had been influenced by gospel music, which was the music of his family, as well as by rock and roll, the musical choice of his peers. The oldest member of Brush Fire, Joe

Partridge, who sang baritone and played banjo or bass as necessity demanded, played saxophone in high school and later developed a honky-tonk piano style that he was able to exploit as a modern country performer. Fleming, Turner, and Partridge formed the nucleus of Brush Fire, which also included, at various times over the years, Mike Head, Russell Owens, John Landers, Gary Sykes, Ken Mobley (who used the stage name Elwood P. Suggins), Jimmy Ross, and Jay Richardson, all of whom belonged to the younger generation of bluegrass musicians.

Although all members of the band were competent instrumentalists, Brush Fire chose to emphasize vocal harmonies, and they quickly built up a devoted following among festival audiences in the Southeast. Equally at ease performing traditional music, gospel songs, and progressive material, Brush Fire's popularity was still at a high level in the late 1980s, some ten years after they played their first festival.[28]

What would later prove to be one of the most important events in the history of country music in Atlanta occurred in 1947 when Bill Lowery, a young man in his early twenties, decided to make Georgia's capital city his home. Born in Leesville, Louisiana, Lowery at an early age embarked on a career as a radio announcer that took him to stations in California, Louisiana, Arkansas, Oklahoma, and Tennessee.[29] Immediately prior to moving to Atlanta he was the nation's youngest radio-station manager, at WBEJ in Elizabethton, Tennessee. Lowery came to Atlanta to open and manage radio station WQXI, which went on the air in the spring of 1948. In the early 1950s Lowery left WQXI for a position at WGST where, in the role of Uncle Eb Brown, a hayseed country-music disc jockey, he developed a large and enthusiastic following among Atlanta-area listeners to that type of music. His warm, jovial, and down-home personality was an inspiration to local pickers, singers, and song writers who sought his advice and help in promoting their careers. Possessed of an extraordinary ability to recognize genuine talent and having extensive contacts in the music industry, Lowery was able to contribute significantly to the advancement of the careers of many aspiring Atlanta artists.

In 1951 Lowery discovered that he had cancer. As a result of being unable to obtain insurance, Lowery, in an effort to ensure a secure future for his family, went into the music-publishing business. Success was swift, bountiful, and perhaps curative, since his cancer went into complete remission. Thirty-five years later his venture had grown into a music publishing, record production, and talent management complex recognized in the industry as one of the largest, most productive, and most profitable music enterprises in the world.

From a modest beginning in an office at WGST, Lowery's base of operations progressed from the basement of his home, through an abandoned elementary school, to a suite of comfortable offices and modern studios located in Century Center, one of Atlanta's many suburban office parks. Still at the helm of the Lowery Group of Music Publishing Companies, the name by which his conglomerate was known, Lowery, in the late 1980s was unanimously hailed as the leader of commercial music, not only in Atlanta, but throughout much of the nation as well. Dubbed the king of Atlanta music, Lowery, in 1969, was recognized as the top publisher in the world affiliated with the Broadcast Music Incorporated (BMI) licensing agency. In 1970 he received three commendations of excellence from BMI in recognition of his contributions in the fields of rock and roll, country, and pop music. He was the first music industry figure to be so honored. Lowery was elected a vice president of the Country Music Association in 1972, and in 1973 he became the first Georgian and second person outside New York and Los Angeles to be named president of the National Academy of Recording Arts and Sciences (NARAS), the organization that annually confers Grammy awards on the nation's top recording artists.

After becoming a full-time music publisher, Lowery's first hit was a country gospel song, "I Have But One Goal," written by Cotton Carrier who later became an executive in the Lowery business. Recorded by Lowery himself, with backing by the Smith Brothers, Tennessee and Smitty, the record sold in the neighborhood of 200,000 copies. Cotton Carrier would not soon forget the birth of his most famous composition. "This was the era of the Weavers," he recalled, "who did 'On top of Old Smoky' where one would read a line . . . and one would sing it. And Tennessee Smith said to me—I'd been writing some gospel songs for them that they had been recording—'Why don't you write us one like that where somebody can read a line and we sing behind them?' I'd had an idea for a song titled 'I Have But One Goal,' so I sat down and wrote it by that pattern so they could do it. So we went over to WGST radio and recorded [it] and Bill published it. Bill did the talking and the rest of us sang behind him. I did work on that record. [I] sang baritone and played rhythm guitar. We had about two microphones—all we had in the radio station. Ken Nelson, the Capitol Records man, came in from Hollywood and sat in the control room. I think the twenty-third time we sang it, Ken said, 'That's it. That's a take.'" According to Cotton, the song was later recorded by several artists, including Molly O'Day, Wally Fowler and the Oak Ridge Quartet, and Wendy Bagwell and the Sunliters.

Although the initial focus of his publishing activities was in the country field, Lowery was not one to have his entrepreneurial domain so narrowly circumscribed. In 1956 he correctly read the signs of the times in the music world and set his sights on capturing a segment of the rock-and-roll market. The first result of this effort was "Be-Bop-a-Lula," a song co-written and recorded by Gene Vincent. It became Lowery's first million seller. Although, as we have seen, he subsequently became a leader in the rock-and-roll and pop fields, Lowery remained in the forefront of country-music publishing over the years, devoting, according to his own estimate, some 60 percent of his effort to this genre. In 1973 his contribution to the country music industry was characterized by *Billboard* magazine as having been "one of the greatest of all time."[30]

Among the country songs that came from the Lowery matrix were "Young Love," a twelve million seller recorded by Sonny James; "Spanish Fireball," recorded by Hank Snow; "Walk on By," recorded by Leroy Van Dyke; "Misery Loves Company," recorded by Porter Wagoner; "Games People Play," recorded by Freddy Weller; Bill Anderson's "Southern Fried"; Waylon Jennings's "America"; and "Common Man," recorded by John Conlee.

Lowery's importance in the field of country music is measured, not only in terms of the songs he published, but also by the talent he discovered, introduced, and developed. For, as he once explained, "all through the fifties I wore three or four hats. I was a publisher. I was a manager. I was a record producer. We later got into our own booking office. We did it all." And against considerable odds, he lamented. For example, he had to go out of town to gain exposure for his artists. "We'd hop in a car and go out to Shreveport [so his artists could] appear on the 'Louisiana Hay Ride.' If WSB had kept their radio shows, we wouldn't have had to do that. We could have stayed right here at home and developed that talent. You see, we have a very sad situation here. The fact that we do not have television, we do not have motion pictures, we don't have a 'Grand Ole Opry.' [We] really don't have any place for our people to [work]. And they need to make a living. We've had a hard time keeping musicians here."[31]

Despite all handicaps, however, Lowery's accomplishments with respect to talent development is impressive. Among those who benefitted from the Lowery touch, the names of Joe South, Jerry Reed, and Ray Stevens stand out.

Of all the artists whose careers Bill Lowery influenced, Joe South was the most enigmatic. Described by his mentor as "one of the greatest of all song writers,"[32] South was born in Covington, Georgia. A Christmas present of a guitar when he was eleven years old helped set him on a course that would eventually lead to success in the entertainment field. When he was fifteen he rode a bus to Atlanta where he proceeded to introduce himself to Bill Lowery and express his desire to be on the radio. Impressed by the young South's bravado and self-assurance, Lowery put him on the air at six o'clock on Saturday mornings where he entertained listeners with only his guitar for accompaniment.

By his own account a reflective and introspective individual, South was dubbed the "Hamlet of Tin Pan Alley, a sort of melancholy Dane of the Top 40."[33] In his songs one finds not only the mark of the poet, but the signs of the philosopher, the intellectual, and the preacher as well.

The numerous hit songs composed by South include "Down in the Boondocks," recorded by Billy Joe Royal; "Walk a Mile in My Shoes," recorded by Ray Stevens; "(I Never Promised You a) Rose Garden," a blockbuster hit for Lynn Anderson that won a Grammy Award as the song most often performed in 1971; and "Games People Play," a double Grammy winner in 1970 (best song of the year and best contemporary song) recorded by Freddy Weller and by South himself.

By the early 1980s South's career had lost the momentum of the two previous decades. Those who knew him during his creative years mourned the slump in his career and waited for the muse again to favor him with a visit.[34]

Jerry Reed, another Lowery protégé, came across as a talented but much less complex individual than South. "I'm so normal it's sickening—really square," he once told a newspaper reporter.[35]

Reed was born in Atlanta on March 20, 1937. When he was eight years old his mother bought him his first guitar and taught him some basic chords. His family were cotton-mill people, and Jerry himself became similarly employed at an early age.[36]

Reed became obsessed with the guitar, and when his boss at the textile mill where he worked gave him a choice of paying attention to his job or playing the guitar, he chose the guitar and lost his job. In later years Reed confessed, "I've dedicated my life to learning how to play guitar relative to what I feel inside and see in my mind. I'm a guitar addict and it drives me crazy when I don't have time to play every day."

After leaving the mill, Reed turned to music full time, playing for dances, in clubs, and at other places of entertainment. He gained considerable experience playing guitar in a band, headed by Kenny Lee, that also included steel guitarist Pete Drake.

Reed got his first break when he became acquainted with Lowery, who agreed to become his manager and encouraged him to pursue his interest in songwriting. Through Lowery's influence, Reed, at the age of seventeen, received a recording contract from Capitol Records.

After a stint in the armed forces where he played in a Third Army band called the Circle A Wranglers, Reed moved to Nashville in the early 1960s. There he made the acquaintance of Chet Atkins and recorded his first album for RCA, *The Unbelievable Guitar and Voice of Jerry Reed*. From that time until well into the 1980s Reed enjoyed a steady succession of movie roles, television appearances, hit songs and records, and numerous awards for his musical contributions.

Reed's movie credits include *W. W. and the Dixie Dance Kings*, *Gator*, *High Balling*, *Smokey and the Bandit*, *Hot Stuff*, *Smokey and the Bandit II*, *Survivors*, and *Smokey and the Bandit III*.

During the 1970–72 seasons, Reed was a regular performer on the "Glen Campbell Goodtime Hour" seen on the CBS-TV network. Other television shows on which he had appeared by 1980 include "Concrete Cowboys," "Jerry Reed and Friends," "Good

Ol' Boys," "The Tonight Show," "Hee-Haw," "The Merv Griffin Show," and "Music Country U.S.A."

From more than forty albums Reed's hit single records include "When You're Hot, You're Hot," "Amos Moses," "Alabama Wild Man," "Uptown Poker Club," "The Bird," "She Got the Goldmine (I Got the Shaft)," and "East Bound and Down."

Reed was named instrumentalist of the year by the Country Music Association in 1970 and 1971. His other honors include Grammy Awards for best instrumental performance for *Me and Jerry*, an album featuring Reed and Chet Atkins, and for best male performance for "When You're Hot, You're Hot." Reed also earned several BMI awards for his songs in both the country and pop fields.[37]

Ray Stevens was "discovered" by Lowery in 1962.[38] Out of a background that included classical, rock, and pop music, he emerged in the 1970s as a country music star. Stevens's psyche combined both the introspective qualities of Joe South and the self-assurance of Jerry Reed. He once explained that he was not uptight about life. "I *was* that way once," he elaborated, "but now I know myself a little better."[39] He once said that "any creative person has to get off alone, walk and think, and get things into their right order. Then he can take action."[40]

By the mid-1980s Stevens had established himself as a comedian as a result of such slapstick hits as "Ahab the Arab," "Freddie Feelgood," "Guitarzan," "Shriner's Convention," "The Doright Family," and his 1974 composition and recording of "The Streak," a topical piece that made the top ten on both the country and pop charts. As both a writer and performer, however, he proved himself capable of more serious and sensitive approaches to music with such songs as "Unwind," "Mr. Businessman," and "Everything Is Beautiful."

Ray Stevens was born in Clarkdale, Georgia, a tiny mill village some twenty miles northwest of downtown Atlanta. A graduate of Georgia State University, where he majored in classical piano, Stevens, as a high-school student, had his own rhythm-and-blues band that played local clubs and dances.

Among fellow musicians Stevens early on established a reputation as a "total artist." He achieved high standards not only as composer and performer, but as arranger and record producer as well.[41]

As the 1990s hovered on the horizon, Atlanta could look both backward and ahead at her role in the country music drama.

The view of the past shows that Atlanta has been in the forefront of the nation's country music scene. In the teens and twenties the fiddlers' conventions attracted national attention and Atlanta was characterized as a center of learning for the art of old-time fiddling. Georgia's capital city made country music history as pioneer radio station WSB introduced to a large portion of the nation the sounds of Fiddlin' John Carson, the first genuine old-time country musician to present authentic old-time country music over a radio station. Other Atlantans and Georgians of a similar musical persuasion soon followed Carson's lead to become among the first of a long list of radio hillbillies. As the major field recording center for early country music, the city for two decades attracted rural-oriented musicians from the entire Southeast. The "Cross Roads Follies," the "WSB Barn Dance," and related radio programs provided attractive showcases for hillbilly artists looking for a powerful radio outlet and the concomitant opportunity for lucrative personal-appearance revenues. These purveyors of mountain music came not only from Atlanta and Georgia, but from surrounding states as well. The last days of live radio gave Atlanta-area country music fans the "Georgia Jubilee," a combination radio and stage show that provided a boost to such local artists as Jack Greene, Bill Anderson, and Billy Joe Royal. The early days of television, overlapping the latter days of live radio, allowed Atlantans and nearby Georgians an opportunity to not only hear, but for the first time to see such local groups as the Sunshine Boys, the Peachtree Cowboys, the Swing-billies, and the TV Wranglers. These are some of the highlights of Atlanta's contributions to the history of country music.

Paying tribute to those who had helped to develop commercial music in Atlanta and Georgia, two organizations came into being in the 1970s and 1980s as both citizens and officials of the state became aware of the area's rich musical heritage. In 1976, then lieutenant governor Zell Miller, in an effort to make the music industry more aware of Georgia, appointed a senate music committee to develop ways by which the state could attract additional music industry. An outgrowth of this endeavor was the Georgia Music Hall of Fame Awards Program, an annual event designed to honor those Georgians, past and present, who had made significant contributions to Georgia's music industry. Those prominent in the field of country music who had been honored through 1989 were Bill Lowery (1979), Ray Stevens (1980), Joe South (1981), Boudleaux Bryant (1982), Brenda Lee (1982), Fiddlin' John Carson (1984), Bill Anderson (1985), Riley Puckett (1986), Jerry Reed (1987), Gid Tanner (1988), Billy Joe Royal (1988), and Harold Shedd (1989). Lieutenant Governor Miller himself was so honored in 1985 as a nonperformer.

Miller, an avid fan of country music, earned the gratitude of all professional musicians for his efforts in the mid-1970s to get legislation passed in Georgia to combat the problem of tape piracy which was depriving recording artists of millions of dollars in royalties.

Atlantan Johnny Carson (not to be confused with the famous television personality), frustrated because his grandfather, Fiddlin' John Carson, and other Atlanta-area country music pioneers who he felt deserved some recognition had not been elected to the Country Music Hall of Fame in Nashville, created in 1983 the Atlanta Country Music Hall of Fame. The first to be inducted were Fiddlin' John Carson, Gid Tanner, Riley Puckett, Clayton McMichen, Roba Stanley Baldwin, Rosa Lee "Moonshine Kate" Carson Johnson, and Anita Sorrells Wheeler Mathis. The annual award ceremonies is a highlight among Atlanta's country music fans and performers, both past and present. The actual ceremony is preceded by concerts, jam sessions, and open stages where the atmosphere and sound of a bygone era intertwine with the modern stylings of present-day country music entertainers.

Other artists who have been inducted into the Atlanta Country Music Hall of Fame since its inception include Lowe Stokes, A. A. Gray, Earl Johnson, R. M. Stanley, Professor Aleck Smart, Hank Penny, Boots Woodall, Cotton Carrier, Bert Layne, Pete Cassell, Mama Wynette, Bill Lowery, Martha Carson, the Blue Sky Boys, the Sunshine Boys, the Swanee River Boys, Boudleaux and Felice Bryant, Jimmy Smith, James Carson, Slim Bryant, Curly Kinsey, Polk C. Brockman, Brenda Lee, Dan Hornsby, Grady and Hazel Cole, Lee Roy Abernathy, Bill Anderson, Harpo Kidwell, Joe

South, Mack Compton, Rev. Andrew Jenkins, Tommy Scott, Lambdin Kay, Bill Gatins, Pop Eckler, Marion Brown, Tennessee Smith, Smitty Smith, Jack Greene, and Buddy Buie.

In addition to his efforts on behalf of the Atlanta Country Music Hall of Fame, Johnny Carson, under the aegis of his umbrella firm, Fiddlin' John Carson Productions, Inc., is involved in other country music ventures. In early 1988 he launched a new Atlanta-based record label, OKeh II. By the end of the year, eight 45 RPM sides featuring four different country music acts—Karen Kirby Merren, Terry Jenkins, Vic Thompkins, and the Generals headed by Ken Kinsey—had been released. Terry Jenkins is the great nephew of Atlanta's pioneer musician, recording artist, and composer, the Reverend Andrew Jenkins. The Okeh II releases Carson had planned for 1989 included two sides by Mike Bryant, nephew of yet another former Atlanta country music artist, Slim Bryant. Counting Carson, and Gid Tanner's grandson, Phil Tanner, leader of a country music band called the Skillet Lickers II, that makes at least four descendants of Atlanta's pioneer country musicians carrying on family traditions in the 1980s.

But the country music scene in Atlanta in the 1980s was quite different from what it was in the period between 1913 and the 1950s. When, in the late fifties, radio and television ceased to be viable outlets for Atlanta's musicians, live country music on a regular schedule could be heard only in the city's nightclubs. Since, at the crucial point in the progress of country music Atlanta had lacked a man with the vision of George D. Hay, the city did not have a "Grand Ole Opry" or a thriving publishing and recording industry on the order of Nashville's to support local talent. "The main country music activity in Atlanta is in the clubs," said Johnny Carson in 1988. "Although it's not thriving like it was during the urban cowboy era, there's still a lot of good country music to be found in the clubs," he added.[42]

The audience for nightclub country music, however, is different from radio and television audiences. It is more limited. There are many devoted country music fans who would never darken the door of a nightclub, even at the risk of never hearing their favorite music again. Because of local liquor laws, nightclub music does not reach children and teenagers. The opportunity for inspiration at an early age by live radio artists is denied the present-day youngster. Such inspiration was instrumental in launching the careers of numerous early country-music artists. Country music enthusiasts of the sixties, seventies, and eighties who wouldn't visit a nightclub had to look elsewhere for places to hear live performances. Available to these folks were the concerts held in country music parks and at bluegrass festivals. By the late 1980s the only surviving country music parks near Atlanta were those at Calhoun and Lake Lanier. Atlanta residents had to travel relatively long distances to attend concerts at these locations. In addition the concert season was limited to the summer months, and the main attractions at the concerts were, in general, not local musicians, but imports from Nashville and other places. However, many of the bluegrass festivals, like those held at Armuchee, Tallapoosa, and Blue Ridge, did feature local amateur artists from the Atlanta area and other places around the state. Again, attendance at the largely seasonal bluegrass festivals involved travel.

Fans of country music who preferred to enjoy their music in the privacy of their homes, as in the good old days of live radio, had to settle for their own album collections and radio stations that played country music records. The artists readily available on records were, for the most part, not Atlantans, but the ever-present Nashville-based pickers and singers. The music heard on local country-music radio stations, likewise, was usually not made by artists who called Atlanta home, but rather, was provided by the top forty tunes of the day on records played in relentless repetition. "One of the frustrating things about promoting records of new Atlanta artists," said Johnny Carson, "is that the local radio stations won't play them. So to get our records played we have to rely on small, independent radio stations around the country."[43]

As Bill Lowery has pointed out so many times, the glaring lack of opportunities in Atlanta for country music artists to develop their careers has made it necessary for local talent, even of the highest caliber, to look elsewhere, mainly Nashville, for these opportunities. "If you want to make a career in country music there's no reason to go anywhere except Nashville," agreed Harold Shedd, a native of Bremen, Georgia, whose aspirations with respect to country music, by the 1980s, had brought him a vice presidency of Polygram Records and an enviable reputation among Nashville's music moguls. On his rise from small-town musician to record company executive Shedd never found it necessary to consider Atlanta as an important stopover.[44] Other Georgians who have bypassed Atlanta on their way to making it big in the field of country music include the Forester Sisters and T. Graham Brown.

And what of the future of country music in Atlanta? Based on recent events, it appears from the perspective of the late 1980s that Atlanta will never pose a serious challenge to Nashville. That opportunity long ago was lost. So what is left to be done if Atlanta is to be a significant force in the country music industry? One hopes that in the coming years the clubs will continue to provide opportunities for the development of local talent. The Atlanta scene would be even drearier were it not for Bill Lowery and his various enterprises, so one cannot help but look to him for continued interest in promoting local country-music acts and ventures. One hopes that others of his ability, vision, and resources will emerge within the next few years. To paraphrase Atlanta's most noted heroine, Scarlett O'Hara, maybe tomorrow someone will come along who can think of a way to reclaim at least partially Atlanta's bygone glory as a leader in the field of country music. For after all, even in the world of music, tomorrow is another day.

Notes and Suggested Readings

INTRODUCTION

1. Bill C. Malone, *Country Music, U.S.A.*, rev. ed. (Austin, Tex.: University of Texas Press, 1985).

2. Robert Cantwell, *Bluegrass Breakdown: The Making of the Old Southern Sound* (Urbana: University of Illinois Press, 1984).

3. Nolan Porterfield, *Jimmie Rodgers: The Life and Times of America's Blue Yodeler* (Urbana: University of Illinois Press, 1979).

4. Neil V. Rosenberg, *Bluegrass: A History* (Urbana: University of Illinois Press, 1985).

5. Elizabeth Schlappi, *Roy Acuff: The Smoky Mountain Boy* (Gretna, La.: Pelican, 1978).

6. Charles Townsend, *San Antonio Rose: The Life and Music of Bob Wills* (Urbana: University of Illinois Press, 1976).

7. Ivan M. Tribe, *Mountain Jamboree: Country Music in West Virginia* (Lexington: University Press of Kentucky, 1984).

8. Gene Wiggins, *Fiddlin' Georgia Crazy: Fiddlin' John Carson, His Real World, and the World of His Songs* (Urbana: University of Illinois Press, 1987.)

9. Charles K. Wolfe, *Kentucky Country: Folk and Country Music of Kentucky* (Lexington: University Press of Kentucky, 1982).

10. Charles K. Wolfe, *Tennessee Strings: The Story of Country Music in Tennessee* (Knoxville: University of Tennessee Press, 1977).

11. *Georgia's Maps through the Years* (Atlanta: Georgia Department of Transportation, n. d.), p. 2.

12. Webb Garrison, *The Legacy of Atlanta: A Short History* (Atlanta: Peachtree Publishers, 1987), p. 2.

13. Ibid., p. 14.

14. John F. Stover, *The Railroads of the South: 1865–1900* (Chapel Hill: University of North Carolina Press, 1955), p. 58.

15. *Forty-Third Report of the Railroad Commission of Georgia* (Atlanta: Foote and Davies, 1916), pp. 158–79.

16. *Georgia's Maps*, p. 3.

17. Dana F. White and Timothy J. Crimmins, "How Atlanta Grew: Cool Heads, Hot Air, and Hard Work," *Atlanta Economic Review* 28 (January-February 1978): 7–15.

18. Population figures are taken from Franklin M. Garrett, *Atlanta and Environs: A Chronicle of Its People and Events*, vols. 1 and 2 (Athens: University of Georgia Press, 1954); Garrett cites as his sources various United States censuses.

19. Blaine A. Brownell and David R. Goldfield, "Southern Urban History," in Blaine A. Brownell and David R. Goldfield, eds., *The City in Southern History: The Growth of Urban Civilization in the South* (Port Washington, N.Y.: Kennikat Press, 1977), p. 8.

20. E. Merton Coulter, *Georgia: A Short History* (Chapel Hill: University of North Carolina Press, 1960), p. 355.

21. John A. Burrison, "Fiddlers in the Alley: Atlanta as an Early Country Music Center," *The Atlanta Historical Bulletin* 21 (Summer 1977): 59–87.

22. Brief but informative histories and profiles of Atlanta's major mill villages can be found in Kelly Jordan, "Atlanta's Mill Towns: Their Past, Their Present—Our Future?" *Atlanta Gazette*, December 17, 1975, 8–13.

23. Ronald G. Killion and Charles T. Waller, *A Treasury of Georgia Folklore* (Atlanta: Cherokee, 1972), p. xiv.

24. Ibid., p. 229.

25. Art Rosenbaum, *Folk Visions and Voices: Traditional Music and Song in North Georgia* (Athens: University of Georgia Press, 1983), p. xi.

26. Augustus B. Longstreet, *Georgia Scenes, Characters, Incidents &c.* (Savannah, Ga.: Beehive Press, 1975), pp. 7–19.

27. J. L. Herring, *Saturday Night Sketches: Stories of Old Wiregrass Georgia* (Boston: Gorham Press, 1918), p. 5.

28. Ibid., pp. 27–29.

29. Ibid., pp. 103–7.

30. Ibid., pp. 187–90.

31. Ibid., pp. 201–5.

32. Ibid., pp. 206–9.

33. Clifton Johnson, *Highways and Byways of the South* (New York: Macmillan, 1904), p. 100.

34. Ibid., p. 101.

35. Pete Lowry, "Atlanta Black Sound: A Survey of Black Music from Atlanta during the Twentieth Century," *Atlanta Historical Society Bulletin* 21 (Summer 1977): 88–113.

36. Ibid., p. 90.

37. Giles Oakley, *The Devil's Music: A History of the Blues* (New York: Taplinger, 1977), pp. 135–42.

38. Bruce Bastin, *Red River Blues: The Blues Tradition in the Southeast* (Urbana: University of Illinois Press), 1986.

39. Catherine Lynn Frangiamore and Pam Durban, "Not Just Whistlin' Dixie: Atlanta's Music 1837–1977," *Atlanta Historical Society Bulletin* 21 (Summer 1977): 15–36.

40. Lowry, "Atlanta Black Sound."

41. Jim Pettigrew, Jr., "From Rhythm 'n Blues to Disco: A Broad Overview of Atlanta Music since 1945," *Atlanta Historical Society Bulletin* 21 (Summer 1977): 114–38.

42. *Atlanta Blues 1933: A Collection of Previously Unissued Recordings by Blind Willie McTell, Curley Weaver and Buddy Moss*, JEMF-106 (Los Angeles: John Edwards Memorial Foundation, Inc., at the Folklore and Mythology Center, 1979).

43. Donald Lee Nelson, "Earl Johnson—Professional Musician," *JEMF Quarterly* 10 (Winter 1974): 169–71.

44. *Welcome South, Brother: Fifty Years of Broadcasting at WSB, Atlanta, Georgia* (Atlanta: Cox Broadcasting Corporation, 1974), p. 46.

45. The biographical information on Lambdin Kay comes from Franklin M. Garrett, *Atlanta and Environs*, vol. 3 (New York: Lewis Historical Publishing Company, 1954), p. 15, and an article written at the time of his death that appeared on page 36 of the *Atlanta Constitution* for September 16, 1965.

46. "Rites Wednesday for Ernest Rogers," *Atlanta Journal*, October 10, 1967, pp. 1A, 4A.

47. Margaret Hay Daugherty, "George D. Hay: The Solemn Ole Judge—A Pioneer P-R Man," *Bluegrass Unlimited* 17 (July 1982): 28–33.

48. Ernest Rogers, *Peachtree Parade* (Atlanta: Tupper and Love, Inc., 1956), p. 86.

49. Ibid., p. 87.

50. Ibid., pp. 86–87.

51. George D. Hay, *A Story of the Grand Ole Opry* (Privately published, 1953), p. 1.

52. Ibid.

53. Ibid.

54. Daugherty, "George D. Hay," pp. 31–32.

55. Karen Luehrs and Timothy J. Crimmins, "In the Mind's Eye: The Downtown as Visual Metaphor for the Metropolis," *Atlanta Historical Journal* 26 (Summer/Fall 1982): 177–98.

56. White and Crimmins, "How Atlanta Grew," p. 9.

57. Garrett, vol. 2, *Atlanta and Environs*, p. 34.

58. Luehrs and Crimmins, "In the Mind's Eye," p. 179.

59. *Saturday Evening Post*, June 26, 1926, p. 188.

60. Luehrs and Crimmins, "In the Mind's Eye," p. 180.

61. Roul Tunley, "Peachtree, Dixie Street of Magic," *American Magazine*, September 1955, p. 34.

62. Ibid., p. 32.

63. John R. Hornaday, *Atlanta: Yesterday, Today and Tomorrow* (No city: American Cities, 1922), p. 377.

64. Edward Robb Ellis, *A Nation in Torment: The Great American Depression, 1929–1939* (New York: Coward-McCann, 1970), p. 9.

CHAPTER 1

1. Oscar Theodore Barck, Jr., and Nelson Manfred Blake, *Since 1900*, 3rd ed. (New York: Macmillan, 1959), p. 126.

2. *Atlanta Journal*, March 31, 1913, p. 7.

3. *Atlanta Constitution*, March 30, 1913, p. 5B.

4. *Atlanta, A City of the Modern South*, compiled by Workers of the Writers' Program of the Work Projects Administration in the State of Georgia (St. Clair Shores, Mich.: Smith and Durrell, 1973), p. 129.

5. For a brief history of these mill villages see Kelly Jordan, "Atlanta's Mill Towns, Their Past, Their Present, Our Future?" *Atlanta Gazette*, December 17, 1975, pp. 8–13.

6. For a brief history of the Atlanta Auditorium-Armory see *Atlanta, A City of the Modern South*, pp. 164–65. See also Wayne W. Daniel, "Farewell," *Devil's Box* 15 (June 1, 1981): 49.

7. *Atlanta Constitution*, April 1, 1913, p. 9.

8. Ibid.

9. *Atlanta Georgian*, April 2, 1913, p. 4.

10. *Atlanta Journal*, April 2, 1913, p. 11.

11. Ibid.

12. *Atlanta Journal*, April 3, 1913, p. 9.

13. Ibid., April 4, 1913, p. 11.

14. *Atlanta Constitution*, April 4, 1913, p. 14.

15. Ibid.

16. Ibid.
17. *Atlanta Constitution*, January 23, 1916, p. 12A.
18. Paul Stevenson, *Atlanta Constitution*, October 31, 1925, p. 12.
19. *Atlanta Journal*, January 26, 1916, p. 8.
20. *Atlanta Constitution*, March 1, 1918, p. 7.
21. Ibid., February 24, 1918, p. 2A.
22. *Hearst's Sunday American*, November 16, 1919, p. 3A.
23. Ibid., February 24, 1918, p. 6A.
24. *Atlanta Journal*, February 18, 1914, p. 4.
25. *Atlanta Constitution*, November 14, 1920, p. 8A.
26. *Atlanta Georgian*, September 25, 1929, p. 6.
27. *Atlanta Journal*, February 18, 1914, p. 4.
28. *Atlanta Georgian*, November 16, 1920, p. 6.
29. *Atlanta Journal Magazine*, January 31, 1915, p. 7.
30. *Atlanta Georgian*, September 27, 1921, p. 7.
31. Ibid., September 28, 1921, p. 9.
32. *Atlanta Journal Magazine*, February 15, 1914, p. 7.
33. *Atlanta Georgian*, November 18, 1920, p. 8.
34. Ibid.
35. *Atlanta Journal*, April 2, 1913, p. 11.
36. Ibid.
37. O. B. Keeler, *Atlanta Georgian*, March 1, 1918, p. 3.
38. *Atlanta Constitution*, April 4, 1913, p. 14.
39. *Atlanta Journal Magazine*, January 31, 1915, p. 7.
40. *Atlanta Journal*, November 16, 1919, p. 4.
41. Ibid., November 19, 1919, p. 8.
42. Ibid.
43. *Atlanta Constitution*, February 3, 1915, p. 9.
44. Ibid., September 28, 1929, p. 6.
45. Ibid., February 3, 1915, p. 9.
46. *Atlanta Journal*, November 13, 1927, p. 2A.
47. Evidence indicates that the name Aleck Smart was a pseudonym. A scholar of old-time music, Professor Gene Wiggins of North Georgia College, was told that Smart's real name was Hogan. According to Wiggins's source, Hogan-Smart "travelled about as a professional photographer (on a bicycle) in the 1930's after the fiddlers' conventions in Atlanta stopped." Letter to author from Professor Wiggins, July 23, 1982.
48. *Atlanta Constitution*, February 19, 1914, p. 9.
49. *Atlanta Journal*, February 19, 1914, p. 4.
50. *Atlanta Constitution*, September 18, 1926, p. 22.
51. Ibid.
52. *Atlanta Journal*, February 28, 1918, p. 9.

53. *Atlanta Constitution*, October 26, 1923, p. 4.

54. Ibid.

55. *Atlanta Constitution*, February 4, 1915, p. 7.

56. Ibid., p. 4.

57. *Atlanta Georgian*, February 6, 1915, p. 2.

58. Linton K. Starr, "Atlanta Expects to Have Greatest Musical Season in Its History," *Musical America*, November 15, 1919, pp. 157–58.

59. *Atlanta Constitution*, November 16, 1927, p. 2.

60. *Atlanta Journal*, September 23, 1928, p. 12C.

61. *Atlanta Georgian*, March 2, 1918, p. 2.

62. *Atlanta Journal*, November 21, 1919, p. 5.

63. The *Literary Digest* article, which appeared on pages 70 and 71 of the issue for December 6, 1924, was reprinted in *Tennessee Old Time Fiddlers' Association Newsletter* 9 (July 4, 1969): 3–5. Professor Gene Wiggins has analyzed Benét's poem "in the context of fiddling and fiddlers' contests, with special reference to that contest which Benét probably read about in the *Literary Digest* before he wrote the poem." See Eugene Wiggins, "Benét's 'Mountain Whippoorwill': Folklore Atop Folklore," *Tennessee Folklore Society Bulletin* 41 (September 1975, no. 3): 99–114.

64. *Atlanta Journal*, April 1, 1913, p. 8.

65. Ibid.

66. *Atlanta Georgian*, April 10, 1917, p. 2.

67. The information for this list of winners comes from stories appearing in the Atlanta newspapers except for the years 1923 and 1925. The winners for these years were listed by Charles Wolfe in "The Atlanta Contests: 1921–34," *Devil's Box* 15 (March 1, 1981): 17–25.

68. Willard Neal, "Piano Tuned with Candy," *Atlanta Journal Magazine*, September 9, 1934, p. 9. Additional biographical data on A. A. Gray was obtained through interviews with his daughter, Mrs. Gladys Langley, at Tallapoosa, Georgia, on June 7, 1979, and his son, Earl Gray, at Bowdon, Georgia, in 1980.

69. Robert Nobley, "Tapescripts: Interview With Troy Gray," *John Edwards Memorial Foundation Newsletter* 2 (February 1967): 27–28.

70. Mrs. Ora Daniel, Tallapoosa, Georgia, June 8, 1979.

71. *Atlanta Journal*, March 26, 1934, p. 5.

72. Undated newspaper clipping in possession of Mrs. Gladys Langley.

73. *Atlanta Constitution*, January 30, 1916, p. 2B.

74. *Atlanta Journal*, November 22, 1920, p. 9.

75. Gene Wiggins, "Uncle John Patterson—Banjo King," *Devil's Box* 13 (September 1, 1979): 9–21.

76. *Atlanta Journal*, September 22, 1929, p. 10B.

77. Willard Neal, "Woman Is Champion Fiddler," *Atlanta Journal Magazine*, September 13, 1931, p. 2.

78. Mrs. Anita Sorrells Wheeler Mathis, interview, Atlanta, Georgia, December 6, 1980.

79. Neal, "Piano Tuned with Candy," p. 9.

80. Neal, "Woman Is Champion Fiddler," p. 2.

81. *Atlanta Georgian*, September 14, 1926, p. 11.

82. *Atlanta Constitution*, November 16, 1927, p. 2.

83. Ibid.

84. *Atlanta Journal*, September 21, 1930, p. 11.

85. Ibid.

86. *Atlanta Constitution*, September 28, 1934, p. 16.

87. *Atlanta Journal*, March 18, 1934, p. 10.

88. *Atlanta Constitution*, September 22, 1929, p. 4G.

89. Dudley Glass, "Our Town, News—Views," *Atlanta Georgian*, September 19, 1935, p. 3.

Suggestions for Further Reading

Burrison, John A. "Fiddlers in the Alley: Atlanta as an Early Country Music Center." *Atlanta Historical Bulletin* 21 (Summer 1977): 59–87.

Daniel, Wayne W. "A. A. Gray, Georgia Old-Time Fiddling Champion." *Old Time Music* 41 (Spring 1985): 9–13.

——. "A. A. Gray: Georgia State Fiddling Champion." *Devil's Box* 13 (December 1, 1979): 44–48.

——. "The Cradle of Country Music." *Atlanta Weekly*, March 4, 1984, pp. 10–15, 18.

——. "The Georgia Old-Time Fiddlers' Convention—A Pleasant Time Was Had by All." *Bluegrass Unlimited* 17 (August, 1982): 42–47.

——. "The Georgia Old-Time Fiddlers' Convention: 1920 Edition." *JEMF Quarterly* 16 (Summer, 1980): 7–73.

——. "Jimmy Jones—Tallapoosa, Georgia's Old-Time Fiddler." *Devil's Box* 14 (March 1, 1980): 25–30.

——. "Joe Collins—The Georgia State Fiddling Champion Who Didn't Own a Fiddle." *Devil's Box* 19 (Winter 1985): 24–28.

——. "Old-Time Fiddlers' Contests on Early Radio." *JEMF Quarterly* 17 (Fall 1981): 159–65.

——. "Old-Time Georgians Recall the Georgia Old-Time Fiddlers' Conventions." *Devil's Box* 15 (March 1, 1981): 7–16.

——. " 'Shorty' Harper: Georgia State Fiddling Champion of 1915 and 1916." *Devil's Box* 15 (June 1, 1981): 43–48.

———. "Women's Lib and the Georgia Old-Time Fiddlers' Conventions: The Story of Mrs. J. P. Wheeler, Georgia's Reigning Woman Fiddle Champion." *Devil's Box* 16 (March 1, 1982): 10–19.

Wiggins, Gene. "The First Atlanta Country Music Hall of Fame Awards." *Devil's Box* 17 (Spring, 1983): 28–30.

———. "Roosevelt's Fiddler: Bun Wright." *Devil's Box* 16 (December 1, 1982): 50–56.

Wolfe, Charles. "The Atlanta Fiddling Contests: 1913–1916." *Devil's Box* 14 (June 1, 1980): 12–29.

———. "The Atlanta Fiddling Contests: 1921–34." *Devil's Box* 15 (March 1, 1981): 17–25.

CHAPTER 2

1. Louis M. Hacker and Helene S. Zahler, *The United States in the 20th Century* (New York: Appleton-Century-Crofts, 1952), p. 353.

2. Frederick Louis Allen, *Only Yesterday* (New York: Bantam, 1959), p. 56.

3. *Atlanta Constitution*, June 3, 1926, p. 3.

4. Ibid., October 25, 1925, p. 16A.

5. Ibid.

6. *Atlanta Constitution*, September 11, 1926, p. l.

7. Allen, *Only Yesterday*, p. 115.

8. Christopher H. Sterling and John M. Kittross, *Stay Tuned: A Concise History of American Broadcasting* (Belmont, Calif.: Wadsworth, 1978), p. 60.

9. *Welcome South, Brother: Fifty Years of Broadcasting at WSB, Atlanta, Georgia* (Atlanta: Cox Broadcasting Corporation, 1974), pp. 7–12.

10. *Atlanta Journal*, March 18, 1922, p. l.

11. *Welcome South, Brother*, p. 11.

12. Ibid.

13. Franklin M. Garrett, *Atlanta and Environs*, vol. 3 (New York: Lewis Historical Publishing Company, 1954), p. 15.

14. Ernest Rogers, *Peachtree Parade* (Atlanta: Tupper and Love, 1956), p. 76.

15. Bob Coltman, "Across the Chasm: How the Depression Changed Country Music," *Old Time Music* 23 (Winter 1976/77): 6–12.

16. *Atlanta Journal*, April 17, 1922, p. 1.

17. Ibid., January 21, 1923, p. 5A.

18. Ibid., February 8, 1923, p. 14.

19. Ibid., July 6, 1924, p. 9A.

20. Ibid.

21. Ibid.

22. Ibid.

23. Ibid.

24. *Atlanta Journal*, June 10, 1925, p. 26.

25. Charles Wolfe, "Roba Stanley, the First Country Sweetheart," *Old Time Music* 26 (Autumn 1977): 13–18.

26. Archie Green, "Hillbilly Music: Source and Symbol," *Journal of American Folklore* 78 (July-September 1965): 204–28.

27. Ibid.

28. *Atlanta Journal*, February 18, 1925, p. 9.

29. In their article "Hell Broke Loose in Gordon County Georgia," *Old Time Music* 25 (Summer 1977): 9–21, Gene Wiggins and Tony Russell refer to the Georgia Yellow Hammers' recording of "The Picture on the Wall/My Carolina Sunshine Girl" as a "hit record which sold over 60,000 copies in 1928 alone."

30. *Atlanta Journal*, March 15, 1925, pp. 1, 6.

31. Ibid., February 25, 1923, p. 11.

32. Ibid., March 11, 1923, p. 6B.

33. Ibid., February 19, 1925, p. 2.

34. Ibid., February 15, 1925, p. 8B.

35. Ibid., July 25, 1925, p. 9.

36. Ibid., February 19, 1925, p. 2.

37. James W. (Bill) Lee, telephone conversation, June 1983.

38. Howard Scoggins, personal interview, June 1983.

39. *Atlanta Journal*, August 30, 1925, p. 7B.

40. Jake Groover also provided information on George Daniell and his Hill Billies band. Ottis Cheatham and Randy Carmichael, both of Smyrna, Georgia, assisted the author in locating Daniell's grave.

41. *Atlanta Journal*, August 10, 1924, p. 6; September 11, 1924, p. 11; April 1, 1925, p. 22; April 22, 1925, p. 22; June 20, 1925, p. 13; July 4, 1925, p. 5.

42. Ibid., January 26, 1928, p. 12.

43. Ibid., November 20, 1926, p. 3.

44. Ibid., March 12, 1927, p. 3.

45. Ibid., September 18, 1927, p. 9C.

46. Ibid., August 14, 1928, p. 8; personal interview with Mrs. Irene Eskew Spain Futrelle, Powder Springs, Georgia, November 6, 1984.

47. *Atlanta Journal*, November 7, 1929, p. 18.

48. *Atlanta Constitution*, August 2, 1926, p. 5.

49. *Atlanta Journal*, August 8, 1926, p. 14A.

50. Boris Emmet and John E. Jeuck, *Catalogues and Counters: A History of Sears, Roebuck and Company* (Chicago: University of Chicago Press, 1950), p. 623.

51. George C. Biggar, "Facts on Radio Broadcasting 1920–1964," in *Country Music Who's Who* (Denver: Heather, 1965), pp. 2, 4–5, 24, 28.

52. *Atlanta Journal*, November 27, 1926, p. 2.

53. *Atlanta Constitution*, October 3, 1926, p. 9B.

54. *Atlanta Journal*, January 23, 1927, p. 9C.

55. Ibid., March 20, 1927, p. 12B.

56. Ibid., May 8, 1927, p. 9D.

57. Ibid., July 4, 1927, p. 8.

58. Ibid., September 2, 1927, p. 22. The lady from Sylva, North Carolina, was Samantha Bumgarner, one of the first women ever to record old-time music for the phonograph.

59. Ibid., November 23, 1927, p. 8.

60. Ibid., September 4, 1927, p. 8A.

61. Ibid.

62. Ibid.

63. *Atlanta Journal*, September 7, 1927, p. 4.

64. Ibid., September 8, 1927, p. 16.

65. Ibid., September 9, 1927, p. 10.

66. Editor's note to George C. Biggar, "The WLS National Barn Dance Story: The Early Years," *JEMF Quarterly* 7 (Autumn 1971): 105–12.

67. *Atlanta Journal*, January 3, 1927, p. 8.

Suggestions for Further Reading

Daniel, Wayne W. "George Daniell's Hill Billies: The Band that Named the Music?" *JEMF Quarterly* 19 (Summer 1983): 81–84.

————. "Georgia's Pioneer Country Music Artists and Early Radio." *Bluegrass Unlimited* 16 (May 1982): 36–43.

CHAPTER 3

1. Roland Gelatt, *The Fabulous Phonograph*, 1877–1977, 2nd rev. ed. (New York: Macmillan, 1977), pp. 69–70.

2. Audio Engineering Society, *The Evolution of Recordings . . . From Cylinder to Video Disc* (New York, n. d.), p. 12.

3. Bill C. Malone, *Country Music U.S.A.* (Austin: University of Texas Press, 1968), pp. 29–30, 37–43. A revised and enlarged edition of this book was published in 1985 by the same publisher.

4. Ibid., pp. 40–41.

5. *Atlanta Journal*, June 15, 1923, p. 4.

6. Kyle Crichton, "Thar's Gold in them Hillbillies," *Collier's*, April 30, 1938, pp. 24, 27.

7. Ibid., p. 27.

8. Malone, *Country Music U.S.A.*, p. 38.

9. Charles K. Wolfe, *Tennessee Strings* (Knoxville: The University of Tennessee Press, 1977), p. 43.

10. Charles K. Wolfe, "The Birth of an Industry," in Patrick Carr, ed., *The Illlustrated History of Country Music* (Garden City, N. Y.: 1979), p. 57.

11. Norm Cohen, *Long Steel Rail: The Railroad in American Folksong*, (Urbana: University of Illinois Press, 1981), p. 33.

12. "Canned Music: Processing the Phonograph Record from the Wax Blank to the Finished Product," *Scientific American* 128 (March 1923): 182.

13. Bill Rattray (with preliminary discography), "Scottdale Boys," *Old Time Music* l (Summer 1971): 22. Corrections to the discography appear in *Old Time Music* 3 (Winter 1971/72): 23.

14. Rattray, "Scottdale Boys."

15. *Atlanta Journal*, January 29, 1927, p. 2.

16. Ibid.

17. Ibid.

18. *Atlanta Journal*, July 9, 1927, p. 2.

19. Extensive discographical data for Dilleshaw's sessions can be found in Charles Wolfe, "The Legend of John Dilleshaw," *Old Time Music* 36 (Summer 1981): 12–17.

20. *Atlanta Journal*, June 3, 1924, p. 8.

21. Ibid., June 17, 1924, p. 12.

22. Ibid., July 1, 1925, p. 16.

23. Ibid., March 13, 1925, p. 22.

24. Ibid., January 16, 1925, p. 18.

25. Ibid., March 14, 1925, p. 11; August 26, 1926, p. 22.

26. For further biographical data on John Dilleshaw see Charles Wolfe, "The Legend of John Dilleshaw."

27. Donald Lee Nelson, "Earl Johnson—Professional Musician" (with discography), *JEMF Quarterly* 10 (Winter 1974): 169–75.

28. Charles Wolfe, liner notes to the Georgia Yellow Hammers, *The Moonshine Hollow Band*, Rounder Records, long-play album no. 1032.

29. Gene Wiggins and Tony Russell, "Hell Broke Loose in Gordon County Georgia," *Old Time Music* 25 (Summer 1977): 9–16; Tony Russell, comp., "A Discography of Old Time Music in Gordon County," *Old Time Music* 25 (Summer 1977): 17–21; Dixie Landress, "I Remember Bud Landress," *Old Time Music* 30 (Autumn 1978): 16–17.

30. Charles Wolfe, Peggy Bulger, and Gene Wiggins, "Roba Stanley, the First Country Sweetheart," *Old Time Music* 26 (Autumn 1977): 13–18.

31. Ibid., p. 16.

32. Norm Cohen and Anne Cohen, "The Legendary Jimmie Tarlton," *Sing Out!* 16 (August/September 1966): 16–19.

33. Malone, *Country Music U.S.A.*, p. 170.

34. Graham Wickham, liner notes to *Darby and Tarlton*, Arhoolie Records, Old Timey LP-112.

35. Robert Nobley, "Land Norris: A Brief Biography" (with discography), *JEMF Quarterly* 7 (Autumn 1971): 122–25.

36. *Old Time Music* 29 (Summer 1978): 16.

37. Guthrie T. Meade, personal communication, November 24, 1980.

38. Donald Lee Nelson, "Uncle Tom Collins: Minstrel Man," *JEMF Quarterly* 8 (Summer 1972): 70–72.

39. Wayne W. Daniel, "Mack Compton—Disciple of Lowe Stokes," *Devil's Box* 16 (September 1, 1982): 46–52.

40. *Atlanta Journal*, February 25, 1927, p. 36.

41. Guthrie T. Meade, personal communication, November 24, 1980.

42. Charles Wolfe, "Lester Smallwood and His Cotton Mill Song," *Old Time Music* 25 (Summer 1977): 22–23.

43. Charles Wolfe, "Bill Helms on the Old-Time Fiddling Conventions," *Tennessee Valley Old-Time Fiddlers' Association Newsletter* 24 (March 1, 1974): 14–18.

44. Charles Wolfe, "Five Years with the Best: Bill Shores and North Georgia Fiddling," *Old Time Music* 25 (Summer 1977): 4–8.

45. Robert Nobley, "Uncle John Patterson—Then and Now," *Old Time Music* 25 (Summer 1977): 24.

46. Gene Wiggins, "Uncle John Patterson—Banjo King," *Devil's Box* 13 (September 1, 1979): 9–27.

47. Charles K. Wolfe, "The Oldest Recorded Fiddle Styles," *Devil's Box* 17 (Spring 1983): 21–27.

48. Nolan Porterfield, *Jimmie Rodgers: The Life and Times of America's Blue Yodeler* (Urbana: University of Illinois Press, 1979), pp. 159–61, 396–97.

49. *Atlanta Journal*, July 7, 1928, p. 3.

50. Porterfield, *Jimmie Rodgers*, p. 219.

51. John Atkins, ed., *The Carter Family* (London: Old Time Music, 1973), p. 39.

52. Atkins, *The Carter Family*, p. 42.

53. Alton Delmore, *Truth Is Stranger than Publicity* (Nashville: Country Music Foundation Press, 1977), p. 38.

54. Ibid.

55. For further information on the Delmore Brothers see Mike Leadbitter, "Wayne Raney & the Delmore Brothers on King," *Old Time Music* 10 (Autumn 1973): 19–23; Bill Harrison, notes to the reissue album *The Delmore Brothers*, County 402, 1971; and Louis Innis, album notes, *Brown's Ferry Four, 16 Greatest Hits*, Starday 3017, 1977.

56. Norm Cohen and Gene Earle, "An Ernest V. Stoneman Discography," *JEMF Quarterly* 16 (Spring 1980): 36–49. The most complete biographies of Stoneman are "The Early Recording Career of Ernest V. 'Pop' Stoneman: A Bio-Discography," JEMF Special Series, No. 1, published by the John Edwards Memorial Foundation at the University of California, Los Angeles, and the booklet accompanying the LP reissue, *Ernest V. Stoneman and the Blue Ridge Corn Shuckers* (Rounder-1008). A brief biographical sketch appears in Bill C. Malone and Judith McCulloh, eds., *Stars of Country Music* (Urbana: University of Illinois Press, 1975), pp. 21–23. Also of interest is Ivan M. Tribe, "The Return of Donna Stoneman: First Lady of the Mandolin," *Bluegrass Unlimited* 17 (June 1983): 16–26.

57. Charles Wolfe, *Nashville, The Early String Bands*, booklet accompanying two long-play reissue albums by the same name (County 541 and 542), 1975. For a discography see "Dr. Humphrey Bate and his Possum Hunters," *Old Time Music* 29 (Summer 1978): 17.

58. Tony Russell, "Homer Christopher and the Rise and Fall of the Piano Accordion," *Old Time Music* 33 (Summer 1979-Spring 1980): 15–17.

59. Charles K. Wolfe, "Man of Constant Sorrow: Richard Burnett's Story, 1 and 2," *Old Time Music* 9 (Summer 1973): 6–9, and 10 (Autumn 1973): 5–11. Burnett's discography may be found in *Old Time Music* 12 (Spring 1974): 32.

60. Donald Lee Nelson, "The Allen Brothers," *JEMF Quarterly* 7 (Winter 1971): 147–52; Tony Russell, "Chattanooga Boys: The Allen Brothers," *Old Time Music* 4 (Spring 1972): 12–14.

61. Clarence H. Greene, Jr., " 'Fiddling Clarence' Greene: Mountain Musician," *JEMF Quarterly* 7 (Winter 1971): 163–70.

62. "The Leake County Revelers, Waltz Kings of the Old South," *Old Time Music* 20 (Spring 1976): 26–30; "The Leake County Revelers on Record," *Old Time Music* 20 (Spring 1976): 31–35.

63. Ray Parker, "G. B. Grayson, A Short Life of Trouble," *Old Time Music* 35 (Winter 1980-Spring 1981): 10–14.

64. Norm Cohen, "Henry Whitter: His Life and Music," *JEMF Quarterly* 11 (Summer 1975): 57–66.

65. Henry Young, "Narmour and Smith—A Brief Discography," *JEMF*

Quarterly 7 (Spring 1971): 31–34.

66. Tony Russell, "The Roane County Ramblers," *Old Time Music* 8 (Spring 1973): 8.

67. Loyal Jones, "The Minstrel of the Appalachians: Bascom Lamar Lunsford at 91," *JEMF Quarterly* 9 (Spring 1973): 2–8.

68. Charles Wolfe, "Grover Rann and Harry Ayers and the Lookout Mountaineers," *Old Time Music* 22 (Autumn 1976): 17, 18.

69. Ivan M. Tribe, John W. Morris, and Leon Spain Mainer, *The Wade Mainer Story*, no date or place of publication, unpaginated.

70. Ibid.

Suggestion for Further Reading

DePriest, Joe. "Cheerful Dan Hornsby." *Bluegrass Unlimited* 24 (August 1989): 32–35.

CHAPTER 4

1. *Atlanta Journal*, March 30, 1913, p. 4.

2. Gene Wiggins, "John Carson: Early Road, Radio and Records," *Journal of Country Music* 8 (May 1979): 20–38.

3. There is some confusion regarding the date of Carson's birth, as discussed by Gene Wiggins in his book *Fiddlin' Georgia Crazy: Fiddlin' John Carson, His Real World, and the World of His Songs* (Urbana: University of Illinois Press, 1987), p. 3.

4. Fred Denton Moon, "55 Years as Fiddling King," *Atlanta Journal Magazine*, April 2, 1933, pp. 1, 18.

5. Charles K. Wolfe, *Tennessee Strings, The Story of Country Music in Tennessee* (Knoxville: University of Tennessee Press, 1977): pp. 25–26.

6. Herbert Wilcox, "Combed His Hair with a Wagon Wheel," *Atlanta Journal Magazine*, June 17, 1945, p. 10.

7. Jessie F. Stockbridge, "Shame to Whip Your Wife on Sunday," *Atlanta Journal Magazine*, April 16, 1939, p. 7.

8. Gene Wiggins, "The Socio-Political Works of Fiddlin' John and Moonshine Kate," *Southern Folklore Quarterly* 41 (1977): 97–118.

9. Willard Neal, "Fiddle Cures Aches and Pains," *Atlanta Journal Magazine*, March 18, 1934, pp. 9, 16. Actually the article gives the date of Carson's first championship bout as 1909. The 1899 date appears in another article, "Fiddlin' John on Broadway" (*Atlanta Journal Magazine*, February 10, 1924, pp. 1, 8), by Bert Collier. The earlier date is presumed to be correct since it accords with other statements about Carson that are presumed to be true.

10. *Atlanta Constitution*, April 4, 1913, p. 14.

11. Ibid., February 15, 1914, p. 4b.

12. *Atlanta Journal*, February 6, 1915, p. 2.

13. *Atlanta Constitution*, August 18, 1915, p. 7. For more on the Mary Phagan/Leo Frank case, the ballad of "Little Mary Phagan," and Fiddlin' John Carson's involvement, see Gene Wiggins, "The Socio-Political Works"; Saundra Keyes, " 'Little Mary Phagan': A Native American Ballad in Context," *Journal of Country Music* 3 (1972): 1–16; and D. K. Wilgus and Nathan Hurvitz, " 'Little Mary Phagan': Further Notes on a Native American Ballad in Context," *Journal of Country Music* 4 (1973): 17–30 (with reply by Saundra Keyes, p. 31).

14. *Atlanta Constitution*, February 2, 1915, p. 6.

15. *Hearst's Sunday American*, November 7, 1920, p. 7A.

16. Ibid., November 14, 1920, p. 2A.

17. Wiggins, "John Carson: Early Road, Radio and Records," p. 26.

18. Ernest Rogers, "John Carson to Celebrate 17 years on WSB," *Atlanta Journal*, March 22, 1939, p. 14. See also Moon, "55 Years as Fiddling King," p. l, who says that "John made his first appearance before the microphone at WSB on his birthday in 1922."

19. Lambdin Kay, "Fiddlin' John Carson, Champ of Champs, Publishes Own Hillbilly Tunes," *Atlanta Journal*, September 13, 1931, p. 8D.

20. *Atlanta Journal*, November 23, 1922, p. 26.

21. Ibid., February 4, 1923, p. 6B.

22. The *Radio Digest* article is reprinted in a booklet accompanying the long-play album *Fiddlin' John Carson—The Old Hen Cackled and the Rooster's Going to Crow* (Rounder 1003).

23. Archie Green, "Hillbilly Music: Source and Symbol," *Journal of American Folklore* 78 (July-September 1965): 204–28.

24. Wiggins, "John Carson: Early Road, Radio and Records," p. 31.

25. Bob Coltman, "Look Out! Here He Comes, Fiddlin' John Carson, One of a Kind, and Twice as Feisty," *Old Time Music* 9 (Summer 1973): 16–21.

26. Norm Cohen, "Fiddlin' John Carson: An Appreciation and a Discography," *JEMF Quarterly* 10 (Winter 1974): 138–56.

27. Coltman, "Look Out! Here He Comes," pp. 16, 20.

28. Ibid., p. 18.

29. Gene Wiggins, *Fiddlin' Georgia Crazy*, pp. 149–272.

30. Kay, "Fiddlin' John Carson."

31. Loyal Jones, *Radio's 'Kentucky Mountain Boy' Bradley Kincaid* (Berea, Ky.: Berea College Appalachian Center, 1980), pp. 29–30.

32. Wiggins, "The Socio-Political Works," p. 104.

33. Ibid., p. 106.

34. William Anderson, *The Wild Man from Sugar Creek: The Politi-

cal Career of Eugene Talmadge (Baton Rouge: Louisiana State University Press, 1975), pp. 76, 78.

35. *Atlanta Journal*, December 12, 1949, p. 32.
36. Wiggins, "The Socio-Political Works," p. 117.
37. *Atlanta Journal*, February 19, 1914, p. 4.
38. Biographical sketches of Gid Tanner may be found in Norman Cohen, "The Skillet Lickers: A Study of a Hillbilly String Band and Its Repertoire," *Journal of American Folklore* 78 (July–September 1965): 229–44; and Malone and McCulloh, eds., *Stars of Country Music*, pp. 27–34.
39. *Atlanta Georgian*, February 3, 1915, p. 3; *Atlanta Journal*, February 3, 1915, p. 4.
40. *Atlanta Constitution*, February 3, 1915, p. 9.
41. *Atlanta Journal*, February 6, 1915, p. 2.
42. Ibid., February 7, 1915, p. 9.
43. *Atlanta Constitution*, March 1, 1918, p. 7.
44. Cohen, "The Skillet Lickers," p. 229.
45. Charles Wolfe, *The Legend of Riley Puckett* (Bremen, West Germany: Archiv für Populare Musik, 1977), p. 6.
46. Ibid., pp. 16, 17.
47. *Hearst's Sunday American*, October 25, 1925, p. 8a.
48. Tony Russell, "The Skillet-Lickers on Record: A Columbia Discography 1926–31," *Old Time Music* 26 (Autumn 1977): 10–12.
49. Cohen, "The Skillet Lickers," p. 229.
50. Ibid., p. 242.
51. *Georgia State Gazetteer*, vol. 2 (Atlanta: Sholes, 1881), p. 92.
52. Louise Calhoun Barfield, *History of Harris County* (Columbus, Ga.: Columbus Office Supply Company, 1961), p. 340.
53. George R. Stewart, *American Place-Names* (New York: Oxford University Press, 1970), p. 256.
54. Catherine Stewart Prosser, "The Lure of Mountain Folk Songs," *Holland's Magazine* (December 1927): 32–33, 69.
55. Ethel Park Richardson, *American Mountain Songs* (New York: Greenberg, 1927), pp. 58, 59.
56. Douglas B. Green, *Country Roots* (New York: Hawthorne, 1976), p. 203.
57. Interview with Gordon Tanner, Dacula, Georgia, March 15, 1980.
58. Cohen, "The Skillet Lickers," p. 242.
59. Telephone interview with Puckett's widow, Blanche H. Bailey, January 24, 1983.
60. *Atlanta Journal*, January 26, 1916, p. 9.
61. Ibid., January 27, 1916, p. 8.

62. *Atlanta Georgian*, April 11, 1917, p. 2.

63. *Atlanta Journal*, April 11, 1917, p. 9.

64. Ibid., July 11, 1923, p. 13.

65. Ibid.

66. *Atlanta Journal*, March 26, 1934, p. 5.

67. Ibid., September 28, 1922, p. 17.

68. Ibid., September 29, 1922, p. 21.

69. Ibid., November 14, 1922, p. 18.

70. Ibid., June 17, 1923, p. 10A.

71. Ibid., November 13, 1922, p. 16.

72. Ibid., October 7, 1923, p. 6B; Ibid., October 9, 1923, p. 18.

73. Wolfe, *The Legend of Riley Puckett*, p. 16.

74. Bill C. Malone, *Country Music U.S.A.* (Austin: University of Texas Press, 1975), p. 51.

75. Wolfe, *The Legend of Riley Puckett*, pp. 6, 17–19.

76. Ibid., p. 7.

77. Ibid.

78. Tony Russell, "Georgia String Bands," *Old Time Music* 4 (Spring 1972): 4–8.

79. Wolfe, *The Legend of Riley Puckett*, p. 11.

80. Telephone interview with Mrs. Blanche Bailey, January 24, 1983.

81. Wolfe, *The Legend of Riley Puckett*, pp. 12, 13; Norm Cohen, "Riley Puckett: 'King of the Hillbillies,'" *JEMF Quarterly* 12 (Winter 1976): 175–84.

82. Wolfe, *The Legend of Riley Puckett*, p. 13.

83. Personal communication with Ernie Hodges, March 9, 1981.

84. Interview with Rev. Jack Cole, Adairsville, Georgia, January 7, 1984.

85. Telephone interview with Mrs. Blanche Bailey, January 24, 1983.

86. *Atlanta Georgian*, February 6, 1915, p. 2.

87. *Atlanta Constitution*, February 3, 1915, p. 9.

88. *Atlanta Journal*, February 7, 1915, p. 9.

89. *Atlanta Constitution*, February 7, 1915, p. 4A.

90. Juanita M. Lynch, "A Legend in His Own Time," unpublished manuscript, 1982, p. l.

91. "Clayton McMichen Talking," transcription of interview with McMichen conducted by Fred Hoeptner and Bob Pinson at Louisville, Kentucky, on July 7, 1959, published in *Old Time Music* 1 (Summer 1971): 8–10.

92. Ibid., p. 9.

93. Ibid., p. 10.

94. *Atlanta Constitution*, October 1, 1922, p. 4A.

95. Ibid., November 8, 1924, p. 22.
96. *Atlanta Journal*, May 4, 1929, p. 16; Ibid., August 23, 1931, p. 8B.
97. *Atlanta Journal*, September 19, 1922, p. 14.
98. Ibid., October 8, 1922, p. 11A.
99. Ibid., January 5, 1923, p. 14.
100. Ibid., September 9, 1923, p. 11A.
101. Ibid.
102. Ibid.
103. "Clayton McMichen Talking: 3," *Old Time Music* 3 (Winter 1971/2): 14–15, 19.
104. "Clayton McMichen Talking: 4," *Old Time Music* 4 (Spring 1972): 19–20, 30.
105. *Atlanta Journal*, February 26, 1930, p. 14.
106. Ibid., May 2, 1930, p. 18.
107. Lynch, "A Legend in His Own Time," pp. 8, 9.
108. Ibid., p. 3.

Suggestions for Further Reading

Armstrong, Randall. "Riley Puckett: Old-Time Guitarist." *Pickin'* 6 (December 1979): 7–8.
———. "Riley Puckett, Country Music's Pioneer Guitarist." *Bluegrass Unlimited* 19 (October 1984): 21–24.
"Clayton McMichen Talking: 2." *Old Time Music* 2 (Autumn 1971): 13–15.
Cordle, Joel. "Skillet Lickin' in Georgia." *Bluegrass Unlimited* 13 (March 1979): 38–41.
Davis, Stephen F. "Uncle Bert Layne." *Tennessee Valley Old-Time Fiddlers' Association Newsletter* 26 (September 1, 1974): 19–27.
La Rose, Joe. "An Interview with Lowe Stokes." *Old Time Music* 39 (Spring 1984): 6–11.
Nevins, Richard. "Lowe Stokes: North Georgia Fiddler." *Tennessee Valley Old-Time Fiddlers' Association* 9 (July 4, 1969): 3–5.
Riddle, Margaret. "A Skillet-Licker's Memoirs." *Old Time Music* 14 (Autumn 1974): 5–9.
———. "A Skillet-Licker's Memoirs, Part 2." *Old Time Music* 15 (Winter 1974/75): pp. 22–24.
Wiggins, Gene. "Gordon Tanner: Fiddler and Fiddle Maker." *Devil's Box* 12 (June 1, 1978): 18–25.
Wolfe, Charles K. "The Legend of Riley Puckett, Parts I and II." *Devil's Box* 10 (December 1, 1976): 17–23; and 11 (March 1, 1977): 52–60.
———. "McMichen in Kentucky: The Sunset Years." *Devil's Box* 11 (June 1, 1977): 10–18.

———. "Clayton McMichen: Reluctant Hillbilly." *Bluegrass Unlimited* 13 (May 1979): 56–61.

CHAPTER 5

1. Don Conger, ed., *The Thirties: A Time to Remember* (New York: Simon and Schuster, 1962).

2. Louis Filler, ed., *The Anxious Years: America in the Nineteen Thirties* (New York: Capricorn, 1963).

3. James D. Horan, *The Desperate Years: A Pictorial History of the Thirties* (New York: Crown, 1962).

4. Jack Salzman, ed., *Years of Protest: Collection of American Writings of the 1930's* (New York: Pegasus, 1967).

5. Caroline Bird, *The Invisible Scar* (New York: McDay, 1966).

6. Edward Robb Ellis, *A Nation in Torment: The Great American Depression, 1929–1939* (New York: Coward-McCann, 1970), pp. 288, 318.

7. H. S. Mariness, "A Dog Has Nine Lives: The Story of the Phonograph," *Annals of the Academy of Political and Social Science* 193 (September 1937): 8–13.

8. J. Krivine, *Juke Box Saturday Night* (London: New English Library 1977), p. 20.

9. Ralph Peer, "Rodger's Heritage," *Billboard* 66, no. 21 (May 22, 1954): 17; Goddard Lieberson, "Country Sweeps the Country," *New York Times Magazine*, July 28, 1957, pp. 13, 48.

10. *Atlanta Journal*, July 24, 1931, p. 4.

11. Bob Coltman, "Across the Chasm: How the Depression Changed Country Music," *Old Time Music* 23 (Winter 1976/77): 6–12.

12. William McKinley Randle, "History of Radio Broadcasting and its Social and Economic Effect on the Entertainment Industry, 1920–1930," vol. 1 (Ph.D. diss., Western Reserve University, 1966), p. 29.

13. I have scanned issues of the *Atlanta Journal* for the four Sundays preceding Christmas of 1929, and I found a total of only four ads for phonographs. In the issues of the *Journal* for the three Sundays preceding Christmas 1930, I discovered only one ad for a phonograph, while radios continued to be widely advertised. However, it should be noted that some of the radios for sale, both in 1929 and 1930, were radio-phonograph combinations.

14. *Atlanta Journal*, December 15, 1929, p. 9D.

15. Coltman, "Across the Chasm," p. 6.

16. Bill C. Malone, *Country Music U.S.A.* (Austin: University of Texas Press, 1968), p. 67.

17. Ibid., p. 104.

18. Coltman, "Across the Chasm," p. 6.

19. *Atlanta Journal*, February 9, 1930, p. 1.

20. *Welcome South, Brother: Fifty Years of Broadcasting at WSB, Atlanta, Georgia* (Atlanta: Cox Broadcasting Corporation, 1974), p. 25.

21. In her master's thesis, "A Study of the Chronological Development of the Three Regional Radio Broadcasting Stations in Atlanta, Georgia" (University of Georgia, Athens, 1954), Jacqueline Ernest Morrison states that WSB "went 'commercial' in the latter part of 1929" (p. 7). In *Welcome South, Brother* we read that "WSB had 'gone commercial' in 1927" although "not much effort was put into selling advertising until a few years later (p. 28)." See also a story on WSB by Ernest Rogers in the *Atlanta Journal*, March 14, 1937, p. 1. Rogers states that "WSB did not enter the commercial field until January 1927, when it became an affiliate of the National Broadcasting Company." Prior to that time the station's operation was "purely a goodwill project."

22. *Atlanta Journal*, November 4, 1929, p. 26.

23. Ibid., February 22, 1931, p. 9S.

24. Ibid., November 3, 1931, p. 8.

25. For a detailed history of one of the larger transcription companies, see Linda Painter, "The Rise and Decline of Standard Radio Transcription Company," *JEMF Quarterly* 17 (Winter 1981): 194–200.

26. *Atlanta Journal*, January 7, 1930, p. 12.

27. Ibid., April 16, 1930, p. 14.

28. "Bluebird Records: 1933–1941 (Part 3)," *Devil's Box* 15 (September 1, 1981): 57.

29. *Mountain Broadcast and Prairie Recorder* 2 (November 1940): 2.

30. *Atlanta Journal*, April 19, 1931, p. 8D.

31. *WLS Family Album*, 1930, p. 43.

32. Telephone interview with Jimmy Maloney, 1980.

33. *Atlanta Journal*, October 7, 1933, p. 7B.

34. Ibid.

35. Ibid., December 29, 1933, p. 23.

36. Charles K. Wolfe, "The Tweedy Brothers," *Devil's Box* 13 (September 1, 1979): 53–58.

37. Pat Ahrens, "The Role of the Crazy Water Crystals Company in Promoting Hillbilly Music," *JEMF Quarterly* 6 (Autumn, 1970): 107–9.

38. Crazy Water Crystals Show with Shorty's Crazy Hillbillies and Colonel Jack, ca. 1934. Radio program transcription from Guthrie T. Meade's collection.

39. *Atlanta Journal*, March 31, 1934, p. 5.

40. Ibid.

41. *Atlanta Journal*, February 17, 1935, p. 7D.

42. Ibid., November 4, 1933, p. 12.

43. Ibid., November 29, 1931, p. 4B. The Carolina Tarheels who appeared on WSB are not to be confused with another group with the same name (composed of Dock Walsh, Clarence Ashley, Garley Foster, and others) that was popular in North Carolina at the same time.

44. Ibid.

45. *Atlanta Journal*, November 20, 1932, p. 8D. Additional information on the personnel of the Carolina Tarheels was provided by Walter Propst of Concord, North Carolina.

46. Letter from Davis's step-granddaughter, Mrs. Katherine G. Smith, of Charlotte, North Carolina.

47. Charles K. Wolfe, *Tennessee Strings* (Knoxville: University of Tennessee Press, 1977), p. 50.

48. Joe La Rose, "An Interview With Lowe Stokes," *Old Time Music* 39 (Spring 1984): 10.

49. Personal communication from Guthrie T. Meade dated September 28, 1983.

50. "The Brunswick 100 Series (Concluded)," *JEMF Quarterly* 10 (Summer 1974): 78–82.

51. *Atlanta Journal*, July 9, 1932, p. 7.

52. Ibid., July 18, 1932, p. 18.

53. *Atlanta Journal*, April 24, 1932, p. 12D.

54. Ibid.

55. Telephone conversation with Marion Brown, February 11, 1980.

56. *Atlanta Journal*, April 22, 1934, p. 5B.

57. Fred Dellar, Roy Thompson, and Douglas B. Green, *The Illustrated Encyclopedia of Country Music* (New York: Harmony, 1977), p. 91.

58. Ibid.

59. *Atlanta Journal*, January 10, 1934, p. 10.

60. Ibid., February 22, 1934, p. 21.

61. Ibid., March 15, 1934, p. 12.

62. Ibid., May 3, 1934, p. 6.

63. Ibid., January 13, 1934, p. 7.

64. Ibid., March 4, 1934, p. 7B.

65. Ibid.

66. *Atlanta Journal*, May 19, 1934, p. 7.

67. Bill C. Malone and Judith McCulloh, *Stars of Country Music: Uncle Dave Macon to Johnny Rodriguez* (Urbana: University of Illinois Press, 1975), p. 145.

68. *Atlanta Journal*, December 23, 1934, p. 5B.

69. Ibid.

70. *Mountain Broadcast and Prairie Recorder* 2 (September 1941): 10.

71. *Atlanta Journal*, December 24, 1934, p. 7.
72. Ibid.
73. Ibid.
74. Biographical data were obtained through personal correspondence with Mr. Atcher, February 2, 1981.
75. *Atlanta Journal*, October 20, 1935, p. 7C.

Suggestions for Further Reading

Morgan, Mary. "Curly Fox—A Living Legend." *Bluegrass Unlimited* 11 (April 1977): 12–16.

Tribe, Ivan. "Curly Fox: Old Time and Novelty Fiddler Extraordinary." *Tennessee Valley Old-Time Fiddlers' Association Newsletter* 27 (December 1, 1974): 8–21.

Wolfe, Charles. "Doc Lew: The Life and Times of Lew Childre." *Bluegrass Unlimited* 13 (November 1978): 26–29.

———. "Up North with the Blue Ridge Ramblers: Jennie Bowman's 1931 Tour Diary." *Journal of Country Music* 6 (Fall 1975): 136–45.

CHAPTER 6

1. Gene Fowler and Bill Crawford, *Border Radio* (Austin: Texas Monthly Press, 1987), dust cover.

2. Letter from George Biggar to Joe Koehler, *Sponsor Magazine*, April 15, 1948. Quoted in Willie J. Smyth, "Early Knoxville Radio (1921–41): WNOX and the 'Midday Merry Go-Round,'" *JEMF Quarterly* 18 (Fall/Winter 1982): 109–15.

3. Information on Bill Gatins's early life was obtained through telephone conversations and personal interviews on several occasions in 1979 with his half-sister, Mrs. George W. Shults of Atlanta.

4. Information on the early days of Gatins's music career was provided through telephone conversations and personal insterviews on several occasions from 1979 to 1984 with Marion Brown of Atlanta.

5. Information on Gatins's later life and career was provided by his widow, Mrs. Ruth Gatins, during interviews conducted in 1979 at her home in Smyrna, Georgia.

6. Information on Red and Raymond obtained from Red's daughter, Mrs. Sherry Higdon, in several letters received during 1980 and 1981.

7. *Old Time Songs and Mountain Ballads*, no city, published by the Red Headed Briar Hopper [Red Anderson], no date, no pagination.

8. *Atlanta Journal*, September 8, 1934, p. 5.

9. Ibid., December 16, 1934, p. 10D.

10. Ibid., February 18, 1935, p. 10.

11. Ibid., July 5, 1936, p. 8D.

12. First-hand information on Pop Eckler has been difficult to obtain. Efforts to contact members of his family were unsuccessful. Most of the information on his career was provided by Curley Collins, Tex Forman, Red Murphy, and Kay Woods McWhorter through correspondence, telephone conversations, and personal interviews conducted between 1979 and 1984.

13. Bert Layne, "A Skillet-Licker's Memoirs," told to Margaret Riddle, *Old Time Music* 14 (Autumn 1974): 5–9.

14. Undated newspaper article in Doug Spivey's scrapbook.

15. *Pop Eckler's Radio Jamboree, Souvenir Program*, September 9, September 16, and July 15, 1939.

16. *Atlanta Journal*, November 9, 1939, p. 41.

17. Ibid.

18. *Fiddler's Gazzette*, November 4, 1939, pp. 1–4.

19. *Atlanta Journal*, June 17, 1938, p. 32.

20. Undated newspaper advertisment.

21. *Atlanta Journal*, December 16, 1939, p. 8.

22. Hoyt Pruitt (October 14, 1982), and Richard "Sonny" Allbright (December 11, 1984), personal communications; clipping from the *Cordele* (Georgia) *Dispatch*, October 13, 1947 (no page number), in Jane Atcheson's scrapbook.

23. Charles Wolfe, letter to author, May 14, 1981.

24. Otherwise unidentified newspaper clipping of an Associated Press story with dateline Covington, Kentucky, March 23 [1970], courtesy Charles K. Wolfe.

25. Tex Forman, numerous personal interviews and telephone conversations between 1979 and 1984.

26. Ruey "Curley" Collins, several letters and telephone conversations, 1980–84. Robin Traywick, " 'Curley' Collins Likes to Whittle and Fiddle," *Richmond Times-Dispatch*, April 13, 1981, p. B-7.

27. Kay Woods McWhorter, telephone conversation, December 11, 1984.

28. Biographical data on the Rice Brothers provided by Paul Rice in interviews conducted on June 7, 1977, Gene Wiggins, interviewer, and April 8, 1980, Wayne W. Daniel, interviewer.

29. Tony Russell, "QRS," *Old Time Music* 26 (Autumn 1977): 19–20; "The Brunswick 100 Series (concluded)," *JEMF Quarterly* 10 (Summer 1974): 78.

30. John Godrich and Robert M. W. Dixon, *Blues and Gospel Records*

1902–1942 (London: Storyville, 1969), p. 395.

31. *Atlanta Journal,* March 2, 1937, p. 13.

32. Paul Rice, Wiggins interview.

33. Paul Rice, Daniel interview.

34. Ibid.

35. Ibid.

36. Paul Rice, Wiggins interview.

37. Paul Rice, Daniel interview.

38. Guthrie Meade, "Rice Brothers Discography," undated, unpublished.

39. Unidentified magazine clipping in Tex Forman's collection.

40. Ibid.

41. *Fiddler's Gazzette,* November 4, 1939, p. 2.

42. *Atlanta Journal,* August 4, 1937, p. 12.

43. Ibid., December 5, 1937, p. 8D.

44. Ibid.

45. *Atlanta Journal,* April 10, 1938, p. 5B.

46. Ibid.

47. Ivan Tribe, "Georgia Crackers in the North," *Old Time Music* 30 (Autumn 1978): 9–12.

48. Interviews, in person and on telephone, with Mr. and Mrs. Bartow Henry, June 2, 1981; July 9, 1981; and other occasions.

49. Interview with Jimmy Smith, October 20, 1982.

50. Ivan Tribe, *Mountaineer Jamboree* (Lexington: University Press of Kentucky, 1984), pp. 173–74.

51. *Atlanta Journal,* December 24, 1939, p. 10C.

52. Doug Spivey, personal interview, October 18, 1981, and numerous letters and telephone calls between 1980 and 1984. Mrs. Marvin Taylor, mail questionnaire, July 28, 1981.

53. Unpublished discographical data provided by Guthrie T. Meade and Charles K. Wolfe.

54. Letter from Professor Toru Mitsui, Kanazawa University, Marunouchi, Kanazawa, Japan, April 27, 1988.

55. Douglas B. Green, *Country Roots: The Origins of Country Music* (New York: Hawthorn, 1976), p. 204.

56. Joel Whitburn, *Joel Whitburn's Pop Memories 1890–1954: The History of American Popular Music* (Menomonee Falls, Wis.: Record Research, 1954), p. 615.

57. Doug Spivey, personal interview, October 18, 1981.

58. Louise Hewitt, "Background of the 17 Dollar and 50 Cent Song and the 'Sunshine' It Spread," *Shreveport Times,* September 16, 1956, p. 3F.

59. Unpublished Rice Brothers discography compiled by Guthrie T. Meade.

60. Paul Rice, Daniel interview, April 8, 1980.

61. Ibid. One claimant to the authorship of "You Are My Sunshine" was Oliver Hood (1898–1959) of La Grange, Georgia. Mr. Hood was a musician and music teacher widely known in the west Georgia area. Surviving family members and musical associates are adamant in their assertion that Mr. Hood wrote the song. Those whom I interviewed consistently place the time of composition as the early 1930s. In 1955 Mr. Hood secured a copyright for a song titled "Somebody Stole My Sunshine Away."

62. "The Colorful Career of Jimmie Davis," *Hillbilly and Cowboy Hit Parade* 1 (1953): 30.

63. Dorothy Horstman, *Sing Your Heart Out, Country Boy* (New York: E. P. Dutton, 1975), p. 181.

64. Unpublished Bob Atcher discography, courtesy Guthrie T. Meade.

65. Letter from Bob Atcher, February 2, 1981.

Suggestions for Further Reading

Cohen, John, transcriber. "Cousin Emmy by Herself." *Sing Out!* 18 (June/July 1968): 26–27.

Daniel, Wayne W. "Bill Gatins and His Jug Band." *Old Time Music* 37 (Autumn 1981-Spring 1982): 8–13.

———. "Cousin Emmy, a Popular Entertainer Country Music History Almost Forgot." *Bluegrass Unlimited* 20 (October 1985): 64–68.

———. "The Pine Ridge Boys." *Old Time Music* 40 (Winter 1984): 8–11.

———. " 'Slimbo' Smith—'Cross Roads Follies' Fiddler: An Update." *Devil's Box* 15 (March 1, 1981): 41–42.

———. "Tex Forman and Curley Collins Remember Pop Eckler and His Young 'Uns." *JEMF Quarterly* 16 (Fall 1980): 132–39.

Kienzle, Rich. "The Checkered Career of Hank Penny." *Journal of Country Music* 8 (1980): 43–48, 61–77.

———. "Hank Penny." *Old Time Music* 28 (Spring 1978): 5–16.

Melton, Ray. " 'Slimbo' Smith—'Cross Roads Follies' Fiddler." *Tennessee Valley Old Time Fiddlers' Association Newsletter* 25 (June 1, 1974): 27.

Wolfe, Charles. "Ernie Hodges: From Coal Creek to Bach." *Devil's Box* 9 (June 1, 1975): 22–41.

———. "Would You Believe: La Follette, Bud Silvey, and Huntsville, 1928." *Tennessee Valley Old Time Fiddlers' Association Newsletter* 26 (September 1, 1974): 54–59.

CHAPTER 7

1. Ernest Rogers, *Peachtree Parade* (Atlanta: Tupper and Love, 1956), p. 74.

2. *Atlanta Journal*, January 13, 1924, p. 7A.

3. Don Naylor, former WGST employee, personal communication, December 20, 1984.

4. *Atlanta Journal*, May 7, 1924, p. 13.

5. Ibid., October 25, 1925, p. 11S.

6. Ibid., February 11, 1926, p. 6.

7. Thornwell Jacobs, *Step Down, Dr. Jacobs* (Atlanta: Westminster, 1945), p. 437.

8. Ibid.

9. *Georgia, a Guide to Its Towns and Countryside*, American Guide Series, Compiled and written by Workers of the Writer's Program of the Works Progress Administration (Athens, Ga.: University of Georgia Press, 1940), p. 105.

10. *Welcome South, Brother: Fifty Years of Broadcasting at WSB, Atlanta, Georgia* (Atlanta, Ga.: Cox Broadcasting Corporation, 1974), pp. 34, 36.

11. Barnwell Rhett Turnipseed, III, "The Development of Broadcasting in Georgia, 1922–1959" (Master's thesis, University of Georgia, 1960), pp. 119, 124, 129, 132, 135, 138. WTJH, which began broadcasting in December, featured hillbilly music, but it started too late to have any appreciable impact on the Atlanta hillbilly music scene of the 1940s.

12. Gene Wiggins, "Not Very Aristocratic," *Old Time Music* 26 (Autumn 1977): 5–9.

13. Earl Bolick, personal interview, Decatur, Georgia, August 19, 1980; Bill Bolick, numerous letters and telephone conversations during 1980 and 1981.

14. Douglas B. Green, "The Blue Sky Boys on Radio, 1939–1940: A Newly-Discovered Log of Their Daily Program, Kept By Ruth Walker," *Journal of Country Music* 4 (Winter 1973): 108–58.

15. Earl and Bill Bolick interviews.

16. Earl Bolick interview.

17. Ivan Tribe, *Mountaineer Jubilee* (Lexington: University Press of Kentucky, 1984), p. 100. According to Bill Bolick the original title was "Black Mountain Blues."

18. Biographical data on the Coles obtained in interviews with Hazel Cole (October 11, 1981) and Rev. Jack O. Cole (January 7, 1984).

19. Ivan M. Tribe and John W. Morris, *Molly O'Day, Lynn Davis, and*

the Cumberland Mountain Folks: A Bio-Discography (Los Angeles: John Edwards Memorial Foundation, 1975), p. 28.

20. Grady Cole, letter to the *Mountain Broadcast and Prairie Recorder* 18 (January 1944): 8.

21. Ibid.

22. Ibid.

23. John Fulton and Frank Gayther, co-managers of WGST, letter dated January 15, 1946.

24. Ibid.

25. Note in Grady Cole's scrapbook.

26. Slim Bryant, letter, *JEMF Quarterly* 12 (Autumn 1976): 109.

27. Telephone conversation with Hoyt "Slim" Bryant, February 8, 1988.

28. Carl Talton, interview at Decatur, Georgia, September 7, 1981, and several subsequent telephone conversations.

29. Johnnie and Stella Pierce, interview, Kennesaw, Georgia, August 30, 1982.

30. George Head, interview, Atlanta, Georgia, November 1, 1980.

31. Tommy Trent, correspondence, October 28, 1982.

32. Jack Holden interview Decatur, Georgia, September 15, 1980, and Fairly Holden interview, Atlanta, Georgia, September 10, 1980.

Suggestions for Further Reading

Bolick, William A. (with introduction and commentary by William A. Farr). "Bill Bolick's Own Story of the Blue Sky Boys." *Sing Out!* 17 (April/May 1967): 18–21.

Daniel, Wayne W. "Bill and Earl Bolick Remember the Blue Sky Boys." *Bluegrass Unlimited* 16 (September 1981): 14–21.

———. "Roots of Bluegrass: The Holden Brothers." *Bluegrass Unlimited* 16 (November 1981): 24–30.

———. "They Left Them to Die Like 'The Tramp on the Street'—The Story of Grady and Hazel Cole." *Bluegrass Unlimited* 20 (August 1985): 69–74.

DePriest, Joe. "The Sweet Fiddling of Pappy Sherrill." *Bluegrass Unlimited* 20 (February 1986): 22–25.

Graham, Keith. "Slim Bryant Became Engineer of Guitar." *Atlanta Journal*, November 13, 1985, pp. 1C, 4C.

"Hoyt 'Slim' Bryant." *Jimmie Rodgers Memorial Association Newsletter* 3 (Spring/Summer, 1984): 1–3.

CHAPTER 8

1. Oscar Theodore Barck, Jr., and Nelson Manfred Blake, *Since 1900*, 3rd ed. (New York: Macmillan, 1959), p. 628.

2. Christopher H. Sterling and John M. Kitross, *Stay Tuned: A Concise History of American Broadcasting* (Belmont, Calif.: Wadsworth, 1978), 197, 313.

3. George C. Biggar, "The Case for Hillbillies," *Billboard* 52 (April 13, 1940): 12, 64.

4. Ibid.

5. Ibid.

6. *Welcome South, Brother: Fifty Years of Broadcasting at WSB, Atlanta, Georgia* (Atlanta, Ga.: Cox Broadcasting Corporation, 1974), p. 36.

7. Telephone conversations with John Lair (January 22, 1980) and J. Leonard Reinsch (January 24, 1980). For information on John Lair's career see Charles K. Wolfe, *Kentucky Country* (Lexington: University Press of Kentucky, 1982), pp. 76–84.

8. *Atlanta Journal*, October 4, 1942, p. 19C.

9. Linnell Gentry, *A History and Encyclopedia of Country, Western, and Gospel Music* (Nashville: McQuiddy Press, 1961), pp. 168–75.

10. *Mountain Broadcast and Prairie Recorder* 2 (September 1941): 10.

11. Jacquelin Ernest Morrison, "A Study of the Chronological Development of the Three Regional Radio Broadcasting Stations in Atlanta, Georgia" (Master's thesis, University of Georgia, 1954), p. 17.

12. *Atlanta Journal*, November 16, 1940, p. 9.

13. Ibid., November 23, 1940, p. 9.

14. Ibid., January 4, 1941, p. 9.

15. James (Carson) Roberts, letter to author, January 2, 1985.

16. Interview of Joseph A. Carrier, Atlanta, Georgia, September 12, 1979, and numerous subsequent personal conversations, telephone conversations, and letters.

17. "WSB Barn Dance" script in Cotton Carrier's scrapbook.

18. Ibid.

19. Information on the life of Bobby Atcheson was obtained through interviews with his widow, Mrs. Jane Atcheson, Decatur, Georgia, October 7, 1982, and his brother, Mac Atcheson, Stone Mountain, Georgia, September 13, 1982, and through a telephone conversation with his sister, Mrs. Lucille Wehunt, on November 6, 1982.

20. Telephone conversation with Boudleaux Bryant, August 11, 1981.

21. Numerous interviews and telephone conversations with Harpo Kidwell between 1979 and 1988.

22. Interview of Mrs. Cotton (Jane Logan) Carrier, Atlanta, Georgia, January 29, 1981.

23. Bill C. Malone, *Country Music, U.S.A.* (Austin: University of Texas Press, 1975), p. 168.

24. Interview of Dennis "Boots" Woodall, Atlanta, Georgia, February 18, 1980.

25. Radio script, courtesy Mr. Don Naylor, Decatur, Georgia.

26. Letter from Don Naylor, March 8, 1988.

27. Louis M. Jones (with Charles K. Wolfe), *Everybody's Grandpa* (Knoxville: University of Tennessee Press, 1984), p. 67.

28. *Time*, December 6, 1943, p. 62.

29. R. M. Schmitz, "Leo Frank and Mary Phagan," *Journal of American Folklore* 60 (January-March 1947): 59–61.

30. Interview of Mac Atcheson, Stone Mountain, Georgia, September 13, 1982. Subsequent quotes attributed to Mr. Atcheson are from this and other personal and telephone interviews with him.

31. Information on Dwight Butcher's life and career obtained from a tapescript (made by Bob Pinson) of an interview with Butcher by Gene Earle on November 5, 1967. The tapescript was published in the *JEMF Quarterly* 5 (Spring 1969): 10–16. Also of interest is the "Dwight Butcher Discography," Ibid., pp. 17–22.

32. Dwight Butcher obituary, *Old Time Music* 30 (Autumn 1979): 18.

33. Taped comments of Hank Penny, October 1979, and biographical sketch of Penny in Cotton Carrier's scrapbook. Subsequent quotes attributed to Mr. Penny are from the taped comments.

34. Interview of Mrs. Rebecca Cassell (Pete Cassell's mother), Lincolnton, Georgia, September 25, 1982.

35. Letter of Mrs. Ruth Spicer (formerly Mrs. Pete Cassell), dated December 11, 1984.

36. Copy in Cotton Carrier's scrapbook.

37. Mrs. Charles Woodruff (Bertha Amburgey) provided biographical data on the Amburgey sisters in a telephone interview on December 15, 1982, and in a letter dated February 3, 1983.

38. *Atlanta Journal*, December 22, 1940, p. 8B.

39. James (Carson) Roberts, mail questionnaire, March 10, 1980.

40. *Atlanta Journal*, April 12, 1941, p. 16. According to the *Journal's* radio log, however, Jimmy Carson had been heard on the "Barn Dance" as early as March 22, 1941.

41. *Atlanta Journal*, December 6, 1941, p. 9.

42. For a more detailed discussion of the relationship between gospel music and hillbilly music, see Wayne W. Daniel, "Making a Joyful Noise

Unto the Lord—The Gospel Roots of Bluegrass," *Bluegrass Unlimited* 19 (March 1985): 58–62.

43. *Atlanta Journal*, March 22, 1941, p. 9.

44. Biographical data on the Swanee River Boys provided by Billy Carrier during an interview, Smyrna, Georgia, July 15, 1980, and several subsequent conversations on the telephone and in person.

45. Information on the Sunshine Boys obtained during interview with Eddie Wallace, Stockbridge, Georgia, September 28, 1982 and telephone interview with Ace Richman.

46. Telephone interview of Ivy Peterson.

47. "WSB Barn Dance" script in Cotton Carrier's scrapbook.

48. Don Eddy, "Hillbilly Heaven," *American Magazine* 153 (March 1952): 121.

Suggestions for Further Reading

Daniel, Wayne W. "Bobby Atcheson: Country Fiddler and Multi-Media Artist." *Devil's Box* 17 (Summer 1983): 29–39.

———. "From Barn Dance Emcee to Recording Company Executive— The Story of Cotton Carrier." *JEMF Quarterly* 15 (Winter 1979): 230–36.

———. "Harpo Kidwell: Portrait of an Early Country Musician." *Journal of Country Music* 9, no. 2 (1982): 26–33.

———. " 'Rocky Top'—The Song and the Man and Woman Who Wrote It." *Bluegrass Unlimited* 16 (April 1982): 20–23.

———. "The Sunshine Boys: A Study in Versatility." *Precious Memories: The Journal of Gospel Music* 2 (January-February 1989): 24–28

———. " 'We Had to Be Different to Survive'—Billy Carrier Remembers the Swanee River Boys." *JEMF Quarterly* 18 (Spring/Summer 1982): 59–83.

Griffis, Ken. "Hank Penny: The Original 'Outlaw'?" *JEMF Quarterly* 18 (Spring/Summer 1982): 5–12.

Kienzle, Rich. "The Checkered Career of Hank Penny." *Journal of Country Music* 8, no. 2, (1980): 43–48, 61–77.

———. "Hank Penny." *Old Time Music* 28 (Spring 1978): 5–10; "Hank Penny Discography," Ibid., pp. 11–16.

———. "Hank Penny Discography." *JEMF Quarterly* 18 (Spring/Summer 1982): 13–22.

Tribe, Ivan M. "James (Carson) Roberts: Thirty-three Years in Old Time Gospel and Bluegrass Music." *Bluegrass Unlimited* 14 (May 1980): 66–72.

———. "The Smith Brothers, Tennessee and Smitty." *Bluegrass Unlimited* 15 (July 1980): 22–25.

CHAPTER 9

1. Alvin L. Bertrand, ed., *Rural Sociology* (New York: McGraw-Hill, 1958), p. 53.

2. Everett M. Rogers and Rabel J. Burdge, *Social Change in Rural Societies*, 2nd ed. (New York: Appleton-Century-Crofts, 1972), p. 250.

3. George Sessions Perry, "Atlanta," *Saturday Evening Post*, September 22, 1945, pp. 26, 27, 47, 49, 50, 52.

4. Ibid., pp. 27, 50.

5. "Industry Spreads in Atlanta," *Business Week*, September 10, 1949, pp. 44, 46.

6. "Surge in the South: The Long Reach of Atlanta," *Newsweek*, March 15, 1954, pp. 59–62.

7. Telephone interviews of Jerry Vandeventer, February 23, 1986, and Elmo Ellis, March 7, 1986.

8. Telephone interview of Don Carroll, February 22, 1986.

9. Telephone interview of Ray Kinnamon, February 3, 1986.

10. Interview of Jack Greene, Nashville, Tennessee, June 14, 1986. For a more detailed account of Jack Greene's career, see Irwin Stambler and Grelun Landon, *The Encyclopedia of Folk, Country and Western Music*, 2nd ed. (New York: St. Martin's, 1983), pp. 276–78.

11. Over the years Bill Anderson has been written about extensively in Atlanta's newspapers. The following are among the more informative of these stories: Maggie Davis, "He's a City Boy Who Writes Country Music," *Atlanta Journal Magazine*, September 17, 1961, p. 38; Paul Hemphill, "Hometown Boy," *Atlanta Journal*, March 24, 1967, p. 2; Dick Gray, "Bill Anderson Digs Baseball, Wants to Act," *Atlanta Journal*, April 8, 1967, p. 1G; Terry Kay, "Georgia's Bill Anderson Glitters in Grand Ole Opry," *Atlanta Journal*, July 24, 1967, p. 15A; Phil Gailey, "Bill Anderson—The Button-Down Hillbilly," *Atlanta Journal/Constitution Magazine*, April 20, 1969, p. 34; Jerry Parker, "U. Ga. Grad Anderson Keeps Secret No More," *Atlanta Journal*, October 4, 1974, p. 13D; Sharon Thomason, "Bill Anderson: Cries and Whispers," *Atlanta Journal/Constitution Magazine*, March 11, 1979, p. 36. See also Stambler and Landon, *Encyclopedia of Folk, Country and Western Music*, pp. 12–14.

12. Bill C. Malone, *Country Music U.S.A.*, rev. ed. (Austin: University of Texas Press, 1985), p. 208.

13. Barbara Smith, "Sunshine Boys Leave for Coast Tuesday," *Atlanta Journal*, November 17, 1948, p. 28.

14. Edwina Davis, "Clothes Make TV, Sunshine Boys Find," *Atlanta Journal*, October 22, 1948, p. 30.

15. Information on Brenda Lee's career was provided by her agent,

The Jim Halsey Co., Inc. See also Michele Greppi, "Brenda Lee," *Atlanta Journal/Constitution Weekend*, August 3, 1985, pp. 32–33, 35; and Stambler and Landon, *Encyclopedia of Folk, Country and Western Music*, pp. 391–92.

16. Undated clipping from *T.V. Digest*, p. 28, in Mrs. Bobby Atcheson's scrapbook.

17. *Atlanta Journal*, December 2, 1951, p. 21C.

18. Telephone interview of Mrs. Christine (Logan) Ogletree, April 6, 1986.

19. For a more detailed account of Billy Walker's career, see Stambler and Landon, *Encyclopedia of Folk, Country and Western Music*, pp. 768–69.

20. Dallas Burrell, unpublished autobiographical sketch presented to author, December 10, 1984.

21. "The Peachtree Cowboys Have a New Home," *T.V. Digest*, February 28, 1953, pp. 4–5.

22. Telephone interview of Ms. Mitchem, January 27, 1986.

23. Interview of Roy Drusky, Nashville, Tennessee, June 14, 1986. See also Paul Hemphill, "Ambition," *Atlanta Journal*, August 13, 1968, p. 2A, and Stambler and Landon, *Encyclopedia of Folk, Country and Western Music*, pp. 200–202.

24. Biographical data obtained from documents provided by Pete Drake Productions. For a more detailed account of Pete Drake's career, see Stambler and Landon, *Encyclopedia of Folk, Country and Western Music*, pp. 196–97.

25. Personal interview of Gordon Dee, October 18, 1988.

26. Telephone interview of Jimmy Smart, October 12, 1988.

27. For more details about the careers of Carl Leming and his various bands, see the following articles by Wayne W. Daniel: "Carl Leming: The Flying Fiddler," *Devil's Box* 14 (December 1, 1980): 35–41; "Flying High: The Dixie Hoedowners," *Bluegrass Unlimited* 15 (February 1981): 20–25.

28. Telephone interview of Mike Fleming, March 9, 1986. A detailed account of Brush Fire's career, along with biographical sketches of each band member, appears in Bill Brown and Jack Sorrells, "Brush Fire, An Emerging Force in Bluegrass," *SEBA Breakdown* (published by the Southeastern Bluegrass Association), Winter 1985, 3 pages, unnumbered.

29. Interview of Bill Lowery, Atlanta, Georgia, January 31, 1986. See also "King William—Atlanta's Music Business Leader," *Billboard*, August 8, 1970, pp. A3-A4; Phil Garner, "Bill Lowery's Greatest Hits," *Atlanta Journal/Constitution Magazine*, December 19, 1971, pp. 6, 7, 12; Art Harris, "Bill Lowery Cranks Out Hit After Hit," *Atlanta Consti-*

tution, November 17, 1975; Bill King, "Lowery Has Been a Big Hit in Atlanta," *Atlanta Journal and Constitution,* November 20, 1976, p. 8A; Bill King, "Artists Pay Tribute to Lowery," *Atlanta Constitution,* November 17, 1977, p. 10B; Keith Graham, "Bill Lowery, Atlanta's Music Man," *Atlanta Weekly,* August 7, 1988, pp. 8–12.

30. *Billboard,* January 27, 1973, p. 58.

31. Interview of Bill Lowery.

32. Robert Lamb, "Hamlet of Tin Pan Alley," *Atlanta Weekly,* March 7, 1982, pp. 6–8, 26.

33. Ibid., p. 8.

34. Ibid., p. 26.

35. Red O'Donnell, quoted in Stambler and Landon, *Encyclopedia of Folk, Country and Western Music,* p. 597.

36. Russ DeVault, "Jerry Reed: All-round Good Ol' Boy," *Atlanta Journal and Constitution Weekend,* May 19, 1984, pp. 30–31.

37. Biographical data obtained from promotional material provided by Jerry Reed Enterprises. See also DeVault, "Jerry Reed," and Stambler and Landon, *Encyclopedia of Folk, Country and Western Music,* pp. 597–98.

38. Linda Lanier, "Ray Stevens Returns Here—'Everything Is Beautiful,'" *Atlanta Journal,* June 16, 1971, p. 20D.

39. Clara Hieronymous, "Ray Stevens," *BMI: The Many Worlds of Music,* December 1970, p. 19.

40. Ibid.

41. For a more detailed account of Ray Stevens' career, see Stambler and Landon, *Encyclopedia of Folk, Country and Western Music,* pp. 704–6.

42. Telephone interview of Johnny Carson, November 17, 1988.

43. Ibid.

44. Telephone interview of Harold Shedd, December 9, 1988.

Suggestions for Further Reading

Hemphill, Paul. *The Nashville Sound: Bright Lights and Country Music.* New York: Simon and Schuster, 1970.

Miller, Zell. *They Heard Georgia Singing.* Franklin Springs, Ga.: Advocate Press, 1984.

Rhodes, Don. *Down Country Roads with Ramblin' Rhodes.* Hartwell, Ga.: North American, 1982.

Appendix:
A Selected Discography of
Long-Play Albums

Anderson, Bill. *Whispering Bill*. MCA 416.
Blue Sky Boys. *Blue Sky Boys*. BB AXM2-5525.
———. *Blue Sky Boys*. Camden Cal 797.
———. *The Blue Sky Boys in Concert—1964*. Rounder 0236.
———. *Precious Moments with the Blue Sky Boys*. Pine Mountain PMR 269.
———. *Presenting the Blue Sky Boys*. John Edwards Memorial Foundation 104.
———. *The Sunny Side of Life*. Rounder 1006.
———. *A Treasury of Rare Song Gems from the Past*. Pine Mountain PMR 305.
———. *20 Country Classics Bluegrass Mountain Music*. Camden Adl 2-0726(e).
Brush Fire. *Brush Fire*. RSR 1191.
Butcher, Dwight. *Dwight Butcher*. Certified 1502.
Carson, Fiddlin' John. *The Old Hen Cackled and the Rooster's Going to Crow*. Rounder 1003.
Carson, James and Martha. *Early Gospel Greats*. ACM 18.
Cassell, Pete. *The Legend of Pete Cassell*. Hilltop JS-6023 (JM-6023).
Childre, Lew. *Old Time Get-Together*. Starday SLP 153.
Cousin Emmy. *The New Lost City Ramblers with Cousin Emmy*. Folkways FT 1015.
Darby, Tom, and Jimmie Tarlton. *Darby and Tarlton*. Old Timey 112.
———. *Early Steel Guitar*. Bear Family 15504.
Drake, Pete. *Steel Away*. Canaan.
Drusky, Roy. *New Lips*. Pickwick.

Selected Discography

Georgia Yellow Hammers. *The Moonshine Hollow Band.* Rounder 1032.
Greene, Jack. *Jack Greene's Greatest Hits.* MCA 291.
Johnson, Earl, and His Clodhoppers. *Red Hot Breakdown.* County 543.
Lee, Brenda. *The Versatile Brenda Lee.* Decca DL7-4661.
McMichen, Clayton. *The Traditional Years.* Davis Unlimited 33032.
Patterson, Uncle John. *Plains, Georgia Rock.* Arhoolie 5018.
Penny, Hank, and His Radio Cowboys. *Tobacco State Swing.* Rambler 103.
Puckett, Riley. *Old Time Greats, Volume 1.* GHP LP 902.
————. *Old Time Greats, Volume 1.* Old Homestead, OHCS 114.
————. *Old Time Greats, Volume 2.* Old Homestead, OHCS 174.
————. *Red Sails in the Sunset.* BFX 15280.
————. *The Riley Puckett Story.* Roots RL 701.
————. *Waitin' for the Evening Mail.* County 411.
Reed, Jerry. *Uptown Poker Club.* RCA, APL 1-0356.
Rice Brothers. *Cliff Bruner/Rice Brothers' Gang.* Victor Musical Industries Inc., Volume 8, VIM-4016. (Rice Brothers on one side.)
Royal, Billy Joe. *The Royal Treatment.* Atlantic/America 90658-1.
South, Joe. *Midnight Rainbow.* Island Records, ILPS-9328.
Stevens, Ray. *Greatest Hits.* Spot.
Sunshine Boys. *The Sunshine Boys.* Power Pak PG 728.
Swanee River Boys. *The Swanee River Boys Finest.* Zondervan ZLP 635.
Tanner, Gid, and the Skillet Lickers. *A Corn Licker Still in Georgia.* Voyager 303.
————. *Early Classic String Bands.* Old Homestead 192.
————. *Gid Tanner and His Skillet Lickers.* Folksong Society of Minnesota 15001-D.
————. *Gid Tanner and His Skillet Lickers—With Riley Puckett and Clayton McMichen.* Rounder 1005.
————. *Gid Tanner and the Skillet Lickers.* Vetco 107.
————. *The Kickapoo Medicine Shows.* Rounder 1023.
————. *The Skillet Lickers.* County 506.
————. *The Skillet Lickers. Volume 2.* County 526.
Various Artists:
Georgia Fiddle Bands, Volume 2. County 544. (Cofer Brothers, Georgia Yellow Hammers, Home Town Boys, Skillet Lickers, George Walburn, et al.)
Hell Broke Loose in Georgia. County 514. (Dupree's Rome Boys, Georgia Crackers, Bill Helms, Lowe Stokes, Shores Southern Trio, et al.)
Work Don't Bother Me: Old Time Comic Songs from North Georgia. Rounder. (Fiddlin' John Carson, Clayton McMichen, Cofer Brothers, Earl Johnson, Lowe Stokes, Gid Tanner, et al.)

Index

Index

Index

Index

Burdine, John, 57
Burnett, Dewey, 61, 64, 65
Burnett, Richard D., 85
Burnette, Smiley, 201
Burr, Henry, 68
Burrell, Dallas, 166, 217
Burrison, John, 4
Bust O'Dawn Boys. *See* Cross, Roy
Butcher, Dwight, 104, 171, 175, 177, 188–89, 195, 196
Butcher, Slim, 188
"Buttons and Bows," 213
"Bye Bye Love," 181

Cabbagetown, 4, 18
Cable Piano Company, 26
"Cacklin' Hen," 21
Cadence Records, 208
Calhoun, Andy, 22
"California, Here I Come," 46
"Call Me Back, Pal O'Mine," 52
Calloway, Jack, 125
Campbell, Archie, 209
Campbell, Cecil, 147
Canada, Harmon, 60
Cannon, "Butch," 144, 161, 163
Cantwell, Robert, 2
Capitol Records, 158, 198, 201, 208, 227, 229
"Carbolic Rag," 72
"Careless Love," 100, 132, 175
Carl, Carolyn, 221
Carlisle, Bill, 202
Carlton, John M., 21, 22
Carolina Clyde, 120
"Carolina Glide," 71
Carolina Sunshine Girls, 168
Carolina Tarheels, 119–22, 140
Carpenter, Harvey "Red," 116
Carpenter, Jesse, 146, 183
Carrier, Billy, 199, 200

Carrier, Joseph A. "Cotton," 177–79, 188, 199, 201, 207, 214, 232; "Barn Dance" emcee, 177–78; comedy skit, 202–4; composer, 226; disc jockey, 179, 212; and the Plantation Gang, 178–79
Carroll, Don, 207, 208–9
Carroll, Jim, 167
Carroll, Johnny, 207, 208, 209
Carroll, Margie, 207, 208, 209
Carroll County Revelers, 82
Carroll Family, 201, 207–9
"Carry Me Back to Old Virginny," 200
Carson, Fiddlin' John, 9, 10, 12, 20, 21, 22, 36, 39, 50, 51, 63, 65, 68, 71, 72, 75, 84, 87, 88–96, 99, 103, 106, 109, 130, 162, 231, 232; birth, 88; death, 96; father of commercial country music, 94; on fiddling, 91; first radio appearance, 92; first record, 93; and hanging of Leo Frank, 90; later life, 96; music of, 94; and political campaigns, 95; repertoire, 94, 95; rivalry with Gid Tanner, 97; songbook, 95; wife, 89
Carson, James (Jimmy), 177, 188, 197, 198, 232
Carson, James and Martha, 197–99, 201, 208; breakup, 198; Capitol records, 198; first records, 198; form duet, 197; marriage, 197
Carson, Martha, 198, 232
Carson, John. *See* Carson, Fiddlin' John

Carson, Johnny, 232–34
Carson, Rosa Lee, 39, 95, 162, 232
Carter, A. P., 83, 156
Carter, Jimmy, 82
Carter, Maybelle, 83
Carter, Sara, 83
Carter Family, 83, 84, 112, 128, 173, 199
Caruso, Enrico, 67
Carver, Cynthia May. *See* Cousin Emmy
"Casey Jones," 20, 39, 103, 137
Cashbox, 214
Cassell, Pete Webster, 142, 159, 171, 177, 179, 187, 188, 191–92, 210, 232
Castleberry, Dottie, 182, 193
"Cat Rag," 82
CBS, 152, 169
CBS-TV, 229
"Celebratin' the Fourth at Uncle Hiram's" (radio program), 62
Chamblie, Henry, 82
Chamblie, Jess, 82
Chancellor Records, 221
Chandler, Bill, 80
Chandler, Doug, 184
Channel 17, 221
Chappel, Jean, 194
"Charleston Polka," 54
"Charlie's Shoes," 217
Chastine, H. L., 155
Chattahoochee, 4, 18
Cherokee Ramblers, 130
Cherokees, The, 209, 217
"Chicken in the Bread Tray," 26
"Chicken Reel," 175
"Chickens Before Day," 19
Childers, Bill, 162
Childre, Lew, 126, 171
Childs, W. B., 21
"Chinese Breakdown," 71, 140
"Chinese Rag," 80
Chitwood, Bill, 76, 77,

Index

Index

Index

Index

"Free Little Bird," 186, 194
Freeman, Belvey, 72
Freeman, Ed, 72
Freeman Brothers, 136
"Freight Train Blues," 192
Fuller, Earl, 47
Fuller, Tiny, 167
Fulton Bag and Cotton
  Mill, 4
"Fulton County Jamboree"
  (radio program), 165–66

Gaines, Roland, 133, 137
Gamble, T. H., 26
"Games People Play," 227,
  228
Gardner, Bob, 196
Garston, Uncle Ebb, 42
Gatins, Bill, 129–31, 136,
  148, 155, 233; death,
  131; Jug Band, 179, 183;
  records, 130–31
Gator, 229
General Phonograph Com-
  pany, 78
Generals, 218, 233
Gennett Records, 82, 85,
  140
George, Clara Louise, 125
Georgia Artists Bureau,
  120, 133
"Georgia Barbecue at Stone
  Mountain, A," 38, 73
"Georgia Black Bottom,
  The," 154
"Georgia Blues," 81
Georgia Boys, 169
Georgia Crackers (Cofer
  Brothers), 154
Georgia Crackers (Newman
  Brothers), 143
*Georgia Fiddle Bands,
  Volume 2*, 79
Georgia Fiddlers' Associa-
  tion, 22
Georgia Grass Roots Festi-
  val, 82
Georgia Hillbillies, 136
"Georgia Hobo, The," 154

Georgia Hot Shots," 104
"Georgia Jamboree" (radio
  program), 117, 121, 128,
  163; program introduc-
  tion, 184–85
"Georgia Jubilee" (radio
  program), 174, 177, 200,
  209, 210, 211, 221, 223,
  231
Georgia Kids, 167
Georgia Mountaineers, 76
Georgia Music Hall of
  Fame, 232
Georgia Old-Time Fiddlers'
  Association, 87
Georgia Old-Time Fiddlers'
  Conventions, 12, 15–
  44, 68, 87, 96, 100, 101,
  105, 113, 136; audience,
  31; description of, 22–
  23; female contestants,
  39
Georgia Playboys, 167
"Georgia Railroad," 103
Georgia Ramblers, 136
Georgia Red Hots, 104
Georgia Theater, 123
"Georgia Wagon," 58
Georgia Wildcats, 107, 108
"Georgia Wobble Blues,"
  82
Georgia Yellow Hammers,
  76, 77
"Gettin' Up in the Cool,"
  54
"Get Yourself a Redhead,"
  191
Gibble, Bige, 60
Gibson Kings, 74. *See also*
  Dilleshaw, John, and
  Brook, C. S.
Gilham, Cecil, 131
Gilham-Schoen Electric
  Company, 152
Gillette, Jack, 119, 147,
  196
Gillig, Al, 161
Gilmer Street, 18
Gilt Edge Records, 160
"Glen Campbell Good-

time Hour" (television
  program), 229
Glosson, Buck, 181, 184
Glosson, Lonnie, 170,
  181
"God Put a Rainbow in the
  Cloud," 60
Goebel, Georgie, 163
"Goin' Down the Road
  Feelin' Bad," 131
"Going Back to Alabama,"
  169
"Going Down to Town," 20
Golden Guitar, 219
Golden Nuggett, 218
"Golden Slippers," 183
Golden Tones, 209
Gone with the Wind, 127
Goober and His Kentuck-
  ians, 177, 178, 182
"Good Night Waltz," 86
"Good Ol' Boys," 230
Goolsby, Jim. *See* Goolsby,
  John
Goolsby, John, 25
Gordon County Quartet,
  76
Gorman, Johnny, 140
Gorsuck, Whit, 124
Gospel music, 199
"G Rag," 77
"Grand Ole Opry" (radio
  program), 9, 10, 65, 78,
  83, 84, 85, 108, 112,
  122, 127, 135, 136, 163,
  167, 173, 174, 179, 185,
  193, 198, 199, 204, 207,
  209, 210, 211, 216, 219,
  220, 228, 233
"Graveyard Light," 170
Gray, A. A., 36–39, 73,
  232
Grayson, G. B., 86
Gray's String Band, 37
Great Depression, 109–10
"Great Ship Went Down,
  The," 154
"Great Speckled Bird, The,"
  197
Green, Archie, 55, 56

Index

Index

Index

Index

Index

Index

Pride, Charley, 218
Pritchard, B. L., 73
Pritchard, Barney, 72
Pritchard, Bonnie, 72
Pritchard, Eunice, 72
Pritchett, Jim, 161; and His
  'Possum Hunters, 161
Propst, Walter, 120
Prosser, Catherine Stewart,
  100
Pruitt, Hoyt, 160, 166, 167,
  168, 171
Puckett, Riley, 12, 53, 71,
  81, 84, 87, 98, 99, 101–
  5, 106, 107, 136, 148,
  159, 161, 162, 189, 191,
  232; death, 105; first
  radio appearance, 102;
  first records, 103; mar-
  riage, 104; repertoire,
  102; and Skillet Lickers,
  103; yodeling, 103
Pure Ivory Band, 220
"Put My Little Shoes
  Away," 132
"Put on Your Old Gray
  Bonnet," 140

QRS Records, 140

"Rabbit Soup," 186
Radio: car radios intro-
  duced, 114; compared
  to phonograph, 110;
  and country music, 110;
  early days of, 45–66;
  early 1930s, 109–26;
  FM reception, 127; lis-
  tening audience, 173;
  post–World War II, 206
"Radio Barn Dance" (radio
  program), 107
Radio Cowboys, 136, 147,
  180, 189
Radio Digest, 93
Radio Farmers' Democracy,
  61
Radio Rangers, 182
Radio Wranglers, 184, 185,
  196, 213

"Railroad Bill," 77
"Railroad Boomer, The,"
  141
Railroads, 3
"Railroad Tramp, The," 80
Rainbow Ramblers, 167
Raines, Sy, 142
Ranch Boys, 202
Randall, Charley, 26
Range Ramblers, 189
Rann, Grover, 86
"Rattle Snakin' Daddy,"
  138, 185
Rattray, Bill, 71
RCA Victor Records, 49,
  76, 77, 79, 81, 83, 84,
  85, 94, 101, 144, 146,
  148, 149, 157, 158, 170,
  188, 189, 191, 229
Record World, 221
Red and Raymond, 129,
  132, 133
Red Barn Records, 170
Red-Headed Briar Hopper,
  132
Red-Headed Music
  Makers, 117
Red River Rangers, 171,
  200
"Red River Valley," 137
Reed, Jerry, 209, 220, 228,
  229–30, 232
Reed, Reidy, 131, 133, 134,
  137
Reeve, Phil, 76, 77
"Renfro Valley Barn
  Dance" (radio program
  and stage show), 127,
  169, 174, 175, 194, 195,
  199
Retonga Medicine Com-
  pany, 159
R.F.D. Club, 61
Rhythm Ranch, 216
Rhythm Ranch Boys, 210
Rhythm Ranchers, 185,
  216
Rice, Hoke, 7, 73, 120,
  122, 140, 190; and His
  Hoky Poky Boys, 140;

and His Southern String
  Band, 140
Rice, Paul, 140, 161, 185,
  190, 201, 213; and "You
  Are My Sunshine," 150
Rice Brothers, 199; and
  "You Are My Sunshine,"
  150
Rice Brothers Gang, 140–
  41
Richardson, Boag, 57
Richardson, Edward, 57
Richardson, Ethel Park,
  100
Richardson, Jay, 225
Richardson, Myrtle, 57
Richardson Brothers, 136
Richman, Ace, 171, 200,
  201, 213
Rickard, James, 83
"Rickett's Hornpipe," 54
"Riding Down the Canyon,"
  141, 157, 190
"Ring Waltz," 102
Roane County Ramblers,
  86
Robert Fulton Hotel, 83
Roberts, Fiddlin' Doc, 197
Roberts, James. *See* Carson,
  James
Robertson, Dave "Specs,"
  119
Robinson, M. Y., 20, 21,
  22
"Rock All Our Babies to
  Sleep," 103
"Rockin' on the Waves,"
  177
Rockmart String Band, 53
"Rock of Ages," 200
"Rocky Top," 181
Rodgers, Jimmie, 65, 83,
  103, 112, 129, 130, 139,
  146, 148, 162, 189, 192
Rody, John, 73
Rogers, Chuck, 120
Rogers, David, 221
Rogers, Ernest, 8, 9, 10,
  49, 92, 121, 124, 142,
  195

Index

Rogers, Jenny, 193
Rogers, Roy, 173
"Rolling Stone Blues," 198
"Rome Georgia Bound," 82
Roosevelt, Franklin D., 127
"Roscoe Trillion," 81
Rose, Fred, 173
Rosenbaum, Art, 5
Rosenberg, Neil, 2
Ross, Dill, 163
Ross, Eddie, 183
Ross, Jimmy, 225
Rounder Records, 79, 158
Roundup Gang, 145
Roxy Theater, 209
Royal, Billy Joe, 220, 228, 231, 232
"Ruby," 186, 187
"Run, Nigger, Run," 20
Russell, Dick, 22
Rutherford, Leonard, 85
"Rye Straw," 21
Ryman Auditorium, 173

"Sailor's Hornpipe," 21
"St. Louis Blues," 102, 106, 192
"Sally Goodin'," 38
"Sally Goodwin," 81
"San Antonio Rose," 128
Sand Sifters, 104
"S'annee River," 20
Santa Fe Trailers, 143
Satherly, Art, 150
"Satisfied," 198
"Savingest Man on Earth, The," 85
Savoy Theater, 17
Scaduto, Felice (Mrs. Boudleaux Bryant), 181
Schlappi, Elizabeth, 2
Schneider, Doc, 123, 124
Schneider, "Vic," 124
Schwarz, Tracy, 187
Scoby, Jess, 124
Scoggins, Howard, 57, 58
Scott, Joe, 131
Scott, Tommy, 233
Scottdale, 4, 5, 18

Scottdale Mills, 5
"Scottdale Stomp," 71
Scottdale String Band, 53, 71–73
Scroggs, Billy, 224
Scruggs, Earl, 173
Sears, Roebuck and Company, 60, 61
Sears, Roebuck and Company Agricultural Foundation, 61, 63
"Secech," 54
Second Greatest Sex, The, 187
"Second-Hand Rose," 219
Seeger, Mike, 186, 187
Seeger, Pete, 186
Seven Aces, 68
Seven Foot Dilly. See Dilleshaw, John
"Shame on You," 173
"Shanghai," 20
"Shanghi Chicken," 21
Sharp, Tip, 170
"Shattered Love," 158
Shaw, Eddie, 166
Shedd, Harold, 232, 234, 235
"She Got the Goldmine (I Got the Shaft)," 230
Shelton, Jim, 53
Shelton Brothers, 195
"Shenandoah Waltz," 163
Sherrill, Homer, 155, 157
Shilkret, Nathaniel, 65
Shook, Jerry, 209
"Shooting of Dan McGrew, The," 62
Shores, Bill, 81, 82
Shores Southern Trio, 82
"Short'nin' Bread," 131
"Shorty," 221
"Show Me the Way to Go Home," 46
Shreveport Times: "You Are My Sunshine" story, 150
"Shriner's Convention," 230
"Shy Little Ann from

Cheyenne," 189
"Silly Bill," 55
Silver Saddle Club, 218
Silvey, John, 36
Silvey, Uncle Bud, 140
Simmons, Charlie, 73
Simonton, J. R., 21
Simonton, R. M., 22
"Since You've Been Gone," 185
"Singing in the Saddle," 144
"Single Girl, Single Girl," 193
"Single Life," 79
Singley, Bonnie, 20
Singley, Cliff, 20
Singley, J. B., 20, 21, 36
Singley, Mack, 20, 21
Singley, Mark, 22
Sing Your Heart Out Country Boy, 150
Sirinski, Koby, 63, 64
Sisson, Allen, 63
"Sitting on Top of the World," 71
Sizemore, Little Jimmy, 163
Skaggs, Dolpha, 138
Skillet Lickers, 71, 72, 76, 82, 98, 99, 103, 107, 162; last recording session, 101; origin of name, 99; on radio, 99, 101; rural drama records, 99
Skillet Lickers II, 233
Skylite Records, 200
Slats, Pappy, 160; and Kentucky Mountaineers, 179
Slaughter Sisters, 63
"Sleep, Baby, Sleep," 102
"Sleeping Late," 85
Slim, Tex, 188
Smallwood, Lester, 81
Smart, Alec. See Smart, Aleck
Smart, Aleck, 30–31, 35, 39, 40, 41, 42, 43, 102, 232, 241n.47

Index

Smart, Alex. *See* Smart, Aleck
Smart, Jimmy, 221
Smash Records, 220
Smith, A. L., 200. *See also* Smith, Smitty
Smith, Carl, 181
Smith, Ed (Eddie), 131, 160, 161, 171, 181, 184
Smith, J. F., 53
Smith, J. W. "Slimbo," 131, 144
Smith, Jimmy, 146–47, 177, 188, 207, 214, 216, 217, 232
Smith, Joe, 188
Smith, John O., 200. *See also* Smith, Tennessee
Smith, Leon, 134, 142, 161
Smith, Marquis M., 65
Smith, Shellie Walton, 86
Smith, Smitty, 171, 208, 213, 214, 233
Smith, Tennessee, 171, 213, 226, 233
Smith Brothers, 201, 208, 213, 226
Smithgall, Charles (Charlie), 134, 167
"Smoke on the Water," 173
"Smoke! Smoke! Smoke! (That Cigarette)," 173
Smokey and the Bandit, 229
Smokey and the Bandit II, 229
Smokey and the Bandit III, 229
Smoky Ridge Band, 30
"Snapfinger," 20
Snow, Hank, 227
"Soldier's Joy," 19, 20, 21, 29, 44, 88
"Somebody Stole My Sunshine Away," 261n.61
"Song of the Saddle," 155
Sons of the Pioneers, 134, 144, 201
Sorghum Band, 30
Sorrells, Anita. *See* Wheeler, Anita Sorrells

Sorrells, Dudley Maddox, 40
"Sourwood Mountain," 103
South, Joe, 209, 220, 228, 230, 232, 233
Southern Agriculturist, 159
"Southern Blues," 71
"Southern Fried," 211, 227
"Southern Moon," 169
Southern Music Publishing Company, 150, 188
Southern Ranch Boys, 219
Southern Sisters, 139
"Sowing on the Mountain," 175
Spain, Irene, 60
"Spanish Fandango," 73
"Spanish Fireball," 227
Spencer, Bill, 177
Spivey, Doug, 134, 160, 195, 196; and "You Are My Sunshine," 149
Spivey, W. L., 148. *See also* Spivey, Doug
Spooney Five, 80, 81
"Square Dance Fight on Ball Top Mountain, The," 73
Square dances, 30
Stamp-Baxter songbook, 134
Stamps, Frank: Quartet, 199
Standard Feed and Milling Company, 166
"Standing by His Side," 170
"Standing by the Highway," 121
"Standin' Neath the Old Pine Tree," 190
Stanley, R. M., 21, 22, 36, 54, 78, 232
Stanley, Roba, 54, 77–79, 232
Staples, Bobby, 160
Staple Singers, 159
Starday Records, 158, 201, 220
Starlight Valley Boys, 209

Starrett, Charles, 201
Steak and Trumpet, 220
"Steal Away," 200
"Steamboat Bill," 49, 103
Steed, "Shorty," 131, 144, 179
Steel-Driving Devils, 136
"Steel Guitar Rag," 177, 184
Stephens, Charles, 167
Stephens, Robert, 106
Stevens, Ray, 209, 228, 230–31, 232
Stewart, Ben, 136
Stewart, Carl, 147
Stewart, Redd, 148
Stewart, Tiny, 148
Stewman, Loy, 166
Stewman, Steve, 166
"Still," 211
Stoddard, Bob, 184
Stokes, Lowe, 33, 36, 73, 74, 99, 106, 233
Stokes, Marcus Lowe. *See* Stokes, Lowe
Stoneman, Ernest V. "Pop," 85
Stoneman Family, 85
Stone Mountain Boys, 168
Stone Mountain Fiddlers' Convention, 76
Stone Mountain Gang, 165
Stop Records, 220
"Story of Adam, The," 130
Straw beating, 34
"Strawberries," 103
"Streak, The," 230
"Streak-o-Lean, Streak-o-Fat," 38, 73
Street, Johnny, 131
Strength, Texas Bill, 216
Strickland, Billy, 183
Strickland, H. R., 53
Strickland, J. H., 21
String bands, 29–30
Stringer, Dewey, 116
Stripling, Chick, 142, 177, 179
Stripling, Gene. *See* Uncle Ned and His Texas

Index

Index

Index

Index

Index

"WSB Barn Dance" (radio program), 13, 14, 146, 170, 172–204, 207, 208, 209, 210, 215, 231; accordion players on, 182; banjoists on, 185; comedy on, 202; emcees on, 177; female vocalists on, 192; fiddlers on, 179; first broadcast, 175; gospel quartets on, 199; harmonica players on, 181; male vocalists on, 188; program, 175, 177; program format, 179; program introduction, 177; sister acts on, 193; sponsors, 176; steel guitarists on, 183; theme song, 192; venues, 176
WSB-TV, 180, 202, 212, 213, 214, 217
WSM, 8, 10, 85, 108, 153, 163, 210, 212
WSMK, 131
WTJH, 153, 165, 209, 210
W. W. and the Dixie Dance Kings, 229

WWL, 189
WWNC, 155
WWVA, 108, 112, 138, 186, 191, 198, 201
"WWVA Jamboree" (radio program), 174
Wyoming Rangers, 146, 147

XERA, 128

"Ya Gotta Quit Kickin' My Dog Aroun'," 98
"Yellow Rose of Texas," 112, 132
"Ye Olde Tyme Barn Dance" (radio program), 62
"Yes, Mr. Peters," 219
"Yes! We Have No Bananas," 141
"Yodeling Blues," 116
Yodeling Cowboy, 136
Yodeling Cowboys, 123, 124
Yodeling Twins, 133
"You Are My Sunshine," 149, 151, 150, 155,

261n.61
"You Can Be a Millionaire with Me," 158
"You Can't Break My Heart," 167
"You Can't Live with 'Em (And You Can't Live without 'Em)," 194
"You Lied About that Woman," 140
Young, Bob, 20
Young, Charlie, 63
Young, Faron, 219
Young, R. H., 21, 22
Young, Roe, 63
"Young Love," 227
"You're My Darling," 190
"You're the Only Star in My Blue Heaven," 157
"You've Got to See Daddy Every Night," 141
"You've Got to Walk that Lonesome Valley," 134
"You Won't Know Tokyo When We Get Through," 159

Zondervan Records, 200

Music in American Life